"*Interpretation for Liberation* is a fundamental book, rich and informed, that introduces in a pedagogical way the nature and function of hermeneutics in philosophy in general and in African philosophy in particular. Through detailed readings of African hermeneuts, Ernst Wolff shows how interpretation engages with the repercussions of socio-historical crises linked to the economic, cultural, and political difficulties of a humanity confronted with the lingering forms of inhuman violence and geopolitical power relations resulting from the slave trade, slavery, colonial conquest, oppression, and underdevelopment, from which nevertheless emerges an irrepressible desire for emancipation and self-affirmation."
—Charles Mbele, Université de Yaoundé

"Ernst Wolff has written a book that vastly expands the boundaries of African Philosophy by doing what is rarely done in the discipline: taking seriously the ideas and discourses of individual African thinkers and engaging them at the most granular level. Henceforth, it is impossible for anyone who practices or writes about hermeneutics as a philosophical method and mode of thinking to claim ignorance of Africans' place in it. With sophisticated analysis, brilliant summaries that never dumb down the complexities of his chosen thinkers' arguments, and critical sections that invite deeper conversation with the authors and their readers alike, Wolff introduces us to both self-identified hermeneuticists and others whose works lend themselves to hermeneutic interpretation. He has made us abundantly aware of the riches that await questors into one branch of African philosophy: Hermeneutics. I give this book my highest recommendation."
—Olúfẹ́mi Táíwò, Cornell University

"This important book provides readers with a critical and vivid account of hermeneutics as a means of cultural and political liberation in African philosophy. First, Ernst Wolff presents the nature of hermeneutics and assesses its role in African philosophical traditions. Second, he offers a fresh and thoughtful reading of some of its major representatives. Combining rigorous argumentation with a rare clarity of expression, this well-researched and brilliantly written book will be of enormous value and significance to students and scholars of philosophy and the social sciences."
—Kasereka Kavwahirehi, University of Ottawa

Interpretation for Liberation
African Philosophical Hermeneutics

Interpretation for Liberation

African Philosophical Hermeneutics

Ernst Wolff

LEUVEN UNIVERSITY PRESS

Published with the support of the KU Leuven Fund for Fair Open Access, KU Leuven internal funds and the Research Foundation Flanders (FWO) (Project number G030523N).

Published in 2025 by Leuven University Press / Presses Universitaires de Louvain / Universitaire Pers Leuven. Minderbroedersstraat 4, B-3000 Leuven (Belgium).
All TDM (Text and Data Mining) rights are reserved.
© 2025, Ernst Wolff

This book is published under a Creative Commons Attribution Non-Commercial Non-Derivative 4.0 License. For more information, please visit https://creativecommons.org/share-your-work/cclicenses/

Attribution should include the following information:
Ernst Wolff, *Interpretation for Liberation: African Philosophical Hermeneutics*. Leuven: Leuven University Press, 2025. (CC BY-NC-ND 4.0)

ISBN 978 94 6270 483 1 (Paperback)
ISBN 978 94 6166 684 0 (ePDF)
ISBN 978 94 6166 685 7 (ePUB)
https://doi.org/10.11116/9789461666840
D/2025/1869/25
NUR: 730
Typesetting: Crius Group
Cover design: Daniel Benneworth-Gray

Table of Contents

Preface. Approaching African hermeneutics	13

Chapter 1. Introduction: Hermeneutics as a trend in African philosophy — 19
1. Hermeneutics: a provisional description — 20
2. The place of hermeneutics in African philosophy — 25
   - 2.1. The place of hermeneutics in African philosophy: using Oruka as a point of departure — 25
   - 2.2. The place of hermeneutics in African philosophy: using Nkombe and Smet as a point of departure — 33
   - 2.3. Preliminary conclusions — 39
3. Hermeneutics: an author-based approach — 41

Chapter 2. On the threshold: from cultural philosophemes to African hermeneutics—Theophilus Okere — 45
1. African philosophy: a historic-hermeneutic investigation of the conditions of its possibility — 45
2. What is non-philosophy? — 50
   - 2.1. Culture from the view of ethnophilosophy and its critics — 50
   - 2.2. Culture as a non-philosophical component of European philosophy — 54
3. What is philosophy? — 56
   - 3.1. The conditions of the possibility of philosophy — 57
   - 3.2. From the philosophical crossroads to the possibility of African philosophy — 59
4. How should philosophy and non-philosophy be linked? — 63
   - 4.1. Working on philosophemes — 63
   - 4.2. Towards a traditionalist or a contextualist view of belonging to a culture? — 66
5. Conclusion — 71

Select annotated bibliography — 72

Chapter 3. Interpretation as a resource for political resistance: Serequeberhan between generality and particularity   75
1. The source: general anthropological claims   77
2. Philosophy in general   78
3. All humans and all philosophy   81
4. African philosophy   84
   4.1. Critique: what is to be avoided   84
   4.2. Advocacy: what is to be pursued   86
5. Improper African philosophy: self-imposed negation of historicalness in Nkrumah and Senghor   89
   5.1. Nkrumah: pathology of extroverted Euro-normativity   90
   5.2. Senghor: pathology of introverted or internalised Euro-normativity   92
   5.3. On the unintentional servants of European Enlightenment   94
6. A new start: from horizon to hermeneutic discourse   95
   6.1. Horizon and vocation   95
   6.2. According mediations their due: expanding and transcending the lived horizon   96
   6.3. Tradition   99
   6.4. Actuality and ideality: normativity and liberation   100
7. From horizon to action   103
   7.1. Original violence with Césaire   104
   7.2. "[Counter-]Violence is no choice" (but a matter of necessity)   107
   7.3. Fusion of horizons and practices of freedom: with Fanon and Cabral   110
8. Conclusion   119
Select annotated bibliography   121

Chapter 4. Critique of African hermeneutic reason: interpretation triggered and oriented by praxis—Okolo Okonda   123
1. Orientation: praxis, hermeneutics, tradition   124
2. Praxis, crisis, development   124
   2.1. Crisis   125
   2.2. Development as "revolutionary praxis"?   126
3. Hermeneutics   129
   3.1. "Every theory of reading presupposes a theory of text and vice versa"   130

	3.2. *"Every reading is oriented toward some kind of appropriation/re-taking [reprise]"*	131
	3.3. *"Every reading and every appropriation is determined by a worldview of the subject who reads and appropriates [or re-takes]"*	134
4.	Tradition	137
	4.1. *Tradition as text*	139
	4.2. *Tradition and the difficult balance between the "already there" and the "not yet"*	140
	4.3. *What is co-extensive with tradition: worldview, ideology, identity*	144
	4.4. *Provisional conclusion on tradition, worldviews, ideology, and identity*	153
5.	Critique of hermeneutic reason: shifting perspectives and complexity as a virtue	154
6.	Ethnophilosophy: contra … and pro	156
7.	Orality	159
	7.1. *Proverbs*	160
	7.2. *Conclusions on orality*	167
8.	Work, critique, and violence	169
9.	Philosophy, singular and universal: the ambition of Okolo's book	174
10.	Conclusion	178
Select annotated bibliography		179

Chapter 5. Implicit hermeneutics: origins, constitutions, projects 181

1.	History versus essentialism as a resource for action in the present: Cheikh Anta Diop	182
	1.1. *From language, through history, to action*	182
	1.2. *Aspects of a Diopian hermeneutics*	186
2.	Critical traditionalism and contemporary social problems: Sophie Oluwole	187
	2.1. *Orality as the core of African philosophy*	188
	2.2. *Strengths and weaknesses of Oluwole's hermeneutics*	193
3.	How truth claims about Africa came to be: V. Y. Mudimbe	197
	3.1. *Making truth claims about Africa (and what this is a sign of)*	198
	3.2. *The variety of Africanist discourses*	202
	3.3. *Reconstructing invention—archaeology as hermeneutics*	207

4. A hermeneutics of total defeat and the small deviations:
   Fabien Eboussi Boulaga — 210
   4.1. Orientation: philosophy by and for Muntu — 211
   4.2. Hermeneutics as a critical unmasking — 212
   4.3. Hermeneutics as interpretation of the conditions of
        self-liberation — 215
   4.4. Hermeneutics as transfunctionalisation and self-affirmation — 217
   4.5. Conclusion — 222
5. Translation as making humanity together: Souleymane Bachir
   Diagne — 224
   5.1. Point of departure: connecting the foreign and the familiar — 226
   5.2. The translator as agent — 227
   5.3. Translatio as transfer: transplanting works of art and
        translatio studii — 229
   5.4. Particularity, universalism, and the ethics of translation — 231
   5.5. Conclusions and questions — 233
6. Conclusion: a wide perspective on what hermeneutics can do — 235
Select annotated bibliography — 239

Chapter 6. Conclusion: hermeneutics as commitment — 243
1. Hermeneutics and philosophical anthropology — 244
   1.1. Understanding, belonging, culture — 246
   1.2. Arts of interpretation — 248
   1.3. Philosophical hermeneutics — 249
2. Negotiating plurality — 250
   2.1. Hermeneutics' two aversions and its founding conviction — 252
   2.2. Generality as supposition and the practical commitment of
        hermeneutics — 252
   2.3. Hermeneutic resources: an ethics of listening and diverse
        "procedures of the spirit" — 254
   2.4. Hermeneutic resources: critique and creativity — 256
3. Between familiarity and strangeness — 259
   3.1. Familiarity and strangeness: the struggle for orientation — 259
   3.2. African philosophy as a compound of familiarity and
        strangeness — 263

4.	Hermeneutics and practice: liberation from what? What for? By whom?	269
	4.1. Hermeneutics as rooted and participating in practice	269
	4.2. Practice and power	271
	4.3. The spectrum of practical engagement	275
	4.4. Understanding the ambiguous practical profile of hermeneutics: ambition and self-restraint	278
5.	Hermeneutics and ethics	281
6.	Hermeneutics among the strategies for liberating the world	285

Notes 289

Index 321

PREFACE

Approaching African hermeneutics

This book is devoted to a fascinating current of thought: African philosophical hermeneutics. Suspended in the tension between Africa's traumatic past and its continuing quest for political autonomy, African hermeneutics draws on old traditions, borrowed ideas, and creative reflection. It pursues intense intellectual engagement with the complexities of life and reflects on what is meaningful or requires criticism. This book shows that there is a wealth of challenging intellectual and existential insights to be gained from studying African hermeneutics.

Aside from some exposure to African philosophy that I had as an undergraduate student, the roots of this book go back to 2005, when I first taught an introductory course on African philosophy at the University of Pretoria. More recently I began gathering material for the present volume in 2014 and started writing the next year. However, the vicissitudes of life prevented me from completing the book during the years that followed, although I did work on the project intermittently. Traces of this research can also be read in other publications on which I worked during the same years.[1] Now, the project has finally come to fruition.

During that first year of teaching African philosophy, I was struck by what seemed to be a remarkable similarity between two visions of philosophy. The first is Paulin Hountondji's argument in *African Philosophy: Myth and Reality* that African philosophy exists in the form of the writings of ethnophilosophers, who describe the language and culture of common African existence.[2] The second is the way in which Heidegger, in *Being and Time*, accords primacy to the intelligence of praxis, while considering the significance of written philosophy, as derived from understanding in everyday existence.[3] Perhaps one may call that similarity a "double hermeneutic", a term I picked up later from Anthony Giddens,[4] and that reflects the fact that interpretation takes place in two distinct but interrelated ways: the constant flux of understanding that accompanies daily human existence and the scholarly attention given to existence. Later, I realised that this first impression of similarity was in fact somewhat misleading. Moreover, an article that I started on Hountondji and Heidegger at the time was never finished, because it soon became clear to me that I was insufficiently equipped to complete it. I leave it to the reader to decide whether the many studies in African philosophy that I have subsequently written have sufficiently built up my competence to deal with a much broader project on African philosophical hermeneutics.

As a subdiscipline of philosophy, hermeneutics is the study of understanding and interpretation. The term "hermeneutics" is thus used both for an approach to philosophical questions generally and, more specifically, for a set of interrelated questions.

This book aims to help readers gain access to hermeneutics as a strand of African philosophy. This simple aim in fact implies five different objectives, each of which has its own justification and its own requirements to accomplish it:

Objective 1: To provide a first overview of hermeneutics to students and scholars in philosophy and the social sciences, including those who have no or little background in African philosophy. While there are many contributions to African philosophical hermeneutics, there is, to my knowledge, no introduction that enables an accessible way to simplify one's first acquaintance with this subdiscipline. As an introduction, this book therefore needs to present the nature of hermeneutics, indicate its place in the broader family of African philosophies, and then present some of the major representatives.

Objective 2: To open a view on the wealth and complexity of hermeneutic philosophy. While there are many studies in hermeneutics, and there are secondary studies that cover aspects relevant to the concerns of the authors discussed in this book, there is a real need to present the works of great African hermeneuts. This requires introducing them on their own terms, but also unpacking the breadth of their argument, rather than merely a section of it.

Objective 3: To present African hermeneuts as philosophers; in other words, to present them not merely as authors with a set of claims, but as authors who offer solid proposals with which we have to engage through philosophical analysis, critique, and appraisal. This requires a detailed examination of their arguments and an assessment of each author's work.

Objective 4: To present central concerns of authors who explicitly identify as hermeneuts and indicate avenues by which the same or related concerns are represented in the work of authors who do not explicitly identify with hermeneutics. Given the centrality of the hermeneutic issues of understanding and interpretation to philosophical reflection generally, there is no reason to expect that these issues are dealt with only by authors who explicitly adopt the term "hermeneutics". There are indeed many overviews of African philosophy in which working on understanding and interpretation is indicated as a justifiable view on hermeneutics, broadly construed. However, I do not know of any contemporary work in which such works of implicit hermeneutics are introduced into an exploration of the landscape of hermeneutics. At the same time, to avoid arbitrariness, the inclusion of all the selected authors requires proper justification, so that the authors' contributions to hermeneutics can be properly profiled.

Objective 5: To offer a synthesis of the divergent views. Each philosopher has their own set of concerns and ways of proceeding and set of ideas that they argue for. "Hermeneutics" can serve as a name for their collective endeavours, but their works do not simply slot together to form a homogenous whole. Separate discussions do justice to this diversity but leave intact the difficult task of laying out an overall coherent picture. Here the commentator can only offer an additional view to that of the authors discussed. While learning from the great authors, the present-day commentator has to follow in their steps to offer a view on what hermeneutics is (about), knowing very well that every reader's synthesis will look different.

The aim of this book is, then, to provide access to African philosophical hermeneutics in all five of these senses. However, the requirements for meeting each of these objectives are not all that simple to harmonise. The layout of this book aims for the best possible combination of these requirements.

Chapter 1 responds to the two aspects of Objective 1. Here, hermeneutics is considered from a high altitude, to present a broad perspective on hermeneutics in general terms. For readers who have never worked in this domain, I offer a provisional introduction to hermeneutics. Then I explore a series of typologies of African philosophy and other works that reflect on African philosophy as a whole, to give an account of the uncertain position of hermeneutics in the field of African philosophies. These overviews also provide a first impression of the accents that African philosophers may put on hermeneutics (or prefer to associate with other subdisciplines).[5]

Chapters 2, 3, and 4 abolish the general perspective on hermeneutics to study three authors who explicitly presented works on hermeneutics. I adopted an "authors" and "classics" approach: the three authors studied here—Theophilus Okere, Tsenay Serequeberhan, and Okolo Okonda—are widely recognised as leading figures in African philosophical hermeneutics. The book chosen for discussion for each of them could be considered a classic in this field.

Chapter 5 continues the author-focused approach and presents five implicit hermeneuts (in line with Objective 4), in a very similar manner as in the previous chapters. The selected texts may or may not be seen as classics of African philosophy (for this reason, the discussions are much shorter)—the point is to read them as contributions to hermeneutics.

Hermeneutics is often considered a difficult mode of philosophy. In numerous ways, I strive in Chapters 2 to 5 to facilitate entry into this domain and thus to remain true to Objective 1. I decided to discuss one author at a time and limit my focus to a classic book or set of essays per author to keep the material manageable and the presentation easier to follow. A systematic reconstruction of the arguments serves to identify and clarify the salient hermeneutic themes. Each author's arguments in the chosen text are clarified with brief references to that author's other works. Each chapter ends with a summary. The bibliography is compiled as a set of suggestions for further reading on the relevant author or on themes touched upon in the discussion. Numerous clarifying endnotes (which may be redundant for those who are already initiated) are designed to orient those who are not familiar with African philosophy. To enhance accessibility, I have ordered Chapters 2, 3, and 4 not in historical order, but in order of complexity.

In pursuit of Objectives 3 and 4, I have devoted the space needed to submitting the "classics" to extensive examination on their own terms, and I have not hesitated to engage at length with their arguments where necessary. While the general structure of each discussion is plainly set out, the discussion also engages with the complexity of the texts, as required for the individual authors (and, need I say, within the limits of my own competence). In adopting this approach, I hope to write also for specialists of philosophical hermeneutics. This objective is pursued further in the concluding chapter.

Finally, Chapter 6 is set aside for a more independent appropriation of aspects of hermeneutics as I see it, but in constant conversation with the authors in the book—as is called for by Objective 5. This attempt at a synthesising view on hermeneutics is my attempt at responding to what I have learned throughout the book (but is obviously impossible to separate from insights drawn from other learning experiences), and serves as a conclusion. In this context, a "conclusion" can only mean a provisional statement of core insights, and does not offer the final word on the subject.

Through its approach to the field of African hermeneutics, its critical analysis and assessment of the selected authors, and the synthesis offered in the last chapter, this book also makes an independent contribution to African philosophy, which should make it interesting reading for specialists of African philosophy too.

The primary objective of this book is not to promote my own views about what constitutes hermeneutics and what should be done with it in African philosophy, but rather to offer the readers help in making up their own minds on these issues. Nevertheless, I must admit that my own convictions come to the fore in several ways. Continuing dedication to writing this book was possible only because I am convinced that hermeneutics is a worthwhile mode of practicing African philosophy. Neither the uncertainty created by divergent scholarly views on its place in African philosophy, nor even the criticism I formulate myself convinced me of the contrary. To the contrary, insofar as the book contains the independent contribution to which I referred above, it betrays my desire to participate in the game. Again, I leave it to the readers to decide what they think.

A last aspect of my own convictions needs to be mentioned, because it has a direct bearing on the material included in this book. If the (early) overviews of African philosophy do not convince one of the fact that English is not the only language in which African philosophy is published, then the sheer volume of francophone texts should do so. I understand that for many anglophone African philosophers, French is a barrier, but I deem it important to oppose the damaging trend in recent handbooks and companions to African philosophy of ignoring the existence of francophone African philosophy. The theme of hermeneutics is an excellent example to illustrate how distorted one's view of a subfield can become if one turns a blind eye to one of Africa's biggest language spheres. This point accounts for the space I devote to a discussion of an author like Okolo Okonda, whose most substantial work is not available in English.[6]

I would like to thank Christiaan Naudé and Idette Noomé for their tireless efforts in editing the text. My gratitude extends also to Mirjam Truwant and the team at Leuven University Press for their kind and professional interaction.

I dedicate this book to Madeleine and Axel Wolff.

Ernst Wolff
Leuven, October 2024

CHAPTER 1

Introduction: Hermeneutics as a trend in African philosophy

> Without any doubt, the problem of African "philosophy"
> refers us back to the problem of hermeneutics.
> —Paulin Hountondji, *African Philosophy: Myth and Reality*[1]

The aim of this chapter is to prepare the terrain for my study of important contributions to African philosophical hermeneutics. Three elements are required for this preparation: an understanding of what hermeneutics is, a perspective on its place in African philosophy, and clarification of how I proceed in the other chapters. Let us look at these three elements more closely:

(1) Since this book is about philosophical hermeneutics, I need to start by telling the reader what the term "hermeneutics" refers to and what specifically *philosophical* work on hermeneutics entails. Since it is not a simple undertaking to render a consensus view on hermeneutics, I begin in § 1 by offering a provisional outline, and then contemplate the exact nature of this outline and its place in the unfolding of the book as a whole.

(2) At first glance, it seems quite easy to situate hermeneutics within the broad range of African philosophies. Need one do more than cite Henry Odera Oruka's[2] 1990 typology of trends in African philosophy, or consult some of the many overviews? In reality, the matter is much more complex. A systematic scrutiny of existing typologies and discussions of hermeneutics in relation to other strands of African philosophy soon reveals that it is neither clear *what* is to be designated as hermeneutics or a hermeneutic tradition in African philosophy, nor easy to establish *which authors* are to be counted as being "in" and which ones as "out" of that tradition.

The aim of § 2 of the Introduction is thus to map the state of this debate. Rendering the different ways in which philosophers and scholars have attempted to interpret the place of hermeneutics in African philosophy has a direct bearing on what one understands African hermeneutics to be. Such an exercise thus turns out to be both

indispensable in formulating the problem explored in this book and in demarcating the field that has to be examined. Moreover, it also suggests the main structuring features of the approach that I adopt to work through the material, namely an *author-based approach*.
(3) There are many different ways in which to approach hermeneutics. While the overview in this chapter approaches it from a broad perspective, as it relates to other forms of philosophy, the remainder of this book adopts the inverse approach: it studies a selection of works from close up and in detail. The third part of this chapter briefly states how I undertake this task.

1. Hermeneutics: a provisional description

There is no simple consensus on what hermeneutics is, or should be. In fact, as § 2 of this chapter shows, hermeneutics is a strongly contested element of African philosophy. Nevertheless, before one can appreciate these differences and in order to make one's way to the debates about hermeneutics, one needs some grasp of what could be covered by the term. For this reason, I start by giving a point-by-point outline of what is frequently understood under the term "hermeneutics".

(1) The general point of departure in hermeneutics is the fact that human beings experience the world around them as meaningful. This includes experiences of confusion or disturbances of meaning. Meaning is found in embodiment and action, in working with things and in engaging with people and living beings, in cultural expressions (oral, written, recorded), in common everyday activities and in specialised practices, in knowledge creation, aesthetic expression or religious conviction, in institutional settings and in innovative initiatives.

(2) Hermeneutics is the study of everything meaningful (including disturbances of meaning), of understanding and interpretation. In a most fundamental way, hermeneutics assumes a secondary position in relation to the general human engagement with meaning, understanding, and interpretation. Hermeneutics aims to give an account of meaning and its absence, and aspires to enhance people's understanding of meaning by augmented efforts of interpretation.

(3) Hermeneutics thus involves specialisation of the general human ability to understand and interpret, and this holds even when hermeneutics

responds critically to perceived meanings or current interpretations. Hermeneutics can be found in different genres of literature, religion, comedy, and so forth. The human and social sciences are all hermeneutic practices, in so far as they strive for enhanced interpretations of the world that people live in. This second order interpretation can never exhaustively or finally capture the whole sphere of meaning, but people cannot live without some form of second order interpretation. The specific form of second order hermeneutics that is recognised by people as having the capacity to enhance their understanding is contingent on people's historical and social context, both of which are subject to change.

(4) Philosophical hermeneutics is a further specialisation of hermeneutics. It typically enquires into the conditions for experiencing events, facts, and interactions as meaningful or meaningless. It strives to give the most encompassing view on the human experiences of meaning, understanding, and interpretation, but also pursues the question of the kind of truth that can realistically be attained through interpretation.

(5) As it is derived from a general human ability, and responds to the exercise of that ability in different spheres of human action, philosophical hermeneutics is never the beginning of understanding or interpretations. In fact, it assumes that, like interpretation in everyday action and in secondary hermeneutic procedures, philosophical hermeneutics also comes from a being that is finite and situated. No hermeneut can step outside of his/her own hermeneutic constitution of a contingently situated and finite being. All interpretation takes place within a given horizon, which limits understanding, but without which it is not possible to gain even a provisional grasp of understanding of anything.

(6) While understanding permeates common life, hermeneutic effort, and philosophical hermeneutics, something remains forever outside of people's limited grasp. This "outside" is not irrelevant, since it still has an impact on processes of understanding in ways that may be realised or reconstructed only long afterwards.

(7) In hermeneutics, everything is subject to flux. The interpreter is a historical being, shaped by contingent historical factors (culture, language, the political situation, and so on), exercising the ability to understand in changing social relations, according to insights about

and practices of interpretation that emerge from changing histories, and that apply to objects of interpretation that are equally subject to change. It is true that some aspects of human life are quite stable or even stagnant, but, whereas a hermeneutic view can give an account of such relative immobility, a view that starts from immobility cannot properly account for the temporality of everything human and meaningful. Interpreting the other also implies interpreting the self, and vice versa.

(8) As a practice, hermeneutics is an exercise in generosity, in the sense that it initially suspends value judgements. One could describe its scientific ethic as one of self-questioning and non-humiliation of the other. This holds even (or perhaps especially) where the work of interpretation has to engage critically with the material it studies. Thus, hermeneutic work is not a pretext for abolishing critique, but a means to pursue the best possible critique. Philosophical hermeneutics has to reflect on how (and to which extent) such a stance is possible, as well as the basis on which a critique may be, and on the difficulties associated with both this stance and the basis for critique.

(9) Hermeneutics surveys the whole range of relations people have with meaning: from the most intimate—even unconscious—attachment, to varieties of distanciation. In undertaking such a survey, it may incorporate explicatory research methods, but it has to do so with the understanding that a philosophical hermeneutics could give an account of the position of explication within interpretation. Hermeneutic work may eventually advocate some interpretations and critique others. These various attitudes in relation to meaning do not form a happy whole, but rather engender a field of tensions and difficult dialectics. There is no pro forma outcome of this conflict. Each time, new configurations of appropriation and distanciation arise.

(10) Hermeneutics pays attention to all that makes it difficult to understand meanings expressed by people of other eras or regions, but it supposes that, in principle, there is always something that can be learned from the temporal, spatial, or cultural other. There may be no direct learning, only translation, which implies that something of what is transmitted will always be lost and something may be created and added. It is a reality of translation that some forms of expression cannot be reappropriated. The cultural and symbolic milieu in which one grows up and in which one may be at home may be shown to

contain strange and unpleasant components; likewise, it is possible to identify attractive and edifying elements in cultural expressions that one initially finds incomprehensible or repulsive.
(11) Meanings and understandings, interpretations and transmissions do not occur in a power-free vacuum, but reflect the specifics of the human and institutional power relations in which they are embedded. As a social reality, the practice of interpretation may itself be an exercise of power; conversely, it may also be an initiative by which to undermine existing relations of power. In addition, the whole sphere of power (action and interaction, and the means and institutions that mediate them) is a domain of hermeneutic study.
(12) In its theory and practice, hermeneutics is extremely attentive to the varieties, differences, and contradictions between cultural expressions. However, in its execution, it cannot rid itself of a number of basic assumptions of an anthropological nature (see the first point), even when this is not explicitly thematised. This recognition of some form of human generality comes to the fore in the inter-human communication of hermeneutic research findings: such communication presupposes that others are able to understand to some degree whatever is communicated. One may call this pragmatic generality or lateral universalism.
(13) Hermeneutics is concerned with all the different practices in which the basic human traits of understanding and interpretation are implicated. For this reason, the field of study of hermeneutics is constituted not only of scholarly and creative practices, but also of social and political realities. In turn, as a human practice, hermeneutics is concerned with the way in which it binds back into these practices. It does so by clarifying or problematising our understanding of history, laying bare abusive arguments and forms of argumentation, and by reflecting on the complexities of projecting courses of action into the future. The historical constitution (or historicity) of human beings as individual or collective agents is part of any research into the abilities and constraints on agency and the complexities of social reality in a specific time and place.

This is the basic position in respect of philosophical hermeneutics with which I enter the field of study of this book. Now, one may ask: where does this outline come from? And how can I claim to know what hermeneutics is before the study from which to conclude what hermeneutics is has unfolded?

The simple answer is that this *is* already a conclusion of sorts on the nature of hermeneutics. It results from my readings over many years, including my reading towards this monograph. It is very much my own synthesis, but it reflects insights gained from many other scholars. This outline of hermeneutics should thus not be misconstrued as a kind of point zero from which I started my research. It is meant as a point of entry into an ongoing process during which this view is constantly adjusted and corrected, because the process requires and enables reading iteratively, to gain fresh insights from those texts already studied, as well as from any new texts encountered.

This outline thus serves as an introduction. The fact that it is only one perspective among many does not invalidate it, because all views on hermeneutics are perspectival. At the same time, one should not overstate this point, since my outline reflects many recurrent traits of hermeneutics.[3] Therefore, the reader should not consider this outline to be a closed off statement, but rather as a point of departure, especially useful to those who are not yet very familiar with hermeneutics. From such a platform it should be easier to follow the contributions made by the specific authors considered in this book. The continual movement from research to provisional conclusions from which to conduct new research and revise the initial conclusions is typical for hermeneutic scholarship: it takes its own established ideas (sometimes called "pre-judices") as a positive given, whence to engage critically with material and to derive new, improved judgements about the nature and value of things. We find a similar way of working in the writings of Sophie Oluwole, who approaches ancient oral traditions in search of philosophy without a dogmatic initial definition of what should count as philosophy (see Chapter 5, § 2).

This then provides a platform, which means that the reader may compare each element with the thought of the authors studied in this book, without any preconceived idea about whether the outline or the author studied represents the fullest scope of hermeneutics. In the concluding chapter, I return to this encompassing view on hermeneutics. The aim there is not to lay bare a single view to which all the views in the book converge. Rather, by documenting my current understanding of hermeneutics, specifically in conversation with the authors considered in this book, I wish to highlight the complexity of the question of the nature of hermeneutics, and stimulate the reader's own reflection on this question.

Having clarified provisionally what I have in mind in speaking about hermeneutics and philosophical hermeneutics, I now need to provide some indication of the "African" aspect of African philosophical hermeneutics. Some authors presented in this book would approach this question by reflecting on what is meant by calling anything "African"—on what "Africanness" means. My approach is different, and consists of profiling philosophical hermeneutics as one strand of the body of thought that is de facto presented as African philosophy.

2. The place of hermeneutics in African philosophy

Approaching hermeneutics by means of an intellectual contextualisation provides me also with an opportunity to survey the current state of research from a bird's eye perspective. I approach African philosophical hermeneutics from the same perspective as that of scholars who try to clarify general trends in African philosophy. Such authors recognise that African philosophy cannot be reduced to a single type of philosophy, but acknowledge that it takes on divergent forms. They help us to understand hermeneutics as part of the landscape of African philosophy by situating it in relation to other forms of philosophy in Africa or, in some cases, by denying hermeneutics a rightful place among African philosophies.

In presenting the major trends and issues, this discussion may also help those unfamiliar with African philosophy to acquaint themselves with some of the major problems it grapples with.

Instead of simply listing discussions of trends in African philosophy, I believe it is more revealing to identify two major propositions, indicating a number of authors who engage with them, explicitly or implicitly. The first of these two points of orientation is provided by Henry Odera Oruka, and the second by Nkombe Oleko and Alfons Smet.

2.1. *The place of hermeneutics in African philosophy: using Oruka as a point of departure*

• *Henry Odera Oruka*

Arguably the most influential typology of African philosophy is Henry Odera Oruka's "Four Trends in Current African Philosophy"[4] of 1978. The first trend he identifies is ethnophilosophy (as it was first named by its critics). Ethnophilosophers strive to identify the philosophy contained in traditional religion and rituals, customs and forms of belief, and especially in oral traditions. In this form, philosophy serves as an expression of collective views of cultural or ethnic groups on the world and human existence.

Second, he notes the documentation of the personal insights of rigorous thinkers who have had no or little exposure to forms of learning from outside Africa. The thought of these sages and its documentation are an instance of African philosophy and serve as a starting point for further philosophising.

The third trend is what Oruka called nationalist-ideological philosophy. It is primarily represented by the political thought of great African statesmen. These authors have developed specific views on how to rehabilitate traditional communalism by combining it with a contemporary humanism and a view on true African freedom. The practical political problems of the present take central place, and if aspects of Western philosophy can help these thinkers to address these problems, then they draw on those aspects.

The fourth trend is somewhat misleadingly named "professional philosophy". It consists of work written and taught by African scholars, most of whom completed their formal philosophical education in Western countries and continue to produce reflective and critical studies in line with the scholarly traditions of the countries where they pursued their doctoral studies.

It is difficult to say whether Oruka did not take note of the texts on hermeneutics that existed in 1978, or whether he judged that they did not yet amount to a trend then. However, hermeneutics does figure in his revised typology of 1990: in his book, *Sage Philosophy: Indigenous Thinkers and Modern Debate on African Philosophy*,[5] Oruka adds two further trends. In identifying in literature a philosophical bent, Oruka wanted to acknowledge the spread of philosophy well beyond the confines of universities. He also wanted to highlight the real contribution to debates on philosophical problems that can be traced in great works of literature by African writers. Such contributions provide fertile material for philosophy, which may in turn be developed further by specialist philosophers.

Finally, Oruka also identified a trend that he called "hermeneutics". This seems to endorse the position of hermeneutics as a branch of African philosophy, and indeed, this claim is often taken simply at face value in the literature on African philosophy. However, when one looks more closely at what Oruka has in mind with this term, the issue turns out to be much less conclusive. According to Oruka, the hermeneutic trend consists of the philosophical analysis of concepts in a given African language to help clarify meaning and logical implications arising from the use of such concepts. Kwasi Wiredu, for example, is already doing this with useful results from an analysis of Akan language. And studies by Kwame Gyekye, *An essay on African philosophical through* (the Akan Conceptual Scheme, 1987) and Barry Hallen and J.O. Sodipo *Knowledge, Belief and Witchcraft*, 1986, are in my judgement, at best, exercises in hermeneutic African philosophy. The two, however, tend to claim that they are reports of the philosophies and wisdoms of the indigenous traditional thinkers rather than the unhindered conceptual analysis of the language of their informants by the researchers.[6]

This description poses several difficulties. First, as far as I can ascertain, Gyekye, Hallen, and Sodipo do not claim to be practising hermeneuts. Second, the components of linguistic analysis and an elucidation of traditional belief and knowledge are insufficient to distinguish them from ethnophilosophy. In fact, Oruka seems to acknowledge as much in the last sentence of the quotation above (a view he reaffirms on page xxvi). Still, a few details do in fact point us in the direction of hermeneutics as I outlined it above: (a) Oruka himself underscores the independent contribution of these authors, as opposed to merely reporting their traditional heritage; (b) these contributions consist of a clarification and elucidation of implications of language and other elements of traditions; and (c) if Oruka is right in saying that Wiredu is "doing this" (hermeneutic work), even when he does not claim to be doing so explicitly, it should sensitise us to the possibility of sometimes finding hermeneutics where it is not openly declared.

But I want to come back to another kind of typology implied in Oruka's initial synopsis. Running across the four major trends (but certainly also the fifth and sixth) is the question of what we mean by calling a philosophy "African". Some philosophers anchor their view of African philosophy in what is uniquely African (and therefore stands in opposition to or differs from European philosophy, which in the early post-independence period was the main other point of reference), whereas others proclaim the universality of philosophy, and rather see an African specificity in the particularity of the authors and/or the context(s) for which they write. Many other scholars espouse a mix of the two stances. We will see throughout this book that the question of the Africanness of philosophy also spreads through hermeneutics and the critique of hermeneutics.

- *Kwasi Wiredu*

Given that Oruka identifies Wiredu's work as hermeneutic, it may be useful to look at how Wiredu in turn went about mapping African philosophies. Section 5 of his entry on anglophone African philosophy for the *Routledge Encyclopedia of Philosophy* is devoted to a "Typology of Current Trends".[7] Wiredu's discussion in many ways simply takes over Oruka's sixfold typology, including the hermeneutical philosophy trend, for which he even references the same examples. What distinguishes his presentation from that of Oruka is that he then engages with these examples from his own work, from that of Gyekye and that of Hallen and Sodipo, in much greater detail than Oruka does. What then makes this exposition of hermeneutics remarkable is that Wiredu does not question the existence of this trend of philosophy in the least, nor the applicability of the term "hermeneutics" to the specific examples Oruka gives, including to his own work. This amounts to strong support for Oruka's application of the category "hermeneutic" beyond works that are explicitly offered under this label. A second remarkable fact is that Wiredu does not even mention the current of thought that explicitly assumes the label "hermeneutic" (as one finds, for instance, in Hallen, see below).[8] And for this reason the differences between two bodies of work—implicit hermeneutics and explicit hermeneutics—remain unthematised.

Wiredu's own introduction to the Blackwell *Companion to African Philosophy*, which he edited, is entitled "African Philosophy in Our Time".[9] Unsurprisingly, its content overlaps with that of his contribution to the *Routledge Encyclopedia*. Again, he does not refer specifically to a hermeneutic trend in African philosophy. However, in the same volume, we find this trend specifically addressed in the article by his "co-hermeneut", Barry Hallen.

- *Barry Hallen*

Because of this discussion of hermeneutics by Hallen, and because Oruka cited Hallen and Sodipo as exquisite examples of the hermeneutic trend, Hallen's overview of African philosophies in *A Short History of African Philosophy* may be instructive here.[10] Indeed, he refers explicitly to Oruka's typology,[11] but does not discuss Oruka's classification at that point. What Hallen does instead is to propose his own characterisation of his and

Sodipo's approach as arising "[a]fter careful consideration of the possibilities, [...] from an adaptation of the philosophical tradition conventionally known as Ordinary Language Analysis,"[12] in other words, as somewhat akin to a strand of anglophone, analytic language philosophy, and as quite similar to Oruka's understanding of hermeneutic work as "philosophical analysis of concepts in a given African language to help clarify meaning and logical implications arising from the use of such concepts".[13] Hallen discusses his and Sodipo's work as part of chapter 4 of his book, but devotes a different chapter to "Phenomenology and Hermeneutics" (chapter 6). The work of Hallen and Sodipo is not mentioned in chapter 6 at all, and from the first paragraph, hermeneutics is opposed to analysis as a different major methodological option in philosophy.[14]

Two further points of Hallen's introduction define his view of African hermeneutics. He strongly emphasises its European roots and not, for instance, the anthropological and common cultural ones[15] Also, Hallen singles out Theophilus Okere, Okolo Okonda, and Tsenay Serequeberhan as major proponents of African philosophical hermeneutics. In other words, unlike Wiredu, Hallen replaces the set of examples initially given by Oruka. The understanding of hermeneutics in the work of Okere, Okolo, and Serequeberhan is indeed different from that of the authors cited by Oruka, and comes much closer to the working outline of hermeneutics I gave above, although there is undeniably some overlap.

In the next three chapters, I focus on the three authors Okere, Okolo, and Serequeberhan as examples of authors who claim explicitly to be doing hermeneutics. Hallen's comments on the hermeneutic dimensions of Africana philosophy written in North America need not detain us here.[16] However, I acknowledge that my own focus on Africa is not a watertight demarcation, as can be seen from my discussions of Serequeberhan and Mudimbe elsewhere in this book.

• *Segun Gbadegesin*

Having traced the meandering path that links Oruka, Wiredu, and Hallen, I want to stop at another author who makes something quite different of Oruka's original typology: Segun Gbadegesin. In his "On the Idea of African Philosophy",[17] Gbadegesin offers a much more detailed and critical discussion of views on African philosophy than that of Oruka, although in essence the broad strokes correspond to Oruka's 1978 typology.

Gbadegesin mentions neither of the two trends Oruka added in 1990, namely literature and hermeneutics. Perhaps the short space of time that separates Oruka's second typology (1990) from Gbadegesin's essay (1991) accounts for his not referring to Oruka's later text; however, this does not alter the fact that Gbadegesin did not think it necessary to add to Oruka's first typology himself.

A few years later, in a synopsis of "Current Trends and Perspectives in African Philosophy",[18] Gbadegesin categorises that part of Wiredu's work that Oruka associated with hermeneutics as "critical cultural philosophy" and, interestingly, devotes space to a summary of some of his own work alongside that of Wiredu, under the same heading. However, here too, there is no mention of hermeneutics.

These two texts of Gbadegesin hint that hermeneutics is of no significance in the landscape of African philosophy. He does not suggest that what Oruka designated by that term is irrelevant, but his silence on the matter implies that apparently there is nothing in African philosophy worth mentioning under the name "hermeneutics". His position raises the question of whether anything is lost by labelling texts works of "hermeneutics" instead of works of "critical cultural philosophy", and how far the range of studies stretches that could be labelled as following this trend.

• *Other contemporary perspectives*

Gbadegesin's view (or rather, his silence) is frequently echoed in contemporary overviews. Adeshina Afolayan and Toyin Falola's *The Palgrave Handbook of African Philosophy* mentions Oruka's category of hermeneutic philosophy,[19] invokes Mudimbe's reference to hermeneutics,[20] and briefly discusses Okere and Serequeberhan under the heading of "situated philosophy".[21] Otherwise, hermeneutics figures only in Peter Amato's chapter "On Vernacular Rationality: Gadamer and Eze in Conversation"[22] as a means of comparison to profile Emmanuel Chukwude Eze's "vernacular rationality", and Amato uses only Gadamer's hermeneutics for this purpose.

Thaddeus Metz's bibliographical overview, "Contemporary African Philosophy",[23] hardly mentions hermeneutics and cites only Serequeberhan's 1991 book.

Issac Ukpokolo writes in the introduction to *Themes, Issues and Problems in African Philosophy*:[24]

> The present volume brings to the fore the very important need to represent philosophical reflections in Africa with emphasis on specific areas of the discipline, such as metaphysics, political philosophy, aesthetics, existentialism, *hermeneutics*, epistemology, gender discourse, ethics or moral philosophy, and other cross-disciplinary discourses.

But if I read correctly, African philosophical hermeneutics is only mentioned once, in passing.[25]

Still, these overviews do not represent scholarly consensus. As part of an (undated) overview of African philosophy for the *Internet Encyclopedia of Philosophy*,[26] Jonathan Chimakonam takes over Oruka's extended typology, including hermeneutics. Some individual authors do confirm the significance of hermeneutics, as I illustrate with examples such as Ademola Kazeem Fayemi and Bruce Janz.

Fayemi's discussion of "Hermeneutics in African Philosophy"[27] not only confirms the place of hermeneutics, but does so in a unique way. He distinguishes between a European history of hermeneutics and an African one, but he simply juxtaposes his discussion of both without any value judgement. Even more interestingly, his understanding of where to find hermeneutics embraces both ordinary language philosophy and the narrower hermeneutic trend (in other words, he simply holds together what Hallen separates into two distinct trends). A third defining aspect of his view is his recurrent insistence on the idea of hermeneutics as a methodology, for which he could expect opposition from many sides.

Janz's[28] short presentation of African philosophical hermeneutics in *The Routledge Companion to Hermeneutics* is also singular in that it embeds our question in the context of intercultural understanding. Janz attributes to hermeneutics ten subtasks. Of these, I would like to highlight the six tasks for which Janz explicitly cites African philosophers as proponents:

> [3] A way of analyzing cultural objects or practices by those within the culture (e.g. Madu 1992);
> [4] A term for some forms of linguistic or semantic analysis (e.g. Odera Oruka's use of the term for Hallen and Sodipo's work; Bongmba 1998);

[5] A way of describing a cultural life-world—intra-cultural, rather than inter-cultural (Okere 1983);

[6] A way of accessing "non-philosophy" (Okere 1983);

[7] A way of uncovering modes of misunderstanding in cultural encounter (e.g. Serequeberhan 1994; Mbembe 2001; Mudimbe 1988);

[8] A method of establishing a philosophical tradition in a place that does not have some hallmark of philosophy (e.g. a textual corpus—Okere 1983; Owolabi 2001).[29]

This list is self-explanatory. However, I would like to draw attention to two things. First, Janz does not only "round up the usual suspects" (Madu, Okere, Owolabi, Serequeberhan, and implicit hermeneuts such as Hallen and Sodipo), but also includes such authors as Mbembe and Mudimbe. What hermeneutics is, or the tasks it fulfils, seems to be the measure of inclusion here, rather than the specific authors' explicit adoption of the label "hermeneutics". Second, hermeneutic analysis and critique functions in such a way that *inter*cultural reflection implies *intra*cultural reflection and vice versa.[30] Admittedly, essentialising and reifying others may well enforce the same kind of view of oneself and vice versa. But hermeneutics understands itself as being vigilant against essentialisation and reification in *both directions at the same time*. If this view is correct, a *hermeneutic* approach to the question of the place of hermeneutics in African philosophy would guard against exaggerating claims of the uniformity of African philosophy, and of African hermeneutics in particular, and it would be equally attentive to possible continuities as to discontinuities between, say, European hermeneutics and African hermeneutics.

From all of this one has to conclude that the position of hermeneutics as part of African philosophy is sometimes confirmed—either in the narrow explicit sense, or in the implicit sense of philosophical language analysis—and sometimes not denied as much as simply implied to be nothing much to speak about.

Thus far I have considered only anglophone texts in this literature review. Hence, for most of the authors cited above, one has to wonder to what extent language was a barrier that had an effect (usually reductive) on their view of African philosophy. For this reason, it is worth undertaking the same exercise from a francophone perspective.

2.2. The place of hermeneutics in African philosophy: using Nkombe and Smet as a point of departure

• *Nkombe Oleko and Alfons Smet*

Nkombe and Smet's overview of African philosophies, "Panorama de la philosophie africaine contemporaine" dates from the same year as Oruka's initial typology (1978).[31] They take as their starting point the argument that African philosophy develops from the tension between (traditional) African wisdom and Western philosophy, and fans out into a wide range of philosophical practices. They identify four major currents:

(1) In the ideological current, "ideology" refers to the thrust of *opposition to* historical ideologies that legitimated the slave trade, slavery, and colonisation, and affirms an original, authentic African culture and personality. This form of philosophy aims at the liberation of Africans, politically, economically, and culturally. This family of philosophies includes the philosophy of African personality, Pan-Africanism, négritude, African humanism, African socialism, consciencism, and the philosophy of authenticity.[32]

(2) The current of recognition of traditional African philosophy also opposes historical prejudices, but especially their anthropological form. This current is found in the work of non-Africans, for which Nkombe and Smet provide ample bibliographical references. This work includes both the quest for philosophical elements in traditional culture and the description of philosophising in traditional culture. To this they add systematisations of traditional African philosophies and the documentation of other forms of traditional wisdom. In the latter two forms, one notes an increasing contribution by African scholars too.

(3) The critical current opposes aspects of the first two currents of thought. It is most notably represented by a critique of ethnophilosophy, but also includes a critique of Western understandings of science and philosophy. Related to this current is a strand of critical exploration of the relation between language (often a foreign language) and philosophy.

(4) The last current, which Nkombe and Smet refer to as "synthetic", stands somewhat apart from the three previously mentioned currents, insofar as it attempts to find contemporary syntheses of thought relevant to contemporary problems. This may be considered a spectrum

of approaches. On the one hand, it detaches itself from the question of the nature of African philosophy in order to document, by means of bibliographies and histories, the whole range of productions and views available in which at least some people recognise that it is of African philosophical nature. On the other hand, without ignoring tradition and history, "synthetic" philosophers pursue new problematics: they primarily undertake the task of identifying, and working on, the philosophical problems of the present. Between these two poles are two quite similar forms of philosophy. "Functional" philosophy "reads" ideas from the past in the light of contemporary questions, and specifically with a view to finding solutions for contemporary problems. "Hermeneutic" philosophy works seriously with African traditions, without taking philosophy as given—it sees philosophy rather as something that is still, and continuously, to be developed. Here an engaged scholar "rereads" the tradition with a view to finding a productive contemporary take on it, rather than a detached rendering of it.[33]

Based on the bibliographical evidence Nkombe and Smet provide for each of the currents, one can see that particular texts can represent different currents. In their demarcation of the four currents, Nkombe and Smet do not hesitate to trace contributions to African philosophy as far back as the early nineteenth century. Nor do they make any distinction, in principle, between authors of African, European, or American descent, and they embrace a broad interdisciplinary view of philosophy (including anthropology, theology, and philosophy in the narrower sense). In principle, these general traits of their overview apply equally to hermeneutics.[34]

- *V. Y. Mudimbe*

Mudimbe[35] engages extensively in "African Philosophy as an Ideological Practice: The Case of French-Speaking Africa" with the way in which Nkombe and Smet articulate the relation between different traditions of philosophy.[36] He appears to be, by and large, in agreement with their panorama of African philosophies, as can be deduced from his (only slightly different) reformulation:

> To be clearer, it seems to me that, on the one hand, investigations to restore traditional African philosophy (second trend) are complementary to the

ideological school—eminently theoretical—of which they are concrete expressions. On the other hand, the critical trend—third school—should be considered as an indispensable stepping stone or, more precisely as the first essential thing without which the fourth orientation—the quest for syntheses, hermeneutic or functional philosophy—would have no meaning, at least as a rigorous philosophical project.[37]

The fact that Mudimbe proposes an alternative schematic representation of varieties of African philosophy and their interrelations does not invalidate the basic overview.[38] Mudimbe's own re-schematisation of the African philosophical varieties starts out from a first major distinction that stretches from a side that includes the more ethnophilosophical and ideological approaches to approaches that he considers "of a strictly philosophical bent".[39] The way in which Mudimbe situates hermeneutics within this second approach is of interest to us, namely as the last step in a process of an increasing complexification of African philosophy:

How is African philosophy in the strict sense presented? As a new field, it is difficult to establish an organization for it as clear as that of the works of philosophy in the wider sense. To begin with, because of the criterion of increasing complexity of philosophical needs, the easiest way would be to take note of its high points in chronological order: (1) a philosophical reflection on the conditions of the possibility of African philosophy, (2) a reflection on the significance of Western science, (3) a reflection on philosophy as a critical auxiliary to the process of African development, and finally (4) philosophical hermeneutics.[40]

While Mudimbe's point remains cryptic, it would be counter to his argument to consider these four trends as reflecting a linear development, let alone as a line of progress. He probably has in mind a chronological succession of the emergence of diverse directions, which implies that the role of hermeneutics in relation to the other three lines has yet to be determined.

Mudimbe's historical window is much narrower than that of Nkombe and Smet. He states that "[after 1956 and] [b]efore 1965, we could hardly count ten significant works [i.e. books, not articles] with an explicit philosophical ambition", but later in the text he considers expanding this number.[41] However, for the remainder of his argument, his reappropriation of their typology can be taken as a confirmation of it. He also agrees with them in not pigeonholing texts, but in rather identifying trends that may appear together in single texts. Moreover, he adopts their interdisciplinary view of philosophy generally. Finally, one notices both in Mudimbe and in Nkombe and Smet the significant place accorded to a francophone bibliography in support of their typology.[42]

• *Kasereka Kavwahirehi*

As part of his survey of francophone African philosophy for *The Oxford Encyclopedia of African Thought*,[43] Kasereka Kavwahirehi outlines the two important historical trends of négritude and ethnophilosophy, and the critiques of these two trends. Thereafter, adopting a point from Mudimbe's schema (above), but through the specific vocabulary he uses, implicitly that of Nkombe and Smet, Kavwahirehi accords a specific position to "synthetic trends" in African philosophy. His exposition pinpoints the place of hermeneutics:

> It is perhaps these limitations that, at the end of the 1970s, motivated the creation of a new philosophical trend that has been described as "synthetic". While shrewdly accepting the contributions of ethnophilosophers and critical philosophers, this movement distanced itself from the controversy raging between the two camps. In fact, according to its disciples, both movements belong, in the words of Mudimbe ("African Philosophy as an Ideological Practice", p. 148), to "a history of African philosophy in the making". By dialectically merging ethnophilosophy and critical philosophy, synthetic philosophers are committed to searching for epistemological foundations and appropriate methods in order to elaborate a new African discourse on the world without renouncing African wisdom. The conference held in Kinshasa in 1983 on the theme of "problems of method in philosophy and social sciences in Africa" clearly illustrated this preoccupation. If the methods discussed at this conference were numerous, particular attention was given to philosophical hermeneutics.
>
> From this point on, scholars would concentrate their efforts on offering a personal rereading of traditions, not, however, with the intention of piecing together the thought of ancestors as such, but rather of reactualizing it within the framework of new systematizations in order to make efficient use of it in the present. In addition, there was a growing interest in examining the functionality of philosophy in terms of the development and the political liberation of Africa (Okolo Okonda, Elungu). This tendency became more pronounced with the collapse of the postcolonial state and the first tentative steps in democracy.[44]

The word "hermeneutics" is used only once, but in a very revealing way. Kavwahirehi's account of "synthetic" trends corresponds exactly to the exposition of Nkombe and Smet. In this context, the position of hermeneutics is historically limited and framed—in respect of both its regional context and the state of philosophical problematics—but the continuities of hermeneutics, both with forms of African thought that precede it and that come after it, are highlighted. It is accorded a *modest* place as a specific philosophical subdiscipline but an *encompassing* role as the coordinator of philosophical concerns—historical and practical—as a whole. From Kavwahirehi's perspective, on the one hand, the place of hermeneutics is so narrow that it can almost be missed, but, on the other hand, it henceforth accompanies all "synthetic" methods. Hermeneutics stands for the project of a continuing philosophical search for modes of thinking that are essentially an *appropriation* of history and a *projection* of the future, each in the light of the other. What we will see is that a large part of philosophical hermeneutics—in the narrow sense—consists precisely in clarifying this "position of synthesis": in Chapter 5, I examine bodies of thought that assume this position as many responses to the question of who is concerned with these issues and by which means they deal with these issues.

Perhaps these conclusions that I draw from Kavwahirehi are a stretch in terms of the content of his text. But it is worth noting that one can find additional support for these conclusions in the literature. On the one hand, while Mutunda Mwembo celebrates the importance of hermeneutics, his *La Quête du sens dans la philosophie africaine contemporaine: L'Herméneutique Zaïroise et le problème de grille de lecture* clearly anchors his claims within the situation of the DRC/Zaïre.[45] Correspondingly, the four main authors he singles out are locally and institutionally related, namely Kinyongo, Okolo, Nkombe, and Tshiamalenga. This confirms the emergence of hermeneutics in different specific localities under specific circumstances (what is said about Zaïre applies, *mutatis mutandis*, to a few other places too). On the other hand, Elvis Elengabeka in "L'Herméneutique au carrefour des rationalités et son impact sur le 'savoir' africain"[46] embraces the view that hermeneutics offers an excellent vantage point from which to interpret all forms of human rationality. This claim is generally supported by authors who self-identify as hermeneuts.

• *Other contemporary perspectives*

One may compare *The Palgrave Handbook of African Philosophy*'s silence on hermeneutics to another volume, also of 2017: a special edition of the journal *Nokoko*, entitled *Philosophie africaine: Ses paradigmes et son historiographie/African Philosophy: Its Paradigms and Historiography*.[47] As a single special issue of a journal, it does not have the same encyclopaedic ambition of *The Palgrave Handbook of African Philosophy*, but it still attempts to give representative views on African philosophy, past and present.

Already in the opening article's discussion of methodology, there is a discussion of hermeneutics, relevant to the work of Nkombe Oleko.[48] This is followed by a kind of retrospective article by Okolo Okonda[49] and an entire article devoted to "The Hermeneutical Paradigm in African Philosophy. Genesis, Evolution and Issues" by Louis-Dominique Biakolo Komo.[50] This article is already noteworthy for my discussion, because Biakolo Komo characterises hermeneutics as "one of the most important trends in modern and contemporary African Philosophy".[51] However, Komo goes much further: by fully adopting the premise that "philosophy is inherently interpretative", he reconsiders hermeneutics as a component of African philosophy as such, or at least as a perspective from which to look at most of the key questions of African philosophy. Accordingly, he construes ethnophilosophy as a kind of precursor to hermeneutics, for which he subsequently discusses what he sees as the main representatives: Okere, Nkombe, Okolo, and Serequeberhan. It is not my intention to endorse Komo's view in its entirety, but to demonstrate how far it is possible to differ from the view that hermeneutics is nothing to African philosophy. Another noteworthy aspect of the volume is its significant orientation towards and inclusion of francophone African philosophy.

However, to ensure that we do not create simplistic schemas, I need to emphasise that not all francophone authors affirm the significance of hermeneutics in African philosophy. Biyogo's four volumes on the history of African philosophy do not include a chapter on hermeneutics and, if I see correctly, they do not even mention such a trend.[52] The massive *Encyclopedia of African Religions and Philosophy*[53] does not contain an entry on hermeneutics, and the online search platform for this work indicates only three occurrences of "hermeneutics" in the text. And if one thinks that a solid background in European philosophy would incline scholars to recognise the hermeneutics trend in African philosophy, one finds a startling contradiction to such a supposition in Heinz Kimmerle's *Philosophie in Afrika, afrikanische Philosophie*.[54]

On the other hand, one could extend the list of authors who *do* recognise hermeneutics.[55] From these, I would like to single out an instructive example: Frederick Ochieng-Odhiambo, *Trends and Issues in African Philosophy*.[56] This book is an important document for my present purpose, because, although it is broadly constructed on the lines of Okere's typology, Ochieng-Odhiambo's chapter devoted to hermeneutics[57] is much closer in content to the view of Nkombe and Smet. To begin with, the key representatives he identifies for hermeneutics are Okere, Okolo, and Serequeberhan. Ochieng-Odhiambo's main argument is thus that hermeneutics has to be understood as an attempt to overcome both particularist and universalist understandings of African philosophy, reminiscent of Nkombe and Smet's position. It is a strong proposition, because instead of merely adding another trend, Ochieng-Odhiambo explains the logic behind the emergence of hermeneutics from the existing problematics in African philosophy itself. In doing so, he affirms another point made by Nkombe and Smet, namely *not* to emphasise the role of European inheritance in African hermeneutics (as Hallen does) at the expense of the role of African scholars working on their own problems in their own context. To conclude, Ochieng-Odhiambo helps us to remain vigilant regarding the overlaps between the different families of typologies presented here.[58]

Finally, it may be interesting also to consider works with a broad encyclopaedic claim on hermeneutics in philosophy generally. The 2019 *Cambridge Companion to Hermeneutics* does not seem to have registered the fact that there is an African hermeneutics (not even in its chapter on non-Western hermeneutics[59]). By contrast, *The Routledge Companion to Hermeneutics*[60] devotes numerous chapters to hermeneutics in settings other than a Western setting, and African hermeneutics figures in the chapter by Bruce Janz, "Hermeneutics and Intercultural Understanding" (already discussed above).

2.3. *Preliminary conclusions*

This chapter certainly does not claim to be an exhaustive overview of the literature, but it suffices to provide a representative view of positions on hermeneutics and its place in African philosophy.

From this we learn that the position of hermeneutics in African philosophy is far from clear. Although it is frequently recognised that there is an important hermeneutic trend, sometimes this fact is not reflected in overviews. Not all reviewers agree which bodies of work reflect the prime examples of hermeneutics: is it the work of Wiredu, Gyekye, and Hallen and Sodipo, or should we rather turn to those who adopted the label "hermeneutics" explicitly, such as Okere, Okolo, and Serequeberhan? Or is this distinction moot, and could we group them all together? When hermeneutics is presented as a trend in African philosophy, its proximity to Western philosophy is a point of disagreement: some authors consider it close to European philosophy (but then, is the leading figure Gadamer or Ricœur?), or as actually closer to English common language philosophy, while others consider the Western heritage marginal and emphasise the originality of the African authors. Some overviews attribute to hermeneutics a small but real position in the African philosophical landscape, while others consider hermeneutics to be an encompassing enterprise that could correct or account for other strands of African philosophy. Some consider hermeneutics more from the perspective of an established methodology and set of ideas, while others emphasise that hermeneutics is a form of philosophising and a synthesis in the making. In general, it seems safe to say that the best attempts at an overview are shaped by the respective author's own scholarly background, current commitments, institutional setting, and language abilities, and tend to reflect a specific time in history.

Perhaps a fair conclusion would be that the presence of hermeneutics is too definite a phenomenon to be denied, but that its precise place in the field of African philosophies remains uncertain and contested. Some authors explicitly embrace the term hermeneutics, but one should also be attentive to contributions made to hermeneutic issues by authors for whom that label was unimportant, and who may have preferred to describe their work in other ways (for example, Gbadegesin's "critical cultural studies" or Nkombe and Smet's general "synthetic" attempt as the development of contemporary African philosophy). Some overviews amply illustrate a *centrifugal* tendency in hermeneutics, in the sense that different observers identify an expanding array of concerns and modes of thinking as hermeneutics, as if hermeneutics is not simply a single form of philosophy. Sometimes this can be attributed to regional and linguistic tendencies in scholarly practice, but often there is no general trend (in other words, authors from the same scholarly, regional, and linguistic background can also have divergent opinions). Nevertheless, the literature also bears witness to the *centripetal* force of hermeneutics, which attracts to it a wide array of philosophies that are concerned with tradition and language, interpretation and practice, and, generally, the question of a philosophical clarification of the real-life problems with which Africans must deal.

Ultimately, this implies that the divergent views on the presence of hermeneutics and the form it takes cannot be harmonised easily, which at least partially accounts for the sceptical silence about hermeneutics in some overviews. As I already indicated in the Preface, my aim with this book is not to pin down, once and for all, what hermeneutics is, nor to advocate what should be done with it in African philosophy. However, despite the uncertainty documented here, I consider the literature referenced under the name of "hermeneutics" to be philosophically rich and challenging, and certainly worth studying. The whole effort of this book is aimed at offering the readers help in deciding for themselves.

3. Hermeneutics: an author-based approach

Having familiarised ourselves with the place of hermeneutics in African philosophy and with the wide range of problems raised in trying to circumscribe its real contribution to African philosophy, we can now clarify the line of enquiry in the remainder of this book. The aim is not to resolve the perplexing issues raised, but to work our way through them. To do so, I must now descend from the bird's eye perspective of the typologist or historian of tendencies to the worm's eye perspective of detailed textual analysis. I do my utmost to adopt this perspective very rigorously, by concentrating mostly on one text at a time, and offering the best possible reading of it.

Still, some clarification and justification are warranted regarding my selection of authors and texts. Above we have seen that one of the important questions regarding African philosophical hermeneutics is who its real representatives are. Some authors explicitly espouse that label, while others, based on the kind of work they do, may be said to belong among the representatives of hermeneutics.

Accordingly, I have devoted considerable space to studying three authors whom one may call *explicit* contributors to hermeneutics: Theophilus Okere from Nigeria (b. 1935, d. 2020), Okolo Okonda[61] from the DRC (b. 1947) and Tsenay Serequeberhan from Eritrea (b. 1952). Their importance as primary early figures of hermeneutics is widely recognised. I study one book by each—three books that may be considered classics of African philosophical hermeneutics. This already suffices to justify the amount of attention I devote to them. At the same time, it should be noted that they are only three authors whom I consider to be major representatives, and that an encyclopaedic study would have to include many other authors. I ordered the three studies, not in chronological order of publication, but in order of complexity: Okere, Serequeberhan, and Okolo. Each chapter serves the double aim of an introduction to the respective author's book and a critical engagement with that book, and each chapter ends with a conclusion summarising the main developments.

I have also devoted a separate chapter to *implicit* contributions to hermeneutics. Here my selection is open to debate. I do, however, hope that it is representative of some of the main kinds of contribution to hermeneutics, broadly construed. The selection includes Cheikh Anta Diop for his view on language and the importance of history. Sophie Oluwole represents authors with a more anglophone sensitivity (in this sense, Wiredu or Gyekye could also be used). The inclusion of V. Y. Mudimbe is justified by his magisterial illustration of the genealogical approach and his effective turning of the African gaze to European Africanism. Somewhat akin to Mudimbe's genealogy is Fabien Eboussi Boulaga's deep hermeneutics of the role of philosophical practice in people's self-affirmation in the wake of the total defeat by colonisation. Finally, Diagne demonstrates the wealth of insights for philosophy and socio-political critique that can be derived from studying translation. Together, they open a perspective on the wide range of possibilities of hermeneutics, spanning the diverse thoughts published by Africans up to the present.

The discussion of works by these authors is shorter than that devoted to the explicit hermeneuts. This asymmetry is intended only to reflect the explicit–implicit distinction, rather than a value judgement on implicit hermeneutics. However, as with the three core hermeneuts, I maintain the same double objective: to give a fair presentation of their contribution to hermeneutics—more reconstructed in the case of the implicit hermeneuts—while retaining the freedom to assess specific points or larger tendencies in the argument.

This selection is far from exhaustive, and could be widened considerably. Let me give a few examples and explain why I decided not to include these—and similar—texts in the present study. Elizabeth Mburu's *African Hermeneutics*[62] focuses specifically on Biblical hermeneutics for African theologians, whereas I wanted to limit my investigation to philosophy. Stanley Uche Anozie's *Hans-Georg Gadamer and African Hermeneutic Philosophy*[63] deals with the novelist Chinua Achebe as the main representative of African hermeneutic philosophy. This is an interesting thesis to explore and is valuable as an attempt to amalgamate Oruka's fifth and sixth trends in African philosophy. However, Anozie's approach is not very representative of African philosophical hermeneutics generally. Finally, Raphael Okechukwu Madu's *African Symbols, Proverbs and Myths. The Hermeneutics of Destiny*[64] could be considered an excellent elaboration on Okere's understanding of hermeneutics. The cultural anthropological concerns that form the point of gravitation in Madu's book is represented in other studies included in my book. Although they are not central to my undertaking in this book, all of these books are fascinating reading. They widen our perspective on hermeneutics and offer a more contemporary view than my emphasis on classics would allow for.

In studying the selected works, I have attempted to reconstruct their arguments on my own terms. In as far as this is the case, the chapters are intended to be used as introductions to these works considered as contributions to philosophical hermeneutics. However, I have also made use of analysis and clarification where needed. Finally, where I deemed it necessary to do so, I freely indicated the implications of the points of an argument and expressed a critique—not in the spirit of a schoolmaster who points out little errors, but to honour the authors as serious scholars.[65] In as far as I elaborated the implications and developed critique, the chapters serve the purpose of an independent contribution to scholarship.

By discussing these texts, I hope to give a few suggestions of how to orient oneself in the landscape of hermeneutics. As already indicated, I mostly focused on one text per author and did my best to let the authors speak for themselves in my reading of those texts. The secondary literature used is primarily other publications by the same author. However, I have included select annotated bibliographies at the end of each chapter for further reading.

My question in this book is what is to be learned about and from African philosophers. For this reason, I do not refer to either European philosophy or post-colonial studies, or African philosophy, unless this is unavoidable (to some extent the select annotated bibliographies provided should compensate for this). Likewise, I discuss the African hermeneuts' use of European authors[66] in general terms where this is necessary to understand their own propositions, limiting my comments on their exegesis of these authors to the minimum.

Now the stage has been set for an exploration of African hermeneutics. If Hountondji was right—back in 1969—in saying that the issue of African philosophy raises the question of hermeneutics, how did his colleagues respond to this call? The first to attempt[67] to address this matter was Theophilus Okere, to whom we turn in the next chapter.

CHAPTER 2

On the threshold: from cultural philosophemes to African hermeneutics—Theophilus Okere

Theophilus Okere's *African Philosophy: A Historico-hermeneutic Investigation of the Conditions of its Possibility* was published in 1983.[1] Although by then several African philosophers had written their own hermeneutic studies, *African Philosophy* originated much earlier. This book is the second part of Okere's 1971 doctoral thesis, *Can There Be an African Philosophy? A Hermeneutical Study with Special Reference to Igbo Culture*, which he completed at the Catholic University of Leuven, in Belgium.[2] With *African Philosophy*,[3] Okere emerged as an important hermeneut, but it is important to understand the book as a product of the late 1960s and early 1970s. This helps us to correctly contextualise the debates the book engages with, and allows us to see Okere as a pioneer of African philosophical hermeneutics.

My reading of Okere's work starts by stating the problem Okere set to work on, namely to clarify the conditions that make philosophy, and in particular African philosophy, possible. Three questions need to be examined to fulfil this task: (a) what is non-philosophy as a source for philosophising?, (b) what is philosophy?, and (c) how does an individual philosopher transition from a shared cultural non-philosophy to philosophy? The three sections of this chapter deal with these questions. These questions also call for an examination of Okere's understanding of culture. The chapter ends with an overview of its findings.

1. **African philosophy: a historic-hermeneutic investigation of the conditions of its possibility**

In his introduction to *African Philosophy*, Okere states his ambitions for the book. Convinced that what had up to that point been published as "African philosophy" was a false start, he takes up the formidable task of clarifying what the "founding of the tradition of rational philosophy in Africa" (v) would actually entail. At the same time, he remains quite modest about his own contribution. Since Okere examines only "how and under what circumstances an African philosophical tradition could emerge", he explicitly cautions his reader against misconstruing the book's argument: it "does not purport to present an African Philosophy" (v). The book aspires to be a preliminary work, a threshold to an African philosophy that would be worthy of this name.

Okere's project in *African Philosophy* is also a polemical one:

> Somewhere in between, on the one hand, the chauvinism of those who claim that philosophy is of its nature a treasure hidden in the secret recesses of highest Olympus inaccessible to non-westerns, and on the other the a priori claims of those who think that philosophy is so natural a thing that if the Greeks had it at all, all people and, therefore, Africans must already have it, this essay finds its place. Its credibility will rely heavily on the meaning it gives the term philosophy. And here the meaning adopted is strictly formal and narrow. (viii)

According to Okere, the appropriate characterisation of his enterprise is "hermeneutic" and the different tasks of this hermeneutics are connected by the phrase "in between":

- With respect to the development of African philosophy, Okere situates his hermeneutic contribution *in between* a critique of past attempts at African philosophy and a new form of African philosophy yet to come.[4] Okere's work is to mark boundaries and point the direction from older ways of doing of philosophy to a new one (cf. vi).
- Regarding the kaleidoscope of philosophies of the whole world, Okere's critical readings fit *in between* a critique of African philosophy and a critique of European philosophy.
- As for the African philosophy to come, Okere advocates for a hermeneutic approach that holds on to "traditional" African culture with one hand, and the critical style of thought named philosophy with the other. Hermeneutics is the *in-between* that links and separates these two forms of intelligent engagement with the world.

Okere's argument in *African Philosophy* is neither a nostalgic exercise to recuperate the author's own tradition nor a servile submission to another's tradition. The citation above from *African Philosophy* (viii) expresses the political dimension of his project. Okere confirms this political aim when he concludes his book (cf. 129–130) by citing at length the Second

Congress of Black Writers and Artists'[5] resolutions on African philosophy. This declaration—and, by extension, Okere himself—aligns philosophy with the struggle against Western hegemony, and with the self-affirmation of Africans and their traditions. The extent to which Okere finally succeeds in bringing this political objective to bear on his project will have to be assessed anew by each generation of readers because, as we will see, his understanding of hermeneutics is open to multiple extensions by those who would like to continue his project.

Equally important in the citation above from *African Philosophy* (viii) is the term "philosophy". Okere is at pains to pre-empt an incorrect understanding of the term, even though he will be really equipped to define it only at the end of his study. According to Okere, philosophy is not equal to thought; not all thought is philosophy. There is something like the "true" definition of philosophy that must be, strictly speaking, distinguished from other forms of intelligent expression and intellectual activity. If such a core of philosophy exists, shared by all philosophising people over the world, it requires a further step, a "qualitative leap" (ix) that separates it from other intellectual activities of people within a specific cultural sphere. But Okere relativises this universalistic claim. On the one hand, "philosophy is not a cultural universal, not to be simply presumed a priori to be part of every other culture" (ix). On the other, where philosophy is to be found, it always grows out of particular cultural contexts (xi). On both points—that philosophy has a universal core and that philosophy is contextually determined[6]—Okere is unmistakably in agreement with Hountondji. If Okere can succeed in arguing that all philosophy is culturally specific, then his universal notion of philosophy is infiltrated by the plurality of human cultures, by which the Greek experience is "provincialised", as we say nowadays, without of course denying or delegitimating that experience. The fact that Okere beholds two quite different bodies of philosophy (more than two millennia of Greek philosophy, and African philosophy that, according to him, is just about to start) does not invalidate the way in which he compares them on an equal footing. The reason for this is the very nature of philosophy, the hermeneutic exploration of which is the theme of his book: every part of Okere's clarification of the "conditions for the possibility" of African philosophy—and in particular the role of its practitioners' cultural background—holds for European philosophy too. This is probably why the amount of attention that he gives to European thinkers in the book does not seem to bother Okere: if there is something like philosophy, its essential core is the same for Europeans and Africans. The particular form that philosophy may take will vary from one cultural context to another, but a pre-philosophical cultural background affects philosophers all the same. From this, I deduce that Okere's argument is based on a conviction that there are at least minimal general anthropological *commonalities.*

However, Okere himself does not present his work from an anthropological angle. Rather, in line with the polemical thrust of his argument, he underscores how cultural *pluralism* affects our understanding of philosophy. This emphasis is understandable and justifiable. Understandable, because Okere echoes developments in the social sciences of his time, which subjected past claims about universal truths and values to severe questioning, notably of the ethnocentrism contained in Western science and philosophy. Justifiable, because Okere's hermeneutic treatment of ethnocentrism has political implications, not only because different "varieties" of rationality influence exchanges between non-Africans and Africans, but also for the ways in which *intra*cultural exchanges in Africa are conceived.[7]

Combining the unsettling force of cultural relativism and applying a suspicion of ethnocentrism to all universal claims of Western values (including those constituting philosophy itself), Okere formulates the main questions to which his book responds: "what are the philosophical implications of the new cultural relativism? What is philosophy, and what exactly is its relationship with culture? How does philosophy evolve from culture?" (xi).

Okere puts forward two approaches by which to tackle these questions. His approach in answering them is essential to his argument and to our assessment of it. He describes the first approach as a priori and it consists of "a study of the hermeneutical movement and of hermeneutics, a study which makes clear both the interpretative (hermeneutical) nature and essential historicity of philosophy. It is a study of principles" (xii). The second approach is typified as *a posteriori* and entails the "examination of some representative 'cases' which confirm the a priori study by showing that each philosophy is the self-interpretation of culture" (xii). In short: a study of principles and an exploration of how those principles work in practice. One should immediately observe, then, that the two approaches set up the study as engaged in a hermeneutic circle. Here, the hermeneutic circle consists in the inevitable to-and-fro from the material from which one draws insight to the formulation of that insight, back to the material to review the general insights, and so on.

But another thing should be noted from the approaches by which Okere sets out to work on his questions: they consist primarily of a critical study of European philosophers. "The hermeneutical movement" to which he refers is represented primarily by Heidegger and Gadamer (and to a lesser extent by Ricœur and Winch); the "representative" cases are representative of European philosophy only. The risk involved in Okere's approach should be evident: for all his protest against the presumptions of ethnocentric Westerners and their philosophy, *African Philosophy* could become another genuflexion to that same supposed superiority, or lead to a portrayal of African philosophy as "a mere branch of the European tradition" (125). Okere seems to consider this risk worth taking and seems convinced that he can escape its negative potential.

In my view, Okere's use of European hermeneuts' work can make sense (that is, be sufficiently coherent to allow one to assess it) only if the conviction of general anthropological *commonalities* silently informs his endeavours. And this is indeed the case. Okere apparently bets that, *if* by studying the European hermeneutic tradition he can show that it subscribes to the principle that the cultural background of philosophers influence their philosophical work (approach 1) and *if* he can demonstrate in some of the most eminent European philosophers' work that non-philosophical convictions and cultural heritage did in fact play a role (approach 2) then

- the relativity of the West in the human activity of philosophy will have been argued sufficiently;
- nobody could deny that for Africans too it holds that non-philosophical convictions and culture may give rise to philosophy; and
- this principle would thus reflect of what the universal human ability of philosophy consists.

This is Okere's ambitious task and his contribution to African hermeneutics in 1983. If he accomplishes this task, it will allow one to conclude that:

> Black Africans, having their own cultures, can have their own proper philosophies by deriving and elaborating them from their own cultures. But it is not enough to have a culture in order to have a philosophy. A mediation, a passage from culture to philosophy is necessary. (xiv)

My exposition of the task that Okere set for himself allows us to appreciate his argument in the subsequent chapters of his book. Instead of following his argument as it develops, I restructure it somewhat, using as guide the key ideas of Okere's "in between" position explained above. In the chapters sandwiched between his introduction and conclusion, Okere is concerned with three questions: What is non-philosophy? What is philosophy? And how are they to be linked? As Okere formulates the issue himself: "It is precisely by reflecting on what actually constitutes philosophy in contrast to what is non-philosophy, that is to culture, that one clearly sees that what we are dealing with is a problem of hermeneutics" (xii; see also 11).

2. What is non-philosophy?

Okere's exploration of the nature of non-philosophy deals with culture,[8] and more specifically, culture as it relates to philosophy, whence its characterisation as "*non*-philosophy". His approach consists of two parts. On the one hand, he endeavours to identify within African philosophy, as he knew it at that stage, components of culture incorrectly identified by the authors as "philosophy", according to Okere. This discussion is found in Okere's critical reading of ethnophilosophy produced during the thirty years before his study. On the other hand, he examines texts of European philosophy, in which he identifies cultural phenomena at work that are not philosophical, even though the entire work in question is presented as philosophy. Here, his focus is, for instance, on Christian influences on such authors as Hegel or Heidegger. In both of these avenues of exploration, the ways in which non-philosophy relates to philosophy—whether through illegitimate conscious inclusion or through unavoidable unconscious inclusion—serve to prepare the way for a double claim. This claim is: not all human cultural expressions or institutions are philosophy, and the fact and persistence of non-philosophy is an unavoidable given of human thought.

2.1. *Culture from the view of ethnophilosophy and its critics*

What do we learn about the nature of non-philosophy from Okere's reading of the ethnophilosophers (he uses Placide Tempels, Alexis Kagame, and John Mbiti) and their critics (especially Fabien Eboussi Boulaga and

Paulin Hountondji)? For our purposes, it is not so much Okere's critical engagement with this debate that is of interest. What we want to know is what understanding of non-philosophy arises from it. Let us therefore give only a short overview of Okere's position in the ethnophilosophy debate.

- Tempels's advocacy of "black reason" against colonial prejudice may have some merit, but the ethnography that informs his own argument is not thereby vindicated (see *African Philosophy*, 4–5). Furthermore, the political critiques of ethnophilosophy by Aimé Césaire or Hountondji are essential to the debate (3). Key questions of these critiques are: who generates "knowledge", about whom, for whom? By following this critique, Okere joins his contemporaries in a project that has become linked to the name of V. Y. Mudimbe arguably more than anyone else's.[9]

- Whereas Kagame's recourse to language as manifestation of African philosophy has the advantage of being based on documented evidence of language, it succumbs to the same idea of a collective philosophy as Tempels did, which Okere rejects as Hountondji does. In the view of both critics, the difference between a *"mentalité primitive"* and a "Bantu philosophy" is insignificant (see 6[10]). Furthermore, if one concedes that there is a close relationship between language and thought, this does not mean that the structure and vocabulary of a language simply is a philosophy—this kind of idea amounts to "baseless and fruitless speculation" (9). If language were philosophy, how would it be possible for people to think different and conflicting things in the same language? (see 9).

- Mbiti's description of the "African" conception of time is not only dubious, but even if it were not, it would still not amount to a philosophy (see 10–11). Besides, as a collective view of time, it does not yet meet the minimum criterion of philosophy, namely that it should emerge from the mental labour of an individual philosopher.

- By "uncritically equating" elements of culture with philosophy, the "African philosophers" (ethnophilosophers, in this case) aim

    to decode for non-Africans the general, subconscious, unarticulated "theory" which will enable them to understand the behaviour patterns and value preferences of Africans or else enable them to adapt their methods of evangelization to achieve optimal results. (11)

In a fascinating paragraph (6–7), Okere develops his position on the point of the "collectivity versus individuality" of philosophy. Although Okere rejects the quest for a collective philosophy as "vain" (6), he nevertheless endorses the anthropological "commonplace", which consists of the claim that "each people, has developed for itself a more or less elaborate, more or less consistent vision of the world—in religion, cosmologies, in language, and other elements for culture" (6–7). What prompts Okere to express caution about this "commonplace" is the "hasty and grotesque conclusions" drawn from it and labelled as philosophy by ethnophilosophers and the resulting misconstrual of what it is to do philosophy. Note that Okere does not entertain the question regarding the degree to which members of a group adhere to common values, nor does he delve into the possibility of dissent or critique within traditional thought (which Oruka later placed at the centre of his Sage-philosophy project). In other words, at the moment when Okere rejects the idea of a collective philosophy, he introduces an idea of a high degree of *homogeneity* in culturally specific "visions of the world". This is not to deny that he identifies a plurality of such "visions" and recognises their relativity (6).[11]

Let us consider this view of limited plurality. I certainly agree that there is not an infinite number of views of the world; the variety of ways of understanding and representing the world is reduced by people's common heritage and interaction. However, the degree to which people adhere to a collective heritage varies and can be established only by field work; the strength and uniformity with which people adhere to a vision of the world cannot be established from the philosopher's office. Furthermore, we have to insist on the socio-theoretical and action theoretical implication of Okere's position. As long as he does not grant that in a traditional setting some people think in ways other than those of others, it is not clear where the hermeneutic exercise from which philosophy is born is to come from. Oruka's study of recognised individual sages would be a way to approach this question. One tempting solution for the emergence of philosophy from Okere's view of traditional culture would be to affirm that Africans in their traditional settings can be helped to come out of this predominant cultural unanimity through confrontation with people from another tradition—other people such as Europeans. The entire practice of his book could be framed as supporting this view. However, this theoretical proposal must be discarded, as it would undermine the central conclusion at which Okere steers, namely that a culturally specific philosophy can grow out of the pre-philosophical traditions of a people and does not require starting-up by foreign influence (see 125). Indeed, Okere's scepticism about cultural mixing is evident at the end of *African Philosophy*, whose argument he claims

> disproves the need for a "métissage culturel" as advocated by some, that is, the necessity to graft African philosophy to the Western tradition in order for it not to become an abortive enterprise. Such métissage would ensure that there would be no development of an African tradition. (127)

Finally, Okere characterises different "visions of the world" as "popular and traditional image[s] recounting the story of the origin and the actual functioning of the Status Quo" (7). How much weight Okere intended to give to the negative connotation of the expression "status quo" is not clear. The following paragraph leads one to believe that it may be quite important to him. Here, Okere cites Socrates' philosophising about the meaning of his own death in opposition to the ambient cultural values, which implies the status quo responsible for his condemnation (see 7). This probably reveals part of the motivation for Okere's insistence on the collective nature of world views: it serves as backdrop against which to describe individual action, which is necessary for true philosophising. But he cannot advance this position without assuming the political consequences of portraying philosophy as (potentially) in conflict with the transmitted or traditional representations of the world and their status-quo-affirming functioning. Rarely does *African Philosophy* deal with this tension. In fact, on the same page (7), Okere portrays the individualism of the philosopher in markedly apolitical and downright problematic terms:

> Philosophy [...] is essentially an individual enterprise and is often a *mise-en-cause*, and a radical questioning of the collective image. By reflection and the questioning of this image, one makes an individual effort to find, that is, to give meaning to one's world. It is quite irrelevant to a philosophy if it founds a school or is used as an ideological instrument of some imperialism. (7)

Evidently, his point is not to advocate a laissez-faire attitude in philosophy, but to emphasise his point of the detachment of the philosopher's thinking from social constraints. One may say that the citation reflects Okere's understanding of the ambiguity of philosophy vis-à-vis political reality.

However, acknowledging the political ambiguity of philosophy as such interferes somewhat with the explicit political function Okere attributes to philosophical hermeneutics.

With all of this said, Okere evidently has no intention of doing away with culture or asking his African readers to leave the heritage of the past behind them. The ethnophilosophers had it right in one respect: understanding African philosophy has to do with our understanding of culture. But only hermeneutics can take care of the role of culture in philosophy appropriately (see 10–11).

2.2. *Culture as a non-philosophical component of European philosophy*

The discussion above should in no way let us jump to the conclusion that one has to look only at Africans to get a view on non-philosophy. In fact, we get a good view on non-philosophy where some would still like to claim that there is only philosophy proper: in the most exquisite examples of European philosophy itself. Okere never presents this as a new revelation; at the time at which he wrote, the issue of how culture influences European philosophy was well explored and Okere draws freely from scholarship on the topic. His point is rather to examine this topic to support his reflection on the place of pre-judice[12] in philosophy and to relate it to what African philosophy should strive to be. One thing stands out immediately: if it is true that the work of the most recognised and recognisable European philosophers can be shown to have taken shape in a non-trivial way under the influence of non-philosophical convictions, then there remains no reasonable way to demand of African thinkers to eliminate all non-philosophy from their philosophy. The point here is not to give a blanket approval of all non-philosophical ideas in philosophy, but to recall the futility of awaiting the total destruction of all non-philosophy in philosophy. For these purposes Okere reopens the dossier on non-philosophy in chapter 5 (section 8) of his book.

Because most philosophers present their thought as borrowing from other philosophers or as opposing them, one may get the impression that the history of philosophy unfolds from its own internal dynamics alone. Philosophy would be built on philosophy, as it were. However, philosophy emerges in a more complex way. To get a glimpse of this complexity, and of the non-philosophy involved in it, one may embark on a kind of "archaeological excavation—unearthing parts of the hidden foundations of the great edifices which are the historical philosophical systems" (82). Such an excavation does not mean that one would attempt to provide an exhaustive explanation for a set of philosophical ideas by tracing the sociological, psychological, and other influences on their authors—in fact, Okere rejects the "reductionist theories of the history of philosophy whether these be Marxist, Freudian, or Hegelian" (82). Okere does not have in view a general theory of the "mechanisms" of the production of philosophy. His claim is rather general in a way that I think it is correct to call anthropological: philosophical reflection is based on and produced from more than just earlier philosophies; it emerges against a non-philosophical background of culture, which consists of "language, history, scientific, or other lore, religion, mythology, values and beliefs, social and individual experience" (82).

One may read this list as a simple indication of the scope of influences that may influence the formation of someone's philosophical ideas. Although Okere does not develop this point further, I think it is worthwhile to consider each element as an invitation for elaboration. Doing so would help one guard against a vague and simplistic view of the non-philosophical. This seems to be the first point of the list of elements: the non-philosophy of which we speak is not simply one thing, but may be any of a number of factors or a combination thereof. It is regrettable that Okere did not expand this point, since a lot of the complexity of remobilising tradition within specific contexts, for which he pleads, is reflected in it. Non-philosophy is not the unique, common treasure of language, in harmony with a common history, in harmony with common experiences, and so on. The elements of non-philosophy sometimes echo one another and can therefore have a mutually reinforcing effect, but these elements can also contradict each other and have contradictory influences not only on each individual, but also on bigger social units and societies. This is not a trivial issue. What is at stake is the question of whether one assumes the cultural homogeneity or diversity of people; whether one approaches the task of hermeneutics from a traditionalist perspective or whether one engages with the complexities of culture and experience, particularly under the upheavals of colonisation and modernisation.[13] Admittedly, here I am speaking, not Okere, but we will see later that his hermeneutics can be developed in the direction of plurality and complexity I deem necessary (see 121).

Back to Okere. From Alphonse De Waelhens he takes the "lesson" from the history of philosophy, that there is only one "universal structure" or common denominator of philosophy, that "[p]hilosophy is a reflection on a non-philosophical experience. Philosophy and non-philosophy have a dialectical relationship with each other. Philosophy reflects on experience, experience contradicts the resulting system [...]" (83). The way in which Okere argues his case with reference to Marx, Hegel, Heidegger, and Plato need not detain us here. More relevant is what we can harvest from these discussions regarding the nature of non-philosophy. We learn that non-philosophy is the "source" of philosophy, but that non-philosophy as it stands, remains insufficient to construct philosophy (86). Non-philosophy is typified as "the non-reflected, that unreflected baggage of cultural background" from which thought develops (88). This is not a concession to irrationalism but, in line with Okere's understanding of the finitude and historicity of philosophy that will be explained below, it does entail the admission that "total rationalism is impossible in philosophy" (88; see also 89–90). Non-philosophy is thus the "frontier and limit(ation) of philosophy" (88). Therefore, as Okere argues with Georg Lukács, the most rational one can be is by respecting the "irrational residue" of every attempt to construct a rational system of thought (cf. 90).

Two tacit assumptions frame Okere's discussion of culture as non-philosophy. First, while his exposition clearly emphasises the plurality of cultures, his discussion of culture seems to presuppose a *monocultural setting*. In other words, the exchanges—peaceful or violent—between different cultural groups that share a single socio-historical context is not taken into consideration. Second, Okere's presentation of non-philosophy sets it up in a dichotomous relation to philosophy: he does not seem to entertain the possibility of a gradual transition from non-philosophy to philosophy or of lingering in grey areas in between.[14] A phenomenological description of the diversity of modes of reflexivity in everyday life would require such a nuanced, gradated approach.[15]

3. What is philosophy?

In this way, our discussion of non-philosophy naturally goes over into the question of what philosophy is. Okere leaves no doubt: the thesis he defends is that "all philosophy is a reflection on a non-philosophical experience"

(98). In Okere's reading, the exact problem with ethnophilosophy is that it was unable to relate philosophy and culture or non-philosophy appropriately, thereby undermining its own status as philosophy. At the same time, it is no trivial matter to ponder that Okere never presents the critics of ethnophilosophy—notably Hountondji and Eboussi Boulaga—as examples to be emulated. In fact, he never entertains the question of the status of *their* philosophy. If he did, one may safely assume that he would have been quite dismissive of a position such as that of Hountondji for the same reason he dismisses that of the ethnophilosophers: Hountondji, he would likely argue, fails to deal correctly with the relationship between culture and philosophy.[16] In this sense one may present Okere's project as finding the conditions for a valid conception of African philosophy against what he perceived as two failed attempts to do so: that of ethnophilosophy and that of its critics (see 121). Let us also mention that Okere does not review alternative conceptions of African philosophy as we may do today retrospectively by considering the work of Césaire or Senghor, Nyerere or Nkrumah, Fanon or Anta Diop, or perhaps Du Bois or William Abraham—each represents a different style of thinking and themes of concern for a true African philosophy. This omission is a bit problematic if one considers the way Okere, after narrowing down his investigation to three ethnophilosophical authors, too hastily concludes "that the search for an African philosophy has not yielded very satisfactory results" (11).

Instead, Okere seeks to define philosophy through the conditions of its possibility and, from that basis, derives what African philosophy could be.

3.1. *The conditions of the possibility of philosophy*

When Okere deals with the question of what philosophy is, the aim remains to determine what *African* philosophy is. For if philosophy depends on the culture of its authors, then there is not only one single philosophy. But because the attempts at African philosophy up to the point at which Okere wrote failed, according to him, he is not even sure that he could point to an example of such a philosophy (see 114, echoing the citation from 11, above). This may then be the reason why Okere does not develop a too detailed picture of philosophy: on the one hand, some common traits of philosophy may be safely derived from the European versions; on the other hand, this exercise is inherently limited because Okere's concern is not to describe the essence of European (or Indian or Chinese) philosophy, but to reflect on the *conditions for the possibility* of African philosophy that can as yet (in 1971) not be described a fortiori.

Is this comment not nit-picking? No, it is important to clarify this point, because if one does not, the impression left by a cursory reading of Okere's book may be that European philosophy is not only a part of the answer to what African philosophy can be, but the entire answer.[17] Furthermore, such a superficial reading may lead to the conclusion that for Okere African philosophy is simply hermeneutics. Whereas hermeneutics is certainly key to his argument, his position is definitely more complex. This complexity is rendered in the title of his paragraph 4.1: "Hermeneutics as mediator between culture and philosophy". How, may one ask, can a form of philosophy (namely hermeneutics) be a mediator between culture and philosophy? It can apply only if hermeneutics, although also referring to a body of philosophical texts, is not simply equated to philosophy. This difference is captured as follows: "it is only within the context of hermeneutics that African culture can give birth to African philosophy" (15). Can only a European tradition of philosophy, namely hermeneutics, give birth to African philosophy? This is exactly *not* Okere's point. The "context of hermeneutics" refers not to a collection of texts, but to a common human experience that is explored in a culturally contingent way in European hermeneutics. The great books of European philosophy from which Okere borrows are not what African philosophy has to be, but speak about a common human capacity, namely of "reflection on a non-philosophical experience" (Okere's definition of philosophy).

Let me summarise. Why do I distinguish two questions, namely "what is philosophy?" and "how are philosophy and non-philosophy to be linked?", when the two are intimately linked in Okere's definition of philosophy? Okere finds no African philosophy worthy of this name (in 1971) and attempts to find the conditions for that philosophy that is still to come (see 121). He therefore turns his attention to the common human ability to reflect on non-philosophical experience. Authors from other intellectual traditions, being equally human, may attest to and analyse this ability. However, the African philosophy to which Okere aspires will draw on the range of non-philosophical experiences typical of life in Africa.

And if all of this is correct, then one may conclude that Okere's book is a contribution to African philosophy (in as far as it reflects on the conditions for the possibility of African philosophy), but that it is not necessarily to be taken as a model to follow (in as far as he advocates for the development of African philosophy as a culturally contingent form of reflection). In other words, Okere presented his book as necessary for the enterprise of African philosophy, but also as a transitional work to be surpassed by an independent African philosophical tradition.

Curiously, if this is true, then the cultural specificity of the European hermeneutics deployed by Okere is a relatively unimportant matter, since it remains first and foremost a tool by which to direct us to the cultural specificity of African philosophy. This is then the ambiguous place of European philosophy in Okere: on the one hand, it is the master teaching the student; on the other hand, it is a dispensable tool freely manipulated by the African scholar. Or to formulate this explicitly as a paradox—the paradox of universality and particularity in Okere: European hermeneutics is an indispensable tool by which to point to something that itself cannot be.

3.2. *From the philosophical crossroads to the possibility of African philosophy*

I think that this interpretative detour was necessary to grasp the "philosophical crossroads" that Okere identifies and to read *African Philosophy* as a preparation to confront his readers with the decision the crossroads implies. African scholars, he claims, have to choose between three possible ways of doing philosophy (see 128–129). The first considers philosophy as "popular ancestral wisdom"—Okere rejects this. The second consists of merely doing philosophy in Western way(s)—Okere refuses this too. For Okere, the only viable alternative is the possibility of an African philosophy. Such a philosophy can now emerge between two forces. On the one hand, a global culture of increasing tolerance to diversity and the quest for ways of co-existence without recourse to force or destruction; on the other hand the self-affirmation of African cultures despite the influence of Westernisation. And Okere's appeal to his readers ends on a tragic note, when he laments that African societies enjoy no real political or economic independence. Still, Okere claims the real possibility of "cultural and spiritual" independence (129). I suppose it is possible to construe Okere's intellectual position here as amounting to a mere defeatist withdrawal into the sphere of folklore and amusement with books. But it can certainly be read otherwise too: given the tragic circumstance of enduring political and economic coercion, he calls on his readers to take up the means of which they dispose to mobilise their resistance to coercion. The remainder of our exposition on Okere's view of philosophy will affirm this reading.

Taken in isolation, then, what is philosophy? A first way to get an idea of what philosophy is, is to contrast it with non-philosophy. Whereas non-philosophical worldviews are collective and spontaneous, philosophy is an individual, first-person effort, according to Okere (see 119–120). Philosophy may be an individual activity, but this does not exclude a common pursuit or the formation of a corpus of works with a mutual affinity or tradition that, again, does not exclude the possibility of divergent individual thought (see 7–8). Philosophy starts with a personal questioning from which it arranges or creates its reflection, like one creates a work of art (119–120).[18] By so doing, one gives meaning to one's world (7); nonetheless, Okere does not make it clear how this differs from the meaning of the world offered by non-philosophy. This personal questioning, however, is informed by the prejudgments and background of the philosopher; in fact, this questioning is *conditioned by* the philosopher's background (culture and history) and *questions* this background, simultaneously (69). The consequence is that

> the real philosopher is like a scientist, who compels nature to answer his own questions, like the appointed judge who compels the witnesses to answer the question he himself poses. [...] We get out of something what we put into it. What we put into it is the prejudgment or presuppositions and motivations, the cultural axioms or prepositions already presumed or declared true within our cultural background. What we get out of it is the judgment, the answer that has its meaning only within the context of the said question, the apparition or manifestation of meaning which is made possible only within this framework. (68)

Okere resolutely affirms that philosophy is two things, two things that give form to his argument as a whole. Philosophy is, or should be, hermeneutics, and philosophy is the mediator between culture and philosophy (15). I have dealt with the ambiguity of this double characterisation and will deal with the transition from culture to philosophy in the next section (§ 4). However, before we get there, one has to recognise the effort that Okere puts into studying the "ontological roots and anthropological implications" (15) of hermeneutics. The core chapters of *African Philosophy* in this respect are arguably chapters 3 and 4, whose titles define philosophy as hermeneutics and as interpretation, respectively. In these chapters,

Okere gives his reading of two major figures of European philosophical hermeneutics: Heidegger and Gadamer.

Following the express design of my study, I do not deal with Okere's reading of these authors in detail. What is at stake is rather what Okere identifies as "the most revolutionary result of the hermeneutical movement" (54). He presents this revolution in dramatic terms:

> Apart from teaching us how best to read and understand ancient authors, and apart from offering us a magnificent anatomy of the art of philosophising, it [the major conclusions of European hermeneutics—EW] becomes the Magna Charta of all those of other cultures who aim to build up a philosophical tradition which will be more than a mere footnote on the pages of Greek and Western Philosophy. (54)

Once again Okere's position is affirmed: the authority of the Western tradition is rejected; the authority of that about which Western hermeneuts speak is affirmed.

The "Magna Charta" consists of a description of the mode of existence of human beings in general, specifically in respect of the way that this mode of existence makes the emergence of philosophy possible. True enough, "philosophy is not a cultural universal, not to be simply presumed a priori to be part of every other culture" (ix). Where philosophy exists, it reveals the "relativity of all philosophy" (xiv). However, the Black Forest German ontological phenomenology by which Heidegger argued, takes nothing away from the universally valid designation of "philosophy as the activation of man's[19] natural inclination and privilege to give meaning to reality. In practice it boils down to a thematic explicitation of an implicit understanding of the meaning of being" (54). More succinctly, Okere concludes that philosophy is "an interpretation, a making explicit of one's understanding of one's self and one's world" (53). If, despite this general fact, or despite what Okere calls the "unity of philosophical attitude and point of view" (76), a variety of philosophies exist, a variety that may become even greater. This variety abounds because the human beings who engage in philosophy are all constituted in the same way, namely as "inescapably time-bound, historical, contextual and relative, relative that is, to this immediate environment" (54). Quite simply put, people are different, and this difference matters in the way they philosophise. That is why, when produced by a historical, finite, contextual being, "man's ultimate interpretation, his philosophy, will be necessarily historical and culture-bound, articulated relatively to his environment and world.[20] His environment will prescribe the terminology, provoke the questions and predetermine the answers" (54).[21]

Following Okere's argumentative strategy one could deepen one's understanding of the hermeneutic constitution of human beings by studying the European hermeneuts (just as, I would add, anyone can do today by studying African hermeneuts, thanks to the work of authors like Okere). Instead, I briefly render the three hermeneutic insights Okere inherited from his European predecessors, three "principles" (see xii) that support his conviction that African philosophy could come into being.[22]

First, from Ricœur, Okere took the insight that symbols and other objectifications mediate the thinking subject's thought. In other words, reflection is the "appropriation of our effort to exist and of our desire to be, through the medium of those works which testify to this effort and to this desire" (115). If this is the case, then one could support the general anthropological claim that spontaneous reflection through symbols nourishes philosophical reflection. And if this is correct, then one may conclude that "[a] philosophical interpretation of the symbols of African cultures would be African philosophy" (115).

Second, from Heidegger, Okere inherits an exposition of the ways in which all human existence has a hermeneutic dimension. Something akin to or analogous to philosophy is part of the fibre of human existence in the world. If this is correct, then "philosophy is already implied by the comprehension of being which is native to all human beings. To philosophise is only to make explicit a set of prejudgements from that symbolic universe which already makes up one's cultural background" (116).

Third, from Gadamer, Okere accepts the argument that philosophy depends on a non-philosophical background. This "unreflected residue" (117) is everything but dead weight. On the contrary, the historicity, pre-judice, and finitude that makes up this background empowers one's reflection on the world. Recognising the centrality of culture in philosophy, Okere exhorts his readers to "go back to one's own roots and sources. The sources, the headwater region of creative and original thought, are one's own culture. No familiarity with the foreign and borrowed element can suffice for the articulation of something so deep-felt as one's understanding of one's self and one's world" (118–119). He goes so far as to present this issue as a "moral question of being honest and true to one's self" (119).

In this section I have presented Okere's view on philosophy. This exposition lands us on the doorstep of the final question: how to arrive at philosophy itself.

4. How should philosophy and non-philosophy be linked?

Once Okere has established *what* philosophy is or could be, the question of *how* to get there follows quite naturally. Schematically, this task can be represented as connecting non-philosophy and philosophy. Keep in mind that Okere set out to clarify this task by defending the thesis

> that Black Africans,[23] having their own cultures, can have their own proper philosophies by deriving and elaborating them from their own cultures. But it is not enough to have a culture in order to have a philosophy. A mediation, a passage from culture to philosophy is necessary. (xiv)[24]

What concerns us here, then, is this mediation, this passage.

The first thing a hermeneut notices is that one's relationship to the world is constituted by one's cultural background; one cannot leave this source behind. However, if one works in a socially, politically, and/or intellectually unequal world, where one is expected to discount certain aspects of one's cultural background in practice, then it is indeed possible to return to these sources, by lifting the imposed parenthesis. It is also possible to return to them in a second sense, namely by noticing and considering the elements of the background with the eyes of philosophical reflection (where that has not been done before). Okere's point is not to encourage his readers to embrace traditional culture as a *form of life*,[25] but rather to consider through *philosophical reflection* the ways in which anyone is constituted by background culture, whatever form it may take.

4.1. Working on philosophemes

With the insights of hermeneutics in mind, we can start making our way towards philosophical reflection. Culture and tradition, Okere argues, are not philosophy, but are not averse to philosophy, either. And here is the crux: "in black Africa"—but one would have to say: in all culture everywhere—"there exists a *reservoir of cultural philosophemes* from which any future philosopher can inspire himself or borrow his share of philosophical raw material" (120, my emphasis). This process of philosophical construction out of cultural philosophemes is creative and critical (see 119). Philosophy can hence be redefined as "an interpretative commentary on reality against the guiding, determining, and suggestive background of a culture" (81). Here, philosophy is hermeneutics and hermeneutics is understood as "an epistemological tool, a method of mediation, and of making the passage between culture as lived and culture as reflected" (15). In a more provocative image, Okere claims that "it is only within the context of hermeneutics that African culture can give birth to African philosophy" (15). Inspiration, borrowing, creativity, commentary, guiding, tool, birth—this is the key vocabulary for the passage from culture to philosophy, which Okere also calls a "method".[26]

The first step of this "passage" having been clarified—recognising philosophy as the interpretation of philosophemes—we can now consider the precise importance of culture in respect of philosophy, an ambiguous matter in Okere's thought. In some places, Okere's appeal to culture is very encompassing: philosophy "is rather a project of appropriation, of assumption and identification with one's total culture in a process of intellectual alchemy from which results a new creation, the meaning of this culture as interpreted by this unique experience which is the philosopher's insertion in it" (xv). In other places, his position is more qualified, in that he assumes that thinking from one's culture does not mean accepting its whole tradition, but rather accepting or rejecting aspects of it on the basis of philosophical questioning (120). While deciding what to make of these two options, we have to consider that our response will have political implications too. We have seen earlier that a culture or worldview describes how the status quo functions, and yet, for Okere, philosophy that emerges from it is not tied to a social project (7). This means that one's assessment of tradition may amount to affirming or undermining the status quo, an effect that would require critical assessment in turn.

I would like to suggest that Okere's rejection of absolute rationalism in philosophy indicates how a philosopher should assume this ambiguous relation to culture and the status quo. By acknowledging that the rational practice of philosophy inevitably contains irrational elements, Okere does not call for a "flight into irrationalism" (88). How should we understand this balance of refusing absolute rationalism on the one hand, and absolute irrationalism on the other? Okere's response is that "for any reflection to take place at all, some data have to be taken initially for granted, without proof, and as it were by decree. They have to be believed or, as is rather more often the case, subconsciously presumed, at any rate, unquestioned" (88). This is the first piece of the puzzle: some part of the unreflected tradition works on us whether we want or not, since this is what opens us to the world in the first place. Consequently, the suspension of philosophy between total rationalism and irrationalism compels us to confer on our heritage the benefit of the doubt, at least as a first step. Let's call it a principle of *hermeneutic generosity*. This initial generosity may well be extended to the whole tradition. Once philosophers recognise that aspects of their culture are "given" and may influence their thinking unconsciously, the hermeneutic work of philosophy can be activated to launch the philosopher on the path from non-philosophy to philosophy. Philosophy "then becomes the gradual appropriation by the reflective reason of this unreflected[27] mass" (88). Although this process of selection and evaluation is guided by the desire for completeness, it can never attain this goal; it is a never-ending process (88).

If I have constructed Okere's view on culture correctly, then it is of no use to try to determine context-independent principles on the basis of which philosophemes can or should be identified, selected, and (re-)appropriated, because this is to be established by each individual philosopher through constant questioning, reflection, and re-questioning in ever new socio-historical contexts. The central role of individual judgement is why philosophy is hermeneutical. The political implication of our assessment of culture cannot be delimited beforehand because, whether we tend more to affirming elements of tradition or more to independent reflection, such consequences can be identified only after we have done the work of hermeneutics.

Okere is quite vague about what the next step in the passage between non-philosophy and philosophy entails. In fact, apart from insisting on the creativity of this interpretative process, he does not say much more. While this passage requires thorough reflection, I can also see some merit in this omission: in the sense that Okere qualifies this mediation as an interpretative process, this silence can be taken as reflecting the constitutive *indeterminacy* of this passage. This indeterminacy can be attributed to the contingency of each philosopher's cultural background and life narrative, which accords a specific profile to the otherwise general traits of hermeneutics shared by all people. For Okere, philosophy "is not an abstract science; it is a statement of meaning by a person committed to life and to reality and eager to relate himself to life and reality" (128).

However, in the conclusion of his book, Okere offers a brief view on how to deal with African philosophemes.[28] In a few short pages, he contrasts examples from Igbo language, ideas on history, and "being" with their Western counterparts. The import of these examples is clear. On the one hand, and in opposition to ethnophilosophy, such examples do not provide an African philosophy yet, but point to possible philosophemes to be worked on by philosophers. In other words, ethnophilosophical research corresponds with the identification and categorisation of philosophemes as the preliminary step of real African philosophy. Whether this preliminary research must be of African origin is not said, but there seems to be no basis on which to disqualify others from collaborating in it. Still, Okere demonstrates that work on such philosophemes of African culture will not yield Western philosophy (124) (even if, by implication, the growth of African philosophy would imply an affirmation of the insights that he drew from European hermeneutics). Growing a philosophy from one's familiar cultural specific philosophemes would represent an act of self-affirmation against the humiliation foreign powers inflicted by dismissing African cultures (128).

4.2. Towards a traditionalist or a contextualist view of belonging to a culture?

A significant question is to ask if Western forms of philosophy could also serve to explicate African cultural philosophemes. On closer inspection, this is just a special case of a general question: can one, with the existing philosophical tools of culture X, embark on the hermeneutic task of engaging with the cultural philosophemes of culture Y, to generate a plausible philosophy for members of either cultural group X or group Y? In short: can philosophy be practised cross-culturally? Okere does not entertain this kind of question.[29] Affirming the possibility of cross-cultural philosophy seems at first sight quite contrary to the spirit of the argument he develops (see 118–119). At the same time, the way in which he uses European hermeneutics to analyse the basic hermeneutic structure of all human beings[30] demonstrates that Okere's own philosophical practice amounts to affirming the possibility of cross-cultural philosophy. I would like to suggest that the response to this question is: yes, but only partially and depending on how we understand "culture". The more cultures are similar, the more it would seem to be possible to engage in such "cross-cultural" philosophical work; the more they are dissimilar, the less plausible it seems. One sees immediately why this question is not a simple brainteaser: it involves the relation of different traditions of culture and of philosophy in a single process of philosophising; it also involves the question of how we understand people's belonging to culture.

Let us turn to this last question, before considering again the possibility of cross-cultural philosophy. Much of the intellectual and political significance of Okere's hermeneutics (related to the passage from non-philosophy to philosophy and to the social role philosophy has to play, respectively) depends on people's "belonging to culture". What does he mean by stating that we belong to a culture? Two responses are possible. Let us call the first the *traditionalist* view of culture and the second, the *contextual* view of culture.

The *traditionalist* view of culture is the predominant voice in Okere's book.[31] It consists principally of his tendency to speak about culture in the singular as a homogenous, ever-present heritage.

- This perspective is that of a human being living in a monocultural context and having a single cultural origin. Furthermore, most often Okere's focus is on the influence of cultural origin and situatedness on philosophy (at the expense of innovation and projection towards the future) (65). Below, we will see that his strategy of illustrating the significance of other-than-Western cultural philosophemes with exclusive reference to Igbo culture reinforces this traditionalist view of culture.
- Okere defines philosophy as "a project of appropriation, of assumption and identification with one's total culture in a process of intellectual alchemy from which results a new creation, the meaning of this culture as interpreted by this unique experience which is the philosopher's insertion in it" (xv, discussed above). Nevertheless, Okere affirms that individuals have *one* culture, and he qualifies people's relation to their culture as an *unavoidably strong* attachment. Apparently, no innovation or imposed violence can make a dent in the "total culture"; change means change of "this culture", which remains essentially identical to itself. Okere even claims that "[n]o amount of emancipation can free one from one's culture and heritage" (59; see also xii). It is difficult to see how such a view on culture can reflect

and cope with the interpretative complexities of plural societies and modernisation.[32]
- Reflection takes place within a horizon of questioning, as is commonly granted. But according to Okere, "all philosophical discourse is first and foremost an answer to the problems and questions raised within a questioning horizon which means always, a culture" (64). In other words, Okere reduces the questioning horizon to culture.[33] No place is left for what is not heritage, that which is invented, innovated, or individualised. Even the questions themselves may be borrowed or imposed by others and circumstances that are not simply part of the interpreter's horizon of familiarity.
- In chapter 5 of *African Philosophy*, Okere focuses on non-philosophical influences on philosophy, often saying nothing about the philosophical transformation of that heritage in turn. He does not discuss how culture changes due to the impact of non-philosophical factors either. In this way, his view of culture is quite rigid and static.
- When all this is said, one may wonder whether Okere internalised Hountondji's and Eboussi Boulaga's critique of ethnophilosophy as much as he claimed, because his view of the passage to a creative, individual, first-person philosophy starts off in a very homogenous culture characterised by consensus.

For all his rejection of ethnophilosophy, Okere's view on culture largely corresponds with that of the ethnophilosophers. Nevertheless, this should not too hastily be considered a contradiction. It may well be (as I indicate earlier) that the process of identifying and analysing philosophemes—which is only the first part of a more encompassing hermeneutic philosophy—corresponds with the practice of ethnophilosophy.

But the parallels between ethnophilosophy and hermeneutics become less clear when one considers Okere's other view of culture. The minor voice in Okere's book portrays culture in a quite different way, which I have termed *contextual*. This view regards elements of traditional heritage in a wider contemporary context of socio-political complexities.[34] The implications of this alternative view of culture for our understanding of what it means to go back to "one's own culture" (118) are significant.

- In the problem statement of the introduction to *African Philosophy*, Okere does mention the impact of pluralism and historicity on the human sciences. True, when plurality is mentioned, he thinks of the

big cultural blocs such as the West, Africa, and the East. But there is no fundamental reason why the real plurality of African societies cannot be brought to bear on his project in the same manner.[35]
- Okere explicitly names the possibility that philosophers will not always accept their tradition en bloc (121). Likewise, whereas culture is most often treated as the *background* of reflection, it is sometimes presented as the *object* of reflection and therefore something that may well be questioned (see, for instance, 68). This may well be true for philosophers; Okere does not see change as something the general public can effect.
- One could be excused for finding in Okere a conservative, essentialist vision of culture, if it were not for the following passage that changes the register considerably. Still speaking about the culture to which we must go back in order to practise African philosophy, Okere writes:

> This background need not be the fossilized, unadulterated past. The black African philosopher is not to become a cultural historian, a laudator temporis acti, or a curator of the ethnic museum, jealously guarding the purity of ancestral heritage and protecting it from the adulterating encroachments of time and evolution. Plato's Seventh Letter demonstrates that some of the philosopher's most abiding inspiration came from contemporary events rather than from the epic Universe of Homer or the mythology of Hesiod. Background for a black African philosopher certainly means traditional institutions, symbols, and values, but also the often violent culture contact that was the colonial experience and its aftermath. It means the present day reality of a new-won and precarious independence, of exterior manipulation and political instability. It means the crisis of traditional religion in confrontation with both Christianity and secularism. It means Africa in metamorphoses—the dramatic change in material circumstances; the upsetting of traditional spiritual values; the moral ferment and ambivalence generated by this upset and the introduction of strange new values; the fact of belonging to the Third World, and the wrong side of the balance of power and wealth in a world dominated by power politics and greed; the crisis of self-respect resulting from the massive foreign invasion into Africa's intimacy, and Black Africa's self understanding as victim in the context of world racism. All this, and more, would form the legitimate background of an African philosopher. (121)[36]

> One can only be astounded that Okere's discussion continues hereafter by contrasting philosophemes from Western culture with those of Igbo culture, as if all of the socio-political complexities that, according to himself, constitute the individual effort of an African philosopher suddenly evaporate to leave the framework of a single Igbo culture in its place. There is clearly no way to reconcile these two views on culture and the relation to philosophy they imply. A sceptic may want to cite to me the passage where Okere presents philosophy as "an interpretative commentary on reality against the guiding, determining, and suggestive background of a culture" (81). According to this definition, culture may be claimed to form the guiding background of reflection and the issues listed by Okere the reality to be reflected on. Indeed, this definition fits the traditionalist view of culture. If this is the last word, then Okere's conservatism would be complete: tradition would provide the exclusive hermeneutic lens through which to look at the world. However, my primary objection is that this is not what Okere says in the long passage cited above. There, he radically enlarges his view of culture and background so as to make place for all the phenomena that constitute the life of people on the African continent today: imposed or desired plurality, hybridity, modernisation, change, together with the stable, transmitted cultural inheritance of societies, and all of the joy and suffering that come with it.[37]

In my view, Okere's major traditionalist voice on culture and his minor contextualist voice on culture cannot be reconciled. And the contextualist view is to be preferred: it is descriptively more plausible, more politically sensitive, and it can, besides, envelope the core phenomena the traditionalist view aims to capture. The contextual view on culture therefore does not negate the significance of cultural heritage as part of the background of philosophy, but situates it in a larger context of socio-political developments.

Having explored the two possible ways of understanding culture as one's own or belonging to culture as the source of philosophy, let's return to the question formulated above: can philosophy be practised cross-culturally? The strength of the traditionalist view of culture is that it points to the limits of such an endeavour. These limits are described by the differences in the cultural background of people of different origins. However, this insight has to be relativised by the long citation above. Next to factors like language, traditional customs, religion, and social institutions, experiences such as political instability, secularisation, exposure to foreign values, poverty, and racism may form part of people's cultural background. But surely significant similarities exist between Africans' experience of poverty and Asians', or the experience of secularisation in Europe and in Africa? One could make the list much longer: unemployment, insecurity, sexism, labour migration, exposure to new communication technologies, modernisation, social diversity, joys of family life, and friendship, and so forth. My claim is not that there are no differences in these experiences or in the ways they inform the thought of people from diverse cultures. My point is that there are significant overlaps of background. And if background cultures overlap in this sense, I see no reason why some African philosophemes cannot inform Western philosophy (and vice versa), or why Western philosophy may not contribute to the explicitation of such philosophemes from Africa (and vice versa).

From this discussion, it should be clear that whatever one's view of culture, it strongly affects how one chooses to proceed from non-philosophy to philosophy. And this is a "core question" of hermeneutics.[38]

5. Conclusion

Reflecting on his life's work and writings three decades after his thesis, Okere concludes: "The preoccupation with culture is a constant. It seems to have been constant ever since I saw clearly from my early work that one's own culture is the Archimedean point from which all thinking and knowledge, all philosophizing, and all theologizing can take place."[39] In this chapter, I have reviewed and analysed how Okere started out on the way from non-philosophy to philosophy. Quite clearly, the question of culture is central, but the specific nature of Okere's philosophy, of his philosophy as a hermeneutics, is determined by the precise way in which he deals with culture and in particular its relation to written and published philosophy. We saw how he rejects equating culture and philosophy, the hallmark of ethnophilosophy. However, he also avoids a stark opposition between the two. The exact articulation is captured by the word "philosophemes", which belong equally to culture and philosophy. Once this term has been accepted, one recognises the rich suggestive power of Okere's text, which is effective even when one does not share his main view on culture. This uncertainty and disputability of the nature of culture and its relation to philosophy may even be inherent to African philosophical hermeneutics as he describes it. Ultimately indeterminate is the relation between the dominant culture and marginal culture of a specific group, between traditional culture and modern variations, between the cultural patterns of African groups and those of the European cultures with which they have been in contact, between the culture of the group and that of the individual. Finally, one should observe the political dimension of this "return" to culture (without, however, exaggerating Okere's explicit elaboration on this theme). While in some places in the world it could be the sign of a conservativism, here it is explicitly a stance of defiance:[40] defiance of a world—and in particular a corner of the world called academia—insofar as it relegates African culture to an anthropological curiosity and parades Western forms of thinking, intentionally or not, as universal.[41] This does not mean that Okere falls into a culturalist pluralism, which would become a war of incommunicable and irreconcilable ideas, because, as I have argued, there is something like a silent supposition of human generalities (if not universalities), which enable exchanges, communication, and debate. In sum, to Okere's mind, the conditions for an African philosophy, or rather of a series of culturally specific African philosophies, are met in 1971. *African Philosophy* stands on the brink of this new possibility.

Select annotated bibliography

Mudimbe, Valentin-Yves. *The Invention of Africa: Gnosis, Philosophy, and the Order of Knowledge.* Bloomington: Indiana University Press, 1988.
    This volume situates the development of ethnophilosophy, against which Okere advances a critique, within a broader survey of Africanist knowledge.

Nkombe, Oleko. *Métaphore et métonymie dans les symboles parémiologiques. L'intersubjectivité dans les "Proverbes Tetela".* Kinshasa: Faculté de théologie catholique, [1975] 1979.
    A hermeneutics of proverbs as an entry to African philosophy, written shortly after Okere's thesis.

Oguejiofor, Josephat Obi and Godfrey Igwebuike Onah, eds. *African Philosophy and the Hermeneutics of Culture: Essays in Honour of Theophilus Okere.* Münster: LIT Verlag, 2005.
    A volume of twenty scholarly studies on Okere's philosophy.

Okere, Theophilus. *Can There Be an African Philosophy? A Hermeneutical Investigation with Special Reference to Igbo Culture?* PhD, Institute of Philosophy, Catholic University of Leuven, 1971.
    Okere's doctoral thesis submitted at the Institute of Philosophy of the Catholic University of Leuven (now KU Leuven).

Okere, Theophilus. *African Philosophy: A Historico-hermeneutical Investigation of the Conditions of its Possibility*. Lanham, MD: University Press of America, 1983.
  African Philosophy is the book discussed in this chapter. It is a reprint of Part 2 of Okere's thesis of 1971.
Okere, Theophilus. *Church, Theology, and Society in Africa: Essays*. Enugu: Fourth Dimension, 2005.
  I add this volume of collected essays for the sake of completeness.
Okere, Theophilus. "My Philosophical Odyssey". In *African Philosophy and the Hermeneutics of Culture: Essays in Honour of Theophilus Okere*, edited by Josephat Obi Oguejiofor and Godfrey Igwebuike Onah. Münster: LIT Verlag, 2005, pp. 353–360.
  Okere's view on his own intellectual work.
Okere, Theophilus. *Philosophy, Culture, and Society in Africa: Essays*. Nsukka: Afro-Orbis Publications, 2005.
  A volume of essays spanning the mid-1970s to the beginning of the 2000s. The essays "Culture and Religion" clarify Okere's understanding of hermeneutics. In 1973, Okere presented "Culture and Religion" at the second Convocation of Bigard Memorial Seminary in Enugu. In 1975, he delivered "Culture" at the College of Science and Technology in Port Harcourt.
Oruka, Odera, ed. *Sage Philosophy: Indigenous Thinkers and Modern Debate on African Philosophy*. Leiden: Brill, 1990.
  An interesting alternative approach to making the transition from African oral wisdom to written, published African philosophy. Oruka's project shares many concerns and assumptions with Okere's.
Serequeberhan, Tsenay, ed. *African Philosophy: The Essential Readings*. New York: Paragon House, 1991.
  A valuable anthology of positions on African philosophy that were published during the fifteen years after Okere wrote his doctoral dissertation.

CHAPTER 3

Interpretation as a resource for political resistance: Serequeberhan between generality and particularity

The Hermeneutics of African Philosophy: Horizon and Discourse is a book of philosophy written by Tsenay Serequeberhan.[1] This elementary fact brings together the two poles between which he set out his whole argument: that of generality (of philosophy in general) and particularity (the particular author). In this book, Serequeberhan attempts to negotiate generality and particularity through a specific understanding of what philosophy is: "philosophy is inherently and in its very nature a hermeneutics of the existentiality of human existence" (117–118).[2] His book can be read as an elaboration of this point. What this elaboration consists of can be presented schematically by stating the central theses of each of the book's four chapters:

1. Humans are historical and interpreting beings.
2. Through ethnophilosophy and "professional philosophy", African thinkers have negated this historical and interpretive aspect of humanity.
3. Colonisation, likewise, is a violent negation of human nature thus defined and calls for violent resistance.
4. It is possible to restore the historical and interpretive nature of humanity through practices of freedom.

In more detail, the content of *Hermeneutics of African Philosophy* can be outlined as follows:[3]

Chapter 1 takes the step from the general anthropological "thesis" (human beings are historical and interpreting beings) to the specific post-colonial African context for which this book is written. This transition is mediated by the key term "historicity" or "historicalness". As I show, these terms refer to human existence that can be grasped only as something that unfolds in changing socio-political contexts. This central trait of human existence introduces a major pursuit of *Hermeneutics of African Philosophy*, which is to philosophise in response to a specific socio-political context. The historical situation of the philosopher is the horizon from which philosophical discourse emerges and this holds no less for African philosophy (see 10).

Chapter 2 zooms in on the debate at that time on the nature of African philosophy. It does so by approaching the debate between "professional philosophy" versus "ethno-philosophy" from a markedly political perspective. Serequeberhan rejects these two alternatives with equal energy. The task he sets out to accomplish in the remainder of his book is to argue for the appropriate way to fill the void left by this double critique. Serequeberhan embarks upon this task by arguing that African philosophy is a mediation between lived experience (which is already hermeneutic or interpretative) and a more conceptual articulation (i.e., philosophy), which enables a more developed reflection on lived experience.

Chapter 3 examines the historical context in which African philosophers cannot but do their work. For this analysis, Serequeberhan enlists the help of Frantz Fanon[4] as a master of hermeneutics. Serequeberhan presents the tension between colonial violence (physical as much cultural and mental), and the violent response in the name of liberation. This is the tension from which the (re-)humanisation of colonisers and colonised must emerge.

The quest for rehumanisation is examined further in chapter 4. It consists of a "return to the source" of human historicity or, in a different philosophical parlance, agency. Here, Amílcar Cabral serves as a second master of hermeneutics, because he, in an exemplary way, analysed—for his particular context—the social transformations through which people acquired the ability to engage in practices of liberation.

It should strike the reader from the outset, that *Hermeneutics of African Philosophy* is characterised by a repeated to-and-fro between general claims about human beings and philosophy on the one hand, and particular claims about Africans, African philosophy, and the problematic of existence on the African continent on the other. To bring this logic to the fore, I first systematise Serequeberhan's general anthropological claims. Second, I identify the basic claims regarding the nature of philosophy in general that he derives from these anthropological claims. Third, I turn to the way Serequeberhan draws conclusions from these basic premises for African philosophy. These three steps will cover, roughly, the introduction, first chapter, and the conclusion of *Hermeneutics of African Philosophy*. Only then will I change gears to see how Serequeberhan engages in the particular question of hermeneutics and liberation. On the one hand, I show Serequeberhan as a diagnostician of what he sees as a misconstrued

African philosophy (especially in his second chapter); on the other hand, I look at how Serequeberhan points the way to healthy philosophical practice (especially in the third and fourth chapters of his book).

1. The source: general anthropological claims

Crucial to the understanding of Serequeberhan's book are the basic anthropological claims he invokes at the beginning of his study (see pages 1–2). The three major claims are that: (a) human beings are understanding and interpreting beings; (b) human existence is temporal; and (c) human existence can be ossified by socio-political circumstances.

All human beings will die; they are mortal. Because we are mortal, we are finite. Because we are finite, we are situated. As situated beings, we engage with people, things, and events around us within the specific and limited horizon in which they appear to us. For these reasons, human beings are *understanding* beings—not merely in the sense that we can and do form an impression of the meaning of things, but also that our entire being is such that we grasp, in one way or another, the world from where we are. And humans can articulate this understanding intelligently, which means that we can *interpret* our world.[5] If the word "horizon" that appears in the subtitle of Serequeberhan's book evokes the situatedness of human beings, then the philosophical articulation of one's being in this horizon is the "discourse" in the subtitle. I underscore from the beginning that with philosophical "discourse", Serequeberhan has very specifically hermeneutics in mind, because: "In contrast to […] 'infinite thinking' hermeneutics enunciates a 'finite' descriptive kind of thinking, which is grounded in the inherently interpretative and mortal character of human existence as such" (123n2).

To interpret and understand depends on a central trait of being human. This core is "existence" or "to be". "Being" or "existing" should not be understood as simply "being there", but as temporal extension, as marked by "fluidity/actuality" (20) or "historicalness" (21). In Serequeberhan's words, "human being[6] is grounded in the particular ontological specificity of the temporalising ecstatic phenomenality of human existence" (20). This anthropological claim, which holds at all times and in all places of human existence, is the "basic premise and grounding thesis" of his book (117). In short, upon this premise the whole argument stands or falls, and it orients the whole argument of his book.

Although being human is essentially temporal, fluid, or historical, socio-political constraints can make human existence more static. Such "ossification" of people's existence is a reality, particularly of the modern world. This was the view of Heidegger[7] and his disciples and equally that of Serequeberhan and the inhabitants of independent African states. In the case of Africa, Serequeberhan argues that the cultural, economic, political hegemony that the West exercises deprives people of their actuality or historicalness, either by ossifying their mode of existence, or by subjecting them to a different mode. Because such ossification and subjection are historical facts, the philosophical articulation of Africans' humanity has from the beginning a socio-political import. The violent imposition of a socio-political order that deprives Africans of their humanity—of their actual existence—estranges people from their meaningful, human core. Such a confusion or estrangement from one's historical and interpretive existence may be called a "misunderstanding" (16). And because this "misunderstanding" is not just and mental mishap, but an existential condition, Serequeberhan finds it to be the origin of the essential problems, the questions, that give birth to African philosophy (as in Okolo; see 24). It is left to the reader to conclude that identifying misunderstanding or distortion of the course of understanding as a source of philosophical reflection is not dissimilar from what is claimed in philosophy elsewhere.

The existential depth of this misunderstanding justifies the prominent place of political philosophy in Serequeberhan's hermeneutics (see 21). This has nothing to do with a blindness to other "subdisciplines" or with arbitrary preference, but is due to the significance of political turmoil as a generator of questions. To summarise: if human agency is the source of all interpretation and practice, then eliminating obstacles to these abilities should be the condition for exercising all other abilities (30). And if these obstacles are primarily political in nature, it requires a politically oriented hermeneutics to help remove them.

2. Philosophy in general

We have now seen how Serequeberhan perceives the existential and hermeneutic constitution of human beings. It should not surprise us that a general claim about the nature of all philosophy can be derived from such a general anthropological orientation. All humans can philosophise and this philosophising attests to the hermeneutic constitution of human beings. As Serequeberhan explains, "philosophy—as, strictly speaking, with all things human—is an inherently interpretative undertaking grounded in the mortal existentiality of human existence" (2).

Furthermore, philosophy is conceptual work and remains "implicated in its own conceptions and formulations" (2). Philosophy, therefore, has to work on its own presuppositions (see 4). Moreover, philosophy as hermeneutics is characterised by the interrelation between "horizon" and "discourse" (see 17). This determination seems to hold for all philosophy, because Serequeberhan illustrates this point with reference to Descartes and Kant, alongside Ya'aqob and Heywat:

> Horizon designates the historico-hermeneutical and politico-cultural milieu within and out of which specific discourses (philosophic, artistic, scientific, etc.) are articulated. It is the overall existential space within and out of which they occur. Discourse, on the other hand, refers to these articulated concerns interior to the concrete conditions-of-existence made possible by and internal to a specific horizon. (18)

Therefore, "philosophic discourse is a reflexive and reflective response to the felt crisis of a lived and concrete horizon" (19, elaborated in 24). Serequeberhan will concur with Marcien Towa's[8] characterisation of philosophy as "[t]he thought of the essential, the methodical and critical examination of that which, in the theoretical order or in the practical order, has or should have for humanity a supreme importance. Such is philosophy in its abstract and entirely general essence" (7, citation from Towa).

All the claims made up to this point hold for all forms of philosophy. But here, Serequeberhan opens the door that leads philosophy in general to the particularity of African philosophy: all philosophical discourse is generated by a *situated* person. Consequently, "[t]he *generality* of this essence [of philosophy, as in the citation from Towa above] is specified by the differentiated *particularity*—cultural, historical, and political—within which a philosophic discourse is articulated" (7, my emphasis). This cultural, historical, and political situatedness determines the "Africanness" of African philosophy (and, by implication, the particularity of other forms of philosophy). All philosophy is written within a horizon and is articulated in discourse; what makes African philosophy a specific, discernible discourse is the specificity of the horizon and the concerns it strives to deal with (7). Another way to say that the specificity of philosophy is determined by its cultural, historical, and political environment, is to say that philosophy is situated within a field of concerns that it eithers counters or advances. That is why the kind of African philosophy Serequeberhan practises throughout *Hermeneutics of African Philosophy*—the kind he demanded of all African philosophers—is marked by the traits of its situatedness within a field of concerns. These traits are specific to periods (such as the post-independence era), places (Africa), and, a bit less clear, agents ("we"). And all three of these determinants converge on a particular problem (such as neo-colonialism or failed independence) (see 8). In this way Serequeberhan resists the temptation of situating Africanness in "colour and race" and rather affirms the general principle that "our being African is grounded in a shared history of subjugation, struggle, and political liberation", as he later writes.[9]

In as far as these concerns differ from those of philosophers who are situated otherwise, they demarcate different forms of philosophy. At least two implications of this approach to the "Africanity" of African philosophy should be indicated at this point:

- Whereas Serequeberhan clearly traces the path from philosophy in general to African philosophy in particular, one cannot miss the fact that the African philosophy thus construed forms again a very sturdy "generality".
- Almost imperceptibly, while passing from philosophy in general to the particularity of African philosophy, Serequeberhan demarcates African philosophy from Western philosophy and other philosophies, which (although never formulated in this way) in practice seems to preclude the possibility that the concerns of Africa may, and may legitimately, appeal to the philosophical minds of people outside this apparent "demarcation". Serequeberhan offers no justification for such a segregation.

Having had a taste of Serequeberhan's idea of African philosophy, we can consider the two sets of general claims together: those about human nature and those about the essence of philosophy.

3. All humans and all philosophy

Against the background of this turn from generality to African particularity, it may surprise some readers to notice Serequeberhan's willingness to take over ideas from European philosophers. He singles out Heidegger and Gadamer for their philosophical expression of Serequeberhan's core anthropological claims (1–2). One should not hasten to see a contradiction in this procedure: he presents these core claims as articulations in a *particular* language, and context, of something that holds for people *generally*. This does not mean that he remains fixated on those German authors either. The truths they express need to be "indigenized" (2). In fact, having done so, one may equally criticise these philosophers to point out their shortcomings (cf. 4).[10]

What Serequeberhan subsequently presents as "African philosophy" does not hold a priori for everything that is offered under the name "African philosophy". Something else parades as African philosophy that is actually a miscreation stemming from the circumstances and spirit of colonisation.[11] This means that "African philosophy" is the name *both* of a very natural human activity for Africans and of a harmful invention to the detriment of Africans. These two manifestations of "African philosophy" part ways in how they deal with the generality and particularity of human being and philosophy.

Let us examine the status or validity of the general claims.

At the core of all particular peoples, Serequeberhan argues, is a general "humanity" (20).[12] The core of Serequeberhan's concern is evidently the humanity of Africans, but his argument compels us to understand that there is only one common humanity. After all, he explicitly rejects such characterisation of Africans as offered by Léopold Senghor's *négritude* or *Africanité*, and rather draws insight from the general anthropological claims he finds in Heidegger. But does this approach not open the door to critics (like Ernest Wamba dia Wamba; see 17), who suggest that Serequeberhan makes himself guilty of adopting a Euro-normative model of human being? Is hermeneutics not a form of neo-colonisation of African thought? Despite the apparent merit of these misgivings, the objection does not hold for three reasons.

First, Serequeberhan shows himself a very able critic of Euro-normativity elsewhere in *Hermeneutics of African Philosophy* (for instance in his debate with Paulin Hountondji and Kwame Nkrumah). However one assesses his view on these authors, one at least has to grant that he understands the problem. Besides, Serequeberhan energetically criticises Heidegger's Nazism and other writers who lack interest in the issues of colonialism and racism in their debates with Heidegger (cf. 131–132n29).

Second, for Serequeberhan the authority of hermeneutics is *not* drawn from the Western expressions given to it, but from the fact that interpretation, as the soul of hermeneutics, is a trait of all human beings. That is why, once crucial traits of the humanity of humans have been identified with the help of Heidegger, Serequeberhan can develop this point with the help of African authors independently of Heidegger, authors such as Towa or Cabral. This is clearly illustrated when Serequeberhan affirms: "The basic premise of Cabral's thinking on colonialism and the anti-colonial struggle, which he formulates as the 'return to the source', is a heteronomous and multivalent conception of history. *For Cabral as for Heidegger*, 'existence is revealed in many ways'" (102, my emphasis).

Third, according to Serequeberhan's views on anthropological generality all human thought emerges from a horizon and all people evidently do not share the same horizon. Serequeberhan could thus respond to his critics by pointing out how his own thought is ultimately rooted in the problematics of African existence (in a way Serequeberhan considers deficient in Nkrumah and Senghor, as I show later). Serequeberhan's entire project is premised on a double claim: one can at the same time reject the "universality" of Enlightenment (38) *and* still maintain an anthropologically general claim about the situatedness of philosophy: "It is this perpetual process of lived self-understanding, peculiar and internal to human existence as such, that philosophical hermeneutics consciously articulates and cultivates" (19).

Together, these points counter the accusation of Euro-normativity levelled by Serequeberhan's critics. Moreover, these points allow us to draw conclusions left undeveloped in Serequeberhan's text.

The first implication of Serequeberhan's position is that African philosophers can use works of European philosophy to understand the humanity common to both Africans and Europeans, provided that the texts are appropriated cautiously and critically. To do so takes nothing away from the historical and cultural contingency of each particular way of exploring that common humanity.[13]

A second conclusion can be drawn from Serequeberhan's explanation that Western philosophy is a poison from which an antidote can be developed. This is perhaps an inappropriate image to describe his idea of how African philosophers relate to Western philosophy (11).[14] More exact would be to say that to the African philosopher, Western philosophy is like a knife that may be put to constructive or destructive use; to the African philosopher, Western philosophy is inherently ambiguous. Both the content and form of argumentation in *The Hermeneutics of African Philosophy* confirm this.[15] Arguably, this conclusion is a special case of a more general principle, namely that any philosopher's use of another is ambiguous and therefore risky.

And if this is correct, I would draw a third conclusion: African philosophy can turn sour too, as we know from Serequeberhan's readings of Nkrumah and Senghor (see § 5, below). Perhaps one should say that all philosophy, coming as it does from humans, can be used to the advantage or to the detriment of any people. And it is for this reason that critical self-reflexion remains part of the vocation of philosophy.

This point deserves to be explained further. In chapter 1 of *Hermeneutics of African Philosophy*, Serequeberhan discusses what he sees as one of humanity's worst afflictions: ossification (20, 22, 81), which means reified, "thingified" (71–75) existence—hence it is also called "nonhistoricity" or "historico-existential inertness" (21). Elsewhere (21), his emphasis is on another metaphor, namely hostage-taking or the taking over of people's historical existence by hegemonic and violent impositions (one may say, imposing a different rhythm or course to this flow of historicality).[16] He calls the latter a "tragicomic obscene duplication of Europe" (21). If the pathologies are pathologies of our hermeneutic existence, then a philosophy that could decipher or "work out concepts" for this "misunderstanding" would also appropriately be a hermeneutics. But what does it mean when Serequeberhan states that Nkrumah and Senghor participate in the lived actuality of contemporary Africa just as much as Fanon and Cabral do (22)? To reconcile this claim with the severe critique Serequeberhan reserves for Senghor and Nkrumah, we can say that there are *two ways of participating in lived actuality*: a healthy way, and a pathological way; or perhaps a proper and an improper way; or, again, a way true to the historicalness that constitutes the core of people's humanity, and ways that deviate from that core because of either reification or taking-over. Serequeberhan seems to tend to such vocabulary when, for instance, he speaks about "our own most distinctive existential actuality" (23), which invites us to consider also its opposite: say, a falsification of our existence.

This conclusion seems to me to be valid for all philosophy and all people. And this is what Serequeberhan seems to suggest when, concluding his exposition of philosophy's rootedness in existence, he claims: "Philosophy [i.e. all philosophy—EW] is thus this critical and explorative engagement of one's own cultural specificity and lived historicalness. It is a critically aware explorative appropriation of our cultural, political, and historical existence" (23)

4. African philosophy

Still speaking of the same human beings and the same philosophy, I now single out their specifically African manifestations.

4.1. *Critique: what is to be avoided*

For Serequeberhan, African philosophy starts as a miscreation of ethnophilosophy practised by Tempels and his followers. At the same time, "professional philosophers'"[17] contestation of ethnophilosophy is as much of an aberration. In Serequeberhan's reading, both kinds of philosophy elevates philosophy to the apex and defining quality of humanity (3). On the contrary, it should come as no surprise that the philosopher who presented philosophy as hermeneutics and hermeneutics as an extension of the common human ability to interpret, would remain rather modest in his claims about philosophy. Serequeberhan offers no idea of philosophy as a particular achievement, let alone an elevation of human nature.

To define the task Serequeberhan assigned philosophy, its particular duty, we must take his critique of ethnophilosophy and of "professional philosophy" as our departure point. In short, he opposes ethnophilosophy's "particularistic antiquarianism" and professional philosophy's "abstract universalism" (5). This opposition serves to identify two important trends that Serequeberhan opposes and in opposition to which he offers hermeneutics as alternative—very much like we saw Okere doing in the previous chapter. However, Serequeberhan is fully aware of the broader spectrum of African philosophies.[18]

The issue here is more than a methodological battle. It also reflects the international socio-political context, which consists of two sides. On the one hand, there is what Serequeberhan calls "the internal self-implosion of *Eurocentric* and *logocentric* philosophic thought, which is constitutive of and interior to European modernity". On the other hand, there is the "onslaught of an African philosophic discourse aimed at redeeming the humanity of the human in colonized African existence" (3).[19] Strangely enough, Serequeberhan devotes practically no attention to the first part about European philosophy—which is quite regrettable and consistent with a general tendency in this book not to thematise the positive developments in European thought after the independence of its colonies. Almost all of his efforts consist in looking at the African side, either by critiquing forms of African philosophy, or by offering his view on what African philosophy should be. In his own philosophical contribution, Serequeberhan explicitly joins Okere, first to identify the gap left once ethnophilosophy and "professional philosophy" have been critiqued, and, second, to consider hermeneutics as a candidate to fill this space.[20]

Hermeneutics has an ambivalent relationship to the history and traditions of Africa: "It is *reverent* in that it is radically open and susceptible to that which is preserved in its own cultural heritage. On the other hand, it is *critical* of tradition to the extent that the cultural elements that have been preserved in it have ossified and are a concrete hindrance to the requirements of contemporary existence" (6, my emphasis). This statement may well seem to be a limited concession to ethnophilosophy. And perhaps it is. But the striking point is elsewhere. It consists of inscribing the act of philosophising in the historical movement that embraces philosophers and their society. In addition, the historical movement of culture is presented as a flow—one that can be obstructed—which will remain throughout a major metaphor for Serequeberhan's view of philosophy too. Later in the book, for instance, he argues with Cabral that we as philosophers and citizens have to return to the "source", but that source is not the archive of traditions, but rather the ability to participate in the flow of human initiative, which includes destroying obstacles (physical, institutional, mental) to such initiative. And initiative thrives on the double relation to history and tradition, through esteem and criticism (6).

Serequeberhan's affinity with Okere's thought is not a question of school or style. It is, apart from their shared view on the anthropological basis of hermeneutics (discussed above), a question of the very vocation and practice of African philosophy. Serequeberhan, in the wake of Okere, claims that "the hermeneutics of African philosophy or African philosophical hermeneutics sees itself, on the level of theory, as the critical-reflexive appropriation and continuation of African emancipatory hopes and aspirations" (6, see also 114). This is the reason why—probably against the readers' expectation—Serequeberhan may look to Fanon and Cabral as masters of hermeneutics (discussed below).[21] They share in the true spirit of hermeneutics as Serequeberhan sees it, namely in maintaining (even if implicitly) that "the locus of philosophic reflection and reflexivity is the concrete actuality and the phenomenal historicity of lived existence" (6). The essentialism of ethnophilosophy and the Euro-normativity of the professional philosophers miss this point, in Serequeberhan's view.

If these major strands of African philosophy miss the point, what is African philosophy, then?

4.2. Advocacy: what is to be pursued

In broad terms, Serequeberhan's answer to this question is plain enough: "contemporary African philosophy is concretely *oriented* toward thinking the problems and concerns that arise from the lived actuality of post-colonial 'independent' Africa" (7, my emphasis). It is less easy to pinpoint exactly what this entails specifically. This grand declaration, which forms the major theme of his "hermeneutics of African philosophy", is more of an ideal than a description. One infers this ideal from the fact that ethnophilosophy and "professional philosophy", both manifestations of African philosophy, lack this "orientation", in Serequeberhan's assessment. His understanding of the ideal or norm of African philosophy, we will see, is subtended (or justified) by his general considerations about hermeneutics.

This is all but a marginal point: Serequeberhan's view of the appropriate way to gain access to the real vocation of African philosophy—and therefore the ideal against which all discourses claiming to be "African philosophy" can be evaluated—is a very specific understanding of hermeneutics. Here, hermeneutics is not just one of the many forms of philosophy. Hermeneutics is what African philosophy really is and should be. One misunderstands this claim as long as one thinks of "hermeneutics" as one of the many sub-disciplines of philosophy. This is not a quarrel between subdisciplines.

Serequeberhan's understanding of hermeneutics is a fundamental one that claims that hermeneutics underlies all sub-disciplines, gives them their point of origin, or leads them back to their source (as set out in the first sections of this chapter). That source consists of general claims about what African people are, the core of which corresponds with what all human beings are. Or, to retrace this argumentative path from the origin: if you know what a human being is, you know what truly engaged thinking is, and you can derive what philosophy is appropriate for people in a particular historical context. And only against this background can aberrations like ethnophilosophy and "professional philosophy" be identified and denounced. The problem with these philosophies is not that they are not written by Africans, or even that they do not speak to certain legitimate concerns of Africans—they do!—but that they have in some way become detached from the source; they could be said to betray that source or (in the terms of the citation from 7, above) to be *"dis-oriented"*.[22] In two distinct ways they miss the fact, according to Serequeberhan, that "African philosophy—even when its protagonists are not aware of it—is inherently, and cannot but be, a hermeneutic undertaking" (2).

These declarations concerning African philosophy allow us to appreciate the importance of Serequeberhan's concise philosophical anthropology and the hermeneutics that is rooted in it. Hermeneutics proceeds not from the mind alone, but from the entire human existence of which it is an integral part. For African philosophy this means two things: *descriptively*, that this philosophy depends on a thin, but general, anthropology; *normatively*, that all African philosophy will be measured against its commitment to this anthropological basis. Such a commitment to a *thin* anthropological core can be undertaken seriously only from within the *thick* situatedness within concerns of concerns, from the "essential problems" of Africa. This hermeneutic vision is integral to African philosophy, but one has to conclude that it applies to any other philosophy.

Once one appreciates Serequeberhan's view of how a thin anthropology is enmeshed with a thick situatedness, all of his claims about African philosophy fall into place. Thus, Serequeberhan concludes that African philosophy is "a critical hermeneutics of the African situation [...] [I]ts specific arguments and formulations [are] grounded in the concrete awareness that philosophy in general and African philosophy in particular is, above all else and necessarily, a hermeneutical thinking through of its own lived historicalness" (118, similarly, 2). The particularities of African philosophical practice and of the rise of African philosophy itself does not preclude it from reflecting a larger tendency in philosophy in general: the "prevalent ascendance of context-oriented modes of philosophizing" (119) or, to reformulate, the ascendance of hermeneutics as the core of all philosophy.

In this constellation of different philosophical discourses, African philosophy has two major tasks. Serequeberhan identifies these tasks by following Lucius Outlaw. On the one hand, it has to work through (or "deconstruct") the Eurocentric, colonial heritage critically. This "unmasking and undoing" (119) involves not only the philosophical heritage, but the entire socio-institutional frame left over at independence.[23] On the other hand, the constructive task consists of an "indigenizing" work in theory that will help revitalise African agency or historicity (119). How to achieve these aims in practice remains undeveloped in *Hermeneutics of African Philosophy*. However, as we read above (in § 1), part of indigenisation means recognising which aspects of other traditions and settings are valid also for Africa.

In sum, African philosophical hermeneutics is, for Serequeberhan, "engaged in articulating the *truth* of its lived present. This 'truth' is, furthermore, nothing more than its own reflexive self-representation on the plane of philosophy, in the service of fulfilling the emancipatory hopes and aspirations inscribed in our 'common history, tradition, [and] universe of discourse' as post-colonial Africans" (120, the cited phrase is from Edward Said). The "post", here, captures perhaps a not-yet-fully-actualised reality, but the hope and aspiration to liberation. Pursuing these aspirations, philosophy responds to the death of those who contributed to liberation (cf. 120). They are evoked in the dedication of the book, where Serequeberhan writes: "This book is also dedicated to the kind memory of my father Serequeberhan Gebrezgi and to my two sons, Nesim-Netssere and Awate-Hayet—to the tragic past and the hopeful future." In the terms of its subtitle, the book articulates in philosophical "discourse" this "horizon" of being situated between memory and hope (2).

This orientation to a specific horizon evidently represents a step away from the universal nature of philosophy (and thus from "professional philosophy"). At the same time, African philosophy is not absolutely unique, because it mirrors and is mirrored by the hermeneutic (i.e. context-oriented) nature of other forms of philosophy. Fanon captures this "in-between" character as follows: "Universality resides in [the] decision to recognize and accept the reciprocal relativism of different cultures [and histories], once the colonial status is irreversibly excluded" (119).[24] Clearly this Fanonian "universality" is worlds apart from the Euro-normative "universalism" of European Enlightenment, which Serequeberhan rejects explicitly (38).[25] Nevertheless, this "in-between" universalism and particularity is no invitation to an indifferent relativism. Rather, Serequeberhan follows Cabral in articulating the global political implications of this position:

> It is the patriotism of those who reclaim their historical existence in terms of and by reference to the historicity of the values inscribed in the charter of the United Nations, a nationalism grounded in the recognition that difference is what constitutes the concrete existence of each nation state and people in their particular and specific historicity. This is what I [Serequeberhan] referred to [...] as the basis for global earthly solidarity. (114).[26]

5. Improper African philosophy: self-imposed negation of historicalness in Nkrumah and Senghor

Up to this point we have seen how Serequeberhan constructs his vision of African philosophy. We have seen that its thin, general anthropological basis, which encompasses human existence, historicity, and agency as mutually implicating, serves as a descriptive and normative reference for African philosophy. The stage is thus set for us to see how Serequeberhan puts his hermeneutics into practice in aiming to fulfil the deconstructive task of African philosophy (as presented in the previous section, § 4). Even so, it may come as a surprise to see where Serequeberhan spends this critical, anti-colonial energy. Not on this or that philosopher from the colonial powers, but on two eminent African philosophers and statesmen: Nkrumah[27] and Senghor. Serequeberhan engages critically with these authors to dispel the invalid claims about the nature of African philosophy and thereby open the way for his positive contribution. In other words, reflecting on African philosophical "dis-orientations" may help to regain the proper, hermeneutic orientation of African philosophy.

From the Introduction of *Hermeneutics of African Philosophy*, Serequeberhan refers to the major debate between ethnophilosophy and "professional philosophy". Establishing the vocation of African philosophy in his first chapter, he revisits this debate in chapter 2 and stresses its political thrust or, as he terms it, the "parallel ideological and political correlate" of the debate (32). For this, the chosen representatives—Senghor and Nkrumah, respectively—are particularly appropriate: they are two recognised authors with major intellectual output (both close to socialism) and both intimately involved with resistance, liberation, and politics, having served as heads of state. Serequeberhan uses most of chapter 2 to demonstrate that these two authors, although in many respects representing opposite intellectual positions, suffer from the same pathology: an undue orientation towards European ideas and value systems. In both cases, an underlying lack of interpretation or hermeneutics accounts for this deficiency.

In each case, the thought of Nkrumah and Senghor will be measured according to the "prior question", namely: "what are the people of Africa trying to free themselves from and what are they trying to establish?" (33). This measure of the advancement of Africa does not suddenly fall from the air, but is for Serequeberhan implied in the hermeneutic-anthropological category of lived actuality, which is the wellspring of all thought and praxis. The prior question does not only serve to identify the level at which Serequeberhan claims to pin-point Nkrumah's and Senghor's fallacies, but also as starting point to construct his own positive contribution. One could reformulate Serequeberhan's question, thinking of Amartya Sen's question, "equality of what?", as "freedom from and for what?"

5.1. *Nkrumah: pathology of extroverted Euro-normativity*

As his point of departure, Serequeberhan observes that Nkrumah declares the decisiveness of "scientific socialism" in the exact terms and theory of classical Marxism-Leninism.[28] No reason to question his intentions, but by so doing, he "occludes the foundational and grounding character of the question of freedom in Africa" and "fails to grapple with the historicity of the African situation" (33). Assuming European modernity as the framework for economics as such, Nkrumah neglects the particularity of African economics or relegates it to the status of a mere addendum to the core European reality. The theory regarding this supposed European truth is held to be a "universal, context-neutral, and value-free-theory"—a "general and abstract" theory, which can be fitted to or serve as framework for any particular situation (34). In Serequeberhan's view, Nkrumah's unqualified use of European theory amounts to Eurocentric theorising (see 34). Formulated otherwise, deploying European theory in such a way overvalues that theory, and the context from which it emerges, at the expense of the contexts to which it is mechanically applied. Now, one should not construe Serequeberhan's critique to exclude the value of European theory or philosophy for other parts of the world (or vice versa). His point is otherwise: the "underinterpretation" of Marxism-Leninism construes it as a "pre-established framework" that holds "automatically and of necessity" to all contexts (34–35). These three failings—underinterpretation, bias, and universalism—*are three major traits of non-hermeneutic reasoning.* Serequeberhan goes further by calling this "colonialism in the realm and guise of theory" (35, 42).

What is imported, or imposed, with this Eurocentric theorisation, this theoretic colonisation, which escaped Nkrumah's attention? In Serequeberhan's reading, Nkrumah lacked recognition of, and engagement with, the fact that Marxism—like all Western leftist discourse on emancipation—is an outgrowth of *European* Enlightenment. In Serequeberhan's view, the Enlightenment was interwoven with the same Eurocentrism that served as support for the destruction of the lives of the colonised. Marxism, for instance, incorporates sees colonialism as a historical necessity of socio-economic reality.[29] Marxism may well be a philosophy or science of liberation, but it nevertheless transmits received ideas of the centrality of Europe to world history. The deconstructive task of African philosophy is aimed at exactly this kind of thinking.

Furthermore, this presumed universalism of scientific socialism, espoused by Nkrumah, goes hand-in-hand with a rejection of "all cultural-historical distinctiveness" (41), notably by critiquing Senghor. But, in so doing, Serequeberhan claims, Nkrumah misses the distinctiveness—in particular the European orientation—of the very scientific socialism he advocates, and in the same move, universalises *this* particularity (41). In other words, Nkrumah's essential error is to underestimate the situatedness of *all* thought.

Looking back at Serequeberhan's critique of Nkrumah, three questions come to mind.

First, without denying the universalist claims in Nkrumah, one has to ask if Serequeberhan is not exaggerating this point. One can quite easily read in Nkrumah's essay, "African Socialism Revisited", how he advocated a reinterpretation of socialism in the light of a traditional African communal ethic, so as to be worthy of the name "African Socialism". Such a socialism would be a response to the particular socio-economic problems of post-independence Ghana, where imported solutions would always be subject to acculturation. This is not the place to start a full discussion of Nkrumah's complex and evolving view of socialism. Suffice to say that further study would have to engage with the correctness of Serequeberhan's rendering of Nkrumah's position.

Second, one may well wonder if there is not a bit of under-interpretation lurking in Serequeberhan's conclusion about Nkrumah's theoretic colonialism. Indeed, one may agree with all of Serequeberhan's critique of Nkrumah, but still deny that it amounts to a form of colonialism. For, is the agent of this thinking not Nkrumah himself? On which basis could Serequeberhan deny it? It seems that the best way for Serequeberhan to qualify his critique of Nkrumah would be rather to say that something is still wrong with Nkrumah's exercise of his own agency, his historicalness is warped, or that he internalised colonial modes of thinking.

Third, one has to ponder where the difference lies between Nkrumah's use of Marxism and Serequeberhan's of Heidegger. Could one not say that Serequeberhan simply took over a pre-established framework from Heidegger? There is certainly in this book insufficient attention to this problem. However, Serequeberhan is not without a solid response. Nkrumah's socialism takes European history and theorising as normative (at least according to Serequeberhan); Serequeberhan does not take Heidegger's thought as normative. He acknowledges the validity of parts of Heidegger's philosophy, but only in as far as Serequeberhan can consent to it, or find other authors who could corroborate significant points. And besides, this generality makes ample space for the socio-cultural, historical, and political singularity of Africans (see discussion, § 3 above). Perhaps the difference between Nkrumah and Serequeberhan is that the latter is better at identifying valid generalities than the former. Besides, both of them agree that general truths are to be grasped only from a specific situation. Serequeberhan would probably argue that Nkrumah is elevating a European singularity to universal status, whereas Serequeberhan would attribute nothing more to Heidegger than that the latter pin-pointed something to which all people have access, even if this instance of German philosophy is not universal but a contingent formulation.

5.2. Senghor: pathology of introverted or internalised Euro-normativity

Serequeberhan's critique of Nkrumah's (and Hountondji's) reading of Senghor does not lead Serequeberhan to accept Senghor's stance. To the contrary, Serequeberhan rejects Senghor's particularism with the same vigour as he rejected Nkrumah's universalism. Let us look at how he assesses Senghor.

Senghor considered humanity to consist of a number of different, complementary races and civilisations (see 43). For him, this basic fact needs to be translated into the political quest to gain consciousness of one's specificity, more specifically, to revive the African values for a world in which African states gradually gain independence. This return to distinctly African values is, as Senghor famously stated, not motivated by the desire to live in a kind of cultural museum, but by the desire to link again with those values that essentially constitute Africans as Africans, which amounts to restoring the very humanity of Africans (44). These values are conceived in a very wide sense. They include a special bond with nature and perceptual immediacy, the latter finding expression in an aesthetics dominated by rhythm and touch (before vision) (44, 46). The defining values of African humanity also entail a specific form of African rationality that, according to Senghor, is synthetic, sympathetic, intuitive, participatory, and mystic (rather than analytical, utilitarian, instrumental, and antagonistic, as European reason supposedly is) (44–45). Most decisively, these traits are not socio-historical constructions; they are rather the timeless, perspective-independent truths about Africans (and Europeans).

It comes as no surprise that Serequeberhan is troubled by this assertion of objectivity. Where would the transhistorical vantage point be from which to make such assertions? Granting the sting of this question, it still seems unfair towards Senghor to claim that his position does not even allow for such a question to be registered. After all, whatever one's assessment may be of the way he thought, one has to acknowledge that he was aware of cultural relativity and the historical circumstances that affect the supposed eternal nature of civilisations. But perhaps not aware enough, for Serequeberhan sees Senghor's discourse as something akin to the crudest Eurocentric cultural theories. The similarities between Senghor's positive image of African civilisation and Lévy-Bruhl's view of primitive mentality are too close for comfort. In fact, Serequeberhan argues that the correspondence is not incidental—it is the same image of the African other, internalised and now valued positively. Or, in Serequeberhan's words, it is "nothing more than the ontologizing of Eurocentric ideas projected and presented as the African's own self-conception" (47). Senghor's stance is therefore an "internalized and ontologized racism" (46). It constructs an African "essence" (47). Its sharp distinctions lead to exaggerated polarisation (48, following Said). And the net effect is a "Eurocentric isomorphism" (49), taking European existence as the norm[30] as much as Nkrumah did, but inverted.

5.3. On the unintentional servants of European Enlightenment

Let us conclude. Nkrumah and Senghor worked in two diametrically opposed ways on the "prior question" of African freedom. The way in which they respectively worked reflects the debate in African philosophy between professional philosophy and ethnophilosophy. For this reason, the political significance of these divergent philosophical stances can clearly be traced in their work. As divergent as their philosophical assumptions and procedures may be, they do converge: "what both of these seemingly contrary positions lack is an awareness of their lived historicity and the requisite historicizing of their thought which goes with such an awareness" (53). Instead, both stances consist of an undue taking-over of a thought pattern or categorisation that originated in *European modernity or Enlightenment*, and in which the humanity and historical experience of Africans are relegated to an unredeemable position of inferiority. Nkrumah does so because he celebrates European standards; Senghor, because he celebrates the figure of the othered African.

That Nkrumah and Senghor, and those who stand close to them intellectually, would dispute this conclusion, is not to be doubted. A full assessment of Serequeberhan's critique falls outside of this study. But what is certain is that this conclusion plays a major role in his subsequent argument. Serequeberhan's argument is informed by the conviction that not only is colonisation a product of European modernity (and that modern European philosophy should be deconstructed because it collaborated in the colonial project), but that African modernity came only through colonisation (stated explicitly in 55). This latter point is not necessarily correct.[31] As much as this conviction has to recommend it, one will notice elsewhere in the book how difficult it is to keep to it consistently. One may, for instance, rightfully wonder how it is that Serequeberhan links up explicitly and approvingly with the Enlightenment philosophical tradition of contractarianism when he considers the role of violence in politics (75–76). That he presents Fanon on the same pages as a creative inheritor of that tradition does not remove the bite of this question. Would one not rather expect Serequeberhan to extend his deconstruction to Fanon too? This question becomes all the more important if one notices how the idea of counter-violence as a therapeutic phenomenon makes its way via Fanon into Serequeberhan's conceptual framework. This partnership with aspects of Enlightenment thought required careful presentation and justification.

6. A new start: from horizon to hermeneutic discourse

After this detour through two exemplary versions of disoriented or pathological forms of African philosophy, we are now ready to press ahead to discover what African philosophy as hermeneutics must look like. I present Serequeberhan's view by focusing on the horizon within which African philosophising starts. First, the horizon of lived actuality is explained as philosophers' socio-political reality from which their vocation derives. I argue, second, for developing the notion of lived actuality and for ways to expand this horizon. Third, I consider tradition as dimension of the horizon and, fourth, the discrepancy between actuality and ideality.

6.1. *Horizon and vocation*

African philosophy is from the outset situated in its socio-political horizon and strives to reconnect with the core of human existence. For Serequeberhan, society, politics, and existence are the philosopher's "lived actuality" or "situated historicity" (7). This situated historicity is not just a factual given, but implies an ideal that "[opens] up the originative historic ground on which, in Africa, the social and political [...] can be established in freedom, that is, within the context of contemporary African historical existence" (35). Working in view of this ideal is the vocation of philosophy.

This "historicalness of the African situation" (35) is given as lived reality to Africans, but philosophical work still needs to explore it very deliberately. And this should start by "stock-taking" (13) of the post-independence period. This "inventory"[32] (23, 115, 154n91) will help to identify the "essential problems" of African existence and therefore of African philosophy. Most of these problems have to do with the subordinate status of Africa as result of colonisation and how neo-colonialism maintains this status of inferiority. These are the problems of what Serequeberhan calls the "concrete totality: post-colonial Africa" (14).[33] Correspondingly, African philosophy must articulate this "concrete totality" through critical self-reflection. In short, if African philosophy springs from a horizon in which it is situated[34] (30), this horizon, or situated historicity, is the concrete totality of post-colonial Africa.

6.2. *According mediations their due: expanding and transcending the lived horizon*

I somewhat belabour this point, because here Serequeberhan introduces a shift in his most basic hermeneutic stance, without ever dealing with this shift. This passage has enormous implications for (a) what one can understand African philosophy to be; (b) the hermeneutics from which philosophy springs; and (c) what Africa and Africans can be.

(a) Serequeberhan repeatedly qualifies the particularity of African philosophy, as distinct from philosophy in general, by referring to the specifics of the "cultural, historical, and political" situation (7). This is perfectly in order, but at the same time he extends that particularity of context to the considerable width of the *entire continent*. It turns out that the horizon of African philosophy is *not that of the individual author* who writes from his/her particular horizon or "lived actuality". Correspondingly what qualifies African philosophy as African is not the place where the philosophy was written or the origin of its author, but general traits of the horizon and lived actuality of the African continent considered as a concrete totality. This totality is decisive in Serequeberhan's understanding of *what African philosophy* is.

(b) The philosopher's particular situatedness is a *generality*, namely the concrete totality of the entire "cultural, historical, and political" reality of post-independence Africa. If one concedes, as one should, the significant similarities between different African countries or societies, this does not yet compel one to equate the particular individual author's "lived actuality" with the general "concrete totality: post-colonial Africa". Let me emphasise that I do not find any problem with philosophising from such a totality or with such general issues in mind. However, orienting one's thought to such general issues is not the same as having such general phenomena present in one's individually "lived actuality". Those mechanisms (news and knowledge of politics and society) that allow me as individual philosopher to transcend the immediate, particular detail of my lived actuality, do have a "generalizing" effect on my lived actuality. Lived actuality includes such elements of my world and I can be said to be *situated among them only by mediation*. I do not think that Serequeberhan would object to this elaboration of his thought.[35] However, we need to consider the implications of accepting the augmenting role of mediation for one's situatedness. First, one does not need to be on the African continent to be deeply concerned about that continent since an understanding of its problems can be mediated to us wherever we are—proof of this is Serequeberhan writing on Africa while based in the United States.[36] I find no reason to ironise this fact, provided that one acknowledges the significance of mediation of information for the phenomenon of lived situatedness. Second, once one accepts this expanded view of situatedness, one would have to accept that any person, anywhere in the world, who is significantly struck by this "stock taking" of independent Africa, can have their lived actuality augmented by concern with the "essential problems" of Africa. When such a person philosophises, he/she then forms part of the concrete totality of post-colonial Africa. Such a person can thus contribute to African philosophy, provided that the form of philosophising does not commit any of the disorienting errors that Serequeberhan attributes to ethnophilosophy or the professional philosophers (see § 5, above). Very concretely, this implies that a European philosopher, doing philosophy in a European style, may be an African philosopher, provided he/she is not Eurocentric. And this conclusion seems to be corroborated by Serequeberhan himself when he approvingly uses European authors to support his African philosophical argument (presumably, while working from the USA). And one may ask again if he is not being overly derogatory in characterising the useful sources of Western philosophy as an antidote to the poison of the wider tradition of Western philosophy.

(c) However, quite contrary to the implications I draw in the two previous points, Serequeberhan claims in a curious passage in the endnotes:

> By the term "African peoples" I mean to refer to the inhabitants of the continent as a whole minus the Whites of South Africa. I use the term collectively, moreover, not in order to level off the variety and multiplicity that constitutes the inhabitants of the continent, nor to establish some "true" African "Essence" *à la* Senghor, but rather to highlight the common experience of European colonialism and neocolonialism that, since the last quarter of the nineteenth century, has imposed on the inhabitants of the continent a shared destiny or a sense of historical place in the antagonistic context of a European dominated world. I exclude the Whites of South Africa precisely because they see themselves as distinct and apart—Apartheid—from the rest of the continent in this specific particular. (136n5)

Serequeberhan is right: he does not establish an African essence *à la* Senghor—but he does establish an African essence *à la* Serequeberhan. It is an essence based on a shared fate, or on what he calls "essential problems". The flipside of all essentialism is *categorical* exclusion. Not only can no white South African have any legitimate African concern (generated from within their midst), but neither can any of them register the legitimate concerns identified by Serequeberhan, nor can they make any philosophical or other contribution to those concerns. Surely the facts fly in the face of such crude generalising othering (one notices that such categorical exclusion is not even extended to the Westernised African elite about whom Serequeberhan is very critical). One can accept Serequeberhan's qualms about white South Africans. After all, the cultural politics that gave rise to the apartheid state contains exactly the kind of Eurocentric and essentialist assumptions Serequeberhan rightly rejects in his critique of ethnophilosophy and professional philosophy. Even so, one has to accommodate the exceptions and degrees of "guilt" even when speaking about the apartheid era (the dismantling of which, Serequeberhan seems not to have noticed at the time). And this holds so much more in the post-1994 era in South Africa.

But my point here is not about white South Africans; the point is about Serequeberhan's essentialism (implicit in his understanding of the African "concrete totality") of which subordinating an other has to be a consequence. Be that as it may, vilifying and essentialising othering is only one pole of Serequeberhan's discourse. The other pole is a beatifying, redemptive othering. Despite the dedication of the book, he devotes only a footnote to the fact that the author's home country, Eritrea, had come out of decades of annexation by Ethiopia[37] shortly before *Hermeneutics of African Philosophy* was published (see especially 136n3). One notices the failing of essentialism when one sees that the phenomenon of internal African aggression cannot be accommodated in a master narrative of African suffering at the hands of external aggressors.[38]

To my judgement, it would be incorrect to conclude that this double critique of essentialism in Serequeberhan amounts to a refutation of his hermeneutics. There are enough resources in his work (as in points a and b above) to be mobilised against these two points of criticism. Rather, attention to these defects helps us to get a picture of the risks involved in hermeneutics. These risks are not "design errors" of the hermeneutics; they are possibilities of the human interpretative condition.

Let us resume our investigation of the horizon from which hermeneutic discourse emerges by considering the connection between tradition on the one hand, and, on the other hand, the discrepancy between the actuality and ideality of liberation.

6.3. Tradition

The horizon of lived actuality "becomes what it is by projecting itself out of its effective past, its lived inheritance" (25). In other words, the affiliation between a philosopher and tradition does not emerge spontaneously. In fact, Serequeberhan argues that between philosopher and tradition there may well exist a relation of tension or mutual questioning (26, 30). Although Serequeberhan does not ignore the fact of cultural traditions, his thought on tradition explicitly does *not* entail some return to an original, undiluted African culture (see 38). Rather, one has the impression that already here, Serequeberhan anticipates the specific tradition that he emphasises in chapter 4 of *Hermeneutics of African Philosophy*, namely the tradition of liberation.

If tradition affords people a first perspective on the problems of the present, the mutually critical relationship between philosophers and the traditions in which they find themselves creates uncertainty, which can be engaged with only at the expense of a certain *risk* (26). What this risk consists of precisely Serequeberhan does not develop further, but elsewhere he gives at least a hint when he explains: "Properly speaking, philosophy has the peculiar characteristic of always being implicated in its own conceptions and formulations. […] It forgets this at its own peril, at the risk of being snared by its own mesh" (2). Seen from this perspective, the risk resides in the ambiguous relation philosophers necessarily have to take up with respect to their tradition. Questioning one's tradition(s) is risky because it may well undermine one's very access to the world. At the same time, not critically engaging with one's tradition(s) means running the risk of perpetuating the estrangements and misunderstandings that the tradition(s) may carry with them. Again, this holds for all philosophers, independent of the traditions they are working from.

Note, by the way, that Serequeberhan does little to examine the possibility of Africans belonging to plural traditions, except perhaps when he discusses the disjunction between the culture of rural people and that of the Westernised elite. This omission narrows his strategic options. Following Cabral, Serequeberhan considers the acceptance of (aspects of) Western science as a regrettable inevitability.

6.4. Actuality and ideality: normativity and liberation

The exercise of introspection and stock-taking, from which African Philosophy has to start, soon reveals a nasty discrepancy between the reality of the post-independence world and the promise that the liberation struggle projected for it. This tension has to be described correctly. It does not consist of a gap between two well defined entities—it is rather a confusion, obscurity, or opacity (16), which calls out for proper definition. Serequeberhan calls the lack of such articulation "misunderstanding", a word he uses in a very specific sense. It is the experience of disturbance or "estrangement of meaning" (16, similarly, 22), also often called "diremption" in *Hermeneutics of African Philosophy*. For Serequeberhan, writing in the wake of Gadamer, this estrangement of meaning is exactly the springboard of hermeneutics: "for us contemporary Africans, that which impels us to thought is precisely the estranged actuality of our present deriving from the colonial experience, the specific particularity of our history" (26).

This horizon includes the actuality of the pre-colonial past as much as the colonial and neo-colonial catastrophes. But it does not stop there—the retrospective and introspective hermeneutics is driven by the prospect of liberation (cf. 19). The stakes of contemporary African philosophy ride on the "misunderstanding" or estrangement due to the neo-colonial condition (26). The lived actuality of continued domination calls for an understanding of that domination and the sources that have to be tapped to find a way out.

But Serequeberhan takes a step further, by attributing to this task a *normative* standard. Finding a way out of the imposed "misunderstanding" and domination is not only the task that *must* inspire African philosophy, it is also the *standard* against which all philosophical and political efforts have to be measured:[39] in as far as philosophy contributes to liberation, it is good. This normative directedness, Serequeberhan calls, with Okolo, "destiny" (27). This destiny is "autonomy and freedom in full recognition of the differing cultural-historical totalities that constitute our world" (28). What is implicated here is the interrelatedness of thought, philosophy, and emancipatory practice:

> In this theoretic scenario, emancipatory *praxis* opens and offers the timely issues and concerns in which a hermeneutical perspective incarnates its interrogative and interpretative explorations. Conversely, and as a rejoinder to the dialectical tensions interior to this relation, hermeneutical reflection opens to *praxis* the proper theoretic space to explore and suggest the normative alignment of its emancipatory projects and practical undertakings. (27)[40]

This is a decisive point. At stake is the very status of Serequeberhan's own work: doing philosophy—provided it is properly done—is an integral part of emancipatory practice. This is how high Serequeberhan sets the bar, for himself, and for philosophy in general. Throughout *Hermeneutics of African Philosophy*, Serequeberhan places human historicalness, understood in the hermeneutic way he exposes, as the measure for correct philosophy. Now we can name the reason for this: because this historicalness is the ultimate source of both hermeneutics and practice and the source of the normative standard against which to measure hermeneutics and practice.

At this point the devil's advocate may enquire about the difference between Serequeberhan's vision of philosophy and the traditions of emancipatory philosophy emanating from Europe. This question is incisive, especially if we think about the philosophy of the European Enlightenment, for we have seen how closely Serequeberhan ties that tradition to colonial violence and how important the deconstruction of those discourses are for him (see § 5.3, above). Some clarification is in order. Serequeberhan courageously gives the devil his due, but limits this concession:

> The heritage of the Enlightenment is for us a borrowed inheritance. We share in it only insofar as we are colonized and neocolonized members of *its* modern European-dominated world and have been drastically affected—incorporated by conquest—into its development and globalization. Sharing in this legacy in this way, our aim is to *destroy* and *go beyond* this European-dominated disclosure of the present. (35–36, I emphasize "destroy" and "go beyond")

This seems to mean that African philosophy as an emancipatory discourse will not do or be the *same* as its European counterparts, but will do or be something *similar*. On examining Serequeberhan's position more closely, one becomes aware of a tension in his view.

On the one hand, he insists on the disconnection between the two families of philosophy—African and European—and reserves harsh criticism for the European side, as is evidenced by the word "destroy" in the citation above. African philosophy "is focused on the theoretic consummation of this demise", that is, the demise of "European colonial dominance and is aimed at the destructuring of the persistence of neocolonial hegemony in contemporary African existence" (29).

On the other hand, Serequeberhan accentuates the task of African philosophy as one of uncovering that which European modernity covers up (see 36). And, for him, this means "simultaneously [to] *transgress* and *appropriate*" (36, my emphasis)[41] the ways in which European modernity discloses the world for Africans.[42] Surely "appropriation", even when paired with "transgression", means something different, and more positive, from "destruction".

Whichever side one thinks renders best Serequeberhan's view on the appropriate way to relate to the *European* heritage—destruction or appropriation—both express the twofold, deconstructive and constructive, task of *African* philosophy (see § 4.2 above). They also head in the same direction: liberation. Here, liberation is not understood as a part of European history, but construed from Africa's own traditions of liberation. Again, "the aim is not to return to some 'true', 'uncontaminated', 'original', African *arche*—as if this were possible or even desirable—but to make possible the autonomous and thus authentic self-standing historicity of African existence in the context of the modern world" (38, similarly, 126n16).[43] The reconnection with tradition is a reconnection with the "autochthonous tradition and history of politico-economic struggles interior to itself [i.e. Africa]" (37). This is what is called "returning to the source" (see 126–127n16), a "world-disclosing" (10) event, by which Africans reclaim their histories (see 36).

In short, if the discrepancy between actuality and ideality[44] is the question, returning to the source is the answer. But this return has a double meaning: philosophical and political. And according to Serequeberhan's fundamental conviction, these two meanings are close allies. Hence the task of African philosophy as hermeneutics is to work out new concepts by which to support and imagine a new historicity (the expression "working out new concepts" is drawn from Fanon's *The Wretched of the Earth*). African philosophical hermeneutics strives to support emancipation, in as far as discourse can help achieve it. Or, in the terms used elsewhere in *Hermeneutics of African Philosophy*, hermeneutics aims to clarify the "prior question" of political praxis, a clarification without which praxis may well be misdirected.

So, Africans just have to return to the source? Yes, but this is more easily said than done! What Serequeberhan aims to achieve is not only to argue for the revitalising return to the source, but to explicate the socio-political embodiment of such a return. The dramatic intensity of this return is captured with the terminological pair: violence and counter-violence.

7. From horizon to action

Launching philosophy from the platform of "historicalness", as Serequeberhan does, consists of an exposition on violence and emancipation. Through this double exposition, the interplay between horizon and discourse will now become clear. For this task, Serequeberhan draws from Aimé Césaire and particularly Fanon to explore the initiating event and logic of the European–African encounter, because both clarify *discourses* on the originative event of the *horizon*—the "concrete totality"—in which African philosophers must work. As with Cabral, Serequeberhan attempts to trace a way back to the alternative to the present horizon: assumed, free agency or historicalness, of which he strives to build out the discourse in *Hermeneutics of African Philosophy*. One may be surprised by Serequeberhan's masters of hermeneutics: Fanon and Cabral. But they are the ones who testify to the historicity of philosophical thought in a way that is intimately interwoven with the political aspirations of African people.

Two statements on violence from the opening paragraphs of chapter 3 of *Hermeneutics of African Philosophy* are fundamental to our understanding of the dynamics of violence in Serequeberhan's thought. First, Serequeberhan claims that modernity in Africa is the result of colonial violence. Second, he claims that this inception of modernity, as a violent encounter between Africa and Europe, is defining for the current African "horizon". The first claim is significant because it points back to the question of philosophy—this is the violence perpetuated by Enlightenment thought,[45] put in practice, and perpetuated inadvertently by the likes of Nkrumah and Senghor. The second claim is significant because it portrays the advent of modernity through colonisation as a historical discontinuity.[46] Together, these claims refer to the moment of emergence of the current African horizon. This event, the advent of modernity, comes from the outside, at the sole initiative of outsiders. It is an imposition.[47]

We now need to zoom in on that founding and defining moment, that break in history that is the source of the current "misunderstanding". Serequeberhan does this with a wager: nobody can guide us better to explore this moment than Fanon. Or more precisely, given the assumptions about the violent, initiating, modernising encounter, Fanon's description of the initial colonial and anti-colonial violence (specifically in chapter 1 of *The Wretched of the Earth*), can be used as companion.[48] But before we get to that point, we have to get an idea of whence this violence originates. To do so, Césaire's *Discourse on Colonialism* and *Letter to Maurice Thorez* serve as guides. Together, Césaire and Fanon set the stage for a tragedy in three acts: first, European violence and its consequence for Africans; second, counter-violence in a Manichean world; and third, the quest for life beyond (neo)colonial violence through a fusion of horizons. This is the structure of *Hermeneutics of African Philosophy*, chapters 3 and 4.

7.1. Original violence with Césaire

Act one opens with Césaire's insight (from *Discourse on Colonialism*) that the relation to the African other constitutes European modernity. This relation, he argues, was hypocritical from the outset, in that colonisation lacked all justification by reason or conscience, even on Europeans' terms (see 57). This irrationality spilled over into violent action. The detail of this claim comprises such facts as military conquest, imposition of lifeforms, negation of cultures, interference in traditions, and exploitation under the guise of an altruistic civilising mission. In this story, philosophers played their role by neglecting the violence suffered for the sake of the expansion of European civilisation (see 61)—be it through the constructions of progressive philosophies of history (Marx, Hegel) or simply the propagation of racist ideas (Hume, Kant).[49] The point that Serequeberhan develops from Césaire is that "the image of the 'primitive' is interior and necessary, to Europe's own gratuitous self-conception. This same 'image' is, however, also used to justify the violent destruction of the specific humanity of aboriginal peoples which it supposedly describes" (62). This is then the first conclusion: the relation of violence between the colonisers and the colonised starts with a unilateral (but complex) initiative from Europe.

This unilateral violence evoked by Césaire had devastating consequences, of which authors like Chinua Achebe and Cheikh Hamidou Kane gave literary recordings: cultural devaluation, existential estrangement, enslavement, colonial administration, imposition of foreign cultures, and subjugation (see 63–67). In Serequeberhan's understanding, the validity of this conclusion stretches far beyond the historical events of colonisation; in fact, it marks the present decisively (that is, at least up to the publication of *Hermeneutics of African Philosophy* in 1994). In Serequeberhan's words, "[t]he un-freedom in which Africa is presently entangled is thus directly rooted in European dominance. This is what Césaire refers to as the 'peculiarity of our history, laced with terrible misfortunes which belong to no other history'" (63). The four decades and course of independence that separate Césaire's *Letter to Maurice Thorez* from the publication of *Hermeneutics of African Philosophy* did nothing to disrupt this basic continuity.[50]

But this conclusion contains a *non sequitur*: Serequeberhan's presentation is about the ideas that justified and maintained colonisation. He has not said a word about the situation after independence. Perhaps his claim about the continuity between colonialism and the situation in the former colonies after independence is valid, but this has to be *argued* first, especially if his discussion continues with a focus on the present. Perhaps Serequeberhan's point is to describe the past as a way to understand the "lived historicity" of the present. However, even then, suggesting that the history of liberation and independence has zero significance for the "lived historicity" of Africans today is not plausible. Thus far, all pre-colonial violence, all violence of independence and post-independence, are excluded categorically from this "stock-taking" of the post-colonial condition. One may perhaps wonder if such exclusions can lead to a viable hermeneutics. Nevertheless, this remark takes nothing away from the unspeakable suffering imposed on Africans.

Let us return to the advent of colonial violence. Irrational, unjustified violence is the origin of the problem; the consequence is lack of ability in Africans to take initiative. What is required then, is: "to *negate the negation* of [the colonised's] lived historicalness and overcome the violence of merely being an object in the historicity of European existence" (57). According to Serequeberhan, "negat[ing] the negation" implies the "primordial violence and [reactive] counter-violence" (57, 73) that describes the master *plot of the colonial and anti-colonial drama*. The colonised, dehumanised, deprived of (authentic) historicity, nevertheless has something left—a residual energy by which to hit back violently. At this point Fanon takes the relay from Césaire as Serequeberhan's ally. Fanon helps to explicate the master plot of violence and counter-violence. The question here is not a description of any particular case, but a typological unfolding, typical of the concrete African totality.

But before we get there, let it be noted that Serequeberhan prepared the ground for a Fanonian vision of the colonial (and even neo-colonial) order as a Manichean order. Serequeberhan's strategy and objective in this respect can be traced from three interesting omissions in his writing.

First, in the catalogue of colonial impositions, Serequeberhan says nothing about written literature that emerged from the imposed educational and cultural systems.[51] In a kind of performative contradiction, Serequeberhan cites Kane and Achebe to sketch the portrait of gruesome violence, but without asking how the insightful literature of Kane and Achebe could emerge from it. My point is *most certainly not* that the rise of the modern African novel should, in I don't know what way, salvage the harm done by colonisation (this argumentative monstrosity has been defeated by Césaire at the latest), but rather that hermeneutic sophistication requires "stock-taking" to be encompassing. An encompassing inventory of the heritage of colonialism would have to include a survey of literature that emerged in its midst, in particular of protest literature. But protest literature doesn't fit Serequeberhan's schema of physical violence and counter-violence. That is, unless this omission is part of his own contribution to counter-violence.

Second, likewise, in his reading of Kane's novel *L'Aventure ambiguë*, whose protagonist Samba Diallo is Muslim, but Serequeberhan does not say anything more about the history of Islam in Africa. He rather implicitly equates Islam with the "enduring traditions of Africa" (65). In general, the role of religion (but for my point Islam is particularly interesting) is not given its due attention in this book.[52] The silence about the checkered history of Islam in Africa facilitates a Manichean interpretation of initial violence.

Third, Serequeberhan says nothing of the alienation, anomie, and exploitation that arose as pathologies from modernity also on the European continent. All Serequeberhan has to say in this respect is that "Europe experienced the dawn of modernity as the age of Enlightenment"

(66). It is only at the expense of a crude distortion of history that one could place the victims of European modernity all on one continent, and the beneficiaries on another.

7.2. "[Counter-]Violence is no choice" (but a matter of necessity)

Act two. As we turn to this choice between two forms of violence, we have to be clear that we are still dealing with the emergence of the "essential problems" of Africa, lest we succumb to the anachronistic use of Fanon, according to which there is no difference between the colonial state and the post-independence (neo-colonised) state. Yet, Serequeberhan seems to have fewer scruples: commenting on a passage from *The Wretched of the Earth*, he writes: "Fanon is describing the colonial situation as it existed *and still exists* in Africa" (67, my emphasis).[53] Whatever social changes occurred since independence, for Serequeberhan they alter nothing about the Manichaeism pattern of colonialism. In this pattern, colonialism produces and reproduces exemplars of two basic categories of role-player colonisers and colonised. Each of them plays out the fixed script of exploitative expansion and reified subjection—each supposes the other and makes the role of the other possible (69). Each time with a different accent, the same dichotomy is reproduced: being and non-being, shaper of history and subject of history, master and servant (73–74). Apart from mutually implying each other, there is no mediation between them, except through violence. Although Serequeberhan emphasises violence as "brute force" (68), he is careful to mention dimensions of colonial violence that are not just physical: violence through economic, legal, symbolic means (68). Under such conditions of oppression, the colonised envies the power, the violence, even the historicity of the coloniser (see 69).[54] In this simple dichotomous setup, the "neo-colonial elite"[55] is a proxy of the colonial powers, working for the "development" of the African territory, which in reality amounts to the imposition of the Western machinery of exploitation (67, 70). Hence, again, the post-independence order is a neo-colonial order, because it maintains a basic continuity with the preceding colonial order.

This dichotomy mediated by violence leads to an outburst of conflict, which Fanon captures succinctly: "The immobility to which the native is condemned can only be called in question if the native decides to put an end to the *history of colonization*—the history of the pillage—and to bring into existence the *history of the nation*—the history of decolonization" (71, cited from *The Wretched of the Earth*). This is the clash between "settlers" who see themselves as agents of history (and one may suppose their proxies in neo-colonialism), and the "natives" who will soon discover the liberating, "therapeutic", and "life-enhancing" effects of the exercise of violence, particularly for their (self-)consciousness (71, 79). Violence is not only the "midwife" of social change (as Marx claimed); it is "the avenue through which humanity is reclaimed", if not created (74, 79). Formulated in Serequeberhan's hermeneutic parlance it is "only in the struggle to contest its subjugation [that] the colonized concretely reactivates its Being as human" (72).

Serequeberhan diverges from Fanon regarding the *agent of counter-violence*. Fanon, one may recall, used a more mechanical metaphor: the body of the "colonized thing" overcharges with energy, which is then suddenly released. This difference is not trivial: in Fanon's image the question of agency is of no importance, in the sense of someone "making history",[56] whereas in the last citation Serequeberhan places agency at the core of his argument. Fanon's image bypasses agency here to present counter-violence as an outburst of energy; in Serequeberhan's argument subjugation is challenged through an initiative of reactivating "being human". But how is such an initiative possible if the colonised had no (significant) agency? Where would the initiative for counter-violence come from? This question persists when Serequeberhan cites Albert Memmi's claim about the colonised having *forgotten how to participate* in the game of history. And similarly when Serequeberhan explains: "So far as he is colonized and remains so, he is nothing more than a *thingified* biological organism with specific life functions" (72). What lacks in Serequeberhan, then, is reflection on the transition from lack of agency to agency. "His master's zombie" (72) who is stuck in a "stunned existence" (79) cannot assert himself/herself through confrontation without thereby revealing that he/she never was a zombie (see 72). In other words, the "self-reflective process" (74) of counter-violence has to come from somewhere, which cannot be a state of zombie-hood of a "beast of burden" (74). The only passage that could suggest a possible response from Serequeberhan to this dilemma, is the following:

> In this regard, as Patrick Taylor points out, it should be noted that, "[u]nderneath the roles into which they are forced, the colonized preserve a human identity and temporal being". This is so however only to the extent that the silent resignation of the colonized is itself a form of passive resistance to

colonial thingification. [...] Hidden under "the roles" forced on the colonized, one finds the smoldering tension of a subjugated and humiliated existence that needs to explode into open resistance if it is not to implode into an interior world of torpid and mystical self-mortification. (75)

"Thingification", then, is a hyperbole, a form of resistance that manifests on the surface as resignation, zombie-hood, stunned-ness, but under the surface smoulders and waits for the appropriate opportunity to ignite. It is not clear to me if this suffices to solve the question of agency in the colonised. And, certainly, these dramatic terms of lack or concealment of agency do not apply to the colonised urban labourers and elite (I return to this issue in § 7.3).

But even if we leave undecided the question of how much agency the colonised has, it is clear that the scope of possible counters to colonial violence is limited: colonial violence, according to Serequeberhan, cannot be opposed by non-violence, but only by anti-colonial counter-violence (see 74). As Serequeberhan peremptorily declares, for the colonised "[counter-]violence is no choice" (78). Now, perplexingly, Serequeberhan provides us with very little insight into what he understands by counter-violence.[57] As far as our focus remains on anti-colonial resistance, the dimension of armed struggle obviously jumps to mind. However, if we consider the fact that he wanted us to think here not only of the struggles *for independence*, but the longer and broader struggles *against all neo-colonialism*, the significance of this question becomes evident. What does it mean in contemporary African countries to oppose neo-colonial violence by violent means? Surely one should hesitate to respond that it is the same kind of outburst of physical force, attributed by Fanon to the first moments of anti-colonial resistance? Admittedly, Serequeberhan suggests at least two forms of symbolic or written resistance. First, in as far as Serequeberhan's African philosophy has a deconstructive task, it undermines Eurocentric thought.[58] Second, he would probably have consented to the idea that works of literature (like those of Achebe and Kane), which defied or defies the established order, is also part of the story of opposition. Serequeberhan does not explore this point. Besides, it is not evident if the word "violence" is appropriate in either case.

But Serequeberhan's focus is so much on a vaguely construed idea of violence that he attributes it even to Arendt. He cites a passage where Arendt actually proposes an alternative to violence (77[59]). For Arendt, liberation starts not in the act of counter-violence, but in an "off-beat" just preceding this act, namely the moments of consultation between resistance fighters as they plan counter-violence.[60] Serequeberhan, on the other hand, probably has in mind very physical forms of violence. He invokes a "bloodbath" (78), "risking of life", and "prolonged war" (79).[61] And one always has to remember that for Serequeberhan neo-colonial violence is a continuation of colonial violence, which means that when he speaks of counter-violence he has contemporary African societies in mind. But how does he think that violence (even "blood baths") can counter the exploitative networks of the globalised economy? Surely if there is a way, this should be elaborated and rendered plausible.

7.3. Fusion of horizons and practices of freedom: with Fanon and Cabral

Act three starts against the backdrop of neo-colonialism. Serequeberhan outlines the possibility of a "beyond", of truly liberated African societies, on two levels. On the macro-level of social analysis, he confronts us with his idea of socio-hermeneutic *fusion of horizons* between sectors of society; on the micro-level of individual behaviour, he will introduce the idea of *practices of freedom*.

(a) The same tragedy, but a different outcome: fusion of horizons

The most salient trait of neo-colonialism is the way it maintains the social divisions brought about by colonisation in African societies. It is still the same tragic play as colonisation, but now Africans play the roles of both coloniser and colonised (see 84). The actors are, respectively, the Westernised urbanites and the non-Westernised rural inhabitants. Those struggling against colonialism must abolish this Western-induced divide and form a new union. This unification or "fusion" has a markedly hermeneutic character: "demographically and sociologically speaking, African liberation movements are born out of the 'fusion of horizons'[62] of these two broad segments of African society" (84). While maintaining the hermeneutic significance for this term, Serequeberhan insists equally on its sociological import: "for me, 'the fusion of horizons' is a concrete historical and ontic process that occurs in engaging real life issues and problems within the context of a specific historicalness" (148n99). In short, for Serequeberhan the fusion of horizons is thus a sociological and hermeneutic term that captures the process by which the "advent of peoples [...] onto the stage of history" (101)[63] takes place. This "advent" may equally be called "decolonization" or "re-Africanization" (102). Advent "does not mean reinstituting a *dead* but an 'authentic' African past, 'living it as a defence mechanism, as a symbol of purity, of salvation'. It does not refer to a 'culture put into capsules, which has vegetated since the foreign domination" (101).[64] Quite the contrary: "The struggle for freedom does not give back to the national culture its former value and shape; [... it] cannot leave intact either the form or the content of the people's culture. After the conflict there is not only the disappearance of colonialism but also the disappearance of the colonized man" (101).[65] Positively formulated, Serequeberhan insists that his point is about seizing collective agency, which "is not an argument for cultural autarchy" (101).

Initially a product of violent intervention, the split society—divided into rural inhabitants and educated urbanites—also contains the two ingredients needed to prepare the downfall of colonialism. In fact, as harmful as this social split is, the roles that the two social groups play become indispensable in post-independence, neo-colonial states:

> Each manifests, in itself, what the other does not have and is estranged from. The Westernized native is acquainted with the world beyond the colony or neo-colony and the struggles of other peoples. The rural non-Westernized native, on the other hand, is steeped in the broken heritage of his own particular African past. In the fusion of these two fractured "worlds" the possibility of African freedom is concretized or made tangible in the form of specific historical movements. (84)

How does Serequeberhan foresee this fusion happening practically? Let us approach this question from the side of the Westernised urbanites. Serequeberhan's disdain for this segment of the colonial and post-independence African society is evident (16, 92, 149n15–16). Serequeberhan's disdain also emerges from his critique of himself as a member of that section of society. This section of society is portrayed as self-interested, perfectly cut off from the concerns of the other section of society, interested only in mimicking European ideas and values. There may be a reform-minded segment of this sector of society, but from the point of view of continued liberation from neo-colonialism, Serequeberhan considers this as negligible. The urbanites rather set themselves up as spokespersons for the aspirations of others while maintaining the status quo. They form political parties, a phenomenon that Serequeberhan sees as an emulation of the colonisers, who are the ones who make history while the colonised undergo history. Moreover, Serequeberhan views the party-formation of the urbanites to be an outgrowth of colonial violence and counter-violence, rather than a means to end this violence (93).

Despite this analysis, Serequeberhan follows Fanon in foreseeing a break-away of a radical fringe from the urban political parties, a group that will then meet the rural masses as equals (94). And then a fusion is to take place "of necessity"[66] in which "the urban and rural native *encounter* each other, *for the first time*, as possible co-protagonists in a process of political struggle and originative history" and this fusion "is the dynamic locus out of which unfolds the dialectic of African self-emancipation" (94). An intermingling of politics, struggle, and ordinary life ensues (98).[67] And from this fusion, people start projecting possibilities beyond what colonialism imposed (100). Serequeberhan explains "in this *encounter* of the urban and rural native, the standpoint of the present is put in question and what is appropriated is not the inert past but the effective historicity of the fusion of these two elemental and dynamic forces. This is what Gadamer refers to as the 'effective-historical consciousness', concretely grasped within the context of the African situation" (100).

At this point it is worthwhile to stop for a number of critical considerations:

- Up to this point, the transition from the colonial situation to post-independence neo-colonialism has hardly been clarified. Yet, it forms the whole backdrop for the shift from violent confrontation to the fusion of horizons needed to cultivate practices of freedom. All happens as if the continuities between colonialism and neo-colonialism are so significant that all differences are trivial. In the same vein, one notices the absence of qualifications about the *degree* to which a post-independence African state may be subject to neo-colonialism. This is important for Serequeberhan's argument, because as soon as neo-colonialism is not the overriding factor shaping society, one has reason to question if the bipolar or Manichean world of colonialism is reduplicated in the post-independence society. This, in turn, questions the validity both of Serequeberhan's portrayal of the typical social structure of the liberation movement and of the means by which neo-colonialism is to be fought.

- The structure of Serequeberhan's argument requires that we accept that the Westernised urbanites perpetuate part of the colonial order. And yet, for some unexplained reason, the conflict between the "colonisers" (a role now played by Westernised urbanites) and the rural "natives" (in Serequeberhan's terms), does not lead to a schema of violence and counter-violence, despite these being presented as "necessary" for liberation from colonisation in chapter 3 of *Hermeneutics of African Philosophy*. Now, a logic of "fusion of horizons" comes to displace it. This change of socio-historical logic is ever more curious, because with Fanon, Serequeberhan has the life and times of the Westernised urbanites *overlap* with the colonial period and the presence of colonial masters (these elites do not arrive only after independence). This historical fact raises questions about the logic that governs Serequeberhan's exposition: colonial Manicheism engenders violence and counter-violence; *or* it produces the fusion of horizons; or the one *after* the other; but one cannot claim that there is no option but counter-violence and then still maintain that there is a fusion of horizons. One measures the extent of this problem by comparing two significant claims. First, the "two segments of African society parrot the estranged and estranging violent dialectic of the colonizer and the colonized [...] But, in this case, the roles of colonizer and colonized are played by the native" (84). Second, the urban elite play an ambiguous role: they "are the mediating link between colonialism and neocolonialism; [but also] abstractly formulate the concrete possibility of African freedom" (92). With the means at their disposal, urban elites *mediate* between the colonial and neo-colonial orders, although Serequeberhan insists elsewhere that only *violence* can mediate this dichotomy. I cannot see how these two claims can be harmonised. And this is not a minor issue: it is this unexplained leap that makes the transition from a violence/counter-violence model to a fusion-of-horizons model possible. It is curious that Serequeberhan sees such a fusion of horizons in this particular stage of the (neo) colonial order as quite natural, when he does not even entertain the possibility of this taking place elsewhere over the entire spectrum of colonial interactions.
- Now that we have a better view on the tension between the two socio-historical logics, it becomes clearer that Serequeberhan's argument requires a clarification of how a fusion of horizons can

emerge from conditions where "[counter]-violence is no choice". Do such fusions of horizon not presuppose a minimum of agency on both sides? If yes, how did the "thingified" colonised people acquire it or how did it persist despite colonial violence? One is left somewhat surprised by the emergence of pedagogy as a way to overcome racial prejudice (see 85). The discussion wavers between the idea that participation in the struggle brings forth this *horizon-fusing ethos* and that somehow *counter-violence* at a certain stage brings forth a "beyond violence" (see 85).

- These questions and uncertainties point to a change in register in Serequeberhan's argument: from the macro-scale of social analysis, to the micro-scale of interaction or practice. It is clear enough that, in Serequeberhan's mind, there exists a relation of mutual implication between the two kinds of exposition. But one would have appreciated greater clarification of the social and theoretical detail of how this mutual implication is to be understood. Claiming that the practices of freedom sublimates or "sublate[s]" (85) the violence/counter-violence schema is an intriguing suggestion, but does not yet do the job.
- All of the points above relate to Serequeberhan's major historical and anthropological assumption: the historical necessity of violence. One cannot state this relation more categorically than Serequeberhan, who agrees with Cabral that violence "is not our invention—it is not our cool decision;[68] it is the *requirement of history*" (79). One may have understanding for the tragic circumstances implied by this claim. However, from an action theoretical perspective, where there is no alternative, there is no agency (only reflex), only continuation of reified existence, and thus no "self-redeeming counterclaim" (78). This makes it very difficult to imagine how agency could emerge from this situation. To give an example from *Hermeneutics of African Philosophy*, how is it that the peasants and nomads have politics and concerns of which the urban rebels initially understand little, but the latter then find in the former "a receptive, eager, and enlightened audience" (95)?[69] Nothing of this speaks of historical necessity. Once again one has to conclude that Serequeberhan, on this point, succumbs to the unhermeneutic attribution of automatic necessity that he criticises in Nkrumah. One may wonder if the idea of historical necessity is not an uncritical appropriation of a Marxist teleology of history.

After these critical considerations, let us now turn to what, to my mind, contradicts the idea of historical necessity: agency. Serequeberhan approaches agency in the form of "practices of freedom". These practices take shape in the fusion of horizons.

(b) "Return to the source": practices of freedom

Serequeberhan takes the terms *"practices of freedom"* or "practices of liberty" from Michel Foucault.[70] Chapter 4 of *Hermeneutics of African Philosophy* considers the social arrangements necessary to encourage practices of freedom: "How does one establish the practice or *ethos* of freedom in the process of liberating one's existence from external—direct or indirect—domination?" (88). Serequeberhan maintains that resistance itself, the struggle for liberation, shapes these experiences of self-formation from which an ethos and practices of freedom develop. Despite the general patterns of reactive counter-violence Serequeberhan describes in chapter 3, he still affirms that each struggle for independence is a singular process, which brings forth contingent practices of freedom. *Freedom*, then, is a set of gradually developing context-determined practices, not the realisation or recovery of a predetermined catalogue of essential human traits.[71] These practices of freedom essentially continue the liberation struggle, but are now more clearly focused on reclaiming history (90)[72] or, as Serequeberhan says elsewhere, reclaiming historicalness or historicity (29, 38). In short, this reclaiming will be nothing but a "return to the source", the source being that core of human existence that is called lived actuality or historicalness.

This return to the source represents the *"concrete implementation*—the practice—of liberty" (88). On the one hand, the return consists of practices of the self on the self (87, following Foucault); on the other, it is the *"praxis of concrete communal self-creation"* (85). Cabral provides Serequeberhan with an invaluable "practical depiction" of communal self-creation (90), but the argument rests on a phrase from Fanon: "beyond abstract affirmations the African liberation struggle is the lived experience of specific national Movements" (102). Consequently, even though Serequeberhan rightly concedes that everything does not have to unfold as written by Fanon (see 95), one has the impression that the entire exposition is informed by a focus on movements rather than, for instance, other forms of collective agency or even the aggregate effect of individual efforts. Be that as it may, ideally the fusion of horizons and the practices of freedom aim to overcome the dichotomies of colonial and neo-colonial societies (85). Let us now see how this may happen, taking up the narrative again from the point when post-independence states are divided between a Westernised urban sector and a non-Westernised rural sector.

To illustrate how this development unfolds, Serequeberhan turns to Cabral. He takes up the story line of liberation, not from the perspective of inevitable, immediate counter-violence, but from a group of Westernised Africans thinking together about their home country, while sitting in the heart of the colonial motherland Portugal (102). Concern for the essential problems of Africa, which defines African philosophy, can indeed take place close to the seat of the colonial power. What emerged from these discussions was a "re-Africanization of [these expatriates'] minds"; the discussions asserted a "heteronomous and multivalent conception of history" (102). This is from the start a stance directed against supposed European developmental supremacy:[73] no developed and underdeveloped peoples, just a plurality of different, but contemporaneously and equally valid modes of existence (see 103).[74] Hence also a first task of "decolonization", which will consist in opposing the modern philosophical metaphysics of history underlying the discourse on development (see 103). Undeniably, criticising this metaphysics of history forms part of the deconstructive task of African philosophy. The point is not against development, but against the imposition of a Western narrative as the standard for "development" everywhere. Consequently, the core of liberation consists of reinserting people's initiative in their particular (group or social) historicity. This understanding of liberation is subtended by an *implicit general anthropological and normative claim*, namely that it is good for humans to act within the framework of their own socio-cultural history. But, at the same time, this generality is limited, because of the recognition of historical plurality.

This history that is retaken charge of is, as we have already seen, only marginally concerned with precolonial traditions. It is first and foremost concerned with the history of colonial oppression and the attempts at liberation (104) or, to reformulate, with the history of being deprived of the source of history and of attempts to reconnect with it. That this vision must incorporate the heritage of the colonial state is inevitable, and part of the tragedy of history, which cannot be wished away. Rather, one's understanding of historicalness of Africans has to be adopted to accommodate this fact: "the negative effects of this aberration can and do become part of the positive historical reality of the colonized once decolonization is actualized" (104). "Decolonisation" is thus neither the return to an authentic past (as set out above), nor the annihilation of the entire colonial heritage. Rather, by implication, it is the process of re-Africanisation of agency and thus may include both the *acceptance* and the *rejection* of parts of colonial heritage, recalling the idea of "stock-taking" (13).[75] At the same time, as Césaire argued long before, accepting or even appreciating part of the colonial heritage should never be misconstrued as retrospective justification for, or implicit consent to, colonialism.

These "Euro-African hybrid" states are plural, not only because of the said division between urban and rural population, but because of different ethnic groups (see 105). Serequeberhan seems to deplore the resultant state of affairs because "[s]uch societies [that are] divided within themselves are impaired actualities for they do not have internal to themselves a common *ethos* that constitutes them as organic historic wholes" (105). One should hesitate at this point. Just previously the plurality of human historicities has been cited as a general and normative fact (see 102). Here, on the national level, Serequeberhan clearly searches for something that he does not even entertain on the international, African level: that divisions are handicapping, that an integrative ethos is enabling. Now, divisions are a "truncation" that have to be overcome through a return to the source (105). This is very significant: at this point, Serequeberhan sacrifices the plurality of historicities he assumes as his premise in agreement with Cabral, for a single, unified source.

This return can be achieved only through the "fusion of horizons". The impulse towards such a fusion results from the restriction experienced by the colonised rural masses and the frustration of unsuccessful assimilation by the Westernised urbanites.[76] However these two forces are bent towards each other by a "decision of conscience" on the part of the urbanites and their subsequent reintegration into the midst of the native masses (106–107). These elites reject their Western cultural legitimacy (108).[77] Nevertheless, the Western cultural baggage—education, know-how, "skills and wider horizons" (108)—does not only accompany the urbanites in their migration to the sphere of the rural masses, but is appreciated by the latter and gradually also enriched by the practical knowledge of the rural people (108).[78]

When Serequeberhan then concludes that "European values and skills are thus absorbed into a new synthesis" (108), it is of considerable significance for the content of his argument, but even more so for the very practice of philosophy he is performing. One may articulate the implication for the author, Tsenay Serequeberhan, by saying that his acquired competence of European philosophy neither disqualifies him with respect to the project of liberation, nor needs to go to waste. In fact, his book on the hermeneutics of African philosophy may well "be absorbed into a new synthesis". Serequeberhan stops just short of stating it in so many words when he explains: "In this dialectic[, the] European culture/history [of the Westernised urbanite] is recognised [by urban and rural natives] as a particular and *specific* disclosure of existence, aspects of which are retained or rejected [by urban and rural natives] in terms of the lived historicity and the practical requirements of the history that is being reclaimed" (109).[79] As far as I can see, this claim would not have been possible if Serequeberhan had not from the beginning accepted the thin, but real, general anthropological assumptions of hermeneutics.

At the same time, not all aspects of rural culture have to be accepted—they too can be ossified (no doubt because of colonial violence). This is because colonisation had also created (or "mummified") the colonised (see 110). Some form of cultural renovation is even presented as a prerequisite for liberation (109). How can one avoid concluding that the fusion of horizons amounts to some form of modernisation, because it leaves intact certain forms of Western knowledge and sheds some parts of traditional culture?

Even if this is correct, this could not be modernisation according to a pre-established pattern. Rather, in agreement with the return to the source of historicity, this "modernization" has to free Africans' "productive forces" (110). Cabral helps Serequeberhan to load this term with a specific meaning: "it refers to the sum total of cultural resources that constitutes a people in the open-ended process of its historical becoming. The term 'productive forces' is thus a formulation which is inclusive of, but not exclusive to, the economic realities of the colonized" (110). One may say that the "production" alluded to here, is that of the making of history. That is why Serequeberhan remains allergic to set patterns for revolution: "Thus 'to know what you want in your condition' is to have a concrete theoretic understanding of one's lived historical situation. For both Fanon and Cabral, then, theory, properly speaking, is always the concrete hermeneutics or interpretation of the needs and requirements of a specific historicity. Their theoretic labors are focused on an engaged hermeneutics of their lived situation" (112).

This liberation is not aimed at an "autistic" introversion. To the contrary, the national project of liberation opens (according to Serequeberhan, following Cabral) to an affirmation of the charter of the United Nations, from the particular side of each country (and continent-wide in an "Afrocentric" way)—in such a way that this nationalism or patriotism would be "grounded in the recognition that *difference* is what constitutes the concrete existence of each nation state and people in their particular and specific historicity", which in turn forms the "basis for global earthly solidarity" (114). Such is Serequeberhan's reformulation of Fanon's notion of universality: "Universality resides in this decision to recognize and accept the reciprocal relativism of different cultures [and histories], once the colonial status is irreversibly excluded" (cited in 119). In this way, Serequeberhan's thought trajectory, which starts from a general anthropology, ends in a general—but plural—humanity and politics.

Having arrived at the end of Serequeberhan's argument, we should remind ourselves that we have not turned away from the central concern of *Hermeneutics of African Philosophy*. The heart of Serequeberhan's enterprise is an enquiry into the practices of liberation and how social changes may give rise to them. This is the way he understands the "prior question" of continued African liberation and contributes to the constructive task of African philosophy. Or, as he formulates it: "Thus, in contradistinction to Senghor and Ethnophilosophy, on the one hand, and Nkrumah, Hountondji, and Professional Philosophy, on the other, this will be our hermeneutical response to the question: What are the people of Africa trying to free themselves from and what are they trying to establish?" (85). And this still perfectly echoes his understanding of what African philosophy is: "African philosophy as the hermeneutics of the post-colonial situation is the critical remembrance, itself interior to the lived emancipatory *praxis* of contemporary Africa, that cultivates, mediates, and revitalizes the origin or the source of this emancipatory *praxis* as the historicity of its effective inheritance" (28).

8. Conclusion

In this chapter we see that Serequeberhan's understanding of hermeneutics is rooted in general traits of human existence. We are temporal, interpreting beings, but socio-political circumstances may constrict and hamper our possibilities of existence. In this way, the condition of our ability to interpret is immediately linked to our political fate.

His view of philosophy is that it emerges from generally shared human traits. However, different varieties of philosophy, in this case African philosophy, take shape because of the divergent socio-historical and political settings from and for which philosophers think. A specific philosopher, contingently situated, can correctly identify general human traits and concerns within the parlance of a specific philosophical tradition. And, accordingly, philosophers may borrow from one another, without necessarily compromising themselves. Even so, borrowing from others, and repeating their errors, can debilitate African thought, as Serequeberhan illustrates with two polar examples: ethnophilosophy and "professional philosophy". The errors of these modes of thinking may well get translated into erroneous political ideas, as he illustrates in his critique of Senghor and Nkrumah. The common denominator in all these cases is an appropriation of Euro-normativity, be it by introvertion or extravertion.

Serequeberhan offers his view of philosophy as essentially hermeneutic and as a means to counter these undesirable avenues for philosophy. He does not attempt to return to a pure, authentic cultural heritage. Rather, by working on interpretation, he strives to tap into the reality of one's lived historicity. Understanding one's socio-political setting is never merely an epistemic exercise; it is also a vocation to respond to that situation. The overpowering socio-political reality in Africa is the violence of colonisation. While Serequeberhan subscribes to the historical necessity of responding with counter-violence, he also sees the possibility in post-independence African societies of a salutary fusion of horizons between the Westernised urbanites and the traditional rural population. From this process, practices of freedom or liberation result, which have a socio-political and anthropological-interpretative dimension.

In all, one finds in this book that Serequeberhan strives to articulate socio-political concerns and hermeneutics together. In his own words: "this hermeneutical undertaking cannot but be a politically committed and historically specific critical self-reflection that stems from the negativity of our post-colonial present" (17).

Select annotated bibliography

Amato, Peter. "African Philosophy and Modernity". In *Postcolonial African Philosophy: A Critical Reader*, edited by Emmanuel Eze. Oxford: Blackwell, 1997, pp. 71–99.
  Amato uses insights from Serequeberhan to interpret the relationship between tradition and philosophy (in Africa and Europe) to clarify the relationship between discourses on modernity and colonisation.
Cabral, Amílcar. *Return to the Source: Selected Speeches by Amílcar Cabral*. New York: Monthly Review Press, 1973.
  A volume in which Cabral describes his understanding of the "return to the source".
Césaire, Aimé. *Discourse on Colonialism*. Translated by Joan Pinkham. New York: Monthly Review Press, [1955] 2000.
  Césaire's classical and authoritative critique of colonialism.
Diagne, Souleymane Bachir. *African Art as Philosophy: Senghor, Bergson, and the Idea of Negritude*. Translated by Chike Jeffers. London, New York, and Calcutta: Seagull, 2011.
  A more sympathetic reading of Senghor than Serequeberhan offers.
Fanon, Frantz. *The Wretched of the Earth* (New York: Grove Press, [1961]1968).
Nkrumah, Kwame. *Consciencism: Philosophy and Ideology for Decolonization*. London: Heinemann, [1964] 1966.
  This book could be read as Nkrumah's own approach to a kind of "destructive hermeneutics" in opposition to a Euro-normative mindset.
Senghor, Léopold Sédar. *On African Socialism*. Translated by Mercer Cook. New York: Praeger, [1961] 1964.
Serequeberhan, Tsenay. *The Eritrean People's Liberation Front: A Case Study in the Rhetoric and Practice of African Liberation*. Boston: William Monroe Trotter Institute, University of Massachusetts, 1989.
Serequeberhan, Tsenay, ed. *African Philosophy: The Essential Readings*. New York: Paragon, 1991.
Serequeberhan, Tsenay. *The Hermeneutics of African Philosophy: Horizon and Discourse*. London and New York: Routledge, 1994.
Serequeberhan, Tsenay, *Our Heritage: The Past in the Present of African-American and African Existence*. Lanham: Rowman & Littlefield, 2000.
Serequeberhan, Tsenay. *Contested Memory: The Icons of the Occidental Tradition*. Trenton: Africa World Press, 2007.
Serequeberhan, Tsenay. *Marcien Towa's African Philosophy: Two Texts*. Asmara: Hdri, 2012.
Serequeberhan, Tsenay. "The Contesting Memory of African Philosophy". Interview with Richard Marshall. https://www.3-16am.co.uk/articles/the-contesting-memory-of-african-philosophy?c=end-times-archive. 12 August 2018. Last accessed 27 October 2022.
Táíwò, Olúfẹ́mi, *How Colonialism Pre-empted Modernity in Africa*. Bloomington: Indiana University Press, 2010.
  Taiwo's reconstruction of colonial "sociocryonics" is a distinctive, historical interpretation of social and cultural "ossification". He also offers a reading of the relationship between colonisation and modernity different from Serequeberhan's.

CHAPTER 4

Critique of African hermeneutic reason: interpretation triggered and oriented by praxis—Okolo Okonda

Composed of independent essays, Benoît Okolo Okonda's 1986 volume, *Pour une philosophie de la culture et du développement*,[1] is unified in its concern with the relation between hermeneutics and practice. The essays' overarching aim is to establish a philosophy of culture and development focused on contemporary Africa (9, 75). From this perspective, *Pour une philosophie*[2] is a straightforward book with a clear goal. However, one is soon impressed by the number of concepts, the attention given to their shifting meanings, and to the complex relationships between them. The reader, following the linear presentation of the argument, is gradually faced with an intricate web of ideas and their relations, a cobweb spun from a single thread where it is not evident where the logical beginning is, or how to progress between notions. This initial difficulty is not due to any failure on Okolo's part. Quite the contrary: the complexity of the text is the result of the author's masterful engagement with the intricacies of the issues captured in the title of the book.

This chapter aims to guide readers through Okolo's book and to engage critically with the views argued in its essays. I take up Okolo's explicit invitation not to consider myself bound by the order of the chapters (cf. 9) and to uncoil the argument as carefully as possible. I do this in two phases. First, I introduce the main themes of the book: praxis, hermeneutics, and tradition (§ 1), before examining each of these themes in detail and how they relate to one another (in §§ 2, 3 and 4). Second, I examine a number of the book's themes from the perspective of the idea-complex as a whole. I clarify this whole in § 5. On the basis of Okolo's arguments against and for ethnophilosophy (covered in § 6), we see how he deals with oral tradition, specifically proverbs (in § 7). The next section, § 8, is devoted to critique and violence. The last section considers philosophy in its universality and particularity. With this approach, I hope to do justice to Okolo's cobweb of ideas without getting trapped in it.

1. Orientation: praxis, hermeneutics, tradition

In Okolo's network of concepts, three stand out and structure his thought throughout: praxis, hermeneutics, tradition. One may be tempted simply to slot in the other themes and terms beneath these three headings: under praxis—crisis, revolution, development, project, destiny; under hermeneutics—text, reading, re-taking (*reprise*), meaning, perspective; under tradition—history, identity, culture, orality. Such a categorisation is not without merit, and can indeed serve as a first mapping of the different components of the discussion. But Okolo is careful to render such pigeonholing problematic. This is why I have adopted the image of a cobweb for the argument in his book: although some concepts are indeed more closely related to others, all concepts are related to all the others; the implications of one concept always bear on the other concepts.

Let us turn to the three core concepts: praxis, hermeneutics, tradition. I suggest we represent them initially as a radically simplified cobweb: as the three sides of a triangle—distinguishable, but inseparable. As a first approximation, *praxis* can be defined as the sphere of human action and interaction, specifically with the objective to improve our living conditions (92). *Hermeneutics* is the interpretation and reappropriation of any text or text-like form of cultural expression (37). *Tradition* is the half-material, half-spiritual cultural deposit transmitted by a group of people (56). The triangle represents the relation between hermeneutics and praxis, but praxis will enjoy a certain primacy. Tradition subtends the relation between hermeneutics and praxis.

2. Praxis, crisis, development

For Okolo, human beings are first of all *acting* beings. His entire argument stretches towards action. But his concern is with something more specific than action in general—it is with action aimed at improving the conditions under which people live (10). This specific form of action he calls "praxis".[3] Perhaps such a delimitation is inessential in theory, but it is certainly practical. At times, circumstances call for urgent action, for appropriate, practical responses to secure a better future. Such a set of circumstances of action is called "crisis". For Okolo, praxis is action in response to crisis. Which crisis?

2.1. Crisis

Okolo views crisis as a compound of heterogenous, but sometimes causally connected phenomena. Those affected by crisis are the "former colonized, oppressed, [... and currently] underdeveloped people who fight for more justice and equality" (46). Crises have a *subjective* dimension, notably a "general identity crisis, due to the presence of a foreign and dominant culture and tradition, and the need for self-affirmation in order to develop one's own culture and tradition" (41[4]). Crises also have an unmistakable socio-political or *objective* dimension, which consists of the "choice between tradition and modernity; conflict between two cultures, African and European; the growth crisis of young countries; the struggle between the emerging bourgeoisie, supported by capitalist imperialism, and the exploited proletarians; etc" (40, see also, 105).

Okolo knows that other philosophers have dealt with the social dimensions of crises. However, some of these philosophical responses are, in his assessment, not only inappropriate, but part of the crisis and are instantiated by "naive ethnophilosophy and unproductive criticism" (41).[5] For Okolo, identifying the philosophical aspect of the crisis has nothing to do with indulgent philosophical navel-gazing. Rather, he recognises that dealing with the crisis within philosophy is an indispensable step of its development towards a philosophy that can deal with the wider social and political crisis. Such philosophical crises echo and amplify political crises, as Okolo illustrates by way of ethnophilosophy. Okolo agrees with criticism that shows

> the link between ethnophilosophy and ethnology in general and the reality of colonialism and neo-colonialism. The people of good will and revolutionary sentiments that have practiced it and still practice it, cannot, in a twinkling of an eye, erase the fundamental trickery [*ruse*] of a science that transforms fantasies into "reality" so that subjugation can live and survive. The unanimity of saying and doing that ethnophilosophy established [as scientific fact] condones [*rend justice à*] the muzzling imposed by our politicians, following our former masters, on our populations, who nevertheless adore the famous palaver, which is often evoked, but never tolerated. (66[6])

Thus, the issue with ethnophilosophy transcends the questions of epistemology and reaches into politics. Politics, whether or not philosophy influences it, is equally ambiguous: it is a source of crisis, but has an important role in responding to the crises.

Likewise, the science and practice of development are ambiguous as necessary, but potentially harmful, allies in confronting the present crises. The theories of development to be resisted are

> based on economism, the dominant ideology of world capitalism: this ideology is ready to sacrifice all the social values to be promoted within the social relations of production to a certain idea of economic progress. The dominant economistic ideology works out a linear, mechanistic vision of development, suited to maintain the periphery in dependence. This struggle [against harmful theories of development—EW] must extend to the theories elaborated in the countries in question: these theories can be the pure and simple expression of the emerging petty bourgeoisie or can simply be deviant. (83, similarly, 85)

This political and economic problem is basically composed of two levels of inequality. The most important type of inequality is the discrepancy between rich and poor countries or between the centre and periphery of global capitalism. Still, as significant as international inequality is, Okolo finds it necessary to guard against a simplification that would oppose rich and poor nations. Because the bourgeoisie can also reside in the global periphery and the proletariat at the centre, class solidarity can cut across national borders (82).[7] Unfortunately, Okolo doesn't work out this point further. To my mind, recognising the overlap of socio-economic interests between societies of different countries is of real significance. First, it allows one to take stock of the crisis properly by, for instance, ascertaining how local elites can sell out national interests to serve foreign interests. Second, it helps to identify possible alliances across national borders to deal with crises more effectively. What Okolo points out, almost in passing, seems to me like the sociological underpinning of globally organised resistance.

2.2. *Development as "revolutionary praxis"?*

To respond to the crises left in the wake of colonialism—crises of identity and tradition, philosophy and politics, economy and modernisation—Okolo offers several directions for praxis. One should be singled out: development. If development is an appropriate response to crisis, then we can understand what Okolo means when he claims that development is not a luxury, but a "summons for our survival [*sommation pour notre survie*]" (85). The response of development should match the complexity of the crises with an equally complex variety of provisions for survival, ranging from the material or economic to the spiritual or cultural (85; 99).

The term "development" implies a state of affairs that is deemed unsatisfactory and must be improved progressively. Yet, Okolo repeatedly points out how this idea of gradual change is actually marked by dramatic breaks. In other words, one has to learn to perceive "development" to entail a "revolutionary praxis". Why this unusual synonymy? Because, on the one hand, development is based on a series of breaks; on the other, it calls for breaking with certain established patterns of development. This needs some clarification.

(a) Development as subordinate to breaks

The idea that development consists of progressive change must be relativised. According to Okolo, the very meaning of development—which has social, political, economic, and educational dimensions—has no exact precedent in traditional African culture and therefore development cannot be pursued in a manner of business-as-usual. The terms of development are imposed from elsewhere (44–45; 105).

African countries were confronted with the question of development through the historical break of colonial conquest. For Okolo, imprudent or rash attempts to respond to this crisis may well feed into neo-colonialism, imperialism, or exploitation (105),[8] and instead of developing anything, this inappropriate development may amount to more destruction (86). In other words, development cannot simply mean following a well-trodden path; development remains a risky endeavour.

To avoid this destructive possibility, development has to be a collective project (39), which means first and foremost that it should be guided by practical reason. Conceded, practical reason should be informed by technical considerations (when Okolo speaks about the "epistemological" aspect of practical reason, he has in mind economics and other disciplines associated with planning development). But especially the *ethical* side of practical reason should come to bear on development (106). Later, we see how the ethical side of practical reason should remain informed by culture and tradition. It is no contradiction to claim that development does not have a precedent in traditional culture, but that this culture has to feed into decisions about development. The desiderata of development are unprecedented; establishing them and qualifying them require a culturally informed approach, about which we learn more below.

(b) The need to break

Articulating the ways in which development results from and implies serious destabilisation does not yet justify calling development a "struggle" (*lutte*), and even less so "revolutionary praxis" (21; 95; 100). One gets closer to the point, by identifying the moment of *radical change* that links the idea of revolution to that of praxis. This is the aspiration to bring about change as "revolutionary [...,] effective transformation of the world" (80), and replacing the changes imposed by the post-independence situation.

"Revolutionary" is thus an appropriate epithet for a course of action that is premised on an "overturning [*bouleversement*] of privileges and points of view" (86). If development is to be a revolutionary praxis, then it should have a political and epistemic component. These two components belong together, as Okolo repeatedly explains:

> The problematic of the "revolution" implies, for its part, the idea of a clear break with the present situation, the idea of a profound transformation of human activities. From all this, we conclude that a true epistemology of the sciences of development cannot be made by the bourgeoisie of the rich countries, but by the revolutionaries of all the countries and especially by those of the so-called "poor" countries. (82, similarly, 81)[9]

To put it simply: the meaning of development as response to the crisis of contemporary Africa should not be read from a handbook on development theory. And although the political work of changing power relations is an indispensable component of dealing with the post-colonial crisis, it is insufficient to reduce the response to the crisis to politics. Reducing development to technical theory runs the risk of merely playing into the hands of established, institutionalised inequalities.[10] Reducing development to political change runs the risk of swopping one set of unjust power relations for another.[11] Still, Okolo is far from rejecting the technical expertise of development or the political struggles to renovate power relations. We need those responses to the crisis too, but we need to buttress and complete them with epistemic or scientific responses. This dimension is required to hold the technical and political initiatives in check and prevent conservative interests from co-opting this revolutionary praxis.

The success of development as revolutionary praxis depends on correctly articulating this epistemic contribution, namely as representing the cultural dimension of society (see 85). This is neither a call for a simple return to pristine traditional culture, nor a celebration of the virtues of scientism. What is it then? We have to remember what we are discussing here: responses to a crisis in a framework in which action enjoys a certain priority. Accordingly, the "epistemic" dimension of the responses requires (a) understanding science as practical response, (b) elaborating the appropriate ways to bring traditional culture to bear on such science, and (c) considering these two points to be intertwined: practice has to take precedence over theory and development requires a culture of liberation (see 95). Thus, scientific work must feed back into the "ethical" practice, as discussed above.[12]

For Okolo, *hermeneutics* will help us think about the cultural and ethical components of development required in Africa. Hermeneutics is not paraded as the response to everything. Its value and importance are only one part within the framework of praxis.

Now we have affirmed, with Okolo, the primacy of action and we have followed action through its crisis induced intensification to praxis aimed at bettering life. In action, people are projected to a future, one may say. And this is correct. But this is only part of the story. As much as Okolo promotes the significance of praxis and argues for his entire philosophy to be in support of a liberating praxis, he will also forcefully resist any reduction of action to the project, or future directed, dimension. This means that as important as development is as practical response to crises, one cannot understand development if you don't see it as interwoven with other dimensions of response. In Okolo's assessment considering development in abstraction (as many do) leads only to deepening the crisis. We therefore have to turn to other dimensions of liberating praxis.

3. Hermeneutics

To focus on hermeneutics is not to shift our attention away from praxis. Crisis is already presented as a "hermeneutic situation" (46) and praxis and hermeneutics are bound by a series of relations of mutual implication, which are only hinted at by the "and" in *Pour une philosophie*'s subtitle: *Exploration of African Hermeneutics and Praxis*. However, it would make more sense to isolate hermeneutics for a moment, and once we have a clearer picture of what it entails, come back to its relation to praxis.

Hermeneutics is the philosophical endeavour of theorising all understanding, interpretation, and application (43). Typically, it constructs a view of these three elements by exploring the circle that repeatedly binds reading (of texts, aspects of culture, tradition), to their appropriation (*reprise*) and to the projection of meaning (105). Okolo helps us to find our way in his view of hermeneutics by developing a set of *three propositions* that also structure his discussion in several chapters:

1. Every theory of reading presupposes a theory of text and vice versa.
2. Every reading is oriented towards some kind of appropriation [*reprise*].
3. Every reading and every appropriation is determined by a worldview of the subject who reads and appropriates (cited from 33, 42, 45[13]).

Of these three propositions, I will now give a synthetic view.

3.1. *"Every theory of reading presupposes a theory of text and vice versa"*

(a) Text

Our starting point is "text", written initially in quotation marks, because it includes a whole range of text-like phenomena (including oral culture, which will be discussed in § 7 below and cf. 36–37). "Text" is defined as any delimited verbal sequence, with a specific style and an identifiable genre (27–28, similarly, 55).[14] Tradition, culture, oral transmissions, works of literature, all count as "text". At the same time, although not exactly text in a strict sense, actions and life situations may also be considered to be "texts" in that they can be "read". Following the traits of verbal sequence, style, and genre, one may easily understand that texts are shaped by a society and a tradition, with all their changeability and contradiction (see 28).

Text is also characterised by its *autonomy*: it is detached from the situation in which it was produced and continues on a trajectory independent of its author and from the initial addressees.[15] Writing—the fact of being written or printed—is the clearest indication and mode of existence of verbal sequences independent of their authors. Okolo observes that entrusting one's ideas to the autonomous text implies already that one assumes that it will be transmitted. The autonomy of the text presupposes a confidence in the possibility that the autonomous message will be delivered for reappropriation. This amounts to recognising transmission, which is a dimension of tradition.[16] In other words, the text-like deposit of culture has to be associated with the collective agency of transmission (see 56).

(b) Reading

Reading a text means "to bring out [*dégager*] the meaning of a text, [...] not to return to the pre-existing meaning which the author had before writing: the meaning of a text does not exist before being articulated and perceived" (36, similarly, 37). If "text" can be understood in a very large sense, so does "reading".

The fact of reappropriating texts through reading presupposes a cumulative history of transmissions,[17] each of which exercised for some time an influence on the meaning of that text. In other words, reading re-actualises a chain of interpretations that accompanies an autonomous text as the reader receives it (see 44).

3.2. *"Every reading is oriented toward some kind of appropriation/ re-taking [reprise]"*

(a) Reading and re-taking (reprise)

Reading, then, is that event by which the meaning (*sens*) of a text is reactivated (37). In no way should it be likened to a disinterested capturing of stimuli emanating from a text-like phenomenon. Or in Okolo's words: reading is not innocent (38). As an effort to reactivate meaning, reading is motivated by the desire to be addressed, accosted, struck, or called to (*interpellé*, 38) by a text.

Okolo calls the act of receiving meaning through reading *"reprise"*. Having no exact English equivalent, this term is analogous to: resumption, repetition, revival, mending. The corresponding verb, *"reprendre"*, aggregates return, retake, recapture, resume, recover, take over, repair, correct. Return, but revival; resumption, but correction. One could perhaps simply use the French, "reprise". Up to now, I have rendered "reprise" as "appropriation", but this term does not always convey the active, creative aspect of "reprise". I will therefore opt for the neologism: "re-take".

Re-taking is quite similar to reading: like reading it is not innocent; it is a re-creation and an actualisation.[18] But reading is oriented to re-taking and should not simply be equated to it. Both are interpretations or appropriations of meaning, but "the difference between interpretation at the level of reading and interpretation at the level of re-taking, is that the former is situated in the universe of meaning-*giving* and the latter in the universe of meaning-*creating*" (39). It is not possible simply to follow Okolo here. Had he not attributed creativity to reading? And what could his general theory of hermeneutics bring to support such a strict distinction between two forms of "non-innocent" appropriation? A plausible solution can be to consider reading and re-taking as two modes of the single activity of interpretation, where reading represents the more passive side of reception, and re-taking the more independent initiative of creative appropriation. Formulated in this way, Okolo's own illustration would still be valid: a proverb can be read and understood—interpreted—without necessarily prompting further philosophical reflection. But the same proverb may be read and interpreted to compare it to other proverbs, to consider the tensions and echoes between them and to confront these views with other arguments on a specific problem (cf. 39). If "reading is oriented to a re-take", as Okolo's second proposition states, then it is because re-taking, more than reading, refers to the creative, selective appropriation and actualisation of meaning gained through reading (44).

Whereas Okolo will most often discuss *philosophical* re-taking, this does not exhaust the possibilities of appropriating meaning through re-taking. Novels (cf. 63) can also re-take a tradition of artistic, cultural, social, symbolic, and other references. Even if we stick to the level of claims-discourse (as opposed to fiction), re-taking a reading can actualise different forms of knowledge: juridical, religious, philosophical, political, and others.[19] In all these cases, "re-take defines and delimits the portion of creation in reading" (38). What is creative in reading belongs to re-taking, and we should think that other kinds of appropriation do not entail creation. As we see later, one of Okolo's objections to ethnophilosophers is that they ignore the role of creation in reading.

The multiple modes of re-taking come with secondary effects. Re-taking inevitably entails selection and selection entails partial forgetting of exactly that which is being re-taken (45). That is why re-taking may require limitation by the more conserving discipline of reading. One of the labels by which Okolo typifies his philosophy captures this vital link between reading and re-taking: *penser à partir de la tradition* (38) or *pensée sur la tradition* (105), that is: thinking from/on (the basis of) the tradition. Thinking from tradition consists of a reading pole, where tradition is the text, and a creative pole, represented here by thought. With this understanding of philosophy, Okolo hopes to unite the wealth of a tradition[20] with "autonomous and responsible" thought (38). Hence the two components of philosophy that Okolo advocates: one in which reading is predominant, best represented by a *historiography* of tradition, and the other, in which re-taking predominates, sometimes equated to *hermeneutics*.[21]

> The first [component of philosophy] consists in situating one's own thought in a genealogy of traditional thinkers; but this supposes beforehand the work of a science of history, applied to ideas, which would reveal to us, if not a succession of thinkers, at least a succession of conflicting ideas, conflicts which marked our traditional social structures [*formations*]. [...] The second form that thought from the tradition can take is of hermeneutic order; it would endeavor to re-take, in a specifically [*propre*] philosophical rationality, the non-philosophical (or philosophical) materials of the tradition: art, literature, symbols, etc. But here it is up to the philosopher to affirm, at the outset, the non-philosophical or philosophical character of these materials [...]. (38)

Below I come back to the relation between historiography and hermeneutics.

(b) Boundaries of creativity

All of this may provoke the suspicion that re-taking—the centre of gravity of Okolo's second proposition on hermeneutics—is nothing better than mere caprice and therefore subjective projection. Indeed, Okolo presents neither reading nor re-taking as neutral or objective account-taking; after all, the sphere of human action and interests that we are dealing with does not allow for such objectivity or precision. And the practical aim of re-taking itself requires commitment to the specific demands of a practical context, rather than perfect impartiality. But with all these conditions stated, one should still be attentive to the number of ways by which this margin of creativity is limited.

First, Okolo assumes that reading is reading *of something*, which sets limits to our creative re-taking thereof. One of the tasks of historical research is to confront hermeneuts continually with the newest state of knowledge with respect to their text (in Okolo's case, traditional culture).

Second, it is plausible to accept that the re-taking is constrained by the interpreter's traditions of re-taking or by those suggested from outside of the interpreter's tradition (44–45). In both cases nothing guarantees that the limitation set to re-taking will have beneficial, rather than detrimental, effects on re-taking.

Third, Okolo insists that interpretation is loaded with conflict about what is interpreted, which means that different people may test one another's re-takes.

Finally, the practical objective towards which we interpret further limits what counts as validly re-taking a text.[22]

Discussing Okolo's second proposition, I have restricted the discussion to the relationship between reading and re-taking. The two form only part of a larger interpretative cycle, which includes also the projection of a future (105). This point leads us to Okolo's third proposition.

3.3. "Every reading and every appropriation is determined by a worldview of the subject who reads and appropriates [or re-takes]"[23]

How we read, interpret, and assess the circumstances in which we live correlates with how we interpret texts and other forms of cultural inheritance. That is why the ways in which people interpret traditions fit with how people understand the most pressing issues they have to deal with (39). These pressing issues are nothing other than the dimensions of the crisis discussed in § 2 of this chapter. But people have different views of the crises in Africa, and so adopt different attitudes towards tradition and conceive diverse practical responses. Some attribute the major problems on the continent to modernity, or that the West imposed a one-sided view of human existence on Africa. Those who define the crisis in this way might take recourse to the values of the past that is seen as an uncontaminated source that can cure Africa's affliction (see 40). Others locate the origin of all problems in the past, consider tradition to be irrelevant to the current situation (rejection is also a re-take), and turn to other means to solve the crisis (cf. 40, but only cryptically presented). A third option states Okolo's own view:

> [O]ur attention to the past should take its starting point from the remarkable contradictions of our socio-economic systems where the traditional modes of production [*modes de production lignagers*] and the international capitalist mode of production *intermingle*: this would situate our present social struggles in the prolongation *and* negation of the traditional social struggles. And our destiny—do we still need to talk about it?—would reside in the struggle for the creation of a new world where equality and justice will reign, a world that will be continuously called upon to resolve the contradictions that it will bring about. But would that be a destiny peculiar to Africa? (31, my emphasis)

Whatever one's view of this short presentation of crisis, and of the requirements for reading tradition, the point is that "tradition is read from a horizon, the one projected by the praxis of a new world to be constructed" (105).

(a) Worldview

Thus far, the need for a practical response to the crisis determines how we read and re-take tradition and everything text-like. In his third proposition, Okolo assigns these tasks of appropriation to "worldviews" (*visions du monde* or *Weltanschauungen*, a term Okolo sometimes uses). Three are relevant here.[24]

First, worldviews have a *descriptive* aspect; they entail an "image of the world, an existential situation" (45). Both an intuitive grasp of the conditions of one's life and a worked-out interdisciplinary account of a socio-political situation are examples of images of the world. Positing a crisis means expressing a worldview.

Second, a worldview comprises some form of verification (*justificatif*[25]), which entails an *assessment* of a situation in comparison to how things were before. This evaluation of long-term tendencies is based on the descriptive function of worldviews.

Third, a worldview entails *projection*, anticipating an individual's or a group's future actions to respond to a situation they evaluate as, for example, a crisis.

All three aspects taken together are hermeneutic (45) if one takes hermeneutics to consist of reading, re-taking, and projection (105). In other words, worldviews and hermeneutic work are internally and in relation to each other dependent on the fluctuating working of interpretation (see the discussion on perspective in § 5, below).

(b) Determined [décidé]

Okolo's third proposition—that readers' worldviews determine how they read—captures the relationship between worldviews and the practices of hermeneutics. Only if one has followed that the worldview is nothing other than our access to our practical situation (that is, our condition as people who have to act), can one follow what this relationship consists of and what Okolo means by claiming that the worldview "determines" reading and re-taking. While affirming the primacy of praxis as life-improving initiative over hermeneutics, Okolo still maintains: "I do not share the opinion that praxis-oriented thought [*la pensée de la praxis*] deals a mortal blow to hermeneutics. I do, however, assert that, in a given situation, it is up to praxis to assign hermeneutics its place and its development. Praxis triggers the hermeneutic process and gives it an orientation".[26] Accordingly, the validity of an interpretation remains dependent on that of a struggle (cf. 46).[27] To conclude: because praxis is accessible only in the form of a hermeneutically structured worldview, all ways to praxis passes through hermeneutics.

Based on these considerations, Okolo concurs with Laurent Ankunde[28] that there is no such thing as knowledge for the sake of knowledge alone, but that the quest for knowledge is motivated by ultimate goals like peace, liberation, or flourishing (76). Okolo also knows that such lofty ideals can be warped and manipulated by forces "from the outside" and from the "inside" (78). We should therefore subject ideology, our own not exempted, to critique, especially because the goal of our action—development—remains badly defined, an idea, a utopia (86).

Thus, we arrive at the end of our preliminary discussion of praxis and hermeneutics. My introduction to this chapter imagines these terms as the two arms of a triangle, which represents the interconnected ideas of Okolo's philosophy. These terms connect to a third: tradition.

4. Tradition

In the introduction I provisionally defined tradition as the half-material, half-spiritual cultural deposit transmitted by a group of people.[29] Let us now try to grasp Okolo's more sophisticated view.

Tradition is a composite of *matter* and *form*.[30] The advantage of this distinction is that it allows us to think of two distinct realities belonging intimately together.

The material aspect of tradition refers to the "things" of culture. Okolo calls it "monuments of all kinds" (56). Later we see that anything text-like falls into this category, which includes also less tangible things like oral culture. These entities form a growing "deposit" left behind by earlier people. What has been lost, destroyed, or forgotten do not form part of this deposit, and in this sense traditions are always exposed to wear and tear. But it is also possible to rediscover and reconstruct parts of the deposit (as we see in Okolo's treatment of historiography below).

Okolo defines the formal aspect of tradition as "the particular spirit, the singular genius of a people" (56). This is not very clear, not least because elsewhere[31] Okolo explicitly rejects this idea in favor of tradition as transmission. Besides, the formulation comes very close to views of collectivities and about interpretative practice that Okolo otherwise explicitly rejects. If the formal aspect of tradition depends on the spirit of a group, what is the role of individual re-taking in reproducing tradition? What is this spirit: a natural attribute, a common (even unanimous!) intelligence, a style of thinking or of creating? Safest is to highlight that the formal aspect refers to the role living, interpreting humans play in transmitting tradition. Indeed, Okolo sees that the material and the formal aspects of tradition are interdependent: "the spirit exists only supported by a steady [*fixé*] deposit, and this deposit has meaning only by the spirit which vivifies it" (56).

Although traditions can be durable (as far as the cultural deposit on which they depend is "steady"), they can be dynamic—living—rather than static. As such, tradition stretches from the past, through the present, to the future or, as Okolo puts it: "the tradition is nothing else than the distance between this 'already there' and this 'not yet' [...]" (56, similarly, 105).

Tradition is also a composite in another way: "[T]radition can be simply sectorial: literary, religious, political, artistic, etc. It can also combine several at the same time. This tradition can remain tribal, intertribal, national; it can extend to the whole continent, or become intercontinental, and thus, be simply human" (56).

With this ampler vision of tradition in mind, it is easier to understand Okolo's insistence that tradition is both something to be *discovered* and to be *invented or created*,[32] while at the same time being simply a given reality in everyday life (42). Tradition is at once the cultural deposit (that is, a text) and its interpretation, an action coextensive with worldview, ideology, and identity.

> —*Note on "culture"*
>
> Of the three major terms of Okolo, "tradition" is the only one that does not figure in the book's title, however, "culture" does. The relation between "tradition" and "culture" thus needs to be clarified. This is an issue, because many formulations in the book present them as two *separate* things. Africa has a culture and a tradition (89), hermeneutics promotes culture and tradition (92, similarly, 95), discourse on development has to be inserted neither in culture, nor in tradition (87), the notion of "destiny" holds the promise, amongst others, of unifying "the philosophy of development, and the philosophy of culture and of tradition" (89) and to guide cultures and traditions to develop their best potential (105). Self-affirmation in the face of a dominant foreign culture has to give rise to the construction of one's own culture and tradition (41). Finally, and most eloquently, Okolo presents "Tradition as the in-between of familiarity and strangeness and culture as the effort of precarious balance [*équilibre*] in this in-between" (9). In a word: they may be similar, but culture and tradition are two distinct things.
>
> Yet, attempting to get a grasp on this difference, one is struck by the *synonymy* with which the two concepts are often used, as for instance in the expression "cultural tradition" (34). Elsewhere culture and tradition are presented in the same breath as objects of re-taking (38, similarly, 52). A history of ideas is needed for survival of both culture and tradition (65). And again, the "wealth of culture and of tradition" (38) are mentioned in one stroke. Furthermore, a number of claims about culture fit as-is to tradition: philosophy of culture and development is charged with the same transformative program as elsewhere a philosophy of tradition and development (75, similarly, 95, 99); or again, hermeneutics forms the junction between culture of the past and the culture to be instated, just as hermeneutics forms the hinge between tradition discovered and created (100).

> Even attempting to equate culture with either tradition as deposit or tradition as reading does not work, since there are instances where both could work.
>
> To conclude: an exegesis of the relation between "tradition" and "culture" leads to *no satisfactory result*. This is the only place in the book where I find Okolo's choice of terminology unuseful. However, at the strength of the last set of considerations, it seems comprehensible to push the interpretation into one direction: taking the two terms to be so close in meaning that treating them as equivalents would not lead to any substantial loss of the argument. Henceforth, everything that Okolo claims about culture will be considered to hold for tradition and *vice versa*. This will have the advantage of elaborating our understanding of tradition.

4.1. Tradition as text

Okolo sees tradition as a text-like phenomenon.[33] Like texts or writing, tradition is anonymous, in the sense of being detached from its progenitors. In fact, most often, we do not know from whom this or that deposit of tradition originated—signed books and works of art are relatively new phenomena (36). Tradition, like texts, belongs to nobody in particular. In principle, anybody can read or interpret tradition, not just the original addressees. In as far as a tradition is deposited, it allows us to examine the rules of their production (37). Like texts, tradition is "multidimensional" (36): it can be interpreted in different "registers": ethical, metaphysical, juridical, political, aesthetical. Consequently, cultural deposits can "transmit" in any number of directions to different readers, which results in diverse interpretations.

Finally, the reference or "world" of texts and of traditions is not simply to be equated with the world of everyday life (37). Okolo's point is not so clear. I take it to mean that the reference of tradition does not simply apply to my particular situation; it can be made to refer to my situation only by an effort of appropriation. Without that appropriation, the deposits of tradition would still have a reference but not yet to anybody in particular. Whatever the case may be, even without this last point, Okolo establishes enough similarities between texts and traditions to warrant his frequent recourse to "text" as a metaphor for tradition. This textuality applies to written and oral tradition (cf. 37, see further § 7) and is as true for African traditions as for any other human tradition (36).

Tradition as a text-like deposit, then, does not have any meaning (37, 43). That is, abstracted from the formal or spiritual aspect of tradition, the deposit may well be material for interpretation, but still needs to be read to reactivate its potential to mean something. This distinction between deposit/text and meaning must be qualified. Repeated attempts to read, interpret, and appropriate texts also get "fixed" in new writing, in new expressions of culture. This means that even tradition, as a deposit, contains something of the history of its appropriation, and is as such also hermeneutically constituted (21, 37). As Okolo describes the process,

> the tradition (monuments–writings–speech) forms an indissociable whole and constitutes an uninterrupted sequence of interpretations [...]. The written word discovers its full meaning only after a chain of interpretations and it then discovers itself as an interpretation and thus as part of this chain. As a counterpart, a moment of the tradition reveals itself [too] to be a moment of the hermeneutic chain. (37[34])

With this, we step back into the spiritual aspect of tradition: the practice of reading. We have to think always of tradition as a cycle of text, reading, and re-taking, together oriented to praxis.

4.2. Tradition and the difficult balance between the "already there" and the "not yet"

Tradition may well be a text-like something, but it is at the same time different from text. This difference resides in the formal aspect of tradition. Or, rather, tradition is the practice that reactivates deposited tradition. That is why reading is so important for Okolo's thought: reading is the traditional practice by which everything text-like—texts, monuments, speech, in short, tradition-as-deposit—is brought to meaning again. If a text retains the possibility of meaning anything at all, it is because the life of tradition (the formal aspect of tradition) consists of a chain of interpretation that carries texts (43). At the same time, if reading and re-taking define the formal or spiritual aspect of tradition, what is read is always a text or text-like deposit (34). In other words, when we turn to the formal aspect of tradition, we naturally examine it in combination with the material aspect.[35]

Even if tradition were only discovered (and not created, too), people would dispute what it consisted of, and what is to be considered more important or central than other elements. This is because tradition is fragmentary, and oral expressions are not accessible to everybody in the same way (35). In a word, reading introduces contradiction into a tradition (53). The fact that tradition is also created merely accentuates this fact. The creative aspect of tradition intensifies breaks, but may also offer solutions to contradictions. Creativity extends and transmits, selects, mends, and invents. In a word, tradition re-takes. Or, as Okolo also writes: tradition is constituted by interpretations (37, 44).

Reading and re-taking of tradition does not happen independently from a living context.

> To read a tradition is not to retrace the whole chain of interpretations to the original starting point—which would be impossible and pointless—but to *recreate* the chain by updating [*actualisant*] it. The whole process is summarized in the term "recreate". It is therefore a new appropriation of the possibilities offered to me by the world of tradition and those I discover in my own universe. (37[36])

That is why reading goes over into re-taking. It is only as an outcome of this entire process that we arrive at the meaning of tradition, which is reanimated in reading and re-taking. In this sense, tradition is not to be found in the past, but in our present doings. More than a mere deposit, tradition is living meaning that stretches to the future. V. Y. Mudimbe, whom Okolo quotes on this point, likewise understood tradition to be a contemporary phenomenon:

> The tradition, just like the past, is in us and not behind us. My tradition as well as my past are in my present discourse [*parole*], this discourse which, marked by concrete details of my socio-economic space, makes me today read my "history" subjectively, and in an inverse movement, reflects the archaeological field of my historical specificity. (92[37])

The meaning to be derived from tradition is situated not in the past, but at the end of a process of transmission and of reactualisation.

Transmitted and received tradition may, thus, be a condition and a horizon of creation by means of re-taking, but tradition neither determines, nor fences off creation. Tradition as a process remains open. Indeed, one of the objectives of discussing oral culture and to advocate the historical (rather than ethnographic) study thereof is exactly to insist on the historicity, internal conflicts, and contradictions that, for Okolo, demonstrate the life of tradition as far as we can look back in time. That is why the whole of tradition has "its own economy of self-perpetuation and self-renewal" (27). This "economy" is the tension between the "already there" and the "not yet" (see 56, explained above), the space in which people create (works of art, literature, or philosophy) and criticise those works (56). Without this openness, which re-taking enables, tradition ossifies and returns to the state of a relic. But when meaning arises from re-taking, it is therefore a mixture of familiarity and strangeness: "this 'familiarity' with the tradition does not suppress the distance to this same tradition" (57). Tradition is the "effort [to find a] precarious equilibrium in this in-between" (9).

This dynamic view of tradition contradicts the idea of tradition as a repetition of rituals bound to the past. This static form of tradition threatens to take over when people claim authority over tradition, imposing strictures on it and fixing it in the past. Tradition can also come under siege: it may be displaced by foreign culture (28) or depreciated when elements of a tradition are forcefully submitted to foreign criteria.[38]

Because tradition cannot live without re-taking and because people draw from *different* traditions, it is not at all simple to distinguish between a threatened tradition and one that is changing under influence of its own creative vibrancy. This difficulty is exacerbated by the instability of people's perspectives (discussed in § 5 below). Whatever the means one uses to assess the desirability of external influence on tradition, importations or new developments of a tradition, these means are themselves products of tradition and as such are subject to creative re-taking.

How does one then determine what it means to achieve a liberated culture (96)? The way Okolo deals with this difficult matter is to develop a view on critique, anchored by praxis (to which tradition and hermeneutics are always oriented). In this respect, Okolo's thought corresponds with other strands of African philosophy, some of which are his explicit intellectual adversaries: "philosophies [in this case, African philosophies—EW] of culture have always also been linked to philosophies of development and revolution and *vice versa*: négritude, African socialisms, consciencism, authenticity, etc" (28).

If the value of external influence on a tradition and of creative re-takings of tradition are measured by the quality of development and revolution they support, then this has a particular impact on the way we understand

Okolo's own philosophical practice. An illustration of this point is warranted. In formulating his views on tradition, Okolo explicitly takes over ideas from Heidegger (56).[39] Reading Heidegger's *Being and Time*, Okolo takes note of what a German philosopher wrote half a century earlier in a markedly different context. In reading Heidegger, Okolo's concern is not to explain Heidegger or to become his disciple. Okolo has a problem, namely the crisis of Africa to which he has a limited contribution to make from his social position as a philosopher. This he does by borrowing as much as he considers relevant to his point. But Okolo understood this praxis such that it *allows for* drawing from outside his own culture in making his contribution to "development and revolution". In other words, what Okolo is *doing* by re-taking, illustrates part of the possibilities of re-taking, namely appropriating elements from other traditions as means by which to innovate on one's own.

But is this the only legitimate view? Suppose we respond that as a philosopher, he is drawing from his *own* tradition—not the tradition of a specific African culture, but the, for Africans, philosophy should mean something similar to what it means for Europeans. One could schematically associate the first vision with that of the early ethnophilosophers; the second with Hountondji or Towa, for instance. Typical for *Okolo's* hermeneutic stance is the assumption of a difficult in-between these two positions: African philosophy is *both particular and universal*. This is reflected in his view on tradition "in-between familiarity and strangeness" and culture as the "effort to maintain a precarious balance in this in-between" (9, similarly, 57). Accordingly, philosophising, as *tradition of philosophy*[40]—by re-taking another philosopher, Heidegger, on this point. One could *reject* this claim only by assuming that for Africans, philosophising should mean sticking to one's local culture (imunising oneself against foreign offers). However, the opposite is equally true; one could *accept* this claim only by assuming that it is all-right when philosophers from Africa draw from European traditions of thought. In other words that an act of culture, strives to cope with this task of maintaining a precarious balance. This is not at all a non-committal position; it is an attempt to grasp the full complexity of the problem. I will return to this question of the particularity and universality of philosophy in the last section of this chapter.

4.3. What is co-extensive with tradition: worldview, ideology, identity

Okolo's terms "worldview", "ideology", and "identity" overlap, and are almost co-extensive, with his understanding of "tradition". In as far as they overlap with "tradition", "worldview" emphasises the relation of tradition to history, "ideology" underscores the relation of tradition to praxis, and "identity" highlights the relation of a traditional society to itself. This is not how Okolo present these terms, but the following schema shows why they are important in the way he defines tradition.

(a) Worldview

Although Okolo uses the word *Weltanschauung* as well as its translation "vision du monde", this does not pose any problem to the reader. What makes for some difficulty is the fact that he uses both to designate two quite divergent understandings of the term.

On the one hand, worldview refers to a concept originally from the toolkit of German Romanticism, but later also re-used (by name, or merely the idea) by ethnography and such currents of thought as ethnophilosophy (16, 27). Here, Okolo understands worldview or *Weltanschauung* to apply to

> a unitary perspective [*regard*] that sees the world, perceives the relationships between its elements, understands them and orders them. It is a perspective that sees not only for the sake of seeing, but for life, use and evaluation. [...] It goes beyond the merely contemplative to include also the behavior that results from this vision. The worldview of a people reflects at the same time the perspective, but also its practical materialization in the monuments, the literary, artistic, philosophical and religious works, the political, military and socio-economic acts. (69)

In essence, then, a worldview is an encompassing view, which is as descriptive as it is practically oriented, and found in ideas, actions, convictions, and artefacts. To this must be added Okolo's problem with it, namely when it is considered to be a *static*, homogenous, or unitary view, generally and (close to) unanimously held collectively by a people (16, 27).

On the other hand, Okolo advocates for the same term, "worldview", an alternative, appropriate understanding, which is *dynamic*: "[w]orldviews must be grasped in their varieties and variations, in their struggles and compromises" (70, similarly, 17). He will also advocate that the suitable science to help us grasp this dynamic conception of worldviews is not ethnography, but *historiography* and more particularly the history of ideas.[41]

One concept, two possible understandings, then. But on top of this distinction, Okolo claims that the term is ambiguous. That is to say that when understood correctly in the dynamic sense, "worldviews" are ambiguous. Ambiguous in that they

> can [1] be the opposite of any rational, methodical and systematic philosophy and translate a simple way of being of a person or a people, it can [2] also mean every philosophy. Still, worldview and philosophy refer to each other and respond to each other. However, the historian of ideas must go beyond the relations between ideas and society to reach the relations between ideas and things, between ideas and ideas. (70, numbering added)

If one accepts that "worldviews" are ambiguous in this way, one must concede that the idea that worldviews are static is retained with the more dynamic definition. Worldviews are both descriptive and practical, part of general culture and specialist science, and cover different domains of life, where the conditions of life feed back into people's views of the world (69). It is the dynamic, ambiguous concept of "worldview" that Okolo characterises as having descriptive, verifying (*justificatif*), and projective aspects (discussed in § 3.2.a, above).

Earlier we saw that "worldview" figures centrally in Okolo's third hermeneutic proposition: "Every reading and every re-taking is determined by a worldview of the subject who reads and re-takes." Now we may conclude that Okolo's understanding of worldview is not only dynamic—in the economy of hermeneutics it is also *dynamising*. In Okolo's words: "This third proposition seeks to underline the operative function of the worldview and the idea of destiny in the hermeneutical process. The worldview is not only what triggers the hermeneutic process, it is also what supports it in its development and what the latter tends towards untiringly" (45).

But how is it possible that a worldview stimulates re-taking, but is itself the result of re-taking? This is not a contradiction: the never-ending to-and-fro between these two poles—interpretation and worldview—is typical for human existence.

Dynamism leads to *variety*. These two traits of worldviews are of equal importance to Okolo. In a debate with Alexis Kagame, he claims that "worldviews overlap as much as they diversify within a society, but they are not always philosophical" (50). He develops this fact of diversity: there are indeed "multiple visions, resulting from the historical vicissitudes of individuals, social groups and peoples", but the variety is also due to different socio-economic of sociological conditions: "fishers do not have the same view of the world as hunters; old people see the world differently to young people" (16, following Njoh Mouelle). But with variety comes sociological contradiction: "worldviews do not simply overlap; they all struggle to emerge on the surface. Of course, their victories and failures go hand in hand with the real power held by an individual, a social class, or a given social formation. [...] The conflicting worldviews generate, orient and block the symbolic and imaginary universes" (16—17, the last statement formulated with support from Nkombe Oleko).

This power-theoretic perspective on contradicting worldviews brings us to the next term: ideology. Okolo offers one meaning of the word "ideology", which refers to "the worldview of a social group" (77).

(b) Ideology

Although Okolo is well aware of the myriad uses of the term "ideology", in his most sustained discussion of the term, he suggests simplifying these uses to "ideology falling short of science and ideology beyond science [*l'idéologie en déçà de la science et l'idéologie au-delà de la science*]" (77). This is how he defines the distinction:

> Ideology falling short of science, is to be understood as any discourse, implicit or explicit, that obscures and masks the real social realities, whatever the pretention, political, religious, philosophical or scientific, and whatever the finality, operational or contemplative. Ideology beyond science fights for a better-being [*mieux-être*], [which is] a project founded on at least a little bit of analysis and committed to correcting itself through permanent contact with reality. What unites the two senses of the term, is the effect intended by any ideology: the mobilization of the forces of production. (78)

This is not a simple distinction. What divides the two forms of ideology is evidently *science*. The citation allows us to derive that science is "founded on at least a little bit of analysis and committed to correcting itself through permanent contact with reality". "Ideology falling short of science" is, thus, uncritical, spontaneous engagement with the world. It may result from closing people's eyes to the world, while misleading them to think that they are indeed seeing. Scientific analysis and self-correction could undo this work of ideology.

Although it remains a very sketchy view of science, this informal characterisation has major strengths. First, it enables Okolo to identify science (and hence the possibility to distinguish between the two forms of ideology) in all human societies in history, including pre-modern African societies. Second, because he does not accord to Western science the role of final arbiter between good and bad ideology, he side-steps the critique that an undue deference to Western culture influences his view of science and is thus itself ideological in the bad sense. Third, although it is often advantageous to be trained in science (of whatever discipline and of whatever tradition), having a professional training is not a prerequisite for practising "science" in the sense Okolo proposes. Forth, his understanding of science is broad enough to encompass the contributions of the natural and social sciences. Fifth, this broad understanding of science allows for mutual critique of one form of science by another (social science by natural science and vice versa; amateur science by professional science and vice versa, etc. cf. 78) without elevating any form a priori to the final authority. One may remain unsatisfied with Okolo's idea of science, but any elaboration would be worthwhile only if it retains these important strengths.

Which sciences does Okolo have in mind? All depends on the context. The most important science for the practice of African philosophy is, for Okolo, historiography. Historiography arms us in the struggle against the ideological trends in disciplines like ethnography or cultural anthropology.[42] However, when we think about development, the interdisciplinary practice of "development science" takes centre stage. Okolo directs much of his criticism specifically against that cocktail of sciences (77). This makes the distinction between his two forms of ideology all the more complicated, because we have to derive that science too can be mystifying and in that sense "fall below the threshold of science".

Although the Marxist background of his notion of "ideology" is manifest, it is less clear what motivates Okolo to reduce the mobilising effect of ideology to the forces of production, as if these forces are the decisive factor that can bring about people's better-being [*mieux-être*]. I take "forces of production" to refer to the entire social reality of human interaction, but recognise the importance of the economic dimension, which is in any case called for, because of the importance of development in Okolo's thought (see § 2.2. above).

What is merely suggested in Okolo's distinction between two kinds of ideology, is that on whatever side of science human ideas and practices find themselves, they are in one way or another ideological. Elsewhere, Okolo articulates this as a general anthropological truth: "ideology is the air that we [human beings in general—EW] breathe. It constitutes one of the essential conditions of durability [*permanence*] and evolution of a given social structure [*formation*]" (78). Hence, the issue is not to distinguish between those who still linger in the obscurity of ideology and those who have seen the light of truth, but rather to distinguish within the same person or group the fluctuating trends of mystification and clarification. Ideology "ceases to be obscuring when it is demystified, made conscious and taken over by an event that is both theoretical and historical, that is, by the science of the given social formation, a science practiced/created [*faite*] by the very people who fight for their freedom" (78). Hence Okolo's repeated insistence on the work of demystification as a "struggle" (*lutte*).

What is the place of this understanding of ideology in Okolo's thought? "Ideology" plays its role in Okolo's attempt to argue that hermeneutics and a "[world] transforming philosophy" (*philosophie transformante*, 75) mutually constitute each other. How can philosophy be more than contemplation; how can it also be "operative" (*opératoire*, 75) or functional (*fonctionnelle*, a term Okolo borrows from Ankunde, 76)? In one way or another, the idea of ideology "haunts" all philosophies that aim at action. For Okolo, ideology mobilises people to act (78). But what is the relationship between an operative, functional, transforming philosophy, and ideology?

Responding to this question requires a better grip on the phenomenon of ideology, which can be given as a series of distinctions (see 78). The first is discussed above: some ideologies fall short of "science", others depend on it. Second, ideologies can be distinguished on the basis of whom they advantage: ideology could be used by a dominant group to hide or justify the status quo or by exploited people to fight the status quo. Accordingly, exploitation can be justified ideologically as "development" from the outside or contested ideologically from the inside. Hence, a third distinction: there are ideologies to be promoted because they are preferable and others to be opposed because they are objectionable. Above, we see how "science" can draw a line between them, so that good or bad ideologies can be either scientific or non-scientific. But the distinction between preferable and objectionable ideologies is also historical and consists of recognising "the place of struggle and of the main antagonists concerned: the bourgeois and the proletarians, rich nations and oppressed nations, etc"[43] (78). Taken together, the demarcations that science and history make seem to me gradually to overcome mere factuality, so that the distinction between ideologies based on truth alone but also on value.

This is this point at which philosophy comes in, where its task is clarified: to distinguish better and worse ideologies. The double nature of ideology obliges us to attribute to philosophy an epistemological and a polemical function (81–84). In chapter IX of *Pour une philosophie*, we find valuable indications of how philosophy and ideology fit together.

Remember that for Okolo development is the major praxis to change African societies. Development is the perspective from which hermeneutics has to read and re-take tradition. In the conclusion of chapter IX, Okolo looks at this relation in the opposite direction: the only to attain development is through "our theories and our ideologies" (84). If I understand Okolo correctly, "our theories and our ideologies" together refer to the complex of intellectual practices formed by philosophy and science (in this case a science of development freed from ideological misrepresentation). Only informed by such theory and ideology can practice be "revolutionary", that is, efficient: "practice alone without theory [meaning here: philosophy—EW] is blind and theory without practice is weak-willed [*velléitaire*]; only their union creates a force capable of lifting the mountains of injustice and inequality" (84).

Thus, ideology projects a future—a new culture to be instated (100) or "real" development (84)—and reaches back to the distant past in which culture or tradition are rooted. Positioned between these two poles is a "theoretico-ideological place [*lieu théorico-idéologique*]" (100). Therefore, the only way to realise such a projected development is to deal with this space. This initiative starts out by reading and re-taking tradition or culture. This is the "theoretic" or even "pedagogical" component of the theoretical-ideological space (100). This re-take of tradition should be such that it mobilises people towards revolutionary or liberating action—this is the more ideological component of this space (84, 100). Both tasks form part of rigorous hermeneutics.[44] Combined, they could promote "self-recognition, [...] [self-] identification and projection" (100[45]) in a hermeneutic process oriented to praxis. That is what Okolo means when he claims that only by "our theories and our ideologies" can we realise real development (84–85). He compares the role African philosophy plays in Africa's struggle for development with that of Marxist theory in the labour movement (84). In either case, theory has a material objective: to reorganise productive resources to empower marginalised classes politically and improve living standards.

As an outcome of African philosophy, development and equality are rather aspirations than a description of historical tendencies. Nonetheless, Okolo takes care to fit his philosophy to African societies and economic conditions:

> Let us consider the famous solidarity, set up as a value and constituting an element of the African culture. It is a consequence of a socio-economic structure, that of the traditional African lineage mode of production. It is therefore inconceivable in the new structures of contemporary Africa. But the ideological reading and re-taking can appropriate it momentarily, to offer to the masses an object of self-recognition and identification, anticipation of the values to be promoted within new social relations of production. It is true that these new values, once installed, will be in negation of the traditional values. Nevertheless, some traditional values read and re-taken in the perspective of the praxis, will serve towards liberation. (101)

However one may assess Okolo's conclusion, we should not miss the wide view he has of ideology. On the one hand, ideology should pre-date our modern way of life. People in traditional societies did not only, like us, "breathe ideology" (78); ideology in such societies was already subject of struggles and relations of domination (21, 16). On the other hand, ideology mobilises us towards the future. In short, ideology is co-extensive with tradition and as worldviews. This was the hypothesis I set out to demonstrate in the opening lines of this section.

But like tradition and worldviews, ideology is always at risk of morphing into something harmful. None of these terms denotes something a priori good. The desirable or laudable versions of each has to be struggled for.

When Okolo declares philosophy to be the "supreme weapon" in the struggle over ideology (83), he is not announcing a happy solution, but just deepening the dilemma of human existence. Like the human and social sciences, philosophy too can succumb to bad ideology (27, 38). The effort to overcome negative ideology and to unleash its positive potential is, therefore, also *a struggle of philosophy against itself.* It is this philosophy, at risk of ideological stagnation or warping, that has to watch over its allies as they strive for "better-being" or development. The disciplines of economics (83) and the less well-defined interdisciplinary practice of development (80) have to be called back to their scientific core, by being stripped of dangerous ideology (81).

Everything hinges on philosophy's capacity to self-correct, to be both involved in the game of generating positive ideology and able to generate a critique of its own ideology.[46] Nowhere does Okolo suggest that this is a simple task. But having explained the urgency of this task, he confidently declares philosophy indispensable for Africa today (84).

(c) Identity

The ease with which the adjective "African" can be used does not lead Okolo to conceive of African identity (or any other kind of identity) as something self-evident or simple:

> What is identity? It is undoubtedly what makes a thing, an individual, what it is and what it remains. In the case of Africa, its culture and tradition, this identity seems fragmented and multiform. It is fragmented because of the multitude of tribes and peoples often divided by the chance of colonial history. Multiform, this identity assumes, in turn and according to the needs, a purely legal character, a cultural, political, geographical, historical character..., and one realizes that the legal or political Africa does not always coincide with the cultural or historical Africa... The identity of Africa is certainly a problem. (89[47])

Above, we saw that the question of identity is a significant component of the contemporary crisis of Africa (41). One of these problems is that attempts to pin-point any identity are sometimes *so contingent* that they cannot apply to the African continent as a whole or, otherwise, that they are *so general* as to apply much wider than the African continent (90).

Another problem is the idea of identity itself. Identity could be recognised by contrasting something with what it is not (e.g., African culture identified in contradistinction to European culture), or with how it used to be (e.g., contemporary culture contrasted with how culture used to be). In this sense, the determinants of culture are, as it were, *elsewhere*. Otherwise, identity could be established by self-recognition. In this sense, identity is determined not by distance, but by *proximity* (91).

From this dilemma Okolo draws a negative conclusion: we have to avoid making identity both a substantial something and nothing at all (91). But what does it mean, positively? How can one grasp what Okolo himself typifies as elusive or "ungraspable [*insaisissable*]" (91)?

Next to the historical dimension of identity, Okolo affirms its future-oriented dimension. This latter dimension he terms "destiny". Destiny does not negate or replace the historical dimension of identity, but situates it more completely. Likewise, the historical dimension of identity serves to balance an excessively future-oriented understanding of destiny. The point is not the past or the future, but the tension between the two. Only by recognising this tension can one establish a dynamic view of *identity as destiny*.[48]

Such a dynamic view is a temporalised view. Temporality is the key to understanding identity as destiny. Hence, in our understanding of identity/destiny we encounter again the tension between the "already there" and the "not yet", where there is neither necessity nor absolute freedom, but rather an ever-reinterpreted past in view of a task that heads towards no fixed end point (92).

To be precise, one does better to speak about "self-identification" than about "identity". Self-identification or self-recognition is the act of dealing with the tension between being there already and not having yet become what is to be. Identity cannot be something purely stable or given: it is repeatedly at stake. Hence the view of identity/destiny as a struggle: "Destiny as a space of struggle and reclaiming [*ressaisie*] seems to be an idea that draws cultures and traditions to the best of themselves and identifies them" (106).[49] But we have already encountered the nature of this struggle for the best possible "in-between" before: it is hermeneutics. In other words, reading and re-taking tradition with a view to praxis is at the same time the event by which people identify themselves.[50] Or, as Okolo writes: "In the African context, the hermeneutics of traditions and cultures offers the theoretical-ideological locus of *self-recognition, identification* and *projection*" (100, my emphasis). Although Okolo considers hermeneutics as a specialist, scientific undertaking, everyone can, and does, practise this form of reading and re-taking within their own context and with the means available to them. Hermeneutics, as the means of Africans' self-identification, does not assign the task of self-identification to specialists alone—it is everybody's domain. If, in Okolo's unassuming definition, identity is "what makes that a thing, an individual, be and remain what it is" (89), then we may paraphrase that hermeneutics is the work of identification, because by reading and re-taking tradition with praxis in mind, any person or group self-identifies as that which they are "destined" to be.

In this presentation of Okolo's understanding of identity, one cannot miss the correspondence with his view on tradition, on worldviews, and on ideology: the same temporal structure, the same "in-between-ness" of what is given and what has to be realised, the same hermeneutic structure, the same stakes and struggles, and thus open-endedness. My hypothesis that "identity" is coextensive with "tradition", in Okolo's thought, is thereby also confirmed. As much as tradition conditions the dialectic between hermeneutics and praxis, identity, in turn, conditions tradition. This position is explicitly attributed to identity:

> African identity, articulated with the notion of destiny, will never be given once and for all, it is a process to be defined beneath the circle "hermeneutics-praxis". A circle that is not closed but that is transformed by a dialectical movement between meaning and action. To say African identity only in terms of "hermeneutics" of the understanding of the past is insufficient. And to project this identity only in the struggle for a better future is to overlook an important point that Marx taught us: The science of revolution and development is part of the science of history. (93)

In his later work, Okolo adopted the term "distributive and narrative identity" both to reject the static, imposed identities of the "ethnographic gaze" and of Western philosophy of history, and to pursue his own reflection on African identity.[51]

4.4. *Provisional conclusion on tradition, worldviews, ideology, and identity*

In Okolo's thought "tradition", "ideology", "worldview", and "identity" are largely coextensive. However, these terms are not simply synonymous. Worldviews, ideology, and identity are shaped by the dual aspects of tradition: deposit and spirit. What tradition is depends on the twin hermeneutic exercises of reading and re-taking exercised in the light of contemporary praxis. Consequently, identity, ideology, and worldview fluctuate between the already-there and the not-yet; each of these three terms imply a hermeneutic process that retains elements that have been transmitted and combines them with novel interpretations or new inventions—each time in combinations and to degrees that cannot be determined in advance. This is neither a philosophy that rigidly affirms tradition, identity, ideology, or worldviews, nor one that dissolves them. It attempts to render in an intellectually plausible way the diversity of positions that people can want to take up between these two extremes.

Okolo's hermeneutics confirms that tradition, like worldviews (hence ideology and identity, too) are dynamic, fragmentary, and heterogenous, and belong not necessarily to groups but to anything ranging from individuals to small associations, through diverse collectives, to the whole of humanity.

5. Critique of hermeneutic reason: shifting perspectives and complexity as a virtue

At the start of this chapter, I suggest a schema of Okolo's thought. This consists of a triangle whose two sides represent the dialectic between hermeneutics and praxis. The third side of the triangle is tradition. Up to now, my main aim has been to examine these three major categories. It should now be evident that the terms are so interrelated that to abstract one from the whole could be done only for the sake of a systematic presentation. Having done so, we can henceforth continue exploring Okolo's thought and allow for more attention to the web of concepts as a whole.

Okolo's concepts are complex because he does not work with a conceptual model of grand categories into which smaller ones should be slotted; his web of concepts serves to reflect human reality in which all aspects interrelate. All concepts are related, and it is worthwhile to reflect on the meaning of each relation. In turn, every concept refers to a reality that, even considered in isolation, represents a multitude of possibilities. "Reading" or "tradition" or "identity", for instance, are not simply one thing; and they are not necessarily beneficial or necessarily harmful to our existence. Each element of this human reality can be assessed differently depending on how it is presented, practiced, and linked with other dimensions of human reality.

These conceptual considerations are important to understand what Okolo requires of his readers if they want to follow what he is doing. Let me illustrate this with how Okolo uses the term "horizon". On page 42 of *Pour une philosophie*, Okolo argues that *tradition* defines the horizon of interpretation, that is, of hermeneutics (and he reaffirms this repeatedly throughout the book). But, on page 105, he concludes that *praxis* is the horizon of hermeneutics. This could be a regrettable contradiction. Yet, in the light of Okolo's web of concepts, it makes perfectly sense to maintain *both*.

When he presents his claims, Okolo does not write as if he is building an edifice of concepts—his understanding of tradition, hermeneutics, and praxis does not allow for this. Rather, he rather writes like someone who is situated in the unstable tension between the concepts and between the range of variable realities to which they refer. In short, he writes in the understanding that he articulates a shifting perspective; he tries to give a reasonable rendering of *what it means to think always from a shifting perspective*. People's perspectives shift for many reasons. The world in which we live changes. We aspire to effect change, and whether we succeed or fail, our actions put us in a different position from which to view our situation. We think from a tradition, re-discovering and re-creating it as we do so, which means that our understanding of our tradition changes, altering our perspective on our actions and the world, whether we realise it or not.

To those who seek absolute stability of orientation in philosophy, this may be worrying. By contrast, Okolo never presents the fact of shifting perspectives as part of the crisis of Africa or, for that matter, any other region. Seeing from a shifting perspective is not in itself a crisis, because it is merely part of human existence. What is a crisis is the variety of harmful ways in which people may let culture stagnate, impose exploitative forms of development, and tamper in other injurious ways with our efforts to find meaningful courses of action in our lives.

Exposing the crises of human existence from a shifting perspective: this is how I understand Okolo when he characterises his thought as a "critique of African hermeneutic reason" (41) or more generally a "critique of hermeneutic reason" (47). He defines "critique" in this context explicitly as a study of the conditions for something to be possible (47). He deploys critique just as much to diagnose harmful developments in human reason. Only when one has understood the essential integration of critique in hermeneutics can one accept the definition of hermeneutics as "everything related to the promotion of culture and tradition" (92).

If critique, in both senses, derives from our *living* hermeneutic condition, it is understandable that we find here no ideal theory. Okolo does not aim at finding perfect solutions in abstraction of crisis, which then have to be applied. Instead, he offers us reflection on what it means to be *submerged in practice(s)* from which we may hope for nothing better than to improve what we have. Therefore, we do well to take note of the caution and moderation with which Okolo finally presents the role and ambition of philosophy in the concluding words of his book:

> Hermeneutics and praxis: between these two terms exists a real and deep relationship. Nevertheless it is a difficult relationship because the interpretation of a tradition is always provisional and because praxis is in perpetual reconquest. The relationship seems difficult and precarious at the same time, since hermeneutics and praxis articulate themselves in the interval between the known and the unknown, the conscious and the unconscious forces. Here the task of philosophy consists perhaps in maintaining leeway, in keeping open the interval. Tilting the balance in one direction or the other, it is to concur with [*render raison à*] the world of the dream or to that of the nightmare. (105–106)

Never does Okolo claim that philosophy or hermeneutics will save us. Their role is to help discard ideas that hamper our attempts to find a liberating praxis, to help direct us to what we dream of and away from the nightmares that are part of our reality already.

A clear illustration of this role of philosophy is Okolo's critique of ethnophilosophy. By the time he wrote, objecting to major tenets of ethnophilosophy was not a novelty anymore. What is of interest is the specific way he articulates his objections, which includes a limited recognition of ethnophilosophy's significance.

6. Ethnophilosophy: contra ... and pro

Although acquainted with other critics of ethnophilosophy (like Okere or Towa), it is to Hountondji that Okolo comes back repeatedly. Hountondji recognised in ethnophilosophy a view of African thought as a collectivist system, to which everybody consents unanimously, that cannot change, and therefore cannot have a history (26). As much as this unanimist view of African philosophy is to be critiqued, it did have the advantage of disputing a certain dominant view of reason that elevated Western particularism to the status of universalism (27) and carried with it prejudice against unwritten, oral reason. Yet, when the ethnophilosophers contest this dominant view of reason by claiming to return to the original unwritten African philosophy, they return in fact to nothing at all. They compile impressive syntheses of divergent aspects of traditional culture (language, expressions, customs), but then project on it the unanimist picture of African philosophy. Instead of translating that information into contemporary debates, they freely invent—but without realising that they invent—a picture of African philosophy that never existed (34, 48). The problem is not the creativity—whoever could object to a philosopher's creativity?—but the invalid claim to a philosophy that would belong to an ethnic group or to Africans collectively.

Perhaps the first question to ask Okolo, insofar as he accepts Hountondji's critique of ethnophilosophy, is if he then thinks that no pre-colonial African philosophy existed. As far as I can see, Okolo considers this question badly formulated or, at least, not the right point to enter the debate. He considers the question still completely open (25), for he declares: "I do not want to limit the meaning of the word philosophy to what it has always meant in the European tradition. I am not presuming anything about its meaning in the context of traditional Africa. It could include philosophical, religious, political or legal ideas, provided they have been thought of at some level of depth" (68).[52] The biggest error of ethnophilosophy seems to be that it has fewer scruples, that it is less cautious, and that it affirms, perhaps too enthusiastically, the existence of African philosophy, projected on traditional African life and thought categories derived from an obsolete ethnographic paradigm.

Inspecting more closely Okolo's critique of ethnophilosophy, and in particular chapter V of *Pour une philosophie*, titled "Hermeneutics and Ethnophilosophy", one discovers that the failures of ethnophilosophy could be summarised in the three propositions of Okolo's hermeneutics (see above in § 3). The first proposition advocates working on an understanding of text and reading. Conversely, ethnophilosophy insufficiently theorises the power and limits of its own practice of reading. Instead of examining the hinge that re-taking represents between tradition and praxis, as the second proposition requires, ethnophilosophy is pursued as if there is no re-taking. The third proposition encourages us to explore how a praxis-informed worldview influences reading and re-taking, whereas ethnophilosophy overlooks its ambiguous relationship to colonial and neo-colonial power.[53]

Even before we look at Okolo's proposal for overcoming these weaknesses, we have to recognise that he has deployed his critique of hermeneutic reason (a critique that studies the conditions for the possibility of reason) as a position from which to critique ethnophilosophy (a critique that exposes flawed reasoning). A succinct rendering of how this latter form of critique functions, is that "[h]ermeneutic critique consists in verifying, in the case of a given practice [e.g. ethnophilosophy or négritude—EW], if the circle of this assertion is closed [*bouclé*] and well closed" (48). I understand this to mean that ethnophilosophy will be evaluated for its ability to take advantage of the most beneficial possibilities offered by the human capacity of interpretation. The circle that has to be closed is the one linking tradition, reading–re-taking, and praxis. Failing to do so sufficiently, Okolo assesses ethnophilosophy as "inauthentic" (105).[54] This term may surprise. Why not "faulty", "defective", or "incomplete"? Although I do not think the term "authenticity" asserts itself rigorously here, it may be accepted as designating an undesirable diversion from what hermeneutic reason can offer us. In this sense, Okolo's hermeneutic critique of ethnophilosophy functions exactly like his critique of ideology: "as much as hermeneutics seems to promote a meaning already there, the critique of ideologies goes beyond this meaning, denounces it as inauthentic and discovers another hidden meaning, the true one" (98–99).

Nevertheless, Okolo's assessment that ethnophilosophy is inauthentic does not amount to declaring the entire enterprise useless or a failure. In a way, Okolo concedes quite a lot to ethnophilosophy: not only is it the *origin* of African philosophical hermeneutics (a point he makes with the support of Ngoma-Binda), but ethnophilosophy *is itself* also a form of hermeneutics (cf. 49).[55] One can say that hermeneutics is not only a critique of ethnophilosophy, but also an attempt to correct and rehabilitate ethnophilosophy.[56]

How then do we arrive at a philosophy that overcomes these shortcomings? Three tasks have to be accomplished.[57] These correspond with the three shortcomings of ethnophilosophy and Okolo's three propositions on hermeneutics, which in turn remain integrated in the larger frame of tradition, hermeneutics, and praxis.

First, *historiography* must replace the collectivist orientation to the African past and traditions. For Okolo, *historiography* is the science par excellence that deals with the particularity of people's and groups' actions. Whereas (in the past) ethnography searched for the unanimously held views and generally practised customs, historiography documents the divergence from tendencies, the contradictions, the tensions, the innovations, in short, the material that real human thought is made of. The reason for looking at the past is to get the "upstream" view of tradition, which reveals the experiences of tradition people have had up to now.

Second is the core hermeneutic task of *philosophising*. Whereas the previous task corresponds more with discovering elements of tradition, the second task occupies itself with the "downstream" re-creation of tradition. Together with the first task, this constitutes "thinking from the tradition" (discussed above in § 3.2).

Third, "thinking from the tradition" needs to be oriented by a revolutionary praxis of development, which entails philosophy's ability to *mobilise* people ideologically.

Should the three-fold initiative succeed, it would reintegrate all the components of a hermeneutically constituted understanding of the world. In this sense, it would "close" the circle of hermeneutics and be authentic. However, in another sense, exactly such a hermeneutic positioning would remain "open" in the sense that the creative moment inherent in hermeneutics remains forever "provisional" and "perpetually reconquering" (106).

If ethnophilosophy is the best place to see the critical working of hermeneutics in action, we need a case to demonstrate the ability of philosophy to overcome these inadequacies. Orality provides an excellent but difficult case study.

7. Orality

The reason why orality is such a significant problem to work on, is because of the importance it had for the first followers of Tempels. They argued that if we cannot show our detractors the philosophical books of our ancestors to prove that they had been philosophising before colonisation, then we can still demonstrate the philosophy inherent in the structure of African languages, in sayings, in narratives, and in elements of worldviews. transmitted to us despite the colonies. In other words, according to this paradigm, the very *possibility of African philosophy is at stake* in orality.

Okolo does not give us an exegesis of orally transmitted utterances. He takes a step back to work out a theory of how such utterances could feed into philosophy. In his theory of orality, he activates especially the first two tasks for overcoming ethnophilosophy (explained above). Combined, they amount to "thinking from the tradition" or, as he calls it in this context, "thinking from the proverb".

7.1. *Proverbs*[58]

In the opening section of *Pour une philosophie*, Okolo joins a reflection on proverbs (chapter I) with a reflection on how to overcome ethnophilosophy (chapter II). In this way, understanding the critique of ethnophilosophy and understanding how to deal with the cultural heritage of proverbs are related.

Although Okolo refers to other aspects of oral culture (like the language, religious convictions, myths, and other narratives), in his book he focuses on proverbs. The point is not to elevate proverbs in this way above other forms of expression, but to zoom in on one element of tradition to make his point. From there on, his conclusions can with some qualification be applied to other traditional forms of expression.

Proverbs lend themselves exquisitely to Okolo's argument. To start with, in taking proverbs as object of study, one is dealing with a distinctive and enduring African heritage. More accurately, it is a heritage of which at least a significant part has emerged, and was transmitted, independently from Western influence. This is important, because one could thus deal with the ideas carried in proverbs as purely African ideas, which could therefore be used as uncompromised building blocks of an African philosophy. Moreover, reflection on proverbs' contribution to African philosophy places Okolo straight away on the terrain of ethnophilosophy. This enables him to engage with this current of philosophy, as it were, from the inside.

Focusing now on the proverbs themselves, they are characterised by *five defining traits*.[59] Proverbs exist as a component of oral exchange. They are exchanged and thus spread over space and transmitted over time. Proverbs have a recognisable stability. They contain ideas about a variety of aspects of life. The last three traits conjoin to make of proverbs a form of literature. In fact, based on these latter traits we may claim that proverbs, though oral, form text-like entities (in the sense explained in § 3.1.a, above).

At this point one may ask if one could not simply systematise the ideas contained in proverbs and then identify their ontological, anthropological, ethical, perhaps even metaphysical—in short, philosophical—presuppositions. In other words, why should one not simply proceed with an ethnophilosophical reconstruction based on proverbs?

Okolo would respond that it is exactly the textuality of oral tradition that prohibits this short-cut approach. The textuality of proverbs makes them an object of hermeneutics, and therefore of reading and re-taking. All philosophy implies re-taking, issuing from reading. Merely systematising what is assumed to be a philosophical system denies two points where interpretation intervenes: the transmitter of oral tradition, and the contemporary philosopher.

To clarify this claim, Okolo enlists the help of two specialists: Njoh-Mouellé and Nkombe Oleko.[60] Because Okolo's develops his view *in relation to* Njoh-Mouellé's and Nkombe's views, his choice of allies is "interested" and "not innocent" (38). But this "interest" does not consist in lining up authors from whom to expect only confirmation of his own views. Rather, Okolo's relation to his interlocutors is such that he can learn from them *and* contradict them. His relation to them is one of hermeneutic reading and re-taking. In this way, the format of his argument already opposes the ethnophilosophical idea of cultural unanimity.

Okolo's argument for what we are dealing with in proverbs is constructed of three parts.[61]

(a) Part one argues that "proverbs do not think" [le proverbe ne pense pas]

Okolo's point of departure is Njoh-Mouellé's study of proverbs. Njoh-Mouellé recognises in proverbs a form of oral literature that, he concedes, captures and transmits practical sagacity (*sagacité*, 14), but neither wisdom, nor philosophy. Insofar as proverbs contain understanding of keen know-how, they cannot be said to be science either (14). Later, Okolo completes the list of negations by also denying that proverbs are politics, law, ethics, and religion (17). But to this general characterisation of proverbs, Njoh-Mouellé adds a simple but decisive observation: they *contradict* each other. This means that the collection of proverbs do not form a coherent whole (15). In a way, these contradictions should not surprise us: the wealth of proverbs was never developed as a systematic whole, but rather formed from a myriad of personal experiences in different situations of life: different between individuals or between groups, between rich or poor, between the old and the young, between fishermen and hunters (16).

As if Njoh-Mouellé's vision of proverbs would not already seem iconoclastic to many ethnophilosophers (16), Okolo amplifies it. The differences and contradictions between proverbs do not only reflect different origins and contexts, but also reflect different interests. Consequently, between proverbs exist not only logical contradiction, but also social contradiction, which means struggle. Okolo maintains that the two kinds of contradiction mirror each other, such that "[t]he contradictions that we read in the proverbs express the contradictions experienced in a given social formation" (16). If that is correct, then we may also suspect that the same power struggles inherent in traditional culture would cause certain proverbs to be transmitted at the expense of others and, in this sense, proverbs may well reflect the interests of only some sections of society (16).

Okolo's point is not merely that ethnophilosophers' idea of proverbs as an implicit philosophical system is an erroneous and naïve reconstruction. Even more significantly, he claims that such a view kills off exactly what it claims to be advocating: traditional African philosophy. Surprisingly, Okolo takes these negative conclusions about proverbs as point of departure to construct his alternative view of philosophy in Africa, a view that applies as much to traditional pre-colonial Africa as to contemporary Africa and, indeed, to any other place in the world.

Njoh-Mouellé prompts Okolo to develop this alternative theory of African proverbs. Having stated that they contradict each other and observing that the same proverb may be used for contradictory purposes or in contrasting contexts (15), Njoh-Mouellé concludes that "wisdom is not to be sought in what each of these proverbs expresses, but rather in the *interval* that separates them; and this interval is unfortunately made of *silence*" (as cited in 14, my emphasis). Whereas some may see in this conclusion the final adjournment of oral African philosophy, Okolo situates the heart of African philosophy exactly here. One has to appreciate this "silence" as

> the meeting place between the impulse coming from the social struggles taking place and the literary process of symbolization and imagination. [...] [T]he social forms that trigger [the process of symbolisations] are not separable from the creative process itself. Conflicting worldviews arouse, orient and block the symbolic and imaginary universes. (17)

To Okolo's mind, this is the core of ethnophilosophy's failure: "they missed what they specifically wanted to show: the fact that the African was capable of assuming at a very high level of rationality his/her condition of being and of existing. And that because they did not seek African philosophy in and beyond the social and historical contradictions of which it must be the expression" (66).

If we accept this seemingly anti-philosophical understanding of proverbs, why then bother speaking about them, except for refuting a strand of ethnophilosophy? Okolo's argument calls for painstaking examination of proverbs (through cataloguing and describing variant forms, changes, the formation of new ones, the disappearance of others, the differences among them, the borrowing from one context to another, etc.), because only through this work can one gain access to how proverbs are *used*: how they reflect individual viewpoints, how views find support to form schools of thought, how proverbs contradict one another, how their use depends on specific contexts, and so forth. (70). In this way one gains access to a history of people's *reflection*. This is the next point.

(b) Part two argues that "proverbs provoke thought" [le proverbe donne à penser]

Okolo develops this point by bringing in his second ally, Nkombe Oleko, but from a different angle. That Nkombe's[62] ideas do not fit snugly with those of Njoh-Mouellé, corresponds with Okolo's argument for the productive potential of discordance, in the use of proverbs and in philosophy generally. Nkombe's understanding of the relation between proverbs and philosophy is quite different from the disjunctive relation that Njoh-Mouellé identifies. This alternative, constructed on a voluminous study of proverbs,[63] traces the *continuity* from proverbs to philosophy, through the intermediary of the sage and the philosopher.

According to Nkombe's study, it is possible to organise the different visions expressed in proverbs in such a way as to systematise the scope of human experiences to which they refer.[64] This means that the agile speaker may well shed light on human affairs by using such proverbs. For the sake of convenience, such an agile user of proverbs is called a "sage" (19–20), but I suppose this refers to any person who uses proverbs in an insightful way. The sage's agility consists of the competence of metonymic reason (which captures a whole concrete situation, or at least an essential part of it, by means of an abstractly formulated idea of a proverb), and of the competence of analogical reason (which compares two concrete situations through the intermediary of an idea expressed in a proverb) (19).

Another trait of reasoning through proverbs is that it effects[65] a normative judgement: by pronouncing proverbs people make ethical assessments about the desirability or objectionability of what is assessed.

Finally, Nkombe's study advances the idea that proverbs are symbols, which means for him that proverbs provoke an "effect of multiple meanings [*un effet de sens multiple*]" (18). And because proverbs can have a variety of meanings, each interpretation is relative to all the other possible interpretations (19). This plurality calls for clarification, which is how the proverb starts provoking thought (in the philosophical sense).

The next step in Nkombe's philosophical study of proverbs is to contrast, and thereby relate, the sage's insightful use of proverbs with the philosopher's work that is as much built on the verbatim form of the proverb as on the use that the sage makes of it. Whereas sages are typically masters of the concrete situation that they clarify with proverbs, philosophers relay these proverbs further by means of greater clarity of expression and systematicity (the philosophical view of proverbs is synoptic) (20). Whereas the sage simply proposes the wisdom of the proverb by applying it to a situation, the philosopher always has to justify claims (19). In short, rather than merely to juxtapose the verbatim proverbs to highlight the silence between them (as Njoh-Mouellé does), Nkombe investigates how proverbs are *used*, and by so doing he indicates the continuity (albeit with difference) in *usage* from the sage to the philosopher.

Having thus presented Nkombe's view on proverbs, Okolo situates himself right in-between Nkombe and Njoh-Mouellé. Okolo argues that proverbs do not "think"—are not in themselves philosophy—but that the contradictions between proverbs is the trace of people who think, who struggle about proverbs' meaning and application. The symbolism of proverbs provokes thought, opens a plurality of meanings that entices the philosopher. Okolo develops this basic view in several ways.

First, whereas Njoh-Mouellé claims that proverbs have no normative intention, Nkombe considers them loaded with ethical judgement. Okolo proposes that ethics is not intrinsic to proverbs, but a product of the philosopher's interpretation. Only through interpretation can "the proverb participate in the practical vision of the world" as part of the ideologies subtending our social life (20). In this way, Okolo declares the difference between Njoh-Mouellé and Nkombe only apparent.

Second, Njoh-Mouellé considers proverbs to be anti-philosophical; Nkombe claims that proverbs feed back into philosophical thought. In Okolo's reading, Njoh-Mouellé emphasises the task of *discovering* philosophy in the silent gap between proverbs; Nkombe need not maintain that proverbs contain philosophy, but that by provoking thought, they stimulate the *invention* of philosophy (21). Okolo combines these two positions into a major standpoint:

> [I]n the problematics of an African philosophy today, one should not limit the question to elaborating the conditions of possibility of creating an authentic and autonomous philosophy, but this question should also concern the methodologies suitable to make us revive the conscious modes of thinking which marked the ideological struggles of our traditional social formations. (21)

This work of African philosophy consists of discovering (by means of historical studies of where we come from) and inventing (through a hermeneutics of creating meaning), and both of these are steered towards praxis (21).

Third, Njoh-Mouellé and Nkombe seem to concur that proverbs reflect an aspect of human reality, but that fixed proverbs then get ideologically stuck (Okolo speaks of a "blocage idéologique", 21). According to Njoh-Mouellé, the proverb does not think further than what it expresses and any user of proverbs, philosophers included, thus are stuck with the contradictory views rendered by different proverbs. For Nkombe, the sage deploys proverbs without tampering with what they express, but accepts that the apparent contradictions are just additions that build out the same original picture of human reality. Whichever side one chooses, Okolo concludes that as long as one sticks with the proverb and its use, there is always the risk that the social contradictions and class struggles reflected in them may only be perpetuated through that usage. This situation provokes philosophical reflection.

Fourth, Njoh-Mouellé and Nkombe agree that proverbs are literature. For Njoh-Mouellé, proverbs are not philosophy and remain "outside" of philosophy (21). For Nkombe, proverbs' literariness gives them an affinity with philosophy. But, if this relation is forced, it risks reducing philosophy to nothing more than literature; on the other hand, if proverbs' relationship with philosophy is expressed too weakly, the philosophical force of proverbs gets lost. Here, Nkombe is caught in a double bind. Okolo's response is to confirm that proverbs provoke thought, but that they do so as much by their portrayal of human reality (when used by the sage) as by the contradictions between them. Proverbs stimulate philosophy, while philosophy retains its specificity compared to proverbs.

(c) Part three investigates what it means to "think from proverbs" [penser à partir du proverb]

This intricate comparison and critique of Njoh-Mouellé's and Nkombe's view of proverbs concludes that it is a justifiable and desirable philosophical practice to "think from proverbs". This thinking consists of two inseparable aspects: thought as received or to be discovered (Njoh-Mouellé's perspective), and thought as initiated or to be invented (Nkombe's understanding).

Now the pieces of the puzzle should start to fit together. Corresponding to how Okolo conceptualises tradition, this to-and-fro between "to be discovered" and "to be invented" captures the essence of the human relation to tradition. In fact, thinking from proverbs is just a special case of thinking from the tradition (discussed in § 3.2 above). What holds for philosophical work from and on tradition holds for proverbs too: "To think from the proverb upstream of the proverb is the work of a science of history, applied to ideas; to think from the proverb, downstream of the proverb, is the work of a philosophical hermeneutics" (22, similarly, 39).

If thinking from proverbs starts with an other-than-philosophical discipline, namely history,[66] it is a clear recognition that proverbs are not philosophy (22). Key to Okolo's hermeneutics is that philosophy depends on history. How are the two disciplinary practices tied? By approaching proverbs with a specific question. I understand Okolo to say that historiography has to study proverbs, identify their contradictions, and the social tensions that the contradictions reflect (27, 70), but that such historiography should be guided by questions that do not belong to the sphere of the proverbs. It is the to-and-fro between historiography and hermeneutics that opens the space of reflection that may overcome ossified ideology (22). This to-and-fro corresponds with reading and re-taking, with discovering and creating meaning (39). Seen from this perspective, the history of contradicting proverbs is not a problem to be solved; these contradictions form part of the diverse symbolic offering of proverbs that nourishes philosophical reflection. Let us examine more closely the relation between historiography and hermeneutics implied in "thinking from proverbs" and "thinking from tradition".

If the philosophical emphasis is thus on re-taking proverbs, something has to be made available to be re-taken. Historiography plays this indispensable supporting role for hermeneutics. The relationship between historiography and hermeneutics is comparable to the relationship between writing and meaning (36–37): historiography continues to provide hermeneutics with its object; it renews its material and thus also its ways of working. As Okolo writes elsewhere, "[c]ultural memory is forever renewed retroactively by new discoveries".[67] Historiography works against the spontaneous and inevitable selection and forgetting involved in re-taking; it restores, while hermeneutics reappropriates (45). Historiography and hermeneutics are not two opposing types of intellectual work. Sure enough, historiography leans more towards recuperating tradition and hermeneutics towards altering or breaking with tradition (59). But history also holds the potential to serve as an antidote to ethnographic generalisation and social freezing,[68] hence Okolo's emphasis on conflict, contradiction, and fragmentation in African oral tradition (29, 38, 49, 66, 70, 82, 89).[69] That is why historiography can enable hermeneutics to do its re-creative work through which tradition is resumed and transmitted. It is therefore incorrect to equate historiography with conservatism and reinterpretation with progressiveness.

7.2. Conclusions on orality

The reason for this detailed study of proverbs was to gain a better understanding of oral tradition and of the significance thereof for African philosophy. One question remains: does Okolo's insistence on the significance of oral tradition not lock up Africa in a distant past, in a world without writing, books or internet, so that the centre of gravity of African philosophy remains a lost precolonial world? The very nature of African philosophy is at stake. What kind of response does Okolo's *Pour une philosophie* allow us to propose to this question?

First, although Okolo understands historiography as an important instrument in research on orality, he never suggested that the backward look reveals a paradise. Neither does he suggest that what historiography offers a destiny we should aim to reach. His is not a culturalist plea for a return to the lost paradise.

Second, historiography helps Okolo affirm a generally shared human ability to disagree (or to agree) on grounds that one may consider justifiable. One can paraphrase Okolo by saying that the error of ethnophilosophy is not that it pays too much attention to tradition, but that it does not do so enough. Historiography outperforms (old style[70]) ethnology by going beyond the commonalities of a group to the intricate detail of their interaction (66, 71). Historiography reveals human possibilities, changes, conflicts, contradictions, and the tensions inherent in tradition that only partially mends its fragmentary nature. Historiography is the first means to resist social freezing.

Third, does the necessity of historiography in interpreting tradition not make African philosophy the domain of specialists alone? On the one hand, no: all people learn something about history, have some experience of contradictory or fragmentary aspects of their tradition, and can recognise social tensions, historical or contemporary. In this sense, thinking from the proverb/tradition is a common human ability. On the other hand, something specific is claimed for philosophical professionals. Not all people have access to the same historical material; not all have the chance to spend time studying such material or to exchange ideas with specialists. The philosopher is placed in a privileged position, and one may rightfully expect of professional philosophers to be generally better at thinking from proverbs than other people are.

Fourth, the historical hinge formed by colonisation—this division into a pre- and a post-—is an obvious temporal reference point for early written African philosophy. However, there is nothing in Okolo that binds him to a schema of "pre- = orality", "post- = writing". Sure enough, his reference to Hountondji to formulate a critique of ethnophilosophy speaks to this new accent on writing. But this does not mean that philosophy exists only in writing. On the one hand, oral philosophising (outside of the sphere of institutionalised professional philosophy) continues in the independence era. On the other, writing forms also a tradition to which the central tenets of Okolo's theory of tradition apply.

Fifth, if we do not need to transport ourselves mentally to a pastoral scene of pre-colonial clan life to do African philosophy, it can still help to return to pre-colonial settings and events, not for the sake of that part of history alone, but as a general return to *all* history. This should logically include recent history whose historiography may be based on written records. To rephrase this point categorically: Okolo's critique of African hermeneutic reason applies as much to people living in contemporary African megapoles as to their parents, their grandparents, and so on. Okolo affirms this point implicitly when he rejects an exaggerated culturalism in philosophy. He affirms it again when he presents a typology of different kinds of African culture according to the modes of production to which they correspond: traditional production, capitalist production, or others (96).

Having followed these arguments, one can understand why Okolo captures the aim of his discussion of orality as "[d]efining the African philosophical places [*lieux*] and the problems they raise, determining the space of interrogation and the interrogations themselves" (105). His point is not to transport himself to any other time or place or, certainly, to reject or malign writing. It is to engage with the world in which he finds himself. His point of departure is a difficult case: if philosophy is alive and well in oral culture, then surely it should not be reduced to a system of unanimous and anonymous beliefs. The shifting hermeneutic perspective on which I insist in § 5 is what restores a more sophisticated view of oral tradition, a view that is not only factually accurate, but also more fruitful for the contemporary philosopher than what ethnophilosophy could offer. Ultimately, in dealing with pre-colonial oral culture, it is the nature of present-day, context-sensitive philosophy that is at stake.

Accordingly, Okolo could identify his core question as, "how to articulate thinking about tradition and from tradition with a reflection on our material development [*devenir matériel*]?" (105). This opens the discussion on praxis, projected action.

8. Work, critique, and violence

The discussion of orality should go a long way to clarify Okolo's understanding of history, tradition, and ethnographic claims. But we need to explore how Okolo deals with problems coming from another front, namely hermeneutics' involvement with praxis.

One could take as entry his reflection on a work (*oeuvre*). This term covers any work of art, literature, and, I think, any attempt to do something well. This seems quite simple. The trouble starts when we ask *how we know* that something has been done well. Let us call the attempt to assess the quality of a work *critique*. Any aspiration to do something well anticipates critique that it tries to deal with in advance. Some forms of criticism, like literary criticism, can be highly specialised. Africa boasts many works of literature of very good quality. But how do we know that they are good? Literary criticism informs us. But whose critique is that: Western or African? Or is there perhaps no real difference?

What started as a simple topic of doing things well, drove us to the intricacies of hermeneutics: we can recognise a work as good only by linking its production to an interpretation, which has to be informed by a tradition of criticism. The three major components of Okolo's book—praxis, hermeneutics, tradition—come together in the question of the work (*oeuvre*).[71]

Sometimes works are texts; sometimes they are text-like (55). In either case, works lend themselves to be read. At the same time, bringing forth a work always depends on a tradition of similar works, but from which the particular work can distance itself. Creating a work and doing something well are acts of re-taking (59, 63). Exactly the same can be said of critique: by bringing something about (an assessment or even a theory of assessment) and striving to do so well, critique may also be considered a work. The work may anticipate critique and in that sense be shaped by critique. In fact, as work done well, it may challenge, or critique, critique itself. In short, "[h]ermeneutics and critique are already in the work [*oeuvre*] itself. Their dialectical interplay guarantees the perpetuity of the tradition" (59).[72]

The reason for this overlap between apparent opposites—work and critique—is because of their hermeneutic structure: they are both forms of re-taking. But because perspectives shift (see § 5, above), work and critique may forever relativise each other. That is why the hermeneutic entanglement of work and critique is characterised as much as by "re-taking" as by "breaking" and "transcending" [*reprise, rupture, dépassement*] (59).

In chapter VII of *Pour une philosophie*, Okolo explores the difficult relationship between work and critique with a reading of Yambo Ouologuem's novel, *Le devoir de la violence*.[73] In this reading, Okolo is interested in the relationship between a work of literature and literary criticism, and that between ethical or political initiatives and our critique of such acts. The first is more a question of textual hermeneutics, the second of the connection of hermeneutics and praxis. But in essence they intersect. This should be born in mind as we now turn to their shared theme: violence—violence as narrated (in literature) or violence committed (in action). In both cases, Okolo frames violence as work (*oeuvre*) that can be subject to *critique*.

Let us take *violence suffered* as point of entry. Part of the crisis of Africa (investigated at the beginning of our discussion) is due to the violence inflicted by Western powers on Africa: slavery, colonisation, post-independence capitalist exploitation. Isolating this fact may create the impression that this violence sets African history in motion. But to this one may want to object—and Okolo places this objection first of all in the mouth of the négritude authors—that, before the beginning of this inflicted violence was a history of vibrant African culture and life according to generous African values. Yet, this picture has two problems.

First, as narrated by Ouologuem, the golden past of Africa was as violent as any other time; the Western interference only changed the look of it.

Second, as valid as the utopian claim of a pre-colonial world may have been to protest against the violence that Africans suffered, a time arrives when the négritude poets of yesterday become the statesmen and executives of today and they never try to re-establish that pristine world. They always strive with might—and ultimately, if need be, with violence—to realise some of the benefits of modernisation (61).

These two rectifications of the idealistic picture of pre-colonial Africa introduce a second kind of violence: *violence initiated*. If violence from the outside is always a "first strike", then violence by Africans may, in principle, be a justified response. But if Ouologuem is right, then Africans have always also initiated violent acts and "[t]he injury [*plaie*] that was colonization was set [*s'est posée*] against the background of an internal tear [*déchirure*] that seems naive to deny" (60). This tear affirms that Africans have always been both perpetrators and victims of violence. This has implications on both levels of Okolo's reading: for the *work* of literature in which violence is narratively presented and for the *work* of action of African people.

Taking the position of a literary critic, Okolo rightly comments that violence committed by Africans is an established (one may say, traditional) theme in literature dealing with Africans (60). In this sense, Ouologuem's *novel* continues that tradition. But it breaks clearly with that tradition in not sparing the Europeans in his exposition of violence, either. Continuity and break—re-take—render, then, Ouologuem's relation to tradition. Any assessment (critique) of this work of literature must analyse how the writer deals with tradition.

But one also has to consider the work of action to which the novel refers. On the level of history or action, Ouologuem's writing also brings about the same effect of continuity and break, this time with respect to perceptions about the nature of action executed by Africans. The un-self-conscious, unreserved way in which he elaborates precolonial African violence breaks with négritude's celebration of the same world: "the ear of a Nègre[74] does not like to hear that négritude, this first unity that colonization has dislocated, is full of contradictions and, moreover, inhabited by violence" (60). The emphasis is perhaps to be placed on the "contradictions" (implied, between being victims and perpetrators of violence) underlying the purported "unity". In short, action and history are shot through with exactly the same experience from which the hermeneutic or philosophical engagement with proverbs emerge, namely *contradiction*.

The point is therefore not that the author can shock his readers by contradicting their expectations. The point is that the issue of violence confronts people with *themselves*. Violence confronts people with themselves, not because instead of being peaceful, Africans are now portrayed as violent—reverting to such a simplistic, traditional trope of African violence is out of the question—but because violent action had at times been a possibility for some and thus remains a possibility for people who have been and may still be victims of violence. This contradiction ignites the question: who am I, descendant of victims of violence and of perpetrators of violence? Who am I that am capable of peace and violence? This question of identity is thus not fixed, but rather characterised by "uncertainty", "hesitation", "swaying" (61), because it draws from a contradictory past and is fed by a contradictory reality. For Okolo, "the person who tries today to untangle contradictions is the same one who, yesterday, untangled and wove others" (53). This conflictual "I" contains the possibility of violence and may be the enemy of Africans (61).[75] African identity is not fixed but composed of a disquieting relation of familiarity and strangeness, similar to what Okolo elsewhere attributed to tradition (57). There is no denying this conflicting identity, only dealing with it (61).[76]

Up to this point, Okolo's argument started out from an African novel and referred to African history and African agents. Nevertheless, he repeatedly remarks that the dilemma of a contradictory self applies more widely, to *all people*. His central conclusion on violence is formulated explicitly in general anthropological terms:

> [V]iolence inhabits humans, like an evil its victim. It exhausts itself with the victim. To strain oneself in an attempt to escape from its frightful pursuits, is to let oneself be torn apart by it, as by a horde of dogs excited by the flight.
> The only way out: to hold the stick and to face the wild beast; because violence has the face of a wild beast, and human beings are its victims. (62)

One should just note that in this powerful image the wild animal that threatens the holder of the stick ... is the holder of the stick himself/herself. The contradiction of violence applies to all people, but this is admitted without the least complacency, since we, humans, are the victims.

What, then, does it mean to confront violence? Okolo explores a variety of ethics of violence.

It is conceivable to respond to the reality of violence by a radical attempt at purity. But Okolo rejects this option for it refuses to recognise the reality of violence and he sees this option as nothing better than a cop-out [*demission*] (63).

Okolo is not much more optimistic about an alternative version of purity, namely that of "involvement without compromise [*engagement sans compromission*]" (63), which consists of pursuing a course of action because it serves a great cause, and persevering independently of how much the cause itself is questioned, even by like-minded people. If the first kind of purity leaves perpetrated violence intact, the second is willing to embark on a violent course of action because it considers its cause justified beyond questioning.

Already these two rejected options of an ethic of violence indicate that Okolo is looking for a critique of work: a means by which to access forms of action.

Having looked at violence suffered, violence committed, violence allowed, violence justified—what alternative remains? In Okolo's judgement, any search for an alternative must recognise the unpleasant potential of violence that accompanies all human interaction. Okolo calls this the "rule of the game". If I follow correctly, he likens life to a game in which one is subject to an order of violence, but that allows for improvisation. From this realisation follows his understanding of playing this game: violence "reigns in fact, but does not establish itself by right, and people can overcome it by engaging fully in a circuit of relationships in which one accepts to play as well as to be played, and not to pose as a manipulative or disengaged spectator" (63). From this follows three styles of playing: the "manipulative" and the "disengaged spectator" refer to the two modes of pursuing purity, to which the only alternative, the third style, is to refuse to flee from this world to one "beyond" this compromised reality, yet without embracing this "guilt" complacently (63). The only alternative is to embark on a course of action that is open to correction. Okolo derives from Ouologuem the name "love" for this alternative praxis, but one could assent to this name only on condition of thinking of "love" as something similar to confronting a wild animal with a stick in a fight for life.

To conclude, the motivation for discussing violence was that it is an issue for both literature and real-life action. Both these forms of work demand critique or assessment. And work and critique are important to us because they refer to the interconnection between hermeneutics and praxis. Violence is the most extreme example of this connection.

Literary criticism can examine works of literature for their attempt to re-take established themes of literature. To work on literature is also to work on the tradition. Such a literary critique can identify the realism of Ouologuem's re-take only by contrasting it, for instance, with the idealism of négritude. But even so, the meaning of such critique depends on the context in which the work is produced, and that is why Okolo's reading of négritude cannot be misconstrued as a facile rebuff: négritude's "idealism" has its place as self-affirmation in the face of alienation (63–64). Similarly, Ouologuem's realism responds to the incompleteness of socio-economic development and real liberation after formal liberation (64). In both cases, what he narrates is the possibility to link with tradition or to break it: to generate tradition through re-taking. But this happens in the space of uncertainty opened by contradiction: "[e]verywhere, hermeneutics and criticism, hermeneutics and praxis give and repel each other at the same time within the tradition they constitute and in which they live" (64).

9. Philosophy, singular and universal: the ambition of Okolo's book

I selected Okolo's book as a significant contribution to African philosophical hermeneutics. As in so much of African philosophy, the question of the relation between claims to reason as universal and reason as particular is an important issue. But we cannot determine how Okolo deals with the issue of African particularity in philosophy without at the same time dealing with the question of what philosophy is for him and the objective of his book.

One thing Okolo granted ethnophilosophy and négritude: they rejected a facile equation of Western particularism with universalism (17, 63–64). But identifying African particularity turned out to be tricky: sometimes such claims actually hold only for a part of African reality; other times they apply way beyond the presumed limits of what is African (90 and see § 4.2 and § 4.3.c above). The close relation between identity—that is, particularity—and tradition has not made the situation easier. We saw that people are related to their tradition in bonds of familiarity *and* strangeness, which means that the personal or cultural identity that is embedded in tradition could thus always be fluctuating and even fragmentary or conflictual. Yet, identity is not for that reason less real (9). Moreover, many of the building blocks in Okolo's thought hold universally, either because they concern objects of study, which have universally similar traits (e.g., traits of text-like things in all cultures), or because people have similar constitutions (e.g., the hermeneutic constitution shared by all human beings).

Still, I think it is worth taking Okolo seriously when he subtitled his book: *Exploration of African Hermeneutics and Praxis*. In one way or another, the adjective "African" is neither vain nor redundant. The following citation gives us some grasp on the matter:

> The problem is finally that of philosophy itself. While affirming its *universality* and rationality, its true being is defined only within a tradition, within the *particular* interplay between the forms and contents of this tradition. Here, philosophy is fundamentally a history and not a unanimous and impersonal system of thought. It expresses the dialectic and the polemic constitutive of a given social formation. We see that it is fundamentally hermeneutic and participates in the praxis. (10, my emphasis; similarly, 45, 93)

What does this mean?

Okolo does not shy away from attributing to philosophy and reason a universal dimension,[77] but his emphasis is on particularity. This particularity is established by philosophy's relation to the philosopher's tradition. Tradition, we repeatedly see, is not simply the cultural deposit, but the fact of "being a history",[78] where history refers to the actions, the solutions to practical problems, the dealing with conflicts, in *specific* contexts. Accordingly, Africans are particular, by being what all humans are—namely hermeneutically constituted beings, confronted with a specific context of interpretation and praxis. Likewise, African philosophy is particular, by being what all philosophy is—a history of hermeneutically constituted practices. This solution will not satisfy everybody. But it is an attempt to define African particularity by steering clear of two pitfalls: fixing African identity in an a-temporal, homogenous essence, and dissolving all specificity. Okolo regionalises (even within Africa) and temporalises particularity: what is "African" has divergent, fragmentary, and even conflicting manifestations, without thereby ceasing to be African.

At the same time, Okolo remains conscious of how this particularity overlaps with others: modes of production (cf. 96), social inequalities, the living conditions of the proletariat (cf. 82), and how culture responds to political crisis (cf. 39–40). Such overlaps are no less defining of what is "African".

But why do such overlaps, especially those with some people living closer to the centra of global power, not simply neutralise African identity? Okolo's hermeneutics allows us to identify at least one reason of great significance: even granting significant similarities does not negate the dissymmetry of relations. Part of the crisis of Africa, a crisis that defines African philosophy in as far as it responds to this crisis, is exactly this dissymmetry:

> What crisis justifies our [philosophers'—EW] recourse to tradition? Here as elsewhere, the *crisis is interpreted differently*: choice between tradition and modernity; conflict between two cultures, African and European; the growth crisis of the young countries; struggle between the emerging bourgeoisie, supported by capitalist imperialism, and the exploited proletarians; etc. (40, my emphasis)

All of these issues concern the West (and other parts of the world) too, and are part of the crisis of the West, *but not in the same way* as they concern Africa.[79] And if one thinks that the response to a crisis calls for re-taking tradition, it amplifies the seriousness of the presence of Western culture in Africa. Western culture, for instance, cannot be said to be invaded by African (or another) culture in the same way as African culture is invaded. This dissymmetry is a marker of African identity, even if it applies in divergent ways in different regions, at different times, and in different social settings on the African continent.

What defines what is "African" is then the to-and-fro between the demands of a practical situation and the attempt to re-take something out of its own tradition. A similar process defines the identity of any other region.

As for African philosophy, Okolo does not divulge any reason to keep it pure, in the sense that it should be stripped of all foreign influence. On the one hand, his thought does not require a quest for purity, because the "Africanity" is maintained by the material, practical situation and traditional basis. On the other hand, such a quest is not desirable: if other traditions can furnish African philosophers with useful material in their search for suitable responses to their practical situation, then so be it. That Africans in this way become inheritors of plural traditions is an inevitable outcome. One should, therefore, not construe these plural affiliations simply as intellectual (self-)colonisation: after all, what is borrowed from Western philosophy is subject to re-taking under the conditions in which African philosophy is practised. The importation involved in such borrowing is also subject to Africanisation (that is, unless such philosophical borrowing consists of mindless repetition, or subjection to foreign impositions, but that would fall short of Okolo's understanding of philosophy).

Finally, the philosophy that comes out of these processes, if they are African, are meant to be of value to Africans. But more! If the hermeneutic constitution of humans is a universal structure, this means that the specificity of the African condition is also a valid point of access to our understanding of humanity in general. Therefore, the work of African philosophers holds the potential of valuable instruction beyond their own traditions and contexts. This is then the implication of maintaining simultaneously that "there exist only hermeneutics of particular traditions" and that Okolo contributes to a "general theory of hermeneutics"[80] (43, 10[81]). One may say that Okolo's understanding of African identity and philosophy is *introvert*, in that it is primarily concerned with the practical demands of the crises of the African continent, but *extrovert*,[82] in the sense that it has the capacity to help us understand also other people and help them to understand themselves (7). This dual orientation of identity and philosophy holds also when Okolo engages European philosophers, because "by confronting these with the unexpected difficulties of a fragmentary and oral culture and tradition, [we] make our contribution to the problem of hermeneutics and tradition [generally]" (35).[83]

From the beginning of this chapter we saw that Okolo offers his hermeneutics in the service of praxis. Praxis informs the hermeneutic re-taking of tradition, by which people self-identify and mobilise. In this sense, particularity remains of decisive importance: "The discourse on development has no reference point but the requirement of truth and the constraints of times and places, times and places that are always *singular*. This amounts to a *particular* moral situation" (87). Still, it would be contrary to Okolo's whole design to establish a hasty equation between particularity and Africanity. The context of practice and normative judgement may be more local (relevant to a country, region, suburb, or specific sector of society), or more global (encompassing concerns that people beyond the limits of Africa share); in some cases, may simply include the whole of humanity (58). In each case, how people identify the particular context of action and the normative dimensions requiring our attention is subject to shifting interpretations and negotiation of conflicting accounts. The ultimate aim of Okolo's book is to make a philosophical contribution to clarifying this task.

10. Conclusion

As much as Okolo writes about interpretation, proverbs, philosophy, and the like, one concern subtends his entire book: in Africa things cannot continue as they are. An acute awareness of urgency and crisis drives *Pour une philosophie*. But it is a book on resourcefulness and the possible ways to act. It is a book about finding and making one's way. This is what hermeneutics is tasked to clarify.

The crises that African countries confront are subjectively experienced, but have an objective socio-political, economic, and intellectual reality. Such crises solicit responses. That is why Okolo's hermeneutics is centrally concerned with human action or, rather, "praxis", which is the active response to crises. Hermeneutics is not that response, but serves to prepare praxis by clarifying how praxis is shaped by tradition, yet always open to improvisation in critical contexts. In this way, hermeneutics opens a view on praxis beyond the confines of the politics of development.

Specifically, hermeneutics engages with all text-like phenomena—theories, actions, elements of tradition—and the reading thereof. Reading is an act of giving meaning to such texts, and opens to a wide array of possible creative appropriations, called re-taking. The work of reading and re-taking is subtended by the interpreter-agent's worldview. In fact, worldview, ideology, and identity are three outgrowths of tradition.

Tradition consists of both text-like cultural deposits and the spiritual reactivation thereof. The reactivation occurs through reading and re-taking, which is the way in which cultural heritage is transmitted. This means that worldview, ideology, identity, and tradition are neither static things, nor insubstantial—they are forever dynamic, mobilised by the ways people identify and re-take their heritage in divergent and changing ways, resulting in fragmentary and conflicting, but also overlapping, identities and cultures. The demands of context motivate this interpretive dynamic, which, through praxis, stakes a claim on the future.

Practice, hermeneutics, and tradition form, then, a conceptual whole that is not only *what is spoken about*, but a description of complex *shifting perspectives from which* people think and act. Hermeneutics is not elevated to the height of an ultimate authority, but is a help in analysis and diagnosis (two meanings of critique, which we will again encounter in the discussion of Mudimbe).

How this double critical potential of hermeneutics functions in practice is illustrated in Okolo's assessment of ethnophilosophy: hermeneutics can identify its weaknesses while recognising its merits. Over and above its critical potential, the constructive potential of hermeneutics can be demonstrated by the way it deals with the wisdom of oral tradition, of which proverbs are an important part. Studying the oral usage of proverbs demonstrates what it means to think from tradition.

The double critical function of hermeneutics applies to the assessment of action too. This holds for action as represented in literature, but also action in practice. In both cases, violence serves as an extreme case.

Okolo's ambition is to present a view on hermeneutics that is a universally valid critique of reason, but which is specifically African, not by being a pure exemplar of an immutable identity, but by creatively re-taking of its own traditions in search of appropriate solutions to specific crises.

Select annotated bibliography

Amin, Samir. *Le Développement inégal.* Paris: Minuit, 1973.

Amin, Samir and Kosta Vergopoulos. *La question paysanne et le capitalisme.* Paris: Anthropos-Idep, 1974.
    These are the two books by Amin that Okolo uses in *Pour une philosophie de la culture et du développement.*

Diagne, Souleymane Bachir. "Négritude". *Stanford Encyclopedia of Philosophy*, Edward N. Zalta (ed.). https://plato.stanford.edu/archives/sum2018/entries/negritude/. Revised version published 23 May 2018. Last accessed 3 December 2022.

  This is a more contemporary and sympathetic reading of négritude.

Mudimbe, Valentin-Yves. *L'autre face du royaume. Une introduction à la critique des langages en folie*. Lausanne: L'âge d'homme, 1973.

  The most important work of Mudimbe that Okolo uses in *Pour une philosophie*.

Njoh-Mouellé, Ebénézer. "Sagesse des proverbes et développement". *Zaïre-Afrique* 15, no. 92 (February 1975): 107–116.

  Njoh-Mouellé's work is extensive, but this essay plays a major role in Okolo's reflection on proverbs.

Okolo, Okonda. *Tradition et destin. Essai sur la philosophie herméneutique de P. Ricœur, M. Heidegger, et H. G. Gadamer*. Lubumbashi: Université Nationale du Zaïre, 1979.

  This is Okolo's doctoral thesis and a significant engagement with three major authors of European philosophical hermeneutics.

Okolo, Okonda. *Pour une philosophie de la culture et du développement. Recherches d'herméneutique et de praxis africaines*. Kinshasa: Presses Universitaires du Zaïre, 1986.

Okolo, Okonda. "Afrikanische Heidegger-Rezeption und -Kritik". In *Zur Philosophischen Aktualität Heideggers 3: Im Spiegel Der Welt: Sprache, Übersetzung, Auseinandersetzung*, edited by Dietrich Papenfuss and Otto Pöggeler. Frankfurt: Klostermann, 1992, pp. 264–272.

  An interesting overview of the African reception of Heidegger, elements of which are referenced in my chapter here.

Okolo, Okonda. *Hegel et l'Afrique. Thèses critiques et dépassements*. Argenteuil: Cercle herméneutique, 2010.

Okolo, Okonda. "From the Hermeneutics of Traditions to the History of Ideas in the Context of Orality". *Nokoko* 6 (2017): 49–80.

  An invaluable retrospective by Okolo on his lifework.

Okolo, Okonda and Jacques Ngangala Balade Tongamba. *Introduction à l'histoire des idées dans le contexte de l'oralité. Théorie et méthode avec application sur l'Afrique traditionnelle*. Louvain-la-Neuve: Academia-L'Harmattan, 2018.

  This book explicitly resumes the reflections on orality and the history of ideas from *Pour une philosophie de la culture et du développement*.

Nkombe Oleko, *Métaphore et métonymie dans les symboles parémiologiques. L'Intersubjectivité dans les "Proverbes Tetela"*. Kinshasa: Faculté de théologie catholique, [1975] 1979.

  This classical study is the second major point of reference in Okolo's reflection on proverbs.

Ouologuem, Yambo. *Le devoir de la violence*. Paris: Seuil, 1968.

  The controversy regarding this novel is not relevant to my chapter. For a contemporary contextualisation, interpretation, and appraisal, see Romuald Fonkoua, "Le devenir écrivain de Yambo Ouologuem: Négrifier la littérature". *Fabula/Les colloques*, L'œuvre de Yambo Ouologuem. Un carrefour d'écritures (1968–2018). http://www.fabula.org/colloques/document6016.php. published 18 April 2019. Last accessed 2 December 2022.

CHAPTER 5

Implicit hermeneutics: origins, constitutions, projects

In the introductory chapter, I presented the landscape of hermeneutics as prior overview studies present it. These overviews have given divergent and even conflicting perspectives on hermeneutics, but it is clear that there is too much evidence confirming the existence and significance of philosophical hermeneutics in African philosophy to ignore it. The best procedure therefore seemed to me to present African hermeneutics and simultaneously show its variety. The preceding three chapters have therefore been devoted to painting a picture of this variety using three key works by authors who explicitly described their own work as a contribution to philosophical hermeneutics: Okere, Serequeberhan, and Okolo. A consideration of their important works, side by side, provides a good sense of the main themes and insights of philosophical hermeneutics. In these works, we saw the importance that their authors attached to the general human ability of *understanding*, and also to the capability to engage such understanding through *interpretation.* Both understanding and interpretation have a traditional dimension: they are contingent on people's culture, history, and socio-political context. But these authors also point towards how understanding and interpretation serve to develop critical views on what is inherited or given, and in this way help to open the way to a more constructive future. In short, these three authors confirm, in essence, the provisional description that I offered of hermeneutics in Chapter 1, § 1, although they develop their vision of hermeneutics in three distinctly different ways.

However, the overviews that I discussed in Chapter 1, § 2, also taught us to look for hermeneutics where it is not explicitly presented as such. For this reason, in the current chapter, I look at five authors who may be considered implicit hermeneuts. They fit this profile, because some of the central questions on which they worked fit into the general picture of human understanding and interpretation. Considering the salient points summarised from Okere, Serequeberhan, and Okolo just now, it is not difficult to see how reflection on language and history, on tradition and the construction

182 CHAPTER 5

of the sciences, and on the uses of philosophy and translation offers promising avenues for further reflection. These are then also the main issues that place Cheikh Anta Diop (from Senegal, b. 1923, d. 1986), Sophie Oluwole (from Nigeria, b. 1935, d. 2018), V. Y. Mudimbe (from the Democratic Republic of the Congo, b. 1941, d. 2025), Fabien Eboussi Boulaga (from Cameroon, b. 1934, d. 2018), and Souleymane Bachir Diagne (from Senegal, b. 1955) on our agenda. Each of them opens up a new perspective on the liberatory vocation of interpretation as we encounter it in African philosophy.

I start each section with a rationale for including the author in question, and an indication of which texts I explore. Then, as in the other chapters, each discussion introduces the author's work, but also leads to more interpretative and critical engagement with it. In conclusion, the salient points of these authors' contributions to hermeneutics are highlighted and further points of interest or critique are offered. To facilitate reflection, I end this chapter with a summary of the five authors' contribution.

1. History versus essentialism as a resource for action in the present: Cheikh Anta Diop

Alerte sous les tropiques[1] is a volume of Cheikh Anta Diop's early essays, which were published from 1948 to 1960. My hypothesis in approaching this volume is that it provides us with a condensed view of what hermeneutics in a Diopian sense is as it gradually takes shape. Let us see how he turns to three foci that are typically associated with hermeneutics: language, history, action.

1.1. *From language, through history, to action*

Diop recalls that he was sensitised to the importance of language from an early age (133). The first texts in this volume offer a lexical and phonetic comparison of Wolof (which he wrote as "Valaf", as he explains on page 19) with other African languages, and with French. His linguistic study was fleshed out by means of analyses of word formation and syntax.

Diop deduces from the linguistic similarities that he traces that the relevant language groups share a common history, and complements this deduction with a hypothesis on the reasons for the separation of these language groups (18, 25). His synchronic, descriptive approach to languages opens the way for diachronic insights. Since linguistic commonalities and differences reflect fluctuating social relations of relative influence, mixing, and tensions (cf. 19), diachronic insights into linguistics allow a glimpse into the history of the broader symbolic order (arts, religions, institutions) and social *history* more broadly. Diop is at his best[2] in his demonstration of how to find elements of the historical constitution of the carriers of meaning (language, institutions, science, art), which stretches as far as the social conditions under which people lived: relations of domination, the contexts of plural cultures, the way religious and political powers are relatively oriented, and so on. Attention to such factors allows for an account of cultural mixing (cf., for example, 26, 27, 30). Moreover, his appreciation of "historical accidents [*le hasard des circonstances historiques*]" (29/*29), logically steers him away from a metaphysics of history, and in the direction of a hermeneutics of historicity (in other words, a general theorising on how people belong to history, to tradition, etc.).

Thus, we see that in studying language and history, Diop's attention shifts organically to *socio-political* considerations. Establishing linguistic similarities serves as a first step in overcoming exaggerated "ethnic barriers" (52). More generally, his history of African languages and the social factors that shaped the relations between them gives an idea of the social function of history in creating an African identity in the "sense of being a historical community [*un sentiment de leur communauté historique*]" (115/*119, translation modified).

Throughout, Diop's pursuit of accurate description is coupled with an attempt to assess or critique (in the double sense used by Okolo) socio-political developments. This can be seen clearly when Diop reflects on the possibility of and means to an African renaissance.

- What is described as cultural mixing or borrowing can be critiqued as subservient filiation or even "contamination" (cf. 34, an example is given in 40–41). For my purposes, I retain from this only his later suggestion (cf. 43) that the core of cultural "contamination" is *imposition*. The implication is that "non-contamination" or "health" does not lie in purity, but has to be conceived in terms of freedom. This view can accommodate a cultural politics of relative purity and mixing, and need not be oriented to an essentialist view of culture.[3]
- What is described as writing according to given standards of excellence can be critiqued as extraversion (cf. 34).[4] He comes back to this point repeatedly in his reflections on education: the colonial language

politics imposed on the African youth and students to write and think in their second or third language means that "we must express ourselves in a foreign language [*expression*] or keep quiet" (35/*35).[5] This point can easily be elaborated to cover power imbalances between urbanites and rural people, rich and poor, and so forth. The flipside of this critique is Diop's insistence on the promotion of local languages for a real African renaissance.

The question of the possibilities of a "renaissance" is a period-specific articulation of a specific question, namely the requirements for a culture and its adherents to flourish in a given context. When Diop documents the existing strengths of Valaf, in the face of ignorance about it, and examines the means by which to advance the language (education, dissemination, literature, the formation of technical vocabulary, a historical consciousness,[6] etc.), he poses the question of flourishing. Here he is working in the same terrain as Okolo, namely the hermeneutic tension between the "already" and "not yet" of specific people in a specific socio-historical context.

The *means* to flourish are quite diverse. In connection with his preceding discussions on language, education, and history, Diop identifies diverse aspects of traditional African culture as "springs [*ressorts*]" for the present (44/*44, translation modified). However, he never reduces the means at our disposal in a culturalist way. In fact, few authors advance a holistic approach (cf. 133) as well as Diop does. His emphatic call for scientific and technological modernisation (42) can even be considered to amount to a call for intensified cultural blending, when it does not simply imply merely taking over elements of other cultures.[7]

In fact, not all work in the symbolic order is relevant for social practice or well-being. Diop distinguishes between *speculation* and *thought* about a situation. Speculation starts and ends in abstract ideas (81). Situated thought starts from what is concrete, but sets aside the time and effort required to clarify complexity, in order to return to concrete situations with a deeper understanding and a more acute awareness of the stakes (82). This view of situated thought is typical of the coordination of action and interpretation in hermeneutics. Hence, the effort of interpretation—hermeneutic work—is not limited to cultural matters such as language, literature, or religion, but also to energy provision, health care, economics, political strategy, and so on (cf. 82–99). The care needed to develop the material conditions for industrialisation (113, 114) is not in conflict with the creation of an "ideological and cultural superstructure" (110/*114) of language and history—the two belong together.

But in order to flourish, people need an impetus, a source for initiative, among the general population, which can only come from people's intensive engagement with their context as a whole. Thinking about the most urgent political needs of his time, in 1952, Diop identifies fourteen aspects of an awareness (*prise de conscience*) of the situation that are necessary. These aspects are then again explicitly articulated in terms of meaning and language performance and an understanding of one's own agency, situated in a specific context in which action could have both meaning and impact. The core of the personal and cultural goods required to start confronting the current situation is already present. However, one also has to reckon with power relations *within* the collective struggle. And thus people have to face a social, political, and economic context of colonial exploitation. Quite clearly Diop's call for preparation to respond to the present situation combines the terms of political initiative with the task of rigorous interpretation: interpreting the colonial-capitalist set-up in fine detail ("every single item of equipment or materials we use in our day to day existence derives from this exploitation", 46/*48), and interpreting the meaning of present action—that is, the practical meaning or intention—in the light of a coming liberation (for example, cf. 68), which is explicitly not a return to a lost paradise that never existed.

In the longer term, aiming culture at action requires working on "national culture". This generally shared symbolic order is harmed by colonisation, but it also has potential for collective resistance against colonisation. From this is derived Diop's advocacy of a politics of a symbolic order, conducted by means of education, science, and history. The link between action and symbolics is most intimate in one's self-understanding as an agent, or "self-confidence" (48), a point we encounter again clearly in Eboussi Boulaga. Indeed, the prime significance of Diop's Egyptology consists in reaffirming African self-confidence through the "idea of a black Egypt having civilised the entire earth" (48/*51).[8] This impulse to self-confidence emanates not only from realising the grandeur of this past civilisation, but equally from the commonality of that past. This is the glorious pole of African identity. The miserable pole consists of identification with the experience of an imperialist imposition of economies of extraction, a fate common to African countries (cf. 57, a point also seen, for instance, in Serequeberhan).

1.2. *Aspects of a Diopian hermeneutics*

Following on from this overview of themes from Diop's early thought, let us make more explicit his contribution to hermeneutics. I start out from a formal consideration. The first texts in *Alterte sous les tropiques* are clearly youth writings, following right after Diop's earliest work in the human sciences. He himself typifies early writings as "childish [*enfantines*]" (133). This is one of the reasons for why a number of his claims are no longer of interest. However, I did not decide to use this volume for anecdotal or biographical reasons. It is an essential point that the complex of issues in this volume, and the urgency to work on them, emerges from the life experience of a young man[9] independently from the scholarly tradition of European hermeneutics. Complex hermeneutic problems emerge from real-life experience (of which scholarly studies may be a later component). In a variety of ways, people give expression to life experience and thereby intensify their engagement with those problems. Philosophical hermeneutics is a second-order reflection that strives for the most sophisticated and learned expression, and struggles with specific questions. But hermeneutics equally pursues the excavation of the most spontaneous human experience, which is why the "infantile" concerns of a young author may well be of philosophical interest. This is a first and significant dimension of Diop's hermeneutics: it does not *start* as a second-order reflection on academic disciplines, but rather grows from the existence and concerns of human beings. The fact that he himself could look back on this work as limited is part of the fact of a shifting perspective that is integral to hermeneutic thinking all the time. This reformulation of Diop's position mirrors his own insistence on situated thought, and rejection of abstract speculation.

One defining aspect of Diop's thought fits in perfectly with this first finding: as theoretical as his reflection on identity and history, culture and renaissance may be, it is rooted in detailed study (whether that involves textual analysis, calculation, or another kind of study), and strives to return to the context of urgent socio-political problems of his time. Diop's hermeneutics is a philosophy that links these dissimilar concerns in a broad reflective movement. Accordingly, there is no contradiction between claiming "1. That they [Africans] must fight for ideas and not for persons; 2. That the fate of a people is first and foremost in its own hands" (45/*47). These two declarations are intended to be mutually reinforcing.

Thinking about the elements of culture or about the components of agency and the context of action is not abandoned, but it is intensified by studying their history. I highlight the Diop who realises this, at the expense of the one who keeps one foot in essentialist thinking.[10] Diop's thought is hermeneutic in as much as the descriptions of "blending" and "becoming" win out against lazy essentialism. Recognising this conflict in Diop's work also equips one to critique him: the contemporary reader does not have to follow him on the detail of his historical reconstructions or geopolitical analysis (see for example, 57–63)—moreover, hermeneutic engagement with these issues today calls for an update. But the crucial point is that any correction of Diop's views would have to follow the same methodological route, but would have to do it better than Diop did. In this sense, Diop's commitment to situated thought, which is characteristic of his hermeneutics, serves as a tool of critique, in both the sense of a study of constitution and of a means of assessment. Any critique of Diop would have to outperform him in the same game.

* * *

In conclusion, Diop's work connects the study of language, history, and action in a broad interpretative framework that is motivated by concerns arising from his socio-political context. It aims at enriching the ability to take initiative in that context. It is attentive to the conditions for, and impediments of, free, flourishing life. His hermeneutics is a critique. He submits his own work to two criteria that his single hermeneutic framework allows him to coordinate: that of the highest academic standards and its ability to feed back into courses of action with a view to liberation. Failing to respect both criteria would either hollow out science to become uninformed activism, or detach research from real-life human concerns.

2. **Critical traditionalism and contemporary social problems: Sophie Oluwole**

A number of general considerations call for an exploration of Sophie Oluwole's lifework from the perspective of her possible contribution to philosophical hermeneutics. When she typifies her own work as "critical traditionalist" ("Africa", 101[11]), she invites her reader to understand her philosophical efforts as situated in the tension between an acknowledgement of the value of cultural heritage, and a reflective judgement of that heritage and its value for contemporary problems. In working out the details of this position, she frequently emphasises that she is not interested in a social-scientific study of tradition, or of her contemporary situation, but is specifically pursuing a *philosophical* approach to both (for example, "Philosophy and Oral Tradition", 100, "Culture, Gender", 95). At least in one place, she seems to characterise her own work as true to a "hermeneutic orientation" ("Africa", 103).[12] True to the tendency in philosophical hermeneutics already described elsewhere in my book, Oluwole advances a position on the nature of African philosophy that is situated in her rejection of both ethnophilosophy and capitulation to Western philosophy (specifically in "Philosophy and Oral Tradition", 99). Here I would like to explore the specificity of her philosophical position as a possible contribution to philosophical hermeneutics. For this purpose, I follow indications from a number of her books and essays (see the select annotated bibliography for this chapter for more detail).

2.1. Orality as the core of African philosophy

Twin ideas reappear throughout Oluwole's work: one should not philosophise in Africa without having established what it means to philosophise as an African, and one cannot establish what African philosophy is without considering the philosophy of precolonial African oral traditions. Admittedly, she sometimes grants in passing that there may be other avenues to follow ("Philosophy and Oral Tradition", 118), but her own philosophical energy is devoted to this project. Interestingly, in opposition to most authors studied in my book, Oluwole's understanding of what makes African philosophy specifically African is its oral tradition,[13] and explicitly *not* the common experience of slavery or colonisation.

In a way, Oluwole stands with one foot in the earliest debates on African philosophy, in that she sets out to demonstrate that there really was precolonial African philosophy. She expends considerable effort in describing and theorising the modality of philosophising in traditions of oral Yoruba wisdom. This requires a study of these orally transmitted "texts", so a specific methodology is required to examine them as a porthole to a living philosophical tradition ("Philosophy and Oral Tradition", xv). The difficulty of this point needs to be appreciated: it requires the scholar, while studying this corpus, to reflect at the same time on what "philosophy" would mean in terms of this same corpus. This is required to avoid (a) testing the corpus using a foreign definition or (b) identifying something that is not philosophy as if it is ("Philosophy and Oral Tradition", xvi). This requires a to-and-fro between the material studied and the question of study, which is indeed typical of hermeneutic procedure.[14] The scholar has to work, as it were, from inside the oral texts, but equipped with a provisional or hypothetical definition of philosophy[15] (cf. also *Socrates and Orunmila*, 8) to establish whether there is any evidence of something that may qualify as philosophy "in any meaningful sense" ("Philosophy and Oral Tradition", xvi, similarly, xviii, xix).

This project requires studying the material in its social setting, taking into account the "custodians" of this tradition (poets, singers, priests) and the form of expression, genres (cf. "Philosophy and Oral Tradition", 4, 13–15) and the practices by which they developed their critical claims. Furthermore, this requires attentiveness to language, oral and written, in the rich variety of their forms ("Philosophy and Oral Tradition", 1), and knowledge of the particular language of the material studied. But working on the language has to be related to the generation of thought (cf. "Philosophy and Oral Tradition" 2). These scholarly requirements already broaden Oluwole's view beyond a lot of work on oral tradition in African philosophy, since it includes being accompanied by a rich anthropology of writing and memorising technologies. These requirements also help to see how varieties of thought could emerge from oral and writing practices (learning, improving, contradicting[16]). Throughout, she remains attentive to ways in which writing, for instance, could narrow down, rather than stimulate thought ("Philosophy and Oral Tradition", 7). In sum, this means that her approach is not committed to an essentialist attribution of equal excellence to all members of society (as rash ethnophilosophy often does). Rather, she can complement her examination of thinking practices with reflection on the real-life advantages of oral and written communication for the transmission of ideas, and the effects of authority on the creation of ideas in both cases (cf. "Philosophy and Oral Tradition", 8–9).

Nowhere does she have to commit to extravagant claims about the excellence of tradition. Her starting point is a demonstration of the existence of precolonial oral philosophy, and that point is not undermined by later judgements of the quality of that philosophy—as she correctly states in "Oruka's Mission", "an inadequate philosophy is philosophy still" (159).

Yet, in her own work, she takes an important additional step in attempting to demonstrate the quality and contemporary value of traditional philosophy.

Having referred to Oruka, it is worth pointing out the proximity of Oluwole's work to his sage philosophy project, a question to which she turned explicitly. This proximity resides in looking for philosophy that exists in Africa independently of Western influence, or is at least very "deeply rooted in the traditional African setting" ("Oruka's Mission", 155), where such philosophy is not the expression of generally held views among an ethnic group, but rather philosophical in formulating the speaker's own personal views, which may or may not be in agreement with those of others. As for the differences, since Oruka works with fieldwork surveys, the philosophers he studied are named contemporary individuals, while Oluwole's studies on classical traditions refer to nameless types of persons, reconstructed from the practice of the traditions that she studies (cf. "Oruka's Mission", 158).

The most accomplished exposition of this project by Oluwole is her book *Socrates and Orunmila*. According to her own explanation, the "literary corpus which is the major source of information on the life and views of *Orunmila*, is the expansive Yoruba oral tradition[17] popularly known as *Ifa*, an edifice conventionally treated as [the] Yoruba religious divination system" (*Socrates and Orunmila*, 12). But this work of comparison also opens up a broader perspective on intellectual cultures, as Oluwole demonstrates in her chapter "Culture, Nationalism and Philosophy". Here she distinguishes general culture from intellectual culture: "An intellectual culture is therefore antithetical to bigotry, fanaticism, narrowness of mind or belief" ("Culture, Nationalism and Philosophy", 23, "Philosophy and Oral Tradition", 103). However, as with culture generally, intellectual culture is plural, which means that cultural expressions other than one's own can be observed and appraised only from one's own perspective. This raises the question of cultural bias: what is irrational to one person may be rational to another. That is why Oluwole advocates inter-cultural philosophy, and that this be practiced in a spirit of "Philosophical/Rational Relativism" rather than "Philosophical/Rational Absolutism" ("Philosophy and Oral Tradition", 119). Nevertheless, a condition for entering into such a dialogue is that both sides need to recognise "[o]ral literature as an expression of an authentic African intellectual culture" ("Culture, Nationalism and Philosophy", 35).[18]

Now, at the same time that Oluwole explicitly rejects the idea that one should attempt a kind of *return* to an original African philosophy ("Culture, Nationalism and Philosophy", 41[19]), her intention in studying old traditions is always to steer reflection to the present, and to the challenges that are posed for the future. The same holds for the work of comparison and dialogue, since this spontaneously opens up the question of the power relations between the societies in which different philosophical traditions are transmitted. With this fact in mind, one can approach Oluwole's contribution to Kolawole's *Introduction to Social and Political Philosophy*. Her contribution, entitled "The Cultural Enslavement of the African Mind", is still anchored by her understanding of oral philosophical tradition, but sheds new light on its nature and relevance.

She insists that the question of an exact understanding of African culture, even in its remotest expressions, is not only a question of scholarly interest, but must share in the incomplete resistance against symbolic violence and oppression. These are questions of a struggle against misrecognition: responding to the question "what are African traditions really like?" is a means by which to approach the question "who are Africans?" ("The Cultural Enslavement", 99[20]). If, as Oluwole argues, it is incorrect to deny that Africans have a traditional intellectual culture and a philosophy, it is equally incorrect to construe the predominance of oral over written culture as a form of backwardness. And if that is granted, I would conclude, there is also no reason to minimise African agency and responsibility (which is not the same thing as underestimating the severity of the political and economic problems Africans have to face).[21] And thus we can see how reflection on tradition opens up reflection on contemporary social and political issues. Accordingly, Oluwole establishes a link between ancient oral traditions and questions of education, development, gender, democracy, and so forth.

Formal *education* of young Africans forms part of a broader drive towards *development*. Both education and development are practical interventions in everyday culture. But instead of simply submitting to imported models and standards for these interventions, one has to reflect first: "What exactly is the nature of this development and why must African youths be asked to run after it?" ("The Cultural Enslavement", 103). A more prudent and context-sensitive education should aim "to develop in the African child the attitude and ability to initiate, critically examine, analyse and synthesize different elements of African intellectual heritage and blend what is set in it with what is relevant in other people's cultures" ("The Cultural Enslavement", 104).

Likewise, while recognising that *gender* inequality is a problem in Nigeria and more generally in Africa (and including philosophy, "Africa", 96, 104), Oluwole discards a response that would consist in turning to Western forms of feminism as a starting point. The specificity of African feminist philosophy resides in its presupposing "the existence of some clearly identifiable worldviews and philosophical positions in which claims about women and of principles that ought to guide their relationships with men have been made" ("Africa", 96). From such a position, the exaggerated patriarchal images of women in traditional and contemporary Africa—a substantial part of which is a Western-imposed colonial heritage[22]—can be undone. The task of dismantling patriarchy in Africa is thus paired with a critique of Western chauvinism (and of Western hypocrisy about its own contemporary sexism, cf. "Culture, Gender", 98, 117). By contrast, in "Culture, Gender", Owulole develops reflections directly from oral tradition, which in essence highlights "male–female complementarity" ("Culture, Gender", 117). Although "Culture, Gender" is not devoid of qualifying comments on certain claims in tradition, these comments do not go as far as Oluwole does in "Africa", where she states more candidly that "[f]eminist philosophy must challenge the basic African assumptions about the nature of reality, man, woman, and knowledge such that they can critically examine the intellectual edifice on which African types of sexism are or were based" ("Africa", 106).

A final example of Oluwole's turn to contemporary issues is her treatment of democratic *governance*. In fact, she distinguishes between (positive) governance and (negative) government:

> Governance when interpreted as state management means the administration of society in ways that will improve the standard of living of citizens as well as promote individual and group interests and aspirations. Government understood and practised as mere authority to exercise force or control on the people may ignore this social responsibility. ("Democracy and Indigenous Governance", 419)[23]

Democracy is not a form of government. To be worthy of its name, democracy has to refer to more than just the fact that non-military personnel hold the positions of government (cf. "Democracy and Indigenous Governance",

420). It evokes the "principles"—"justice, freedom, equity and liberty"—according to which a country is governed, whatever its constitution may be, and assesses how well that governing is done ("Democracy and Indigenous Governance", 420). If one considers governance in this way, it is possible to demonstrate that the difference between governance and government is not only reflected in the languages of Nigeria, but that traditional culture already institutionalised aspects of the principles of democracy (cf. "Democracy and Indigenous Governance", 420–421). These principles include a division of ruling power, the selection of competent leaders, institutionalised checks and balances of power, decision-making through consensus formation, and others. Furthermore, Oluwole can then identify material from oral tradition that supports the right to life, to property, to work, to free movement, equality before the law, the right to a fair trial, women's, children's, and adults' rights and respect for women, the right to political participation, the "rights of slaves" [sic], and reciprocal responsibilities between diverse social groups ("Democracy and Indigenous Governance", 424–429).

While I recognise the significance of restoring our view of traditional societies and undo the symbolic violence inflicted on them, it is less clear what the turn to tradition contributes to contemporary political issues that we did not know about or adhere to before. In addition, in Oluwole's attempts to provide insight into contemporary problems with reference to her knowledge of ancient tradition, she sometimes acknowledges some reservations about her qualifications to do so. Thus, she claims that *as a philosopher* her competence resides in assessing what is *said* about social matters, rather than what is *done* by social role players (cf. "Democracy and Indigenous Governance", 423). Elsewhere she delimits the role of *philosophy* in feminism, as broadly construed: "Philosophy is a concern with human thought rather than a concern with the direct analysis of social actions" ("Africa", 107, also "Culture, Gender", 95).

2.2. *Strengths and weaknesses of Oluwole's hermeneutics*

In this discussion, I have tried to render the basic problem and approach of Sophie Oluwole's philosophy. Next, I would like to synthesise her specific contribution to philosophical hermeneutics. I do so in two steps. First, I look at a number of weaknesses in her philosophy, an issue I have thus far bracketed out. Then I offer a few comments on its strengths.

My reason for turning to the weaknesses of her philosophy is not scholarly honesty alone, but also that these failings are hermeneutically instructive. I suggest that each of these points could be attributed to a slip in hermeneutic vigilance and that we could thus refine our understanding of philosophical hermeneutics by paying due attention to them.

First, Oluwole neglects the state of research on her own domain of specialisation, the oral traditions of Africa, when she claims that "[t]here has been no direct and serious study of African oral texts and societies to establish most claims about the existence and style of African philosophy" ("Philosophy and Oral Tradition", 100). In fact, work on proverbs by Nkombe Oleko predates her own work by more than two decades. She also misses the complexity of reflection on the performative aspect of proverb usage in oral culture as we have seen, for instance, in the work of Njoh-Mouellé or Okolo.[24] Taking more cognisance of this prior research would have helped her to guard against harvesting ideas on human rights directly from proverbs. She cites, for instance, the proverb, "It is understandable that the slave[] runs, it is equally understandable that the owner looks for him/her" ("Democracy and Indigenous Governance", 427), and deduces from it nothing more than the idea that slaves had rights. Instead, she could have considered how the usage of such a proverb by a slave owner could easily have functioned as condoning slave ownership.[25] Generally the lack of attention to the socio-political usage and implications of the cited proverbs undermines Oluwole's argument for their contemporary relevance.

Second, one often gets the impression that Oluwole considers (ancient) traditional culture to belong naturally to all *contemporary* Africans, as when she opines: "Many blacks were consequently never taught anything about *their own* culture at school" ("Philosophy and Oral Tradition", 17, my emphasis). I obviously do not deny the fact that in African schools many children do not learn about African traditions. However, Oluwole misunderstands the way in which human beings acquire culture. A cultural heritage that has not been transmitted to me, and that I have not actively received, cannot be called *mine*, no matter how much it made up part of the most intimate existential self-understanding of my parents. Children who have not learned that tradition have instead acquired other aspects of culture, whether that refers to learning through formal schooling, or learning how to survive on the street. That is *their* real culture. Claiming that they did not receive their only true and valid culture trivialises the cultural formation that children have acquired and insufficiently addresses the question of their overall schooling. Oluwole should rather be more precise and say that the children have not learned *her* culture,[26] and then argue why that is a comparative loss to them and to the broader society. This also implies that *all* philosophising on the basis of a presumed cultural treasure has to be complemented by reflection on what it means to think from people's de facto culture. It also requires reflection on the politics of culture acquisition in education that separates de facto culture and a particular cultural ideal. My point is not in any way to deny the tragedy of a loss of cultural treasures through an interruption of chains of transmission, but to emphasise the need to understand what we mean by referring to any human being as a *cultured* being.

Third, Oluwole fails to develop a hermeneutics of the present and its problems on a par with her requirements for a hermeneutics of oral tradition. Sometimes one has the impression that in turning to traditional wisdom, she also turns to traditional society, for which she gives advice, leaving most issues of contemporary urbanised Africans untouched. And when she does touch on these contemporary issues, her comments tend to neglect the hermeneutic effort to connect precolonial wisdom with urban post-independence reality. For that reason, her comments are often superficial, uninformed, and unhelpful (cf. "Culture, Gender", 112). At other times, a spirit of apologetics wins over one that recognises the tensions in tradition and even what requires contemporary critique of tradition from us. Although she mostly escapes the pitfall of unanimism (explicitly rejected in "Philosophy and Oral Tradition", 99), as in her discussion on "paradoxes and apparent contradictions" in traditional wisdom ("Culture, Gender", 111), she attributes a kind of authority to traditional culture that is reminiscent of an ethnophilosophical style of thinking. When the debate finally shifts to contemporary issues (as in "Culture, Gender", 120), one can hardly see why the detour through traditional culture was necessary. Finally, she does not refrain from essentialising the West (cf. on sexism in "Culture, Gender", 96–98), and she also sometimes embraces a very uncritically traditionalist stance of cultural purity. She refers, for instance, to "[o]ral literature as an expression of an *authentic* African intellectual culture" ("Culture, Nationalism and Philosophy", 35, my emphasis) and elsewhere discards cultural mixing *in toto*: "[T]he authentic African alternative has now been greatly *polluted* by Western views" ("Culture, Gender", 119, my emphasis).[27]

Let me summarise in a more positive formulation the insights on hermeneutics that Oluwole's weaknesses help us to identify: academic self-understanding improves from the widest scholarly contextualisation; language utterances ("texts") need to be interpreted in the context of practices; humans as the understanding and interpreting beings that philosophise and for whom we philosophise have to be understood in the full complexity of their culturedness and traditionality (or their relative absence). Whether one approaches contemporary socio-political problems from tradition or by contemporary social scientific means, this endeavour cannot work without a proper hermeneutics of contemporary society and of one's interpretative efforts; tradition needs to be appropriated critically and not as an authority to be protected; essentialism necessarily warps our understanding of matters and skews our judgement. These are the significant points of hermeneutics that must be considered as visible as an absence in Oluwole's work.

But since her work is more than the weaknesses, let us now turn to the strengths, which are equally instructive on what is best in philosophical hermeneutics.

First, Oluwole advances an understanding of truth as provisional and uncertain (cf. "Philosophy and Oral Tradition", 11). Therefore "knowledge and wisdom cannot be absolute" ("Culture, Gender", 111). She opposes the "confusion of 'rational' in the sense of being [...] 'logically or empirically undeniable' with 'rational' as 'reasonable in view of evidence'" ("Oruka's Mission", 156). Accordingly, philosophy cannot assume any supreme position among forms of knowledge, but is "only one of the several rational endeavours of man" ("Culture, Nationalism and Philosophy", 39).

This view of the provisional nature of all claims to wisdom is supported by the identification of "paradoxes and apparent contradictions" ("Culture, Gender", 111) within a single tradition, which also warrants a rejection of any idea of unanimism ("Philosophy and Oral Tradition", 99). This means that even within a given tradition, people hold different perspectives, thereby relativising the strength of one another's truth claims. The same happens with differences between cultures. Where Oluwole seeks wisdom from ancient traditions, this therefore needs to be accompanied by a critical procedure, and hence her own positioning as a "critical traditionalist" ("Africa", 101). Such a critical stance would, I think, require scholars to adopt a suspension of judgement and willingness to learn as a first, prudent stance towards all forms of cultural expression and claims of wisdom. In any case, a dogmatic "revivalist" return to traditional culture has to be avoided, because it requires sidestepping critique and prudent self-relativisation and provides "inadequate solutions" ("Culture, Gender", 118) to contemporary problems. It would be more realistic, considering the limitations of human insight, to strive towards a progressive elimination of contemporary errors ("Culture, Gender", 118).

Her modest view on the rationality that philosophy can hope to achieve does not render Oluwole's work powerless or feeble. She is forever testing the limits of what may with validity be called "philosophy", not only in the eyes of spokespeople of Western philosophy, but also in the eyes of those of African philosophy. Exactly this assumption of a weak—I would say, hermeneutic—understanding of human rationality affords her a perspective from which to critique excessive claims and the chauvinistic behaviour that may result from them.

This form of thinking (with a detour through tradition) advocated by Oluwole opens up and aims to find its ultimate legitimation in the contribution it can make in responding to contemporary problems. The first political gesture is to dismantle falsely imposed ideological distortions of what Africa is and this contributes to self-affirmation.[28] Whether the challenges of the present really call for such a detour and what its exact contributions would be remain to a large extent to be established by scholars who pursue Oluwole's project further.

3. How truth claims about Africa came to be: V. Y. Mudimbe

Mudimbe's *The Invention of Africa* grew out of a survey of African philosophy (cf. ix[29]) to a broader study of the varieties of knowledge discourses by Africans, and by scholars of different origin on Africa and Africans, which he calls "Africanism" (ix). Thus, his book covers the whole field of discourses that aspire to make truth claims about Africa: from popular discourse in everyday culture, to philosophy and scholarly discourses of all types. This is reflected in the book's subtitle: "Gnosis,[30] Philosophy, and the Order of Knowledge". Accordingly, this book covers the whole range of human hermeneutic experiences, from unspecialised traditions to a variety of traditional and contemporary disciplinary specialisations, such as philosophy, theology, and anthropology, as well as to an overarching critical reflection on these disciplines.

A second orienting strategy of this book can also be considered hermeneutic: it does not start out from a set of criteria for truth, or for the legitimacy of claims, to sieve out what is subsequently explored. Instead, its intention is to study the entire field of discourses that were ever presented as having a truth content on matters African. By considering this material historically, or more specifically "archaeologically", Mudimbe traces the "progressive constitution of an African order of knowledge" (xii). This allows him to examine the socio-historical and epistemological conditions for the possibility of these discourses (cf. ix) and for generating any scholarly claim regarding Africa today.[31] Mudimbe's way of working may differ from that of, say, Okolo, but this way of working does correspond to some extent with the first sense of a "critique", as a study of the conditions of the possibility of discourse.[32] Indeed, these two forms of critique figure at the end of *The Invention of Africa* in the phrases "examination of its own historicity" (Critique I) and "permanent reevaluation" (Critique II) (186).

3.1. Making truth claims about Africa (and what this is a sign of)

At the heart of Mudimbe's study is a major concept: "Africa". It is a study on the conditions of the possibility of making truth claims of various kinds on "*Africa*". These conditions are complex and historically mutable, and the claims made based on such conditions are diverse. Together they reflect the meanings of what is evoked by the term "Africa". This is also the sense of the term "invention" in Mudimbe's title: *The Invention of Africa*. For each person who wants to understand what is meant by "Africa" or "African", these processes of creating the meaning of that term is a necessary passage.[33] These processes inevitably accord an important place to Western, especially European, scholarship, because of the availability of written documentation and because of the role such documentation and scholarship subsequently played in African scholarship, either by being imposed or by being borrowed (as we will see later in more detail). Accordingly, *The Invention of Africa* also explores the shift towards Africanist discourses made by African scholars.

As an initial point of departure, and most of the way, this procedure suspends, as I have already indicated, the question of the truth content, instead focusing on Africanist discourses as "signs of something else" (ix).[34] This way of dealing with parts of discourse as having multiple references is typical of a hermeneutic procedure. Accordingly, discourse can be studied at face value (that is, on its own terms) or in a diagnostic way (as if discourse is a symptom of something else). This diagnostic form of interpretation is typical of the two ways in which we have considered hermeneutics to be "critical": both in studying the conditions for the possibility of meaning and in laying bare the pathological effects of meaning.[35] While this double critique opens up the reading to include the socio-historical conditions, with their power effects, domination, exploitation, and resistance, it marginalises the question of truth (a fact to which we will return in a moment). But let us first insist on an important implication: if discourse lends itself to these two forms of critique, that critique may apply to the kind of scholarly discourse in which Mudimbe engages as well. This is the next fundamentally hermeneutic dimension of his text: even while adopting a kind of meta-perspective on Africanist discourses, *he cannot step outside* of the flux of discourses, since his own writing is another discourse that depends on a set of conditions of possibility (Critique I) and can be read as a sign of something else (Critique II). All philosophical hermeneutics grants the fact that there is no zero-position from which to think—interpretation starts out from within a milieu of situated, perspectival interpretations.[36] This only amplifies the question of truth or assessment of claims.

I have stated that Mudimbe starts by suspending his judgement on the truth content of the discourses he studies. In his second chapter, "Questions of method", he clarifies some of this methodology, or rather, the scholarly "attitude" he assumes. This attitude is supposed to help him overcome the essentialist schemas of traditional anthropology and African inverting replications of them. Two authors help him shape this attitude. From Michel Foucault he takes the perspective on human sciences in which the role of agents—the researching, writing, and evaluating scientists—is downplayed, to zoom in on the *effects* of the scientific enterprise. This perspective sets aside explicit normative evaluation of these effects, but still identifies the "conquering horizons" of the history of social sciences (cf. 27–28). This perspective is reinforced with reference to Claude Lévi-Strauss, to reject the notion of a normative reference for culture (no culture is normative for another), while still providing a means for self-analysis (cf. 33).[37] However, the clarification of his scholarly attitude or epistemic stance is incomplete without the component provided by African authors, from which he singles out elements from the theologian

Engelbert Mveng and the philosopher Paulin Hountondji. When Mudimbe refers to the work of these authors as "amplifications" of Foucault or Lévi-Strauss, he does not mean that they repeat what these European authors have written, only more emphatically. Instead, he has in mind both a discontinuity (now we are speaking about African authors, *not* European ones) and a continuity (there is thus a kindred attitude in the approach to different cultural expressions, which resides in a style of "epistemological vigilance", 36).[38] Therefore, whatever the continuities may be, the "amplifications" do something different. Mveng's epistemological vigilance finds expression in a critique of African discourse that remains true to patterns of thought of the colonial era, and in the assumption of "scientific sovereignty" (36) as a complement to political sovereignty (36). This stance prioritises an Afrocentric agenda, but does not require the denial of an "epistemological filiation" or a pursuit of the "decolonization" of human and social sciences through a kind of purification of African methodologies (cf. 37). In Hountondji's words, the task of African scholarship includes *"demythifying* the concept of Africanity" and *"weaken[ing]* resolutely the concept of Africa", in order to strip the term of its baggage, inherited from anthropology, and to free it to explore the phenomenal richness of African traditions (cited in 37). In as far as these two forms of amplification retain European filiation, they are re-takings (in Okolo's sense), and in that way re-narratings of the African self and African priorities—the story of the accumulation of knowledge told without, and from outside, the traditional centres of academic culture. This is the assumption of sovereignty by "rearrangements".[39] Through the assumption and exercise of this scholarly stance, these authors implicitly instruct us on the "importance of the subject in social sciences" (23), that is, both the subject of those studied, and that of the scholars. To conclude, the whole second chapter of *The Invention of Africa* describes Mudimbe's stance in relation to matters of anthropology, which, whether implicitly adopted or explicitly advocated, subtends all other disciplinary Africanist discourse.

This brings us back to the important place that European discourses occupy in Mudimbe's book. The reason for this is the significant role that colonial history has played in the generation of a variety of Africanist disciplines. It is well known that the "colonizing structure" extended over the "physical, human, and spiritual aspects of the colonizing experience" and consisted of "the domination of physical space, the reformation of the *natives'* minds, and the integration of local economic histories into the Western perspective" (2). This suffices as a reminder of why and how knowledge on a myriad of matters African was required by colonisation (cf. 83), which in turn draws our attention to the European socio-political and historical background of European Africanist discourses. Finally, the "colonizing structure" accounts for the construction of a theoretical dichotomy of the centre and periphery, each with its own set of people, institutions, cultures, knowledges, religions, modes of production, temporal trajectories, and so on (cf. 189).[40] Clearly, this dichotomy has always implied an elevated valuation of the centre and a trivialisation of the margin (cf. 3–4). As useful as it is to identify this step in Mudimbe's thought, it would not strike the reader as anything new. Moreover, the important place that Mudimbe accords European scholarship may even create the impression of a Eurocentric orientation—later I show why the opposite is true, and that there are also African discourses that are independent of European filiation. However, for now, I only want to point out that his description of a dichotomous order does not commit Mudimbe to a simplistic Manichean reconstruction of science during the colonial era and its aftermath. Rather, his description of the complex forms of discourse and their historical development reflects his commitment to reveal the ways in which people transgressed—however modestly it may have been—the crude colonial fiction of a dichotomy, even when this dichotomy was forcefully imposed.

The discursive version of this dichotomous dissymmetry may be termed "epistemological ethnocentrism"[41] (15, cf. 185). However, one should be careful to distinguish two related, but heterogenous, dimensions of this "ethnocentrism".[42] The first is *"epistemological filiation"* (19), which refers to the continuity of epistemic practices with those of Europe at a certain point in its history.[43] The essential point of epistemological filiation is the fact that, as agents of truth claims, African scholars think from a specific context, from inherited practices, with transmitted understandings of truth in mind, and that most of these bear the traces of European contexts, practices, and understandings of truth that shaped those of Africans. Epistemological filiation refers to this continuity and stretches as far as these continuities can be pointed out, even when people adapt and revise these practices. Epistemological filiation speaks first of a scientist's situatedness and historicity and is therefore not something that one can simply step out from all at once.[44] To my mind filiation is an ambiguous fact. While it exists to some extent inevitably, it is not therefore necessarily innocent: its mere functioning may already have ethnocentric effects, for example, when the institutional power of formal teaching and research marginalises traditional forms of knowledge acquisition and transmission. At the same time, filiation does not mean determination, because it accommodates the possibility of engaging with the European material and its appropriation in ways that do not entail a "capitulation of otherness" (174). In short, filiation also allows for borrowing without a loss of sovereignty.

On the other hand, epistemological filiation is often entangled with an *"ideological connection"*, which is the second and unambiguously nasty dimension of ethnocentrism. This connection refers to the kind of attitude adopted or demonstrated in a discourse, and in which the idea of an a priori (European) superiority is reflected.[45] It is possible to recognise one's epistemological filiation even while trying to rid it of all remnants of self-proclaimed superiority; but there is no ideological connection that does not depend on epistemological filiation. Mudimbe goes even further, by calling ethnocentrism both the virtue and weakness of anthropology, and thus of all social science and philosophy (cf. 19): the epistemological filiation is part of scholars' basic openness to what they study and to their critical self-reflection, which can, conversely, be closed off by ideological warping. Thus, Mudimbe himself knows that he is enacting epistemological filiation in writing his book, but to him the question is to confront this fact, rather than to deny it. The task is to recognise epistemic filiation, to study it, but to relativise its possible harmful effects.

3.2. *The variety of Africanist discourses*

With these preparatory clarifications in place, we can now work through a host of Africanist discourses of which Mudimbe traces the emergence and development: anthropology, theology, anthropology, négritude and authenticity, and philosophy. But the list could be extended to include geography, art, psychology, literature, and more.

Consider, for instance, the bundle of discourses that purport to be "anthropology" and a critical engagement with the heritage of the professional and amateur practices of "anthropology". Mudimbe reflects on the origin of the persuasive power of anthropology by assessing heterogeneous dimensions of its contemporary practice: (a) he takes into consideration the (potentially) best sources (rehabilitating missionaries as amateur anthropologists), (b) identifies the root of binary categories in Enlightenment philosophy, early professional anthropology, and even Greco-Roman culture[46] (cf. 68–71), and (c) highlights a turn in European views of others from the 1920s, when the repression or denigration of the other on terms of sameness began to be relativised (cf. 80, 83). Other antecedents to the changes mentioned in (c) (cf. 80) and the historical and scholarly reasons for them (75–78)[47] need not detain us here. In sum, these are the early conditions for the possibility of retelling the story of the science of anthropology in the ensuing decades.

Mudimbe pursues this exploration of "re-tellings" of the relation between self and other, with another parade of a succession of figures. He traces the complex combination of lived experience of the négritude authors and their filiation to European modes of thinking,[48] but then highlights how Sartre's "Black Orpheus" amplified the effect of their poetry and thought by demonstrating how "whites become [the] object of [the] black gaze". Sartre gives a new impetus to négritude by means of a political and identitarian reinterpretation, and thereby provides a stimulus for the formation of discourses on African authenticity at that time.

One such type of discursive self-affirmation is found in African nationalisms, which, in turning to practical political liberation, partially complemented and partially contradicted the self-image propounded by négritude (cf. 87–88). The first significant proponents of African nationalism were to a significant degree "assimilated" Africans (cf. 88), which implies that Western ideas formed a substantial part of the mixed origin of nationalism. Gradually, African nationalism also came to draw on influences from Afro-American writing, Marxism, and newer tendencies in anthropology. Nationalist discourses advocated the need to centralise and homogenise a national identity, at the expense of marginal ethnic cultures and identities and plurality. In this respect, the emergence of African nationalisms is a "turning point in the history of the West" (88) in the sense that it represented "ideologies of otherness" (cf. 40, 85, 86) that could speak back to the West. Another challenge to the West grew out of the African appropriation of Marx, which in many cases resulted in an Africanisation of Marx and the formation of African socialisms, where communalism supplanted communism (cf. 92–96).

A second bundle of discourses that Mudimbe documents is *theology*. He traces the transmission of Christian religion by Western missionaries and their African successors step by step (44). In his exposition, it is less the personal faith conviction than the theological discourse with truth aspirations that takes centre stage. Mudimbe offers a view on the metamorphoses of this type of discourse, which he regards as interlarded with anthropological prejudices and anthropological research, and as used with the intention of "dominating or liberating African people" (44). Again, Mudimbe attempts to unpack the wide range of different variables embodied in historical tendencies.[49] In doing so, Mudimbe examines

> the articulation between missionary language and its African echo or negation,[50] and the ultimate consequences of this relationship for anthropology. The investigation is appropriate in view of questionable hypotheses about missionaries' positive or negative contributions to African ideology, and, in general, of the controversial interpretations of this relationship in the crisis of African Studies. (44)

These processes of "echoing or negating" are described in detail by comparing the colonial ideology of "developing" Africans by colonial rule to the early Western missionary theology of salvation (which he shows to be very close to a colonising discourse). His point is to demonstrate the formal equivalence between the imperial and the ecclesiastic discourses, whereby, knowingly or inadvertently, missions brought with them a kind of Euro-normativity that ensued in a trivialisation of everything African. Subsequently, partially under the influence of changes in anthropology,[51] African theologians reshaped this inherited missionary theology through "acculturation" into a theology of indigenisation. This change is also reflected in the African clergy's increasing appropriation of ecclesiastical responsibility. The first phase of this change was radicalised from the 1960s onwards and was complemented by intensified self-aware nationalist and authenticity accents. Thus, the "African successors" gradually formed a "theology of incarnation", which linked theology closely with politics (cf. 59).

This reconstruction of changing truth discourses and their power-effects has specific hermeneutic consequences. Mudimbe concludes his discussion by stating:

> [I]nsofar as the new African discourse perceives its own course and fate in terms of epistemological rupture [...], we may stop at this claim and interrogate its situation. That can be done through three questions: Who is speaking? From

which context? In what grids and in what sense are the questions pertinent? I propose that one of the best ways of answering these questions might be a careful rewriting of the relationships that have existed between African ethnography and the politics of conversion. (64)

In other words, Mudimbe's reconstruction of the history of discourses generates core hermeneutic questions and should therefore be seen as an indispensable partner to hermeneutic practice.

A third bundle of discourses is *philosophy*, the examination of which is the kernel from which *The Invention of Africa* developed. Philosophy partook in the colonial "taxonomic grid of human cultures" (136), echoing Lévy-Bruhl's view of a dichotomy between people gifted with logic and those waiting (forever?) to be endowed with logic by others. Philosophy was either Western, or it was not philosophy at all. In as far as modes of philosophising were then taken over by Africans through colonial education, this filiation leads one to conclude that "[m]odern African thought seems somehow to be basically a product of the West" (185). However, this still leaves unanswered the question of the originality of the manner in which African scholars engaged with this heritage.[52] However, the story of the European influence on philosophy on the African continent does not stop there; African philosophy can be studied as a sign of yet something else. The significant turn in anthropology in the 1920s (alluded to above) resulted in a shift in the Western gaze on ethnic groups and their prevalent ideas. This shift included the use of philosophical categories (ontology, ethics, metaphysics, etc.) to describe these ideas and hence attribute it to peoples. Tempel's *Bantu Philosophy* and its reception by African philosophers is an important event in this respect. But this milestone of written African philosophy is a problematic step forward: it still flirts with a bipolar view of human reality, while being critical of this view—it presents an "inversed figure of the same" (180).[53] Mudimbe critiques the collective attribution of ideas to ethnic groups and the corresponding fallacy of an implicit philosophical unanimity, the core of which would be an ontology of a vital force (cf. 152). But Mudimbe also recognises in these writings the formation of a tradition of thought where authors, while remaining methodologically indebted to Western forms of thinking, test and try to improve on existing literature, practising an interest and sympathy for African culture (e.g., 145).

African philosophy is more than Western heritage and anthropology. Bearing in mind authors such as Césaire, Hebga, and Eboussi Boulaga,

Mudimbe highlights the complexity of the development of African philosophy by recalling the fact of a "variety of racially and culturally oriented enterprises, some of which arose independently from the thesis of an African ontology" (152) and fed into African debates about identity. To this should be added the critique of ethnophilosophy and the power imbalances that this mode of thinking reflects (cf. the critique of Hountondji, Towa, and again Eboussi Boulaga), but also the critique of the critique of ethnophilosophy with its claims regarding the power imbalances that the first critique feeds into.[54] To the network of tributaries flowing into the variety of African philosophies, one may add studies on Ethiopian thought, the influences from Anglophone Western philosophy, debates in the human and social sciences, and debates on Marxisms (cf. 162–168).

Within this turbulence of intellectual currents, Mudimbe also identifies the emergence of an internally varied *hermeneutics* (172–173[55]). While he does not claim so explicitly, in the same discussion Mudimbe's proximity to hermeneutics is undeniable. This can be seen from his summary of the core of his own approach in reading intellectual history and its contemporary stakes in the following three-fold hermeneutic agenda:

> (a) to understand and define the configuration of scientific practice in social and human sciences as an ideological locus determined by three major variables—time, space, and the (un)conscious of the scientist; (b) to analyze and understand African experiences as formed on the basis of a particular history and as witnessing to a regional *Weltanschauung* [worldview]; and (c) to think about and propose reasonable modalities for the integration of African civilizations into modernity, this in accordance with critical thinking and scientific reason, for the purpose of the liberation of man. (175)

I have now presented three bundles of Africanist discourses surveyed by Mudimbe. Whatever their form may be, they all contribute to the manifold event of the "invention of Africa". We have to understand this phrase in both senses: Africa and Africans are being invented, but they are increasingly agents of invention, inventors. This double-sidedness of the invention of Africa already encapsulates a firm stance against the idea of ethnic unanimism and in favour of contextual, situated research. But this invention goes in *two directions*: "This critical reading of the Western experience is simultaneously a way of 'inventing' a foreign tradition in order to master its techniques and an ambiguous strategy for implementing alterity" (171). This means that Africans are inventing not only Africa, but also Europe—which may be done through extraversion or re-narrating Africa for oneself (*récit pour soi*), or a combination of the two. Africanist discourse is thus stretched in this to-and-fro, this dialectics, of invention. The stakes of this dialectics are high: they mark the difference between subservience and sovereignty.

Allow me, in conclusion, to come back to Mudimbe's underlying scholarly attitude, which he establishes by suspending the question of truth-content in order to perform his archaeological study of discourses. As it stands, all his study can point out is the succession of and variations in scholarly practices, without any judgement about the quality of their truth content and any progression in that truth content. The question is then: how long can one maintain that suspension of judgement of the truth-content before the turning to that which is referenced by scholarly discourses (*la chose du texte*), that which they claim to be clarifying? The fact is that, not only these discourses, but also Mudimbe's own text, are about *something*. Any truth claim has to submit itself to the measure of *that about which we speak* (cf. 183). This "something" is the historical object of violence, that which has been silenced, and to which some aspire to give the best possible expression and support on the path towards increasing liberation.[56] Acknowledging that discourse aspires to reference something outside of itself does not, in my mind, amount to surmounting the discursive mediation of our relation to reality. However, such an acknowledgement would refuse to reduce the history of sciences to an ever-changing juxtaposition of empty claims and referenceless points of view. Something transcends the discourse, even when we can grasp its theme only through discourse. Moreover, since there is something beyond the discourse towards which the epistemic ambition still aspires, the contradiction between discourses of whichever kind may serve as a mutual correction (cf. 184).

3.3. *Reconstructing invention—archaeology as hermeneutics*

Let us now look back at my reading of *The Invention of Africa* above to synthesise a set of final insights into Mudimbe's hermeneutics. While his study should span discourses of all types, he instead zooms in on developments in the human and social sciences and related argumentative practices such as négritude and nationalism. We have seen that Mudimbe adopts an approach that sets the question of truth aside, to study the conditions of the possibility for discourses to arise (Critique I), which opens up to a diagnostic reading (Critique II). However, the suspension of judgement about truth makes it impossible to practice Critique II fully. The study is historical, and therefore social, considering the situatedness and perspectival nature of all discourse, and therefore presented from a situated and perspectival point of view (out of which hermeneutic scholars never pretend to be able to lift themselves, a fact that is echoed by the "epistemological filiation" of scholarly discourse).

A theme that follows from Mudimbe's argument right through is the place of anthropology—as either explicit or implicit assumptions—which infiltrates Africanist discourses. In Okere, Serequeberhan, and Okolo we have repeatedly seen how their arguments reflect a view of anthropological generality and specificity (as also discussed in Chapter 6, § 1, below). What Mudimbe provides us with is a *historical* (or archaeological) approach for studying the constitution of that very underlying anthropology, whether that be in the work of African, European, or other authors.

Now let us consider again Mudimbe's suspension of judgement on the truth content and his focus on what discourses are signs of. In a sense, one may suspect that, all along, Mudimbe longed to lift that suspension—after all, he did not explore just any discourses on Africa, but considered it worthwhile to focus on those that had undergone some form of formalisation and laid claim to enhanced accuracy or verifiability. Thus, even granting the value of studying discourse as part of a social reality, at some stage—and as an intervention in that reality—people may want to seek the means to distinguish truth from untruth, or at least, to distinguish better renderings of matters from weaker renderings (as we saw above). This is the place where Diop's insistence on science comes in. Diop cannot escape the situatedness of his own scientific discourse, but Mudimbe cannot simply abandon the question of the assessment of truth content. Indeed, Mudimbe's discursive performance is premised on the expectation that his readers will take *his* discourse not merely as another invention, but as an insightful, truthful, accurate perspective. And, indeed, his whole scholarly performance testifies to his allegiance to a certain understanding of truth. This "truth" is established by his pursuit of the most accurate, sophisticated, and impartial rendering and diagnosis that he as a finite, situated, and perspectival scholar was capable of at a specific time. Such is the pursuit of truth in hermeneutics.

Another remark about Mudimbe's performance in this book relates to the two directions of invention mentioned above. His book, *The Invention of Africa*, is dedicated to the study of Africa, however, one soon recognises how much he has to say about Europe. This is a book on Africanism, but in discussing this, the author takes a step back, making it not a book about Africa, but a book about speaking about Africa—bringing it strongly into the ambit of hermeneutic competence, but without in the least letting go of the interpretive contributions made by other sciences. This means that he asks questions such as: What is happening when people make truth claims about Africa? Or even, what is happening to us when we make such claims? And since a lot of Africanist scholarship issued from Europeans, this is (partially) a study of how European academia exposes its biases in speaking about its other. One may therefore equally characterise Mudimbe's book as a contribution to "Europe-ism".[57] This insight then equips me to clarify why I could announce earlier that the amount of attention to European views in this book does not amount to a kind of Eurocentrism: it is because this book on Africanism is, in as far as it examines European discourses, a *critique of European orders of knowledge*. By never obliterating the traces of his own "epistemological filiation" with European disciplines, Mudimbe's study of discourses demonstrates how we may examine those European discourses as "signs of something else" (ix). That something else stretches beyond the curiosity to know, right into international power mechanisms, those of the past or contemporary ones.

But we may unpack even further Mudimbe's position among the vast array of discourses that he explores. Considering the historical development of strands of ideas, Mudimbe thinks about the "confused intermediary area" between often too simplistically applied socio-historical categories, namely "tradition" and "modernity" (191). He rejects the notion of a perfect break (which would support the dichotomous pattern of colonial thinking and its static view of African culture), but also the idea that this intermediary space is filled only by submissive acculturation. But one already notices that in whatever way this space will be filled, it will have axiological implications. Mudimbe's approach is to recognise differences in culture, but to follow Janheinz Jahn in elevating the intermediary to what one is seeing at this moment (in Africa, but by implication also elsewhere). This intermediary is a "neo-culture", which is neither a pathological version of tradition, nor a tortuous road to a pre-established modernity, but something in its own right.[58] When contemporary Africans consider themselves "legitimate heirs" (193) of tradition, that credits them with the authority to receive from their tradition what they deem fit, and to mix it with whatever they consider appropriate from other traditions—resulting in "neo-culture". This is Mudimbe's view too.

And this is the position from which, despite his apparently free-standing posture, he *participates* in the history of Africanism. His book is itself a contribution to "neo-culture" and to an understanding of the human abilities from which it may arise. Take, for instance, the valuable epistemic attitude which he gratefully learned from Foucault and Lévi-Strauss: nevertheless, this attitude is not copyrighted by Europeans, nor locked to expansion by Africans. We saw such expansion, in the mixture of taking over and creation, which Mudimbe termed "amplification". In a similar vein, Mudimbe's relation to his own epistemological filiation—to European and African scholarship—is an attempt at amplification. Hence his book implicitly testifies to the space of manoeuvring of agents despite their historical conditions. This is supported by Mudimbe's own accounts of the changes in disciplinary tendencies (for example, in anthropology, theology, and African identity discourses). Thus, the study of conditions of possibility accounts for the restrictions under which people thought, without making a deterministic framework of those conditions. The very complexity of developments documented by Mudimbe rather serves as a caution to remain aware of the intricate relations of mutual influence and independence between historical events and the succession of ideas (cf. 188).

While Mudimbe's whole historical account and his own performance evokes the possibilities of agency and change, even amid the most formidable external constraints, his study stops short of drawing further political implications.

4. A hermeneutics of total defeat and the small deviations: Fabien Eboussi Boulaga

Generally, African philosophers tend to be well aware of the socio-political environment in which they work. But the work of Fabien Eboussi Boulaga[59] stands out for its emphatic understanding of philosophy from its context. Rarely is the violent tragedy so plainly articulated as when he writes:

> "Nobody would consent, as they say, to go backwards. Realism and objectivity that are the beginning of wisdom oblige one to admit the fact of one's historical

backwardness [*retard historique*] and, hence, one's dependence and debt to those who objectively help now to gradually bridge the gap. That one's self-pride might be mortified at it is of no importance and does not change the facts of the matter" (79/*78, translation modified[60]).

This realism about loss and the factors that caused it has a direct impact on his view of philosophy. Many an African philosopher would hesitate to spell out the consequences of this position as frankly as he does: philosophy, as Africans encountered it at first, is part of the machinery by which traditional life has been irremediably destroyed; this philosophy was encountered first as a presumed articulation of the essence of that civilisation and as part of its system of education. From this perspective, philosophy is first and foremost encountered as a powerful instrument—"[p]hilosophy is an attribute of power" (8/*2)—and since the power in question is exercised by the Western conqueror, Eboussi Boulaga concludes that "to declare that philosophy is Western is just redundant, a pleonasm" (8/*2, similarly, 100/*97[61]). His view of the devastation brought about by colonisation is so encompassing and penetrating that one may wonder if any view of philosophy *as African* could still emerge from this context.

And yet, from this most painful awareness of defeat arises the sharpest view of nascent resistance, including that in philosophy. Following Eboussi Boulaga's thought from this perspective allows us to see that it is precisely this intense preoccupation with the contextual specificity of philosophising that gives it a hermeneutic character.

4.1. Orientation: philosophy by and for Muntu

In the strictest sense, Eboussi Boulaga does not understand *Muntu in Crisis* as a book of *African* philosophy. The "Muntu" in the title refers, at most, indirectly to human beings living in Africa or people who share some general African cultural traits. The human being called "Muntu" refers to those survivors who have had (and in many respects still have) to face the effects of "total defeat" (16, 67, 79, 152). It is one thing to survive; it is another to find real ways to realise the "desire to be by—and for—oneself" (41/*37) after defeat. And this "desire" is Eboussi Boulaga's main normative reference: all modes of existence are henceforth assessed for the contribution they make to Muntu's "reprise de soi": their renewed self-affirmation in practice.[62] If there is something like African philosophy, it would, in Eboussi Boulaga's view, be worthy of this name neither because it is practised by Africans, or on the African continent, nor because it remains true to authentic traditions,[63] but because it contributes to the self-affirmation of Muntu. Whatever does not contribute to this quest, however minimally, is trivial in Eboussi Boulaga's eyes and is therefore "uninteresting" (11/*5).

Thereby we have already discovered three key principles in his own interpretative work on philosophies—and these are three principles of hermeneutics. First, no philosophy can be properly understood without being contextualised. Second, this contextualisation is not, in the first instance, a matter of the history of ideas matter, but a contextualisation within socio-political events. In other words, when we examine the content of a philosophy, we have to ask what is being *done* in making its claims. Third, the value or interest of a philosophy is measured by its contribution to a renewed practical self-affirmation of Muntu.

However, following the hermeneutic stretch of this book requires a slower entry into its complexity. For the purposes of this discussion, I examine three moments in Eboussi Boulaga's argument: (§ 2) the critical unmasking of existing points of view, (§ 3) the identification of the conditions for the (minimal) exercise of freedom, and (§ 4) the exercise of that freedom.

4.2. *Hermeneutics as a critical unmasking*

Eboussi Boulaga's review of philosophical options available at the time of writing *Muntu in Crisis* is of course a means by which to position his own contribution. However, it is much more than that. It also extends his explanation of the far-reaching effects of colonisation, and it practises one of the modes of interpretation that he advocates in his book. It is particularly this last point that is of interest to us here. Eboussi Boulaga demonstrates what hermeneutics as critical unmasking looks like though a critical reading of the two main forms of philosophy available at the time when he wrote, in the mid-1970s: ethnophilosophy and the practice of Western philosophy by Africans, which he calls school philosophy.

One finds an excellent orientation to this strategy of interpretation in the opening statements of his "Problematizing" (11/*5), which also serves as an orientation to the project of the whole book. If one wants to understand the existing attempts at African philosophy, Eboussi Boulaga proposes that one should start by gathering *all* material that appropriates to itself the label of "philosophy". Then one has to consider the conditions under which these texts have been written.[64] Doing so then reveals that a tension emerges between the claims made in the texts and what really happens in the process of making claims. Through these texts, the authors strive to affirm their humanity under colonially imposed conditions and its lasting aftermath. However, unbeknownst to them, their best efforts at demonstrating their autonomous reasoning remain subservient to an oppressive social system by echoing some part of its ideological justification. This means that these forms of thinking betray the aspiration towards real self-affirmation (11, 85).[65] The key to this hermeneutics is thus situating the *text* within the process of *philosophising*, which is itself contextualised within the prevailing relations of power. In other words, Eboussi Boulaga always distinguishes between two levels of truth (cf. 14), one in the discourse, and the other in the speech act as part of a socio-historical unfolding (for example, 27). This distinction implies that one under-interprets philosophies by studying only their *what*; one must also study their *how* and *why*. Although the importance of the *what* is not thereby denied, the real significance or "interest" (11) of a philosophy can be read only from the *how* and *why*, which determine the profundity of that philosophy (cf. 23).

If we approach Eboussi Boulaga's critique of ethnophilosophy from this perspective, the main point is not his critique of the kinds of claims made, or the even harsher judgement that ethnophilosophy fails as a philosophy (60–62). Instead, the hermeneutic of unmasking demonstrates that ethnophilosophy claims to let the common population speak, and claims to demonstrate the prevalence of philosophy in traditional culture, but actually creates only an illusion of self-affirmation. On closer inspection, according to ethnophilosophers, philosophy is something that traditional people are said to *have* (31)—not to *do*—and they have it *collectively*, as if the homogenous ethnic group forms one single subject, in whose midst no contradiction emerges, because all people's views harmonise together into a global "concordisme" (40–41/*36). This amounts to self-negation through internalisation of the master's categories (those of ethnocentric anthropology), thereby implicitly confirming the stereotypical views of indigenous populations, making them and their culture palatable and manageable to the powers of the day (cf. 37, 39, 47).[66]

The school philosophers, as heirs of Western philosophy, have an altogether different understanding of philosophy. However, their practice can be assessed in a similar way. Again, the principle holds that

> when the conditions under which a would-be philosophical discourse is produced are not explicitly stated, it smuggles them into the fabric of discourse as its determinants and turns out to provide an ideological confirmation of the prevailing balance of forces and to become subservient to the powers of the moment. (86/*82)

In the case of school philosophy, this becomes evident when one considers the institutions where this is practised. The school and university—where education in philosophy is located—conform to the same model of indirect rule prevalent in other colonial mechanisms of rule. Here the intermediary is the (philosophy) teacher, who acquires the competence and accreditation to speak for (Western) philosophy from the dominant powers. The hypocrisy of the civilising mission is thereby carried into philosophical practice: while it proclaims itself to be the free practice of universal reason, philosophy de facto functions as a traditionalised deference to Western authors, requiring unfailing adherence from the African philosopher. In addition, African philosophers have to set aside all particularities of their context and concerns, and in consequence pursue a philosophising that has little ambition to address burning issues. African philosophers' subservience is entrenched by the fact that this position requires them perpetually to await assistance and to aspire to assimilate (cf. 101/*98). This situation smothers any emancipatory potential of philosophy, and the position of self-negation for survival becomes "second nature" (101/*98).

For all his critique of ethnophilosophy and school philosophy, Eboussi Boulaga has some sympathy with their efforts: ethnophilosophy starts from a moral rejection of initial defeat (67), and this is its "truth" (85), and the school philosophers' embrace of their fate in a spirit of *amor fati* is understandable, as it is born from the need for survival (100/*97). But after all is considered, this is not sufficient to salvage their work; in both cases philosophy is an "uninteresting" practice. Consequently, the conclusion arising from Eboussi Boulaga's survey of the then existing philosophical offerings is not a choice for either ethnophilosophy or school philosophy, but a damning critique of both. If, as we will see below, in the end, school philosophy comes out looking somewhat better, this has to be understood only as a next step that depends on what Eboussi Boulaga advocates as a strategic response to the problematic nature of school philosophy.

4.3. Hermeneutics as interpretation of the conditions of self-liberation

If ethnophilosophy is thus compromised to the core, and if the transmitted Western philosophy is in fact an "attribute of power" (8/*2), does this indicate a dead end for philosophy in (post-)colonial countries? To justify his rejection of this option, Eboussi Boulaga invites us to have another look at Western philosophy as it is practised by Muntu. After all, for all his critique of the school-philosophical epigones, Eboussi Boulaga never discredits Western philosophy *as philosophy*, whereas he declares ethnophilosophy to be both "uninteresting" and philosophically void.

As a first step, he limits himself to how claims are generated, from the perspective of a practising philosopher. Eboussi Boulaga identifies the common denominator of all inherited philosophy as an exploration of the emergence of truth, at the highest level of abstraction. This reflection is so abstract that it could be rendered in terms of the relation between spirit and being. This relation fans out over all subfields of philosophical enquiry, in epistemology, logic and metaphysics, to ethics and politics. All are subtended by an anthropology of human beings as rational and aspiring to free expression of this rationality in theory and practice (cf. 180). And overall, "[t]o philosophize is to recognize this circular motion from self to self, through the mediation by things or by detours through others" (179/*180, translation modified). This circular movement consists of different "procedures of the spirit [*opérations de l'esprit*]" (179/*180[67]) that move in two directions: an outward movement (from the self to what exists, to what is given, or to what has passed), and an inward movement back, through which the spirit appropriates the gains of the outward movement for itself in view of its present and future.

To each of these procedures there is a corresponding series of disciplines or forms of intellectual effort.[68] The outward movement begins by establishing the facts relevant to any enquiry, contextualises them, and improves understanding by interpretation and commentary. Then it compares, hierarchises, and judges elements to establish their relative merits. Finally, through reasoning, it establishes relations of logic, dialectic, or synthesis between the interpreted fact. Running in the reverse order, the inward movement establishes the foundation and orientation of what has been mediated, articulates various elements in a positive discourse that assesses their practical relevance, and projects the findings into a concrete reality to test their validity. A lot of what is commonly understood under hermeneutics, narrowly conceived as the art of interpretation, corresponds to the outward movement; hermeneutics more broadly conceived as the effort of appropriation and application corresponds to the return movement inward.

To a considerable extent, Eboussi Boulaga is willing to grant the significance of this phenomenology of intellectual efforts. The problem that he perceives lies elsewhere: it arises when this whole "procedure of the spirit" is spent on a secondary object, which is philosophical texts. In other words, the point of contention is not the claims made in these texts, but the risk that discipline specific work on them closes scholars into a sterile book-centred activity. I understand Eboussi Boulaga to say that this is what makes scholarly work an instrument that perpetuates the apparatus of unjust power. But this does not exclude another possibility:

> Because of its general character, this framework or schema has the potential for an emancipatory practice of philosophy if, instead of the individual mind, one sets up a real person, you and me, needy and historical beings; if, in the place of the Spirit, we place collective, historical entities [*personnalités*] who strive to assume ownership of themselves, to gain autonomy and to realize "freedom"; if, finally the horizon is actual humankind, at large [*l'humanité concrète, mondiale*], striving to self-reflection through the effects of technology, but also from a political will, and the provision of the necessary conditions of a freedom, which is indivisible and cannot be restricted without being renounced. Thus, it is only the concrete history of liberation of human beings, such as they are empowered at last to apprehend what there is and to order their existence according to its norms that can take reflection away from its abstraction. (184/*184, translation corrected)

One may say that Eboussi Boulaga's problem is not with the exercise of these (hermeneutic) procedures themselves, but with the reductive purpose for which they are being deployed in a bookish philosophy.

One and the same philosophy is, then, an occasion for fatalistic, sterile reproduction, and one for opening this abstraction to real reflection. At first glance, the two forms of philosophy may look quite similar. The difference resides in the assumption, however minimal, of agency over self-negation.

Another way to put this is to say that philosophy has to be approached from the perspective of action—philosophising—and this must be inserted into the medium of ethics (185/*185). This implies that we now have to widen our perspective from the generation of philosophical claims in the mind of a philosopher to this same activity as it relates to the broader social reality. Then the double potential of philosophy reveals its positive side more clearly. By putting the philosophical "workshop" at the disposal of those who are motivated by the quest for self-liberation and the demands of historical practice, the series of intellectual procedures described above may become tools for self-attestation (184). This positive potential emerges first, not as a group phenomenon, but as a "permanent self-education [*pédagogie personnelle constante*]" (184/*184).

Up to this point in the process, what becomes visible is little more than a *possibility*, inscribed in the ambiguity of philosophy that was imposed as part of the colonial machinery. However, the gain of this possibility is not trivial. What Eboussi Boulaga has done is to confirm the anthropological basis for the possibility of reactivating abstract procedures of the spirit in the service of engagement with real-life issues. This is the basis of hermeneutics that we have encountered in other hermeneuts' work too. What makes the difference between a stagnant, mechanical repetition and real research is that repetition smothers the human ability to interpret, to engage with the particularity of a person's context by whichever means that person has available, whereas real research stimulates that ability to interpret and engage with particularity. In foregrounding the possibility of non-stagnant engagement with real-life issues, the limits of situatedness and human finiteness have never been abolished or denied.

The next section serves to explore this possibility further.

4.4. *Hermeneutics as transfunctionalisation and self-affirmation*

The positive hermeneutic moment in Eboussi Boulaga consists, then, not in forgetting about the massively reductive stronghold and imposed "interests" of which philosophy has made itself an instrument, but in defending the significance of *deviations* (*écarts*) from this status quo, no matter how minute they may be. That is why (as I have argued above) the kind of philosophy in which self-affirmation may arise may at first glance look very much like that in which self-negation is at work. The question is this: we have, since the beginning, made every effort to assess a philosophy according to what is *done* by and with it—what then is really at work in that philosophising?

Eboussi Boulaga sets out to demonstrate that "[u]nder the cover of the same words and practices [as those used in Western philosophy], diverging objects are pursued; perhaps more accurately, philosophy is caused to play new roles and undergo a functional transformation [*une transfonctionnalisation de la philosophie*]" (128/*124). And although he makes this point here specifically in respect of Western or school philosophy, elsewhere he pursues a similar transfunctionalisation (cf. 144/*142) in relation to tradition, the hallmark of ethnophilosophy. Eboussi Boulaga's whole argument depends on the possibility of effecting such shifts or deviations (*écarts*). These shifts could be considered modes of what Okolo called re-takings (*reprises*).

From the perspective of practising school philosophy, such surreptitious change occurs in two ways, both of which represent a first attestation or self-affirmation:

> Attestation is brought about in two manners, [a] by the irruption of other codes, unexpected and incongruous, into [*au milieu de*] the canonical code of philosophy, [b] by the connection and correlation to philosophy of quite different sets of experiences. The first process is metaphor, whereby the repressing meaning of desire makes eruption, the second is metonymy operating deflections signifying that philosophy does not meet the deriving need behind the appeal to it, and it must open up to the totality of the real. (125/*120, numbering added)

Transfunctionalisation happens in the "metaphorical" mode when apparently irrelevant or incongruous references make a second meaning "irrupt" from the midst of philosophical discourse. Eboussi Boulaga identifies several such irruptions: (a) a singular form of *expression*, the uniqueness of the philosopher and the context from which he/she thinks (125/*127); (b) the expression of emotion or sentiment that reflects how authors are affected by issues; and (c) ways in which race and power infiltrate outwardly universal, disinterested thinking. My impression is that in all the forms that Eboussi Boulaga identifies, that which is said in philosophy acquires a different meaning through the person who says it and the way it is said.

Transfunctionalisation occurs in the "metonymical" mode, by displacing the locality from which philosophy is written, including shifts in the *locality* to which an author has been assigned (125/*127). This new topography of philosophy has to be understood in all possible senses: geographically, culturally, socially, and politically. While the ambiguous nature of philosophy (discussed in the previous section) could create the impression that all one has to do is just apply the standard philosophising on different materials, one now notices that the changes of author and locality introduce different concerns, and generate different questions. And because of this, both these new questions and attempts to work on them shift the *function* of philosophy from being co-opted as an instrument of indirect rule to seeking to gradually overcome the self-negation implied in accepting Western philosophy under the regime of school philosophy (as described above). Correspondingly, gradually, Eboussi Boulaga has slipped in an additional set of criteria for the meaning and validity of philosophy, all of which amount to the demand that philosophy should contribute to people's renewed practical self-affirmation [*reprise de soi*].

What holds for the practice of school philosophy cannot—at least in Eboussi Boulaga's view—simply be transposed to ethnophilosophy, because ethnophilosophy lacks too much in real philosophical rigour. However, this does not mean that ethnophilosophy was wrong in examining the potential of tradition in self-affirmation. In fact, tradition can be demonstrated to be "usable and operational in the search for elucidation and the framework of a situational reflection" so that "tradition may transform its function" (144/*142). In other words, tradition may also be transfunctionalised from the extraverted ethnology that ethnophilosophers have made of it.

Adopting a better understanding of what constitutes tradition is essential to the transfunctionalisation of tradition. Eboussi Boulaga, fearless of being accused of iconoclasm, maintains that "there was no African tradition at first, because there was no African at all" (145/*143). "African", as applied to traditions, is an ex post facto generalisation created after the crisis of "total defeat".[69] Those who have in common suffering this violence become, in effect, linked in their shared striving to overcome its effects. Accordingly, Eboussi Boulaga understands tradition as "a being-together and a having-in-common that call forth a common destiny by dint of an acting together" (145/*143, translation modified). Once again we see Eboussi Boulaga's steadfast orientation to the experience of total defeat.

Correspondingly, in response to total defeat, this definition understands tradition in terms of a project, of action, of temporality, rather than as a static ontology and identity, as tradition was often presented by ethnophilosophers or anthropologists (cf. 144).

But this temporalisation is not simply good news, because, as we have seen, the *past* brought a destruction of traditional inheritance, and the imposed *present* and *future* is a modernisation according to others' terms and interests. Again, Eboussi Boulaga anticipates and grants this point (cf. 149). Thence come the rather modest roles he allocates to tradition. However, despite their modesty, these roles are not roles without significance. Working with tradition has to assume the critical task of safeguarding the memory of a history of trauma and destruction. However, while one understands that the cumulative and transmissive effect of such "vigilant memory" (156/*154) accords it a form of traditionality, it is not clear to me why this task is not primarily given to historiography. Tradition also has to serve an affirmative task as a model of (self-)identification. This requires overcoming the view of tradition as merely a fixed inheritance, and opens it up as a treasured resource from which to live and to create. One could thus say that Eboussi Boulaga splits "tradition" into a more negative function as the memory of extreme crimes, and a positive function, which pluralises inheritance through creative transmission.[70]

However, this positive function of tradition is still limited by the conditions imposed by a future that is qualified in advance: the immediate future has to be modernisation. But drawing from all the resources of tradition, and seeking a synthesis of its negative and positive functions allows for a third function, namely projecting a utopian view beyond the immediate future. The flipside of the crimes committed against Africans is the dream of a world in which people's needs are met, knowledge is disseminated, and wealth and power are steered by popular participation (cf. 158–159). This utopia may still be out of reach, but it should already start informing our decisions in the present.

To summarise, according to Eboussi Boulaga,

> a living tradition is an active interpretation. It judges, asserts, denies. It is not satisfied to be interpreted as an object of interpretations. [...] Tradition, indeed, calls for a given being-together to build a common destiny. Therefore, it is not only origin-oriented but it is also end-oriented, looking always in the direction of the future, for it is to be accomplished within circumstantial bounds. It is then capable of supplying utopian models of action. (158/*156)

The hermeneutic thrust of Eboussi Boulaga's understanding of working with tradition thus becomes undeniable. The three-fold understanding of working with tradition amounts to working on self-understanding and unfolding that understanding in practice.

Thus, we can see that the transfunctionalisation of both school philosophy and tradition serves the purposes—the "interest"—of Muntu as outlined right from the beginning. But we cannot conclude this discussion without enquiring about what Eboussi Boulaga leads us to understand about *his own position* while speaking about the work of philosophy in this way.

What we have looked at in this and the previous section as the anthropological condition for the possibility of shifts and a phenomenology of transfunctionalisation through diversions from the status quo is what Eboussi Boulaga himself calls the method of the book (128/*124, a point that is somewhat lost in the translation). In other words, we should understand it as a clarification and legitimation of the practice he tries to unfold in the book, as he understands it. What Eboussi Boulaga calls his "method" is therefore also a kind of genealogy of his own competence to make the claims that he does.

Much of the book takes the form of a philosophical argument, including its "epistemological filiation" to Western philosophy (as Mudimbe[71] would call it). But gradually one notices how Eboussi Boulaga grants even his adversaries—ethnophilosophers and school philosophers—their position as Muntu. And although a lot of the transfunctionalisation still remains to be done (and nowhere does Eboussi Boulaga claim to have done it all), one cannot overlook the displaced topology from which the book draws its main concerns, questionings, and criteria for assessment. These provisionally small deviations or differences (*écarts*) demonstrate Eboussi Boulaga's ability to read and appropriate both school philosophy and tradition in ways that differ from what these two main paradigms propose. And this ability to engage in a critical, context-sensitive, alternative appropriation is a key aspect of the hermeneutic thrust of his book.

Finally, we have seen that Eboussi Boulaga always understands philosophy as a historically situated practice. By bringing about small shifts in the domain in which he is able to do so, Eboussi Boulaga aspires to turn philosophy into a "miniature schematization of a protocol of action" (151/*149). His explicit desire is for this kind of work to be transposable to other domains of culture and society (cf. 9). And thus we find that what is hermeneutic in his work is intimately linked to his understanding of practical engagement.[72]

4.5. Conclusion

Without claiming that I have covered all the hermeneutic aspects of his work exhaustively, I have identified three hermeneutic moments in Eboussi Boulaga's reflection about the prospects of philosophising in the wake of total defeat. All three of the hermeneutic moments are to be understood in relation to this "inaugural myth" (116/*112). This devastating experience and the question of the margin to manoeuvre after that connects the three modes of hermeneutics. Eboussi Boulaga's intention in relating philosophy to this foundational trauma is to situate his own philosophising always in tension with philosophy or hermeneutics as an exclusively bookish activity. But this tension does not deny the importance of scholarly work—on the contrary: it is part of the motivation for engaging in such work with renewed energy. Eboussi Boulaga's question is how the stakes of existence for Muntu in general can be seen to be the real stakes for philosophy in particular. Philosophy is, after all, part of the social existence of Muntu. This is not, however, the kind of grandiose theorising in which the philosopher leads an ignorant society. Eboussi Boulaga's proposal is constructive, but modest: while African philosophers may generally succumb to the same power effects of (post-)colonial societies, philosophising holds the promise of forming a miniature model of a protocol of action. This is not a celebration of in-the-end and despite-all-adversity invincible heroic philosophers; but nor is it a lamentation of fatalism. It is an interpretation of the stakes of life that does not stop with the valid and necessary exposure of the overpowering forces of exploitation and domination, but one that is pursued strenuously and rigorously to raise awareness of the minutest initiations of counter-initiatives.

The core of the hermeneutic stretch of *Muntu in Crisis* is set out in the three propositions that guide Eboussi Boulaga's study from the beginning (cf. 11), and that he captures later more briefly as follows:

> They all purported to welcome the questions that root "philosophy" as an autonomous discourse constituted by a type of intelligibility under the constraints of its production and through the practice of people who work it out in a set position within their own society. In this perspective, as much as to texts, to a corpus and discourse, "philosophy" refers to historical and social reality, to the relations of force that produce it. (85/*81)

Eboussi Boulaga's book is hermeneutic in working on discourse, studying the finest details of its rhetoric and the composition of its claims. But it is hermeneutic also in interpreting how the social and institutional setting of philosophical practices affects the meaning—the "interest"—of philosophy. Moreover, it is hermeneutic in remaining forever attentive to the ambiguity of practices—all practices in principle, but here specifically the practice of philosophising—an ambiguity spanning the extremes of collusion with oppressive machinery and even oppressive civilisation on the one hand, and the liberating practice of gradual emancipation on the other (117). This tension reflects the real stakes of philosophy in Eboussi Boulaga's view—laying bare those stakes that call for practical responses is the hermeneut's contribution to steering our attention to practice.

A number of important implications for hermeneutics may now be drawn from Eboussi Boulaga's thought.

- Eboussi Boulaga's position keeps a difficult balance between thorough critique—never letting any of the remotest potential knock-on effects of power go unnoticed—and doing justice to his contemporaries. How is it, then, that he displays intimate knowledge of the art of crafty deviations (*écarts*) but makes no mention of this in the work of his own contemporaries? Strictly speaking, he has to recognise that some people before him have carried out such deviations—it is difficult to deny this in the work of Hountondji, Césaire, or Fanon, for example. But the moment he concedes this point, it diminishes the sharpness of his critique. And in the extension of this way of thinking lies the recognition that Western philosophy is more than an attribute of power of the colonisers, and, similarly, that ethnophilosophy is not, as a whole, a mode of compulsive extraversion.
- The possibility of such positive initiatives is rooted in an understanding of human abilities (and their defeat) common to all people. This commonality makes it possible to initiate the first steps of self-affirmation from within Western philosophy and from within tradition. Transfunctionalisation is neither a creation out of nothing, nor a restoration of cultural identity. In both cases, it requires a critical reappropriation to meet the needs of a specific context. The same understanding of commonalities in human nature makes it realistic to hope that small shifts in philosophy can serve as an indication of what is possible elsewhere. Nevertheless, this "general anthropological" substrate never overrides the cultural and historical specificities of Muntu.

- An important implication of this point is that if African authors can transfunctionalise philosophy, in principle, so can anybody else. Who the author is or in which context he/she is working is beside the point in this matter. The real question is whether individual philosophers, with their own particularity and from their own context, are supported or disabled by institutional powers to undertake such a task, or whether, despite disabling conditions they can already effect small deviations in respect of the traditions and institutions of power from which they work, to support a renewed practical self-affirmation of the oppressed. This is at least part of what is required to overcome pervasive racism, including by those who are not its direct victims.
- The validity of Eboussi Boulaga's critique and solution—not for his own time but for ours—always depends on our continued interpretation of the conditions under which people work. These conditions are quite diverse. And we remain true to the spirit of his thought by not simply taking over his thinking, but by actualising it. Thus, for each specific context, we have to enquire how unfree people are or to what degree their history subsequent to the crimes perpetrated against them has seen substantial liberation. The freer people are, the less the critique as Eboussi Boulaga articulated it holds, and the more rehashing that critique amounts to lazy victim-playing. Likewise, the greater the degree to which people are still unfree, the more it is inappropriate to exaggerate the potential of the small changes, and the more unfair it is to hold up to people the conditions under which they live as of their own making, adding insult to injury.

5. Translation as making humanity together: Souleymane Bachir Diagne

A superficial view of translation reduces translation to rendering what is said in one language in another language—a kind of repetition, but in a different code, for some or other practical purpose. However, anyone who has attempted to undertake a piece of translation knows how much effort may go into getting to understand what is said and searching or creating the best means by which to give real expression to this in another language. Typically, translation is situated between languages and requires both understanding and interpretation. For this reason already, reflection on translation has its place in philosophical hermeneutics. This is the place that Souleymane Bachir Diagne's book *De langue à langue. L'hospitalité de la traduction*[73] takes in the present study.

A sceptic who would grant translation only a small place in philosophical hermeneutics can be challenged on this basis of two aspects of Diagne's argument. First, Diagne implicitly invites us to consider his book from the angle of hermeneutics at the point when he defines translation as the "movement of understanding"[74] (113, similarly, 22), and typifies translators as "interpreters of themselves and of their culture" (67). According to these claims, translation is essentially bound up with the core concerns of hermeneutics—understanding and interpretation. Second, Diagne widens the perspective of philosophical enquiry on translation to "transplantation, *traduction*, translation" (87), "transfer" (114) and "tradition" (several places), in other words, to the widest array of phenomena by which meaning is transmitted, appropriated, and transformed between generations and between people of different places and times. To this list of translational phenomena, Diagne adds three terms in the Wolof language for translation: decanting (*transvasement*), unravelling, and disentangling (68), thereby emphasising the entanglement of translation with interpretation. In sum, "translation" becomes a point of entry to a series of questions we have already dealt with in studying the other authors considered in this book. Our perspective on "translation" is thereby opened up from the hard work of generating a text in a different language from the original, to the relation between different modes and places of linguistic practice, with all the socio-political implications that this relation may have. Thus, although translation is not hermeneutics, it gives us a valuable perspective from which to consider issues of prime hermeneutic concern.

A declaration of the intention of *De langue à langue* allows us to deduce a number of important aspects of Diagne's argument and to set the agenda for our discussion of it:

> This book presents a reflection on translation and the capacity to translate, its power to create a relationship of equivalence, of reciprocity between identities, to make them appear, that is, to appear together on an equal footing, by making it possible for people to speak to and understand each other from one language to another language [*de langue à langue*]. (14)

Accordingly, translation emerges from the plurality of languages and aims to cross the gap between the familiar and the foreign (§ 1). This relation of equivalence has to be created, a fact that refers to the capacity or agency of the translator (§ 2). But the demands on translation change when the object of translation (for example, a work of art or forms of learning) is transferred from one context to another (§ 3). The equivalence established between the original and the translation raises the question of the particularity and the universality of human discourse and culture; it also raises questions regarding the ethics of establishing the "equal footing" (§ 4) that Diagne refers to.

5.1. Point of departure: connecting the foreign and the familiar

Translation is the art of giving to understanding what is otherwise not accessible to it. It starts out from a distance that has to be bridged, two positions that have to be "compared"[75] and "put into relation" (52, 161).[76] The "trans" aspect of translation stands for establishing this connection. The presence of what is foreign in relation to what is familiar creates something like a differential force-field, the bridging or traversing of which is captured by the Latin word *translatio* and the series of derivatives cited above.

It would therefore be correct to liken translation to the construction of a bridge between the foreign and the familiar. However, gaining access to what is not directly graspable requires effort: the effort to encounter what initially appears strange, the effort to find appropriate ways to transmit, the effort to create a place for the foreign in what was familiar. For this reason, Diagne repeatedly refers to the encounter with others through translation as a challenge or a test (*épreuve de l'étranger*, 113).[77] Responding to this test amounts to an intervention in the differential force field, giving new shape to it. The intervention becomes itself an intermediate or "third space" (64), which can take on divergent meanings, depending on the nature of the differential:

- between speakers of two different languages, between dominated and dominator (raising the question of the agency of the translator),
- between two kinds of expression, for example, art and philosophy (raising the question of the relation between translation and aesthetics),
- between different eras and places (raising the question of the transmission of forms of science, the *translatio studiorum*).

But the image of a bridge is also defective. As an intervention in the differential force-field, translation is not merely a conduit, but also potentially effects changes in both the "start" and "recipient" base. In respect of the "start", translation is not necessarily restricted to repetition of what has already been said, but forms a real poetics (19). On the "recipient" side, it can give raise to hybridising effects (119), meaning that the "recipient" side itself becomes a moving target. As long as "translation" evokes the simplest paradigm of saying something in another language, these effects may remain fairly modest. However, as soon as one considers the whole spectrum of *translationes* and the large socio-cultural complexes that are involved in them—as Diagne suggests we do—the significance of these effects of translation becomes more clearly visible.

While translation in the narrow sense pursues strict fidelity to the "foreign" and to the "familiar", it already contains the potential to manoeuvre to deal with the openness or relative indeterminacy of "bridging the gap". The cumulative effect of all the manoeuvrings of all processes of translation running through history gives Diagne's theory of translation a definitively dynamic character.

However, we need to return to the relative indeterminacy as it is inscribed in even the minutest tasks of translation, for it is here that we witness the role of the translator in translations.

5.2. *The translator as agent*

There are many practical reasons for which one would wish a translator to play as small a role as possible. These reasons may be laudable (for example, maintaining fidelity to the original text) or not (for example, to achieve more effective manipulation of others, cf. 71). However, whatever the motives may be, the view of the translator as conduit or a medium (a *"truchement"*, 65), should not blind us to the fact that the translator is always faced with a series of actional possibilities. The relative indeterminacy that typifies the third space of translation creates some leeway, opening up an array of possible variations, including divergence, error, betrayal, and even premeditated violence (102, see, for example, 163). The possibility of such drifts accounts for a dramatic intensity inscribed in the task of responding to what is strange—that is, the task of translation.

Although Diagne's book is ultimately oriented more to the positive possibilities of translation, he repeatedly evokes negative ones too. An example of violent translation is the translation of the Quran that was prepared under the auspices of Peter the Venerable (b. *c.* 1092, d. 1156), and that was prepared to serve the polemical purpose of exposing directly to the reader's eyes—but in warped rendering—the untruth of its message (164). The services of translation in the broader colonial project also come readily to mind. Here translation was supposed to make the inner life of colonised people accessible to the understanding of administrators to allow them to administrate more efficiently (73). In such a context, translation aims at appropriating aspects of culture, to simplify them and to uphold a condescending practice (73[78]). Below, we come back to this link between translation and domination. But before that, let us have a look at the positive side, for it is on this that Diagne spends most of his time, unpacking the possibilities of the translator.

The first important case used to illustrate the agency of the translator is derived from historical and literary studies on the position of the translator in colonial administrations (53–66). This material allows Diagne to foreground the initiative of the translator, as opposed to performing the task of a mere conduit (*truchement*) in the service of efficient management of local populations: "colonial administration cannot prevent those who occupy the privileged position of intermediaries from also becoming mediators" (63). While the intention is that the translator should be only an instrument in the service of his employers, this "instrument" gets a life of its own. And by doing so, the translator prises open the available space of uncertainty and manoeuvring further.

Something similar happens when African authors adopt the former colonial languages for the purposes of creating literature—Diagne has in mind especially the "literature of translation" (69). Re-narrating orally transmitted stories in writing in these colonial languages may seem to be an act of linguistic surrendering. However, in Diagne's view, the works of Senghor and Sadji, Bernard Dadié or Birago Diop instead bear witness to the emergence of an altogether new creativity. Not only does this act reinforce the perennial transmission of stories, but it transmits the creative force of these stories right into the host languages (78). One need not deny that such writing does a service (some would say an undeserved service) to the receiving languages, which may give rise to the impression that some hold of this literary practice as merely a continuation of subservience to the master and a deformation of the original tradition. However, Diagne argues that this literature holds the possibility of "inseminating" (82) the host language, and in that sense effects a "deconstruction" of the host language's logic of proud self-sufficiency (74).[79] Diagne's understanding of this deconstruction is not that it is a form of reprisal by which the former enemy is conquered; instead, he sees it as a strategy by which the relation of enmity is dismantled. The value of a literature of translation is that it furthers the establishment of reciprocity (74): "It's not because they [the authors of a literature of translation] were Africans and their work somehow represented an indigenisation of translation. It was because they had been able to decentralize the imperial language, to impose on it the gentle violence of métissage that exchanges [*commerce*] from language to language creates" (75).

Whichever way one assesses Diagne's position on this point, our perspective of any translational initiative is always codetermined by the socio-political context that necessitates translation in the first place (87) (see the theme of translation and domination in § 4 below). But before that, let us widen the view on other ways in which the third space of translation is traversed.

5.3. *Translatio as transfer: transplanting works of art and translatio studii*

Above we saw that Diagne perceives the domain of translation to stretch as wide as the differential force-field between the foreign and the familiar. Having examined how the translator can take a position in this force-field, let us now consider two other ways of traversing it: in the domains of art and philosophy. In the case of art, the focus is on the same object as it is transferred from one context to another with the translations that it invites in each locality; in the case of philosophy, the object itself is translated, but this equally has an impact on the world in which this process is undertaken.

Diagne is not complacent about the colonial histories that led to the massive presence of African artworks in Europe, but he examines their "transfer" with another objective in mind: to demonstrate their role in mediating between the worlds from and to which they are transferred. They are, of course, appropriated by people in quite divergent settings, ranging from the original artists and their world(s) to the world of European art collections and museums, and the places where these works of art will henceforth be kept on their return to Africa. The appropriation and integration of elements of African art by "primitivist"[80] European artists implies that these artists' creations always include some form of reception of a creative impulse[81] of which the artists are not simply the origin. These artists de facto become translators (95, 100) of the artworks' suggestive force into a new artistic register. At the same time, this process illustrates again the possibility that translation can transform the very medium of reception or, as Diagne puts it elsewhere, the hybridising effect of translation (119), which creates a form of "neo-culture" as Mudimbe would say. Diagne goes even further by attributing a "decolonizing" quality to the establishment of reciprocity through translation (102).

But the subsequent transfer, the restitution of art to Africa, has equally significant implications for the translation of a work of art. Now, restitution implies resocialisation, which requires a new appropriation or a new translation by those who will henceforth be the custodians of works created long ago (104). In fact, Diagne foresees a long route of translation still ahead for these works (106), for as long as such appropriations may continue to testify to the creative force carried by these works.

Let us now turn to the second modality of transfer, that of learning. Diagne uses the term *translatio studii*[82]—transmission of learning—to designate the ways in which bodies of written learning are transferred from one centre of learning to another over long distances and long stretches of time (114). In this book, he is not interested in tracing all such itineraries or studying them in detail, nor does he present a grand history of philosophy to underpin his argument on the lines of transmission. He rather explores the *fact* of such transmission, of the de- and re-localisations of learning with their translations, and particularly the fact that there is not just one such line of transmission.

Taking the transmission of Greek philosophy as his prime illustration, Diagne takes note of the traditions that claim the significance of the transmission of the centre of gravity of philosophy from Ancient Greece, through the Latin world into the modern European centres of learning with their respective languages. Now, Diagne insists that there are other route(s), notably the one that passes from Greek through Syriac to Arabic (115).[83] He makes this point not only to correct thinking on the number of strands of transmission, but to show that if there is another branch of transmission, this relativises any claims the first branch may have to exclusivity. Thus, his argument questions the motives and instrumentalisations of claiming exclusivity for the first branch. In this way, he demonstrates that the geopolitics of those who claim excellence as final inheritors of the *translatio studii* is suspect and needs to be subject to critique (117).

This does not mean, however, that the second branch is unproblematic. The transfer of learning imposes the work of translation (from one language to another), which then requires modifications (hybridisations, 119) of the receiving language, and possibly people's mode of thinking (about themselves too). These modifications may be assessed as an intrusion by some, and as enrichment by others. Arabic, as little as Greek or Latin, can claim to be the ultimate expression of human rationality, which implies that it too is relativised by its encounter with other languages. In other words, there is no privileged language of philosophy—the linguistic nature of philosophy consists rather of *multilingualism* and *translation*. Hence, nowhere does Diagne attempt to establish which of the two branches is superior, or to invalidate either of them. Except for debunking the Eurocentric branch's claim to exclusivity, the two branches can simply co-exist. In fact, the tendency in Diagne's argument throughout the book is to use translations to mediate between the fruit of both branches.

This juxtaposition of traditions raises the question of the relation between them.

5.4. Particularity, universalism, and the ethics of translation

From the moment one considers the relation between a foreign and a familiar language, and from the moment one considers bilingual or multilingual contexts, the question of their mutual relativisation is implicitly brought into play. Instead of embracing the unresolved juxtaposition and relativism (132), many people commonly prefer some form of auto-immune rejection, or artificial simplifications such as nationalism (18), which overemphasises differences, and that they see no way beyond their own solidified boundaries (see, for instance, how Diagne rejects with equal vigour occidental "ontological nationalism" and African "ntu-logical nationalism", 123 and 128).

It is not surprising, then, that Diagne calls on translation as a way to mediate between divergent expressions and languages. Translation sets up a third space between these expressions and connects them through complex practices of reception, understanding, interpretation, and creation. But how are such practices even possible? Diagne does not accept the possibility of any third or universal language, not even that of a universal logic, which would be accessible to all people from their respective particular languages. All claims to an overarching universalism (*universalisme de surplomb*) are illegitimate and should remain suspect because of the violence that claims to such universalism serve. The only alternative (also to relativism) is a lateral universalism (*universalisme lateral*).[84] Such a universalism is not a given, but has to be *made*; it is not primarily theoretical—in fact, it is in the first instance practical: "the universal will have to be forged and experienced in human languages […] and in their encounter, which is translation" (121[85]). In other words, Diagne assumes a middle position between relativism and an overarching universalism in the form of his "model" of translation: "Because languages do not enclose us in incommensurable grammatical philosophies, the philosopher in general, and the African philosopher in particular, will think as a translator, from language to language" (132). The importance of this statement is underscored by the fact that it concludes with the words that Diagne also used in his book's title.

The universal that saves us from relativism is thus neither a given, nor something that can be discovered. It can be *made*, but only on the condition that one assumes in advance that relativism can be overcome. This is done by adopting a principle of charity in acting towards others.[86] By striving to communicate and participate, one will find some way to communicate and start to participate. Conversely, one can refuse to communicate, instead insisting on what is not yet understood, imposing one's will, distorting the other's expression, and hypocritically pretending to participate in exchanges between equals, and so forth. Any such tactics would impede the work of understanding and interpretation through translation. Again, Diagne's point is not that the encounter with the foreign ceases to be a test, but to show how it is possible to negotiate one's way through that test at all. Reflecting upon this possibility is not a way to dispel the strange confrontation with the other, but to subject oneself in honesty to the test of the stranger. Instead of writing off this strangeness as "untranslatable", the commitment to the principle of charity allows one to recognise "untranslatables" as a never-ending task for translation (132–133), and, I would add, it is possible to succeed in this translation to a non-trivial degree. Finally, structural factors can bedevil us as we try to translate—that is why the possibility of translation always needs to be *reaffirmed in the face of domination* (cf. 15–19): "The existence of a hierarchy between languages, and of relations of domination between them, is a fact that any reflection on a humanism of translation [*humanisme de traduction*] must take into account" (15).

It is only from this perspective that one can finally understand that there is nothing moralistic in Diagne's claim that respect, charity, and anti-inequality are the drivers for translation (19, 101), that the essence of translation is generosity and hospitality (102, 164), and that translation aims at "making humanity together [*faire l'humanité ensemble*]" (50). It is indeed from understanding how our very rationality depends on this practical attitude and pursuing such an ethics of translation that we can develop an understanding of what *translational violence* is (164). These are the means by which a philosophy of translation equips us for a critique of domination. Accordingly, Diagne remarks: "Humanity is not the object of our nostalgia, but our horizon and our task" (165). And he knows very well that translation is only part of such a project (165).

5.5. Conclusions and questions

In this section, we have seen the wealth of insights opened by considering a special figure of the understanding and interpreting human—the translator. But Diagne's argument is not only about a specific profession or even about a trait of intellectual work more generally. One of the unspoken premises of Diagne's book is that translation is a general human experience and capability. His exploration of themes of translation—by means of perspectives derived from different cultural spheres and languages, each translated by him to connect them—is an excellent demonstration of this point. Each whole human being is not a translator, but translation broadly conceived forms a considerable part of human co-existence, and more specifically, it operates in all domains in which we encounter the differential force-field between the foreign and the familiar.

Translation deals with utterances—oral or written—but in principle also with the whole of human cultures, as is testified to by Diagne's exploration of art.[87] Translation is a capacity, and it is deployed within a broader or narrower margin of creativity. While the original (the object, creator, context, or references) is always the starting point, Diagne's emphasis is on what each person can do with it in a new context (for instance, with repatriated works of art; see 104, 106). Translation can always be done in different ways. In this aspect of his argument, Diagne joins most of the authors considered in this book in considering tradition both as an inheritance and as constant creation (cf. Okere, Okolo, etc.).

While Diagne understands the "ambivalence" (82) of the social role of the translator and of the work of translation, his principal objective remains to speak out "in praise of translation" (19), and to meet this objective, he shifts this ambivalence to the background to some extent. The fact that translations serve as media, and that translation always remains a difficult task, to be accomplished within trying circumstances, should have invited him to delve deeper into the compromises that translations may entail. Translation is not always either only true or only a betrayal—it is often a combination of both. For instance, while one may readily grant Diagne's plea in favour of a literature of translation, there is no reason to exclude the possibility that this form of literature can at the same time represent a form of extraversion. Although Diagne is attentive to the role of the translator in the context of colonial administration, he does little to allay the criticism by someone such as Fanon against those who serve as mediators in a Manichean world. Even if we accept Diagne's argument for the practical construction of universality and the ethics of generosity that is required to construct it, we need not agree that the essence of translation is simply hospitality and generosity. The essence of translation could very well be the never-ending struggle of translation with its own ambiguity and the divergent possibilities opened up by that ambiguity.

We have seen how Diagne uses the idea of *translatio studii* to decentre a Eurocentric view of philosophy and even of human intelligence and cultural excellence as such. However, he does so merely by pointing out another important tradition—starting out (as Bacon did) from the Greeks—and he does not consider altogether different traditions. Diagne confronts one branch of tradition with another branch, but not with another tree. The argument in favour of written African philosophy does not deter him from focusing on clarifying the relation between the *translatio studii* (which leads from Greece to Timbuktu) and the oral traditions of Africa (which was so important to Oluwole) or other written traditions (recall Diop's advocacy of the importance of ancient Egyptian culture).

As a matter of clarification, let us return to the question of emancipation, which we follow throughout my book. Insofar as translation hinges on agency, agency depends on a context (often one of domination) and confronts us with another variant of the emancipatory intent of working with interpretation and understanding. What is this emancipation from? From simple Manicheism, condescendence, being taken possession of by others, domination, and essentialism. Translation is a subtle means of resistance, but it is aimed at the heart of domination. On a high level of abstraction, one could say that translation offers a liberation from "what is", in pursuit of "what may become", and of "what still has to be constructed". This is not a magic recipe, but without translation, as Diagne conceives of it, it is hard to see how humanity could escape a never-ending struggle.

Finally, one may page through Diagne's book and ask why I have classed him among the African philosophers. One cannot discern in Diagne's text an explicit desire to present himself specifically or exclusively as an African author. Engagement with other African authors and issues of the African continent is only one aspect of his book. Have I made myself guilty of an incorrect attribution? My position is rather different. Diagne is an author of African descent, and at least some of his concerns stem from Africa (for example, African artworks and their transfer, the specific form of Islam in Western Africa, translation under colonisation, the appropriation-insemination of colonial languages, etc.). For the rest, one has to be attentive to the fact that his philosophical practice situates him forever at the crossroads between different modes and cultures of thinking—his philosophical practice is that of translation. Translation as a philosophical practice does not invalidate anybody as a contributor to African philosophy; in fact, it demonstrates how meaningless the essentialised attribution of "Africanness" can be.

6. Conclusion: a wide perspective on what hermeneutics can do

None of the five authors discussed in this chapter—Diop, Oluwole, Mudimbe, Eboussi Boulaga, or Diagne—present their work, generally, as hermeneutics, but all can clearly be seen to work on core issues related to understanding and interpretation. Each of the five works takes a specific direction in its exploration, giving us a wider view on what hermeneutic enquiry amounts to.

In line with hermeneutics, generally speaking, Cheikh Anta Diop starts out from language as something held in common (to the members of a linguistic group), but also as something particular (to those who know that specific language, compared to those who do not). Language registers part of a social history and plays an important role in community formation. But it also serves as a medium to express people's understanding of the world, themselves, and others. Where two languages cohabit, one may often expect violent imposition of one language at the expense of the other. More generally, cultural difference offers fertile soil for generating inequalities. Hence, proper study of people's cultural situation in relation to that of others is a means by which hermeneutics can open up that situation to critique. For Diop, such critique serves to find the best description of people's practical problem, and in that sense informs practical responses to a critiqued socio-political situation. Diop's vision is sensitive to the potential in tradition and culture, but it also includes innovation and improvisation in a holistic approach to contemporary problems, which spans even the economy, energy provision, or health care. Hermeneutics can thus amplify people's awareness of the stakes of their situation and their understanding of what is to be done about that situation. At the same time, proper interpretation reveals the complexities of action, not only because action requires means to respond efficiently to the other, but also because of the complexities of collaboration around a common goal. Diop's interdisciplinary studies and reflection on political practicalities are situated in the force-field between a history of collective suffering and a future that is accessible only through an iterative assumption of the initiative to act.

Hermeneuts, in their attention to the common human reality of understanding, include everyday language in their field of study. Orality plays a defining role in Oluwole's approach to African philosophy. For her, orality is not merely a different kind of "text": it includes a host of practices of memorisation and argumentation, and these are set in specific social contexts of transmission and curating. From these practices, intellectual culture gradually detaches itself from general culture, a separation from which philosophy emerges. Her anchoring of African philosophy in oral traditions is not a kind of return to some pristine essence, but is intended to clarify contemporary social relations. Relations between different intellectual cultures span mutual critique and symbolic violence. Insisting on the virtues of oral intellectual traditions amounts to affirming people's equal dignity and ability (all else being equal) to take charge of their fate, on terms not simply imported, but decided upon by those directly concerned. Whether in the domains of gender, development, or governance, Oluwole also draws insights from the oral tradition with a view to understanding contemporary problems better. Although sometimes her work errs in paying one-sided attention to tradition, at other moments, her work underscores the relativity and finitude of philosophy, and the contradictions contained in each tradition. This weak, hermeneutic view of rationality can in turn unmask exaggerated claims to truth and insight.

Mudimbe starts out from the array of discourses by which people have advanced truth claims about matters African, and asks about the historical formation of such discourses and the socio-historical and epistemological conditions that made them possible. The resulting study is critical in reconstructing the conditions from which each form of discourse arises, and in identifying of what each kind of discourse is a sign or "symptom". This draws our attention especially to the colonial setting from which many of the relevant discourses emerged. This setting resulted in knowledge discourses being oriented to Europe, at least in the form of epistemological filiation, but also in the more negative ideological connection to a supposed European superiority. He traces the meandering receptions and improvisations of knowledge discourse through anthropology, theology, and philosophy (where hermeneutics holds an important place). These disciplinary discourses represent strands in the complex history of the invention of Africa, by Africans, and others, and by implication, a critical reinvention of Europe in turn. Mudimbe's apparent free-standing descriptions nevertheless silently presuppose the reader's desire for truthful representation. Thus, he performs the two dimensions of critique mentioned above, and these make up part of an African "neo-culture".

Eboussi Boulaga understands philosophy as a part of the machinery by which some parts of the world have been subjected to total defeat. Whatever else philosophy may still mean to and for the victims of this defeat is to be measured by philosophy's role in their self-affirmation and ability to regain autonomy. His philosophical approach starts out from socio-political contextualisation, aims to clarify what is to be done, and is measured in terms of its contribution to the improvement of Muntu's fate. This work is undertaken, first, through a critical unmasking of existing philosophical propositions, notably those of "ethnophilosophers" and of Western-educated "school philosophers". The key to this unmasking is the contradiction between the self-affirmation claimed in these philosophical discourses, and the performative subservience of the discursive practice itself. This subservience could take the form of adopting false views on African culture as unanimist or accepting the model of indirect rule continued through academic means. The possibility of self-affirmation resides in the human ability to engage in intellectual effort, which reaches outward to interpret the world by, and appropriates what is found through, a series of "procedures of the spirit". This intellectual circuit has an ambiguous potential: it can close down on itself by remaining centred on the repetition of ideas and the production of more books; but it can also be an act of self-attestation and the resumption of initiative through new interpretations. This ambiguous potential is what allows for shifts or deviations from the agenda set by the inherited school tradition of philosophy, but also from the remnants of tradition. By letting the present concerns of Muntu burst into them, philosophy and tradition are transfunctionalised from being a means to indirect rule to being a means to self-affirmation. In both forms of transfunctionalisation, the perspective of a history of trauma opens up to a creative assumption of the future. While philosophy is only part of the response to the fate of Muntu, its significance stretches beyond its own practice in that self-attestation through transfunctionalisation forms a "miniature protocol of action" for other domains of free action.

Diagne's contribution to hermeneutics is focused on bridging the gap between the foreign and the familiar. The gap may take the form of a variety of dimensions of power, time, place, literary genre, and, of course, language. Hence, the transition from one side to the other is established in complex ways, including translation, transfer, tradition, or transplantation. Consequently, translation is more than mere repetition, since it allows for a margin of creativity, through which both the "original" and the "recipient" language can be changed. This places the translator in a position to choose between actionable possibilities in relation to the original "text", ranging between fidelity and symbolic violence. Diagne highlights the creativity through which a translator could change the nature of interaction between the practitioners of dominant and dominated languages. This is possible because the translational "third space" is a space of creative hybridisation between different discourses, languages, or cultures, and holds the potential of promoting equivalence and reciprocity. This potential is not based on some universal language that would guarantee the consistency of an "overarching universalism", but resides in the human ability to translate and thus create a "lateral universalism", which is the uncertain but real possibility of overcoming the absolute relativism of juxtaposed cultural forms. The commonality between humans that can thus be formed requires an ethic of translation, the core of which is generosity and hospitableness, as well as resistance to inequality and domination.

Looking back at the domains covered in this chapter, one gets an impression of the impressive range of concerns confronted by hermeneutics in its wider sense. One learns perhaps as much from the dead ends as from the productive work advanced by these authors. The time has come to change the perspective from the authors-based approach followed up to now to integrate insights and develop them into an encompassing view on hermeneutics. This is the aim of the concluding chapter.

Select annotated bibliography

Cheikh Anta Diop

Coquery-Vidrovitch, Catherine. "Cheikh Anta Diop et l'histoire Africaine". *Le Débat* 208, no. 1 (2020): 178–190.

    The author situates the development of Diop's thought in relation to his own political aspirations, the state of relevant scientific debates during his lifetimes, and the more recent reception of his main theses.

Diop, Cheikh Anta. *Alerte sous les tropiques: articles 1946–1960: culture et développement en Afrique noire*. Paris: Présence Africaine, 1990. English edition (1996), *Towards the African Renaissance: Essays in African Culture & Development, 1946–1960*. Translated by Egbuna P. Modum. London: Karnak House, 1996.

    A collection of Diop's articles on language, tradition, and history (with inroads into that of ancient Egypt) as resources for self-confidence and initiative in a modernising Africa.

Diop, Cheikh Anta. *The African Origin of Civilization: Myth or Reality*. Translated by Mercer Cook. New York: Hill, 1974.

    Selections of Diop's major works of Afro-centric historiography (*Nations nègres et culture* [1955] and *Antériorité des civilisations nègres* [1967]), overlapping in orientation with *Towards the African Renaissance*.

Obenga, Théophile. *African Philosophy—The Pharaonic Period: 2780–330 BC*. Dakar: Per Ankh, [1990] 2004.

    Similar to Diop's Afro-centric view of African history, this book considers ancient Egypt, focusing directly on the question of philosophy.

Sophie Bosede Oluwole

Kazeem, Fayemi Ademola. "Sophie Oluwole's Hermeneutic Trend in African Political Philosophy: Some Comments". *Criticism* 13 (2013):158–177.

    This book offers a reading of Oluwole's work as a contribution to the hermeneutic trend in African philosophy, with specific attention to its relation to political philosophy.

Nkombe Oleko. *Métaphore et métonymie dans les symboles parémiologiques. L'intersubjectivité dans les "Proverbes Tetela"*. Kinshasa: Faculté de théologie catholique, [1975] 1979.

    A classic hermeneutic study on proverbs and their relevance for philosophy. It is valuable as a comparison to Oluwole's work from outside of the Yoruba tradition.

Oluwole, Sophie B. "Culture, Gender, and Development Theories in Africa". *Africa Development* 22, no. 1 (1997): 95–121 [cited as "Culture, Gender"].

Oluwole, Sophie B. "Culture, Nationalism and Philosophy". *Studies in Intercultural Philosophy* 3 (1997): 23–42 [cited as "Culture, Nationalism and Philosophy"].

Oluwole, Sophie B. "Philosophy and Oral Tradition". Lagos, Nigeria: African Research Konsultancy, 1997 [cited as "Philosophy and Oral Tradition"].

Oluwole, Sophie B. "Oruka's Mission in African Philosophy". In *Sagacious Reasoning: Henry Odera Oruka in Memoriam*, edited by Anke Graness and Kai Kresse. Nairobi: East African Educational Publishers, 1999, pp. 149–162 [cited as "Oruka's Mission"].

Oluwole, Sophie B., "Africa". In *A Companion to Feminist Philosophy*, edited by Alison M. Jaggar and Iris Marion Young. Malden: Blackwell, 2000, pp. 96–107 [cited as "Africa"].

Oluwole, Sophie B. "The Cultural Enslavement of the African Mind". In *Introduction to Social and Political Philosophy*, edited by Jeje Kolawole. Lagos: Samtech Communications, 2000, pp. 95–111 [cited as "The Cultural Enslavement"].

Oluwole, Sophie B. "Democracy and Indigenous Governance: The Nigerian Experience". In *Philosophy, Democracy and Responsible Governance in Africa*, edited by J. O. Oguejiofor. Münster: Lit, 2003 [cited as "Democracy and Indigenous Governance"].

Oluwole, Sophie B. *Socrates and Orunmila: Two Patron Saints of Classical Philosophy*. Lagos, Nigeria: ARK Publishers, [2014] 2017 [cited as *Socrates and Orunmila*].

Oruka, Odera. *Sage Philosophy. Indigenous Thinkers and Modern Debate on African Philosophy*. Leiden: Brill, 1990.

This is Oruka's central statement on "sage philosophy".

Presbey, Gail. "Sophie Oluwole's Major Contributions to African Philosophy". *Hypatia* 35, no. 2, 2020: 231–242.

An overview of Oluwole's philosophy with a useful, albeit incomplete, bibliography of her writings.

Valentin-Yves Mudimbe

Agzenay, Asma. "V. Y. Mudimbe's Archaeological Reading of Africa's Difference in Cultural History". In *Handbook of African Philosophy of Difference* (*Handbooks in Philosophy* series), edited by E. Imafidon. Cham: Springer, 2020, pp. 129–147.

A critical reading of *The Invention of Africa*, especially for its use of Foucault's understanding of archaeology.

Coquery-Vidrovitch, Catherine. "Valentin-Yves Mudimbe, *L'Invention de l'Afrique. Gnose, Philosophie et Ordre de La Connaissance*". *Cahiers d'histoire. Revue d'histoire critique* 151 (2022). http://journals.openedition.org/chrhc/18064. Last accessed 25 March 2024.

Written for the publication of the French translation of *The Invention of Africa*, this review situates the book in relation to other post-colonial studies.

Fraiture, Pierre-Philippe. *V. Y. Mudimbe: Undisciplined Africanism*. Liverpool: Liverpool University Press, 2013.

An overview of Mudimbe's work up to the date of publication.

Kavwahirehi, Kasereka. *V. Y. Mudimbe et la ré-invention de l'Afrique. Poétique et politique de la décolonisation des sciences humaines*. Amsterdam and New York: Rodopi, 2006.

This volume studies Mudimbe's entire oeuvre.

Mudimbe, Valentin-Yves. *The Invention of Africa: Gnosis, Philosophy, and the Order of Knowledge*. Bloomington: Indiana University Press, 1988.

Mudimbe, Valentin-Yves. *The Idea of Africa*. London: Currey, 1994.

The follow-up volume to *The Invention of Africa*. The Preface to this book is a valuable commentary on *The Invention of Africa*.

Fabien Eboussi Boulaga

Fabien Eboussi Boulaga. *La crise du Muntu. Authenticité africaine et philosophie.* Paris: Présence Africaine, 1977. English translation: *Muntu in Crisis: African Authenticity and Philosophy.* Preface by Kasereka Kavwahirehi. Trenton: Africa World Press, [1977] 2014.

Eboussi Boulaga, Fabien. *L'Affaire de la philosophie africaine. Au-delà des querelles.* Paris: Editions Terroirs/Karthala, 2011.

This volume collects Eboussi Boulaga's most important essays, starting from his early critique of Tempels, "Le Bantu problématique".

Collective, coordinated by Kisukidi, Nadia Yala, *Eboussi Boulaga: Défaites et utopies.* Special issue of *Politique africaine* 164, no. 4 (2021): 5–100.

This special issue explores Eboussi Boulaga's work from several angles. The abstracts are available in English on the Cairn platform: https://www.cairn-int.info/journal-politique-africaine-2021-4.htm

Procesi, Lidia and Kasereka Kavwahirehi, eds. *Beyond the Lines: Fabien Eboussi Boulaga, A Philosophical Practice/Au-delà des lignes: Fabien Eboussi Boulaga, une pratique philosophique.* Munich: Lincom Europa, 2012.

A volume of studies about and for Eboussi Boulaga. It contains Eboussi Boulaga's full bibliography.

Mbélé, Charles Romain. *Système et liberté dans la philosophie négro-africaine moderne.* Dakar: Panafrika/Silex/Nouvelles-Sud, 2018.

Mbélé situates Eboussi Boulaga's work in relation to other great Cameroonian philosophers and in relation to the major socio-political concerns of African societies today.

Wolff, Ernst. "Working under Cover. Eboussi Boulaga and the Practice of Social Critique". In *Philosophy in the Shadow of Racism* (forthcoming).

Souleymane Bachir Diagne

Diagne, Souleymane Bachir. "L'universel lateral comme traduction". In *Les Pluriels de Barbara Cassin ou le partage des équivoques*, edited by Philippe Büttgen, Michèle Gendreau-Massaloux, and Xavier North. Lormont: Le Bord de l'Eau, 2014, pp. 243–255.

An important articulation of Diagne's understanding of "lateral universalism".

Diagne, Souleymane Bachir. *The Ink of the Scholars: Reflections on Philosophy in Africa.* Translated by Jonathan Adjemian. Dakar: CODESRIA, [2013] 2017.

Four essays in which Diagne gives his view on the most important questions of contemporary African philosophy.

Diagne, Souleymane Bachir. *Open to Reason: Muslim Philosophers in Conversation with the Western Tradition.* Translated by Jonathan Adjemian. New York: Columbia University Press, [2014] 2018.

Diagne, Souleymane Bachir and Jean-Loup Amselle. *In Search of Africa(s). Universalism and Decolonial Thought.* Translated by Andrew Brown. Cambridge: Polity, 2020.

This debate can be read as clarification of main aspects of Diagne's thought.

Diagne, Souleymane Bachir. *Le Fagot de ma mémoire.* Paris: Philippe Rey, 2021.

Diagne, Souleymane Bachir. *De langue à langue. L'hospitalité de la traduction.* Paris: Albin Michel, 2022.

Diagne, Souleymane Bachir. *From Language to Language. The Hospitality of Translation.* Translated by Dylan Temel. New York: Other Press (forthcoming).

Fall, Papa Abdou. "Souleymane Bachir Diagne, le penseur du propre et de l'universel". *Akofena* 4, no. 6 (2022): 437–444.

Fall emphasises Diagne's correction of the idea of universalism, which includes reflection on the relations between self and other and on creolisation.

Thiérard, Hélène. "Multilingual Literatures and the Production of Universality through Translation: Cassin, Diagne, Tawada". In *Minor Universality. Rethinking Humanity after Western Universalism/ Universalité mineure. Penser l'humanité après l'universalisme occidental*, edited by Markus Messling and Jonas Tinius. Berlin/Boston: De Gruyter, pp. 173–189.

This article studies Diagne's views on translation and universalism, by situating it in relation to contemporary proposals in this domain of enquiry.

CHAPTER 6

Conclusion: hermeneutics as commitment

In the preceding chapters, I sought to introduce the reader to the world of hermeneutics in African philosophy. Moreover, in considering each author, I strove to expand the discussion, as far as possible, by means of a critical examination. The result is not a comprehensive or fixed set of doctrines, but a sense of a number of directions in which philosophers have explored the fact of human understanding and interpretation. That is why I have refrained from declaring what hermeneutics is, or what its real task is—in line with what I indicated in the Preface. The aim was rather to offer the reader an orientation to the different proposals for and contribution to hermeneutics, to equip readers to decide for themselves.

Having now looked at three major hermeneuts and five more authors whose work represents substantial contributions to hermeneutics, the value of Chapter 1's literature review should be evident. Studying the landscape of publications on, or relevant to, understanding and interpretation makes it possible to identify several overlapping concerns and views. There is a series of family resemblances that allow a tradition of hermeneutics in African philosophy to be identified. However, opinions may diverge on what the most typical approaches to hermeneutics are and who the most defining authors are. Views on the relative significance of European hermeneutics for African hermeneutics also vary. Some consider hermeneutics a narrow perspective on specific problems, whereas others consider it to be the broadest perspective on all philosophical problems. Some consider hermeneutics to be a rounded offering of ideas, while others insist that it is a project of synthesising, and that the realisation of this synthesis is still ongoing. Finally, by omitting hermeneutics from their discussion of African philosophy, some authors by implication question the significance of hermeneutics in and for African philosophy.

In Chapter 1, I concluded that the presence of hermeneutics in African philosophy is too clear to deny, but that its precise place in the field of African philosophies remains uncertain and contested. Throughout this book, my approach has been to *reflect* this uncertainty about hermeneutics, rather than to impose order on its divergent forms and relevance. Nonetheless, there are two ways in which the construction of the present book implies my own position. On the one hand, by devoting a whole book to hermeneutics in African philosophy, I unquestionably side with those who consider it a significant, albeit small, part of the African philosophical offering. On the other hand, through my choice of authors, I tried to represent the variety of views on hermeneutics and the centrifugal and centripetal effects of philosophical hermeneutics (see Chapter 1, § 2.3), rather than to demarcate a narrowly defined core. (African) hermeneutics is not the summation of the opinions of the authors studied. It is the interpretation made by each author of whatever could be studied, assessed, and concluded.

In this concluding chapter, I want to follow their lead. To do this, I need to assume a more independent position. Therefore, the aim is neither to summarise the book, nor to present the definitive synthesis, although I do implicitly confirm the preliminary orientation of the typical convictions and concerns of hermeneutics offered in Chapter 1, § 1. Admittedly, I already began to present my personal view when, in discussing each of the selected authors, I extended the presentation with a critical engagement with their argument. But in this chapter, I want to take a view on hermeneutics as a whole and reflect on what I have learned.

In as far as this chapter draws on insights from African philosophers and reflects on a subdiscipline of African philosophy, it is my contribution to African philosophical hermeneutics.[1] This contribution focuses on five issues: (§ 1) the relation between hermeneutics and philosophical anthropology, paying special attention to everyday understanding, practices of interpretation, and philosophical hermeneutics; (§ 2) managing the difficult coordination of cultural specificity, translation, and commonalities between people; (§ 3) the structural uncertainty of hermeneutics, suspended in complex relations between familiarity and strangeness; (§ 4) the orientation of hermeneutics to practice, especially liberation; and (§ 5) the relation between hermeneutics and ethics. In the concluding remarks (§ 6), I reflect on hermeneutics as a part of African philosophy, and its wider contribution to philosophy in general and to humanity.

1. Hermeneutics and philosophical anthropology

As much as philosophers have insisted on the cultural and linguistic differences between people, and on the difficulties of and failures in communication between people, hermeneuts widely agree that *spontaneous understanding and efforts of interpretation are general human abilities*. Admittedly, not all people understand equally well (and this raises the fraught question of what good understanding is), and practices of interpretation are extremely diverse. Nevertheless, except in extreme cases of pathology, human beings perceive the world surrounding them, consisting of things, people and other living beings, and symbols, as *meaningful*, and they have some understanding of that meaning. Moreover, as wide as the experience of meaning stretches, just as wide are the difficulties of understanding, because of misunderstandings, confusion, disappointed expectations, differences between languages, cultural plurality, and so on. Each of these compels people to reflect on what is understood or misunderstood. And so prevalent is this reflection that it gradually gives rise to practices of interpretation that may acquire a fair amount of independence in relation to the original everyday understanding: in education and theology, in art or science.

Such typically human experiences of understanding and practices of interpretation correspond to what Giddens calls a "double hermeneutic" (as I have already evoked in the Preface): that which is initially spontaneously grasped as meaningful (the first hermeneutic) then itself becomes the object of secondary, more intentional practices of deciphering (the second hermeneutic).[2] For the sake of convenience, I refer to these two levels of hermeneutics as *understanding* and *interpretation*. Moreover, *philosophical hermeneutics* adds a third layer to this: this layer is the attempt to provide a systematic account of understanding and interpretation, and of a host of issues that follow from them. In this sense, philosophical hermeneutics is thus distinct from everyday understanding (because it is a discipline-specific practice rather than a spontaneous engagement with the ambient world). It is also distinct from interpretation (because it involves a meta-reflection on the origins, constitution, and limits of practices of interpretation). And yet, it is inconceivable that people could participate in philosophical hermeneutics if they themselves did not have vast experience of understanding in everyday life. It would be equally inconceivable that they could subject interpretations to a philosophical meta-interpretation if they had no prior experience in practices of interpreting understandings. For this reason, when I speak about "hermeneutics", I refer to all three dimensions of engagement with meaning.

Everyday understanding is not philosophical hermeneutics, and practices of interpretation are not simply a form of philosophical hermeneutics, but philosophical hermeneutics always remains dependent on understanding and interpretation—not only as the objects of its study, but as constitutive dimensions of its own practice. Different philosophers give different articulations to these relations: some insist that there are strong proto-philosophical qualities in everyday understanding and in non-philosophical practices of interpretation; others insist on the specificity of philosophical research and argumentation, and therefore see hermeneutics as relatively independent from ordinary understanding and interpretation. Therefore, where I refer to everyday understanding, practices of interpretation, and philosophical hermeneutics as *"levels"* of hermeneutics to reflect the way in which they depend on the other, the term "level" does not imply a hierarchy. The three levels simply reflect three quite different, but interdependent, forms of human engagement with meaning.

None of the authors in this book presents philosophical hermeneutics in terms of this three-level model, but it is not difficult to find support for these levels in their work.[3] Let us reconsider the three levels in more detail: understanding (§ 1.1), practices of interpretation (§ 1.2), and philosophical hermeneutics (§ 1.3).

1.1. *Understanding, belonging, culture*

People understand the world because through their perceptions and actions the surrounding environment presents itself as meaningful. Meaning presents itself to people as finite, situated beings, which implies that they are also perspectival beings.[4] By implication, then, understanding can offer only a limited grasp of people, their experiences, and environment—not an all-encompassing truth. Understanding therefore of necessity reflects the finitude and situatedness of each person. Living a life of spontaneous understanding certainly includes experiences of incomprehension, meaninglessness, or confusion, in varying degrees of intensity and significance.

However, human beings are also socialised. They represent and communicate their understandings and transmit views, ideas, languages, objects, and modes of doing from generation to generation. Understanding thereby acquires a cultural dimension; the ways in which people understand, the ways in which they become familiar with the surrounding world, mark them as belonging to cultural groups, with or without their active pursuit of belonging. And although people can alter aspects of their cultural belonging, they cannot change everything at the same time.[5] This simple statement hides a complex reality that is a core object of study in philosophical hermeneutics.

African hermeneuts are unanimous in confirming the significance of culture and tradition for hermeneutics. They are almost equally unanimous in maintaining that the ethnophilosophical equation of culture with philosophy cannot be sustained. In particular, they reject the idea of "concordism" (Eboussi Boulaga)—the assumption that all who belong to a shared cultural tradition also think alike. Moreover, they tend to reject claims that culture is static or homogenous. In other words, even if people are socialised and their understanding of meaning is shaped by the culture(s) transmitted to them, each person's view of reality has a significant degree of uniqueness. Although humans are shaped by culture and tradition, under more peaceful circumstances they are less like prisoners in iron cages than like people moving in clothes. And this space of manoeuvring creates some divergence of opinion and may cumulatively result in gradual changes of culture. Naturally, when domination prevails, the scope for altering imposed cultural forms intentionally will narrow significantly.

Typically, then, hermeneutics criticises misrepresentations of tradition and culture, but without in the least underestimating the significance of tradition and culture for philosophy. Okere's position is a good example in this respect: he considers everyday culture as the "Archimedean point" from which any thought (and philosophy in particular) can be launched, because culture already contains philosophy-generating potential, which he calls "philosophemes". Philosophemes are not philosophy, but they provide many opportunities and provocations for further reflection. I would want to underscore that such philosophemes may be fairly stable transmitted elements (practical insights, forms of socialisation, proverbs, etc.), but they may equally arise from an unexpected confluence of circumstances that creates unexpected views on matters.

Several hermeneuts confirm that African culture holds such potential for stimulating reflection, and that African philosophy can (and does) spring from the familiar terrain of belonging. A variety of stances can be adopted in relation to such belonging, spanning the extremes that one may call the "archivists" and the "artists". The archivists emphasise the importance of gathering, documenting, conserving, and transmitting a valuable cultural inheritance, for the sake of philosophy and life in society more broadly. Oluwole's advocacy for the value of oral traditions represents a very bold version of this approach. The artists emphasise the significance of adopting, adapting, transforming, and innovating a heritage. They foreground the creative potential, that which can be made from this inheritance.

I come back to this point below, to consider also how non-belonging, strangeness, or disruption can generate philosophical reflection.

1.2. *Arts of interpretation*

Where hermeneutics is defined as the art of interpretation, it mostly refers to the second of our three levels of hermeneutics. It is called an "art" because one is not born with it, one has to acquire it. It refers to relatively standardised practices that some master better than others do. Arts of interpretation have in common that they take the domain of meaning as their object of study—through documentation, categorisation, analysis, and even explanation, with a view to understanding better, to clarifying. But arts of interpretation typically delimit their perspective or their field of study, whence the multitude of different arts of interpretation. Practices of interpretation strive to establish facts as accurately as possible and lay out clarifications as rigorously as possible, but interpretation is especially needed for domains of uncertainty, complexity, ambivalence, and repeated questioning.

Large parts of the human and social sciences consist in practicing arts of interpretation. However, one should not think only of modern academic disciplines. Some forms of narration, of theological argumentation, or instruction in handiwork, for instance, also take the form of arts of interpretation.

One of the salient features of philosophical hermeneutics is that authors often acknowledge their dependence on insights derived from one or more of the arts of interpretation. In fact, there is often no clear boundary between where the work of such arts ends and the philosophical work resumes. This often gives hermeneutics an interdisciplinary character. For example, a substantial part of Mudimbe's work is an interpretation of Africanist discourses on other disciplines. Diop's thought is subtended by linguistics and Egyptology. Diagne draws on the intertwined histories of Islamic theology and philosophy. Perhaps most importantly, whether they thematise this or not, all the authors I have looked at work with an understanding of *socio-political history*. They experienced some of this history first-hand, but their work presupposes competence on a much longer history and wider geographical space, knowledge of which a responsible philosopher could only obtain by consulting the best research available in history.

1.3. Philosophical hermeneutics

Given the important place accorded to understanding and interpretation, it becomes less easy to describe and insist on the specificity and necessity of a third level of hermeneutics. The first element of the domain of the third level that I would like to emphasise may be called *phenomenological anthropology*. By this I mean a description of the general characteristics of human beings and societies, in as far as they condition the fact of understanding and interpretation. This echoes Serequeberhan's understanding of hermeneutics as anchored in a reading of human existence. Surely this already requires many insights from other interpretative disciplines. But I know of no discipline that focuses as much on the entire domain of understanding and interpretation as philosophy does—this then is the second specificity of the philosophical enterprise: its striving towards *integration and exhaustivity*.

Third, any art of interpretation begins to "spill over" into philosophy when it starts to reflect on its own *epistemology and methodology*. Philosophical hermeneutics too engages with such questions, but tends once again to do so on a more general level. It is typical of the philosophical engagement with questions of understanding and interpretation to attempt to formulate *assessments*, for instance, in finding ways to expose an abusive imposition of understandings, or in searching for the most appropriate directions in which to develop aspects of interpretation. This may be the fourth defining element of philosophical hermeneutics. It opens up the question of the relationship between hermeneutics and practice that is examined in more detail below.

Philosophers typically engage in the task of hermeneutics in dialogue with other parts of their philosophical tradition, but it is not clear to me how significant this engagement is for the task of philosophical hermeneutics. Furthermore, if we look back at the different means by which the selected authors have made their contributions, we see that they have often used the tools of other sciences. One could then describe much of what is being done in philosophical hermeneutics as involving anthropological, historical, sociological, and political perspectives on the human capacity for understanding and interpretation with a reconstructive and critical ambition.

Since many forms of philosophy involve the human capacity to understand and engage with the interpretative sciences, many of them have a hermeneutic aspect. This is what leads some people to consider hermeneutics as central to all the work of philosophy. In line with this contention, we saw in Chapter 1 that Nkombe and Smet's view of hermeneutics as an encompassing project of ongoing syntheses reflects this position. They were followed in this by Mudimbe and Kavwahirehi. We also saw how this wide perspective on hermeneutics invites one to draw, question after question, closer to a hermeneutic approach, resulting in hermeneutics' *centripetal* effect. This does not take away from the fact that views differ on what hermeneutics ultimately is, and the ways in which people work in it, resulting in the *centrifugal* effect of hermeneutics. Here, one needs only to juxtapose Mudimbe and Oluwole, for instance, to see how different hermeneutic work can be.

2. **Negotiating plurality**

So far, I have largely bypassed a central aspect of hermeneutics: its recognition of plurality. Not only does hermeneutics affirm linguistic, cultural, economic, and other differences, but it examines the impact that these differences have on differences in how people grasp reality. In various ways, all African hermeneuts recognise some form of plurality. In rejecting ethnophilosophical unanimism, they highlight the differences of opinion among members of a (shared) cultural sphere. By advancing hermeneutics as an effort by individual authors (even if they are supported by others), they admit a plurality of takes on the world. By clarifying the conditions for the possibility of African philosophy (as Okere, Serequeberhan, Oluwole, or Eboussi Boulaga do), they are overtly or implicitly asserting that there is a difference between African philosophy and other forms of philosophy, as well as the full intellectual right of African philosophy to be considered on a par with any other form of philosophy. In tracing the historical development of disciplines of knowledge (as Mudimbe does) or the transfer of learning (as Diagne does), one acknowledges the gradual change of modes of interpretation, which one might call temporal and spatial plurality. Finally, emphasising translation, deviation, re-taking, and other forms of creativity in the process of interpretation, suggests that one can expect authors' socio-political diagnoses to differ, and that authors would generate a plurality of views on the initiatives to which hermeneutics should lead.

The net effect of these pluralities is they disrupt the schematic three-level picture that I present of hermeneutics in § 1 above. Plurality within a single person's view may well render the ambiguities and complexities of what is understood, but it undermines certainty, making it difficult to assume a single strong position. The plurality of languages, cultural practices, and institutions also makes it difficult for people to understand one another and can require tremendous energy and devotion to be dealt with. Plurality creates complex juxtapositions of competing and sometimes irreconcilable points of view; any arbitration may turn out to be nothing more than yet another view parallel to the others. Plurality can also generate tension and power disparities between adherents of different positions, and these differences cannot always be undone through debate. In cases where views or institutions have to be confronted or even dismantled, a plurality of strategies to achieve such ends may undermine effective action. And since our understanding of matters often focuses on what is important, precious, or urgent to us, mere acceptance of plurality in principle is not always compatible with our efforts to lead life with integrity.

Thus, while there is much to be said for appreciating diversity and accommodating divergent views, in practice, plurality remains equivocal and can pose real difficulties to the best efforts to merely understand, interpret, and make headway in interaction. My point here is obviously not to vilify plurality, but to acknowledge the difficulties that emerge from its presence.[6] This enumeration of some of the difficulties associated with plurality should also convince us that dealing with them requires a complex understanding of the problems and complex proposals to *negotiate*[7] our way through them. This will remain the task of hermeneutics as long as there are human beings. Here I would like to unpack the nature of negotiating of plurality. I first identify two ways of avoiding such a negotiation of plurality (§ 2.1), and clarify generality as the presupposition that supports interpretation in a milieu of plurality (§ 2.2). Then, I point out four hermeneutic resources that can be used to carry out this task. Hermeneutics (a) is an ethics of listening, and (b) gives itself diverse means by which to augment this capacity (§ 2.3), (c) develops self-qualifying and probing capacities of critique, and (d) supports the creative process of "taking a step" towards new understandings (§ 2.4).

2.1. *Hermeneutics' two aversions and its founding conviction*

Generally speaking, hermeneutics is averse to two radical responses to the difficulties of plurality. Both amount to abdicating the task of negotiating plurality.

The first kind of avoidance consists in accepting plurality wholesale in a kind of nihilistic relativism where everything and its opposite are of equal value. Pursuing this line of argument consistently would entail holding voids of meaning or the collapse of meaning as equal to experiences of value. Indiscriminate violence would be merely one manifestation of human existence among many. Discourse would be reduced to mere linguistic effects, without any regard for what it may refer to, or fails to refer to; or it may reduce discourse to mere power effects without any regard for the relative preferability or objectionability of that discourse.

The second kind of avoidance consists in an artificial reduction of plurality by stereotyping, essentialisation, ahistorical renderings of what is historical, or one-sided explanations. Let me already anticipate § 4 below by pointing out that such reductions are not found only in scholarly writing, but also make part up of a socio-political reality—in this respect, part of the vocation of hermeneutics is to help unmask such reductions and undo their consequences.

How tenable these two positions really are in practice is a question I need not deal with here. The point is that as soon as one diverges from either position, the question arises what the nature is of the (minimal) hermeneutic engagement with plurality that such divergence implies.

2.2. *Generality as supposition and the practical commitment of hermeneutics*

A lot of what hermeneutics is, or aspires to be, results from adopting positions between the two extremes named in § 2.1. All such positions entail dealing with plurality. It would be *incorrect* to say that hermeneutics is inspired by a naïve optimism regarding the possibility of unhindered dialogue, mutual understanding, or a tendency of views to converge. In fact, hermeneuts are acutely aware of how difficult it is to negotiate plurality, so one of the tasks of philosophical hermeneutics is to give an account of why this is the case. But the pursuit of understanding and interpretation is premised on a conviction that attempting to bridge the gap between elements of plurality *is not simply futile*. This negative formulation is essential for understanding what hermeneutics is about.

The assumption that efforts to negotiate plurality are not simply futile is both a key *supposition* of hermeneutics and a *practical commitment* that accompanies the work of interpretation throughout. Sometimes this supposition is explicitly stated and argued for. But whenever interpretation is carried out, meanings are clarified, or points of view are arbitrated, this supposition is at least implicitly at work. Above we saw that the human ability to understand is rooted in everyday practical existence; here we see that interpretation itself is practical in the sense of performing a commitment to possible understandings. This assumption could be articulated as follows: wherever human beings express meaning, *this meaning will not forever remain completely inaccessible to other human beings*. Engaging in interpretation within a milieu of plurality without a commitment in line with this assumption would amount to a performative contradiction. Without performing—setting into effect—this presupposition, it would still be possible to understand spontaneously, but all engagement with plurality, disruption, confusion, would become futile. Again, proceeding in agreement with this assumption does not commit the interpreter in any way to unrealistic views about the transparency of others and their cultural artefacts. The practical commitment to interpretation is compatible with the practical limits of interpretation.

Given that this commitment is a practical one, we may well attempt to excavate the hidden reasons as to why it is not simply experienced as an arbitrary decision. Any such excavation would have to be undertaken in full awareness that the decision to make this commitment is not the same as a theoretical conclusion. If we nevertheless proceed to identify the hidden reasons for making such a practical commitment, I would venture that they have a strong anthropological component. Through such a practical commitment, we recognise, implicitly or explicitly, that, (a) however diverse human beings may be, they share at least some minimal (but significant) *generalities*; moreover, (b) by working on the differences, *commonalities* can gradually be constructed. Recognising such generalities, or acting in anticipation of commonalities being created, in no way negates the specificity of each point of view. Indeed, one approaches this thin generality only through the thickness of one's own particularity.[8] Similar to Diagne, I do not subscribe to a thesis of a universal language or cultural universals to which all people would somehow have equal access. But claiming the reality of lateral universalism,[9] or the possibility of finding and expanding generalities between people, presupposes that interpreters or translators assume from the start that something in the other's way of being human is similar to their own way, whatever the differences may be, and that it is not futile to seek to build out this similarity.

The set of generalities that an interpreter may consider it realistic to assume may differ in number and extent, depending on the material of interpretation. For this reason, it is not all that simple to unpack a single set of anthropological constants that accompany all understanding. However, significant parts of what I have presented under the headings of understanding and interpretation (above, §§ 1.1 and 1.2) may well make part of it. Insofar as we concentrate on philosophical hermeneutics, the work of the authors discussed in this book amply illustrate how such commonality (between diverse people) informs their work, as I have repeatedly pointed out.[10]

2.3. Hermeneutic resources: an ethics of listening and diverse "procedures of the spirit"

In committing practically to the possibility of negotiating plurality, one can draw on a number of resources.

First, since hermeneuts hold that finitude, situatedness, and perspectivism characterise all people's openness to the world, hermeneutics has to be an *ethic of listening and humility*.[11] Of course, not all interpreters lend an ear to what they study with humble self-restraint, but this failing contradicts the factual limitation of their understanding and is likely to compromise their effort to bridge plurality. A hermeneut does not think that the other(s)—however strange they may appear—are ignorant or silly, but starts by making an effort to grasp the other as well as possible. For this reason, one may also describe hermeneutics as an exercise in patience. Only after making this effort does the process of assessing other points of view start, which may in turn lead to combinations of appropriation and rejection. However, even our severest criticism does not exclude recognition of what is meaningful in the other's stance. Conversely, understanding does not mean approving.

One can neglect this ethic of humility by refusing to listen patiently to others. But one can also do so by identifying too quickly with those one is supposed to listen to. It is not uncommon for people who seek to think in solidarity with the exploited or oppressed, to homogenise them as a group or overhastily to identify with them. It is troubling when philosophers misuse such identification as a way artificially to augment the authority or their claims (as if standing for a good cause relieves the philosopher of the work of rigorous argumentation). It is particularly vexing when such identification is used to delegitimate the arguments of other conversational partners, who may equally want to practise philosophical solidarity. Intellectual integrity and an ethic of humility requires that we respect the complex variety of conditions under which people (about whom we reflect) live, distinguish solidarity from identification, and lend an understanding ear to potential partners in pursuit of such a cause.

But even with good will, understanding others does not necessarily come easily. As a second resource, interpreters have at their disposal a wide range of intellectual procedures to accompany this patient listening. One of these is the ways of working in the interpretive practices of specific cultures and the interpretive sciences that are now very widely institutionalised in universities and other research institutions (see above, § 1.2). One could represent the wide array of intellectual efforts—as Eboussi Boulaga does when he speaks about the *"procedures of the spirit"*—as moving in an outward and an inward movement. Reaching outward, the widest manageable perceptiveness is sought through dialogue and conducting interviews, establishing texts, surveying cultural artefacts, setting up archives, cataloguing phenomena, reviewing literature, describing interactions, institutions, works of art, and so on. Reaching back inward, interpretation consists of an analysis of cultural forms, arguments, and styles, as well as of comparisons (Oluwole, Diagne), a reconstruction of events, tendencies, generalities, and causal connections, a historiography for contextualisation or genealogy, and so on. The process also requires documentation and an articulation of the findings, in debate with the present state of interpretation offered by others, in the form of arbitration, assessment, or critique. And when this has been done, the changing state of findings from these outward and inward movements set each other in motion again, in an unending circle of mutual clarification and correction.

While both the outward and inward efforts ideally serve to maximise attention to what is, and the most rigorous representation of it, any form of documentation and analysis requires a particular perspective, and therefore involves a form of reduction (for example, not everything is archived; the documentation of research results is limited to what is relevant to the original research question). One of the aims of continuous interpretation is then to minimise harmful effects that may arise in this way.

But there are also ways of meta-interpretation that compel interpreters to reconsider their basic suppositions and approaches, the methodologies of their efforts reaching outward and inward, and the normative orientation of their practices. Consider, for instance, the fact that African artworks in European collections were indeed interpreted by artists, art historians, anthropologists, and others in the way I describe, but that questioning their very presence in these collections calls for a significant rethinking of these modes of interpretation (in this respect, revisit Diagne's comments on the restitution of artworks). As this example illustrates, such meta-interpretation may be generated on the basis of public opinion or on the basis of second order reflection arising from the relevant sciences themselves. Typically, philosophical hermeneutics would strive to find an encompassing perspective on as many of the fundamental problems of interpretation as possible and pursue reflection on them as far as possible. When African hermeneuts orient hermeneutics towards problems of cultural diversity, self-affirmation, and liberation, they demonstrate this function of philosophical hermeneutics. In assuming this role, hermeneutics is more than a philosophy of interpretation. It is also a model for social scientific research that seeks a balance between the simultaneously valid (but sometimes conflicting) demands of a researcher's autonomous reasoning and the intelligence circulating in a population, and between critique justified by institutionally set scientific practices and critique justified by citizens' opinions.[12]

2.4. *Hermeneutic resources: critique and creativity*

The above paragraph evoked the effective presence of *critique in interpretation* in three ways. Let me state it more explicitly.
(1) Pursuing interpretation according to the best insights arising from the relevant practices entails distinguishing between more and less successful practices—such critical assessment is part of the practices themselves. Furthermore, analysis and genealogy, broadly construed, are practices of critique.

(2) While the reaching outward and inward involved in interpretation depend on each other, they also proceed independently. This may result in their mutual destabilisation in the iterative interpretative process. The demand to renew any of the procedures of reaching outward in the light of the procedures of reaching inward, or vice versa, amounts to critique.
(3) Meta-perspectives can critique existing practices, the relation between the normative assumptions or the socio-political ends of interpretative practice.

One of the tasks of philosophical hermeneutics is to scrutinise all of these workings of critique so as to assess their potential in opening up, or expose their obstruction to, the meanings that are to be interpreted. In speaking about interpretation and its relation to critique in this way, I have presented a kind of progressive process of accumulation and correction of insights. And often it is this kind of process. However, interpretations are also advanced in contexts where alternative interpretations already circulate. Advancing a better interpretation therefore often amounts to relativising or delegitimating other interpretations; it may also consist in uncovering the harmful effects of certain forms of understanding on social reality. Thus, advancing a contrasting interpretation offers people a perspective from which to *"take distance"*[13] from existing views, which could serve as an opportunity for people to undo something of their *"belonging"* to a tradition, to a culture, to established views, or to accepted practices. In the work of several authors (for instance, Okolo, Mudimbe, Serequeberhan, or Eboussi Boulaga) we have seen this *double working of hermeneutics as critique*: saying what certain ideas amount to (Critique I) and enabling us to "take distance" from it (Critique II). However, it seems accurate to say that wherever interpretation is rigorously pursued, it generates these two forms of critique. Let us consider *critique*, then, to be the third resource of hermeneutics in negotiating plurality.

It should not escape our attention that critique, understood in this way, could increase the plurality of views. In opposing the second mode of avoiding negotiating plurality (see § 2.1 above), hermeneutics opposes simplifications arising from ahistorical presentations, exaggerated essences, and artificial oppositions, and instead offers complex explanations rather than simple ones.[14] Hermeneutics seeks maximum complexity and is most questionable where this fails. And thus hermeneutics as a critical practice generates a greater plurality of views. This is not a contradiction, but a necessary step in the quest for the best possible negotiation of plurality. On the other hand, a critique that retains no commitment to the possibility of improving understanding would succumb to nihilistic relativism, the first form of avoiding to interpret plurality. To put this in a more positive way: critique invites us to re-enter, albeit differently, the cycle of interpretation, to commit ourselves to new ways of negotiating plurality. We could—and often should—suspend judgement, but we cannot do so indefinitely. At some point, we also need to *"take a step"* from an existing understanding to a new one. Let us call this the fourth resource of hermeneutics in negotiating plurality.

By "taking a step", hermeneutics attempts to establish what was not there before in terms of clarity, comprehension, sophistication, communicability or commonality—all forms of negotiating plurality. In this book, we have seen a number of figures for this dimension of the hermeneut's work. Through translation, a passage is forged between languages that initially do not communicate with one another (Diagne). By re-taking the inheritance from another era, this legacy is revivified (Okolo). By transfunctionalising the intellectual practices of others or of an apparently stagnated tradition, new potentials of insight and orientation can be generated for today (Eboussi Boulaga). The cumulative effect of such creative steps can be seen in the progressive changes of Africanist discourse, as described by Mudimbe as "amplifications". It can also be seen in a creativity that finds its energy through working with what one has received as a cultured being and as a human being with the potential to act, as Serequeberhan argues in his view on post-colonial states as re-Africanised, that is, as Euro-African hybrids.

I began this discussion of plurality by pointing out some of the difficulties generated by diverse forms of plurality. The plurality-generating effect of critique and the possibility of establishing new links invite us to point out another difficulty with plurality. This is that plurality is not only a problem, for if it were, one could work to reduce or ignore it—plurality is sometimes also an opportunity. A single, static, or dominant view may be challenged by confronting it with others. One can learn from others. New ideas may be generated by confronting conflicting ideas, and so on. But making the best of the constructive potential of plurality requires drawing on various arts of interpretation, translation, re-taking, and a set of complex virtues: willingness to cooperate (without compromise), openness (without laissez-faire), and humility (with self-affirmation).

3. Between familiarity and strangeness

I started the previous discussion by enumerating a series of manifestations of plurality that are reflected in all forms of human understanding and interpretation. The work of African hermeneuts generally testifies to this. In this section, I want to come back to this terrain of uncertain understanding and interpretation, but now from the perspective of how people are oriented in it. To be more precise—as beings who are sensitive to meaning and for whom their existence is a source of concern, humans are continually engaged in relations of familiarity and strangeness[15] to themselves and their surroundings. In § 3.1, I examine people's complex suspension between the ties of familiarity and experiences of strangeness. This presents the field of meaning as ambiguous. The uncertainty of orientation opens up to different strategies of negotiating familiarity and strangeness. Very often this negotiation plays out in a range of hybridities. This point is examined further in § 3.2, where African philosophy is considered as compounded of familiarity and strangeness. This is perceptible in the quest for better self-understanding and in the construction of commonalities—among African philosophers and between African philosophers and philosophers of other regions. While African philosophy retains an epistemological filiation with Western philosophy, this filiation does not preclude independent philosophising.

3.1. *Familiarity and strangeness: the struggle for orientation*

Familiarity arises from the socio-cultural milieu in which one is born, in which one is socialised, and that one gradually expands through one's own initiative. This is one of the most elementary givens of human existence, and it is absolutely fundamental for hermeneutics: familiarity with our social, material, and cultural environment is the primary fact of understanding. Without it, no further understanding can be acquired, and no meaningful interpretation of the world can be undertaken. So fundamental is this fact that we may say that people *"belong"* to a world (a term already used above). Belonging evokes ties of familiarity, support, know-how, or a sense of an embracing environment. Arguably one of the most salient characteristics of hermeneutics, as compared to many other approaches to human cognition and knowledge, is its careful attention to the significance of belonging as a dimension of human existence.

Hermeneutic work on aspects of everyday life—on practices, customs, languages, culture, social institutions, or social interaction—all derive from this fact.

Nevertheless, hermeneuts also understand that humans belong so much to a sphere of meaning—they may be so familiar to their lifeworld—that it becomes almost invisible. Excavating this dimension of overfamiliarity as part of human existence requires effort. A disconcerting result of this effort is that what is most familiar may appear strange or foreign once it is thematised. That to which one intimately "belongs" may in fact be the unhealed wounds of trauma or an acquired ability to cope with injury. And these in turn may have a lasting impact on people's ways of feeling, seeing, conceiving, thinking, and so forth. Here, too, familiarity is indissociable from strangeness, albeit in a different way. Thus, considered from the perspective of both positive and negative experiences, we can see that although hermeneutics is oriented to belonging, it is *not simply a philosophy of homecoming*. And once the strangeness in the very heart of our familiarity has been recognised, it turns out to accompany almost all modes of our existence. In fact, to be oriented by meaning turns out to be oriented to diverse experiences of familiarity *and* strangeness.[16] The experiences of negotiating plurality—discussed above—are lived through as changing landscapes of familiarity and strangeness.

This landscape covers a discouragingly wide range of permutations and ambiguities. Consider the following examples. Through violent events, people may become estranged from their most familiar, intimate ability to use their initiative, as Serequeberhan and Eboussi Boulaga argue. Or they may lose aspects of "their" culture and history—what was once familiar may become strange—to such an extent that they may have to reappropriate it again to draw self-affirmation from it (as Diop argues with reference to ancient Egypt) or acquire it anew to reintegrate it into their living traditions (as Oluwole argues with reference to Igbo oral wisdom). Whether this occurs under the extreme conditions of colonial violence or in a calmer encounter with books of Western philosophy, Africans encounter not only *others as strangers*, but through these encounters become aware of *themselves* in ways that require adaptation and readaptation—the emergence of African philosophy speaks to this working on a *strange self-awareness*. At the same time, many things that have become familiar and even cherished are a familiarised or domesticated strangeness, as when one considers the use of colonial languages for science or literature (as Diagne points out).

The relations between the familiar and the strange can be "ossified" through coercion or internalisation (cf. Serequeberhan, Okolo). But they can also be dynamic. When Okolo speaks about development, or Eboussi Boulaga comments on transfunctionalisation, they evoke different figures of a transition from what is familiar to what is still unfamiliar, and in that sense is strange: Okolo suggests that the shift from the familiarity of harsh living conditions to socio-economic development cannot but include the adoption of cultural forms that did not exist locally before; Eboussi Boulaga shows that familiarity with once foreign colonial education has to be transformed into something new and still unknown.

And these are only two figures of a wider understanding that human life generally, and in striving to flourish more specifically, rarely consists of a mere affirmation of what is familiar. To exist means to orient oneself *between the familiar and the strange*, especially under conditions where people have to struggle to find their orientation, or even survive. The hermeneutic effort, integrated in all our action and thought, attempts to act as a mediator in the friction between the familiar and the foreign. The outcome of such efforts is that one *"becomes"* Wolof, and should even pursue blending [*métissage*] (as Diop argues) or that the translation of literature and transfer of knowledge results in linguistic and cultural "hybridization" (in terms of Diagne's argument). What is foreign or strange is appropriated and is integrated into the familiar, changing the familiar into something different from what it was before.

From all of this, we learn that the human condition of being related to meaning creates a vast variety of effects of familiarity and strangeness, belonging and distance—including ambiguities of familiarity in strangeness and strangeness in familiarity. Again, there are ways by which to dismiss this complexity—whence, for instance, the temptation of essentialism or a categorical discarding of all mixing. Although these reactions may be understandable in the context of experiences of disorientation, it can amount to incorrectly attributing the culture of people's predecessors—culture lost through destruction or abandonment—to one's contemporaries and thereby downgrading whatever culture these contemporaries may currently have (Oluwole is certainly not the only scholar to fall into this trap, as I argue further below in § 3.2.b). But this mistake is not a failing of hermeneutic thought itself, as the authors who reflect on hybridisation demonstrate (see above). Nor does mixing (the appropriation of others' means) exclude criticism of those others (as Eboussi Boulaga or Mudimbe have shown).

From these divergent experiences, it is evident that it is not possible to merely apply formal criteria to assess the desirability of this or that orientation within the experiences of familiarity and strangeness. In other words:

- Belonging is not good in and of itself, and conversely, nor is a relation of strangeness necessarily bad. Through force, one can be familiarised to humiliation (through internalisation—as highlighted by Serequeberhan) or to violent imposition (through the practical need to adapt—as highlighted by Eboussi Boulaga). On the other hand, above, we saw that the ability to step back even from constructive familiar meanings is an important resource for reflection and is indispensable to advance either interpretation or critique of imposed or ossified forms of understanding.
- But nor is belonging bad, and estrangement good. The primal orientation that basic familiarity with surroundings may provide is a sine qua non for all understanding. Moreover, tradition remains a treasure trove available for creative reactivation and a basis for positive self-affirmation. On the other hand, estrangement is also experienced in violence, deprivation, the destruction of tradition, language, and institutions, and other disorienting events.
- Finally, neither purity (relatively continuous, unchanging forms) nor hybridity is simply good. Purity spans an ambiguous space which includes both fidelity to a valuable heritage, and a contracted stagnation, or an artificially imposed freezing.[17] Conversely, hybridity spans the ambiguous space between rebellious transfunctionalisation or creative tampering with the master's code, on the one hand, and on the other hand, compromise or submission.

Given the *ambiguity*[18] of familiarity and strangeness, and all the permutations of the relations between them, arguably the most prudent way to proceed is to seek the most accurate possible descriptions of this complexity and suspend judgement on it, as long as can be tolerated in practice. At least, that seems to be the implication of the hermeneutic approach (detailed in § 2). This does not mean that hermeneutics is tolerant to the injustices that its domains of description may entail, but it does imply that the correct normative "diagnosis" will always rely on a correct description. This is at least part of what hermeneutics can do to help negotiate in the fundamentally *uncertain* tension between the familiar and the strange, in all their manifestations.[19] What is at stake in their juxtaposition or transition towards hybridisation are fidelity, custodianship, living tradition, self-affirmation, opposition to forceful impositions, resistance to artificial enmities, and many other concerns that weigh on people's receptiveness to life as meaningful.[20] One excellent domain to explore this uncertainty is African philosophy in its relation to Western philosophy.

3.2. *African philosophy as a compound of familiarity and strangeness*

The contributions to African philosophical hermeneutics that we have studied demonstrate amply the effort to find an orientation in the complex field of familiarity and strangeness. The prevalence and intensity with which this problem is dealt with is one of the most salient aspects of African philosophy generally. And, although it is not explored here, this struggling with orientation is not at all alien to other philosophies.[21]

Here I want to pursue this exploration by looking at the need for commonality and solidarity as part of the question for philosophical self-affirmation. This question in turn requires further reflection on the meaning of epistemological filiation in African hermeneutics.

(a) Familiarisation with oneself, commonality, and solidarity

Our philosophers generally concur that philosophising is an important way, among others, for Africans to re-affirm their dignity and agency. Undertaking this task attests to Africa's confrontation with an other, often, a violent other. From the outset, this basic vocation requires the mediation of diverse forms of friction between familiarity and strangeness. It is much too simplistic to schematise this task as starting out from what is "ours" and "familiar" to deal with what is "theirs" and "foreign", because the encounter with others destabilises our self-understanding. As a result, the work of excavating what is most intimate and has to be re-affirmed can itself uncover something that is non-evident—if not strange—because the conditions for its simple familiar acceptance have been damaged. And when one looks for help to deal with this task collectively, the question arises of who constitutes the other with whom the closest alliances can be concluded. Simply calling a philosophical practice "African" and using the term "African philosophy" in the singular masks the complexities of transforming strangers (because they are from other cultural or geo-political contexts or because they are from diverse regions of the African continent or its diaspora) into familiar partners with a collective vocation. The reference to a "common fate"—important as it is for African philosophy—is a shortcut, because the fate of the exploited and humiliated is not restricted to the outlines of this continent. Okolo's evocation of global solidarity makes this point. Besides, in philosophy too, Africa has to be invented, as Mudimbe has abundantly demonstrated. The commonality between people that is enacted in solidarity, or named with a word, "Africa", is not simply a given, but has to be established.[22]

An understandable strategy in assuming this task consists in identifying African languages and traditions as points of orientation. However, this strategy too calls for vigilance, since culture is sometimes itself the object of manipulation by the powerful (whence the significance of Mudimbe's genealogy of anthropology, for instance). A second strategy for advancing views on African philosophy consists of taking aspects of European philosophy as a point of reference. The philosophy of the others (which in some cases have been imposed, appropriated, or indigenised) is not to be considered universal philosophy. Simply making the best of this "second" culture would overlook its real ambiguity: on the one hand, the transmitted canon of Western philosophy contains violent distortions of the self and other that emerge from overstating the universality of Western thought; on the other hand, this canon still testifies to what philosophy could be anywhere in the world (as we have seen, African hermeneuts confirm this when they acknowledge anthropological generalities in the work of their European counterparts). In other words, the familiar also has to be (re-)discovered in the philosophical practice that was introduced to the continent as one of the mechanisms of its defeat (as Eboussi Boulaga has argued). Again, we see that on the level of philosophical practice, the familiar is not simply a given, but has to be sought, discovered, or established.

On the other hand, through the very way in which they argue, all the authors studied here challenge the claim that philosophy is incompatible with fidelity to African cultures or modes of existence.[23] What is more, they present their works *to be understood*. In other words, the ways in which they present their work anticipates the possible reception by both their compatriots and any reader of good-will elsewhere in the world.[24] By doing so, they performatively confirm the commitment to lateral universalism[25] as the assumption underlying the mediation of the familiar and the foreign. Recognising this commitment in no way makes philosophy a universal discourse, because, as explained above, the mode of its practical performance is always shaped by the authors' thick participation in their own particularity.

The basis for lateral universalism is also the deepest root of hermeneutics: this resides in the assumption that negotiating the familiar and the strange is not futile in the long run (see § 2.2, above). This practical anticipation, which may for some time initially appear counter-factual, makes it possible to identify or establish commonalities between people despite the most prominent differences of culture, social context, or economic, military, and political means. It is because, and in so far as, philosophers of different backgrounds assume at least some points of common humanity that they are not wholly unfamiliar beings to one another, no matter what their mutual strangeness may be. To the hermeneut's mind, this is the reason why some insights of the other can, and may, be appropriated. For this reason, one has to be careful in claiming that African philosophical hermeneutics starts with African students who studied German and French authors at Western universities. It would be more accurate to say that those same students had been understanding and interpreting even before they entered any university whatsoever, and would have been doing so even if they remained illiterate and did not engage in any formal education.[26] After all, the origin of Western philosophy too resides in the same way in the hermeneutic existence of its philosophers. The point here is not to deny, gloss over, silence, or trivialise the role played by European authors in African philosophers' understanding of philosophy—Mudimbe's term "epistemological filiation" captures this relationship well—but to situate the possibility for such filiation in human commonality.[27]

(b) A further look at "epistemological filiation"

The possibility of commonality, then, resides in a practical assumption of the possibility of finding and establishing commonality. But, in practice, every such attempt to negotiate the familiar and the foreign takes a specific form. In the case of African philosophers, it is true that, by force or by choice, many of them have acquired competence in Western philosophy, and that this is visible in their own practice of African philosophy, even when they seek the maximum orientation to the fate of muntu, local traditions or oral wisdom. Whence the identifiable "epistemological filiation" to Western modes of thinking.

Such filiation is the reason why philosophical hermeneuts often critique their "professional" or "school" philosophical colleagues for an unreflective adoption of Western philosophy. When these hermeneuts themselves then also make use of Western scholarship, it is with a definite resolution to engage with the task of reflection, and not merely to adopt a culturally specific mode of reflection. Epistemological filiation *as a mode of philosophical effort* consists not so much of a wholesale taking over, but *rather of selective borrowing, debate, and critique* of aspects of European philosophy. Consider, for instance, the fact that African hermeneuts (a) select from diverse Western traditions of thought; (b) choose different authors for reference within hermeneutics (Heidegger, Gadamer, Ricœur, Habermas, and others); and (c) use diverse parts of these referenced authors' work; (d) combine insights derived from them in different ways; (e) reflect critically on the validity of these works; and (f) relate the gathered insights in different ways to modes of African thinking. Admittedly, there are many studies containing mere scholarly exegesis (see Smet's bibliography[28]), but each of these has to be assessed on a case-by-case basis and cannot be a priori considered epigonic performances (and let us not forget that such uncreative repetition is part of the Western scholarly landscape too). But the point is that epistemological filiation *includes* philosophical debate and independent reflection.

Evidently, the most visible manifestation of epistemological filiation pertains to the *practices and institutions* through which scholarly works are produced: the setting within universities, the founding of scientific journals, publishing in such journals and in monographs, forms of referencing, the communication of research results in conferences, the relative separation of academic philosophy from other domains of social life, the practice of philosophy by salaried employees (often as civil servants), the continued use of English and French, and so on. And this holds for the entire spectrum of African philosophies, from ethnophilosophy through hermeneutics to "professional" philosophy. Of course, much of this is the outcome of the way in which the first generations of Africans who could attend schools (where philosophy was part of the curriculum) or universities encountered philosophy. Nobody can disabuse one as well as Eboussi Boulaga does from a too rosy perspective of this encounter. However, considering the relative freedom to improvise available to doctoral students, and much more so to lecturers and researchers at post-independence institutions, it is not possible to attribute this whole package of practical and institutional similarities to unimpeded external imposition. Since there is a sufficient margin of divergence from this Western model, and since there is an increasing body of texts in which experiments are performed on diverging from this model (which could thus serve as examples for continued experimentation), the extent of formal continuation of Western epistemological practice has to be interpreted as *willing* adoption, at least to some degree. It is by the *modes* of adoption that philosophers testify to African agency in academic practice. This can be seen in almost all the authors studied.[29]

This "re-taking" (in Okolo's sense) or creative appropriation can therefore not be "pure" African philosophy; nor is it mere repetition of Western philosophy. From the perspective of its epistemological filiation, one should consider African philosophy as a wide variety of ambiguous practices: it is not a simple transmission of local traditions nor servile mimicry of what is imported, but is constituted of always new forms of negotiation between the familiar and the strange. Failure to see this closes one off from one of the main sources of innovation and creativity in African philosophy, and can lead only to essentialising simplifications of both African and European philosophy. By contrast, hermeneutics examines the full scope of emerging modes of thinking, be it in Africa or in Europe, in their fullest ambiguity, with the hope of deciphering the most liberty-enhancing possibilities among them. As little as filiation to Western modes of thought prevents Africans from understanding those modes of thought, so little does an orientation to African pre-philosophical culture, traditions of thought, or contemporary concerns make it impossible for non-Africans (however one would define them) to follow works in African hermeneutics. And there is no reason to think that there is nothing for non-Africans worth learning in African hermeneutics. The hybridisation that results from creative filiation is an outcome of the effort to link the familiar and the strange.

From this perspective, its attention to tradition—or rather, a specific understanding of tradition—may be one of the hidden pitfalls of African hermeneutics. It is true that people's traditions potentially stretch as far back as reconstructable history; but it is not true that all of the accumulated culture of that time span is appropriated by each present-day recipient. It is correct that the rehabilitation of precolonial traditions (and whatever has remained of them, despite colonisation) is an important project; however, this is not to say that they *are* the culture of contemporary living Africans. One should distinguish between the potential treasure and what is at this moment appropriated from it.[30] And one should also distinguish between historical traditions and the myriad of traditions that are forming and continue to morph into new forms, especially in the big cities throughout the continent. Okere, even Okolo, Oluwole, and others, do not make this latter distinction sufficiently. One has to grant that reinterpretations of the remotest aspects of culture do not exhaust reflection on living traditions. Although Serequeberhan sometimes presents a reductive view of African tradition (as only one singular tradition), his insistence on contemporary practices and traditions of initiative goes some way to illustrate my point.[31] What is needed is a hermeneutics that could spend its interpretative work on the really *existing traditions of Africans living today* to demonstrate the clarifying potential that such work has from that point. The degree to which older or now marginal forms of tradition have to be (re-)introduced into contemporary culture is for each person to decide. But neglecting contemporary African culture cannot do justice to our contemporaries as cultured beings. Besides, by turning too much to pre-colonial culture, one closes off possible discussion with people on other continents who live under comparable circumstances and work with similar concerns.

By promoting communicability, hermeneutics is already a kind of "miniature protocol of action" (Eboussi Boulaga), in that it helps to discern what opposes collective self-affirmation and opens a view on possibilities of solidarity that would otherwise not be visible. Again, one could invoke here Okolo's reference to trans-national solidarity against economic inequality, or Serequeberhan's idea of a "global earthly solidarity" as relevant examples. Solidarity, properly understood, may emerge from a similar fate, without thereby erecting a community of fate that automatically includes some and excludes others.[32] Solidarity can also emerge through people's ability to be concerned for the life of far-off others. In as far as translation can be undertaken in many different directions, it serves as an illuminating complement to hermeneutics as a protocol of action.

The conclusion to be drawn from all of these forms of engagement is that any adoption of African perspectives calls for a varied assessment of the value and legacy of Western philosophy and the products of Western culture generally. One might say that this heritage is ambiguous in its effect and potential, and, today, the nature of its impact depends on the ways in which African scholars appropriate or reject, connect with, or critique it—in short, creatively engage with it. But this ambiguity is also typical of the contemporary relation to African traditions: as treasures to be reactivated, or as artificially ossified forms. The point is that hermeneutics generally proceeds by augmenting people's awareness of the web of uncertain relations in which they find themselves.

4. **Hermeneutics and practice: liberation from what? What for? By whom?**

Thus far in this chapter, and in numerous ways throughout the book, we have seen a certain proximity of hermeneutics to practice. In this section, I want to engage more fully with this issue (in § 4.1), by recalling that hermeneutics is rooted in practice, and that philosophical hermeneutics has to understand itself as an institutionalised practice, and, as such, as part of a socio-political reality. As discussed in the next section (§ 4.2), this implies that the act of understanding, the arts of interpretation and philosophical hermeneutics, engaged as they are with meaning, cannot be understood in abstraction, divorced from the nexus of power.

This then raises the question of the kind of impact that hermeneutics can, in turn, aspire to have on social reality. The point here is really its effect on the quality of life of people generally—in short, the question of liberation in the fullest sense (§ 4.3). It turns out that a socially sensitive hermeneutics would have to find a balance between an ambitious vocation to promote people's liberation and realistic self-restraint, due to the specific nature and limits of what hermeneutics can realistically hope to contribute (§ 4.4).

4.1. Hermeneutics as rooted and participating in practice

Overlooking the constitution of hermeneutics in practice also means missing one of its core dimensions. I insisted above on the fact that human existence generally is constituted as meaningful, that being human entails having an understanding of the meanings one belongs to or is confronted with—this implies that practice is an integral part of this view of human existence. This has been strongly affirmed by Okolo and Serequeberhan. People understand their natural and material world by traversing, using, eating, admiring, neglecting, cultivating, or suffering from it, and so forth. They understand animals and other people through their interaction, caring, conflict, habits, procedures, relaxing together, and so on. All of these modes of *doing* are symbolically shaped and mediated, but the inverse is also true: the milieu of symbols is carried by actions and interaction, as well as their extensions, which are media of symbolic transmission.

When people stand back from these everyday practices to interpret them, the interpretations are also ways of *relating to* the material studied. Such relating does not happen only in human minds: it involves reading books, narrating stories to others in appropriate situations, accumulating evidence to be catalogued, exchanging views and debates, and so forth, according to a rich variety of culturally specific practices. And if this does not convince one of the practical side of interpretation, then one needs to recall that the capacity of interpretation in most contexts takes on relatively standardised forms, each with their standards of excellence, which must be mastered through education and practice. In many contexts, one needs to be accredited as a legitimate interpreter—accreditation qualifies someone to assume a specific role, to act in institutions and to relate to other people in specific ways. Anybody may, for instance, form an opinion on a legal dispute and is in that sense an interpreter of the law, but not everybody is formally qualified and institutionally authorised to act as a lawyer or a judge. Thus, interpretation is set in the dense web of social life.

Besides, hermeneutics as the art of interpretation typically *applies to* phenomena that are difficult to interpret, which include the wide range of human action and interaction invoked above. This covers also the symbolic mediation of action and the extensions of action in texts, artworks, rituals, and so on. And what holds for the arts of interpretation, holds also for philosophical hermeneutics.

Finally, while the work of hermeneutics requires a certain withdrawal from practice, indefinite suspension of all practical engagement is only one mode of doing that work. Hermeneuts generally accept that the work they do clarifies the domain they work on and that, even if only in an indirect way, our capacity to act benefits from this work of clarification. Many hermeneuts (among them several of the authors discussed in this book) consider the feedback of hermeneutic work into practice and the contribution to improving people's living conditions to be an integral part of their vocation as hermeneuts. I will come back to profile this ambition, but only after further clarification of the relation between practice and hermeneutics.

4.2. Practice and power

We have seen that recognising the intimate interwovenness of understanding, interpretation, and philosophical hermeneutics with practice compels us to consider how they are situated within their broader social reality. Taking both the practical nature and social extension of hermeneutics seriously makes it impossible to overlook dimensions of *power at work on all three levels of hermeneutics*.

Thus, for instance, the spontaneous disposition or habitus of people's understanding interaction with the world takes shape under the influence of others and of social facilitation and constraints. In the vast terrain of possible arts of interpretation, some acquire higher social standing or influence than others. Furthermore, the social processes that allow some people to access training in these arts and obtain accreditation as competent practitioners in them depend on decisions by people who are in power and who accord power to the beneficiaries of that accreditation. Some people, groups, or institutions have more influence than others on shaping the social and cultural world, by making some objects appear more valuable, significant, or edifying than others; by organising the flow of resources; and by instituting rules and organisations. The kinds of relationship established between different cultures, languages, and knowledges in a region also depend on the exercise of power and contribute to the distribution of relative quantities of cultural, linguistic, or epistemological power. Foreclosing some initiatives in response to interpretations of the practical requirements of a specific context requires institutional power arrangements and efficient symbolic means. Moreover, the transmission of ideas requires implicit or explicit collaboration, access to appropriate means, and influence on the potential contexts of reception.[33] The list can easily be extended indefinitely. The point is not to reduce understanding, interpretation, and philosophical hermeneutics to the sole factor of the exercise of (or subjection to) power, but to emphasise that the *whole sphere of hermeneutics is permeated by the exercise and effects of power*. Sometimes this array of power is exercised in a consciously planned way; sometimes we need to think rather of the unintended consequences of the aggregate of social interactions. And while the aspect of power in understanding and interpretation is sometimes more significant than at other times, it is hardly ever possible to step outside of it.

Now, part of hermeneutics on all three levels consists of grasping the dimensions of power in each context. But whoever speaks about power, speaks about the effects of power, and these are rarely understood merely as neutral increments of energy. Very often, people's immediate grasp of, but also their interpretative take on, relations include the asymmetrical effects of power as a source of concern: such differences are considered fair/unfair, just/unjust, justified/illegitimate, proportionate/arbitrary, and so on. In short, the understanding and interpretation of power develop *descriptive and evaluative dimensions*, and often the one has an impact on the other. One needs to think only about the term "violence" to see how inseparable the descriptive and evaluative dimensions can be.

These basic points about power hold for all contexts. It is not difficult to see that the phenomena touched upon here would become all the more intense under conditions of sudden, broad, and deep *disruption* of people's lifeworld, as in colonisation. This radical experience of disruption is an important common point of reference for all the authors studied here;[34] it can hardly be imagined what African philosophical hermeneutics would have looked like without the events of colonisation. However, this does not minimise earlier tragedies, notably the long history of slavery. And nor does it make light of the traumas of the post-independence era—on the contrary, hermeneutics engages with the historically formed living conditions of people today. Since we have seen how intertwined hermeneutics is with practice, we should avoid the error of considering this orientation of hermeneutics as merely an intellectual decision. It is true that, since some African philosophers do *not* orient their practice in this way, we know that doing so requires a decision. But for hermeneuts, the way their work is rooted in everyday understanding makes the reference to the living conditions of everyday life unavoidable.

Accordingly, one of the initial tasks of hermeneutics is "stock-taking" (Serequeberhan). It consists of interpreting the history of destruction, but, conversely, it also highlights what remains of African culture, traditions, languages, modes of doing, and capacities to act. Each author gives his/her specific articulation of these points. Contrast, for example, Eboussi Boulaga's point of departure in "total defeat" with Oluwole's insistence on the remaining strength of pre-colonial oral culture.[35] Or compare Okere's initial doctorate, of which half is an anthropological description of Igbo culture, with Serequeberhan's refusal to orient his hermeneutics to pre-colonial culture and his emphasis on returning to the source of autonomous action. But on a high level of abstraction, all these authors start from the ambiguities of a historically formed reality and attempt to find a way through conflicting possibilities of initiative in the present. Orienting hermeneutics to a history of destruction does not amount to reducing the life of all contemporary Africans to suffering; it simply reflects the fact that the general context of interpretation is one of far-reaching social disruption. Again, while hermeneutics thus requires accurate analyses of this context, these analyses are generally understood to have normative significance: the factual—historical trauma and its contemporary aftermath—is what ought not to be. And in this way, a hermeneutics of the living reality of Africans today is a hermeneutics of concerns of *things that are at stake*.[36] Saying that hermeneutics draws much momentum from the experiences of destruction does not refer to an artificial adoption of pathos as a style, but identifies a commitment to the ambient world as a world of concerns (rather than merely detached study).

When hermeneuts study culture, this refers to the widest range of human practices, beliefs, oral transmissions, and so forth. But the ultimate meaning of reflecting on the wasted treasures (physical or spiritual) of culture is to better understand the traumatised and dysfunctional lives of people and the difficult work of finding means by which to reconstruct a more just and ordinary mode of life in society.

For this reason, in hermeneutics, one thinks *from the midst of the interrelated aspects of a present reality*, dealing with concerns from the lived world, including reflection on the humans who have to face the demands of that world. For instance, hermeneuts inevitably think of the self too, when they consider the other (and vice versa). They reflect on forms of expression in relation to their context, which in turn can be understood otherwise in the light of new expressions. The present is interpreted in relation to the past, but the past is already interpreted with a view to the future. Action is recognised to be traversed by meaning, but meaning is also dependent on action. All of these examples illustrate the situatedness of interpretation, to which I have referred above. It makes the position from which we interpret to be one that moves, and the relations that are construed to be ambiguous. Thus, for instance, the attempt to recuperate elements of tradition could affirm identity, which is a valuable strategic element of positive self-respect and collective action, but can succumb to the dangers of an ideology of purity and immutability, with its own violent exclusions. Many hermeneuts recognise the violence that has inserted them as academics in unfairly privileged ways into the circuit of Western learning and science, but they are not blind to the fact that alleviation of many needs in independent countries requires some form of modernisation, which requires the implementation of some forms of Western technology and know-how,[37] and that, even when this implementation is successful, is likely to have adverse effects on the remnants of indigenous culture. In all, the image of a cobweb that I applied to Okolo's work is relevant to the position of hermeneutic reflection generally: not only is it situated in the midst of diverse realities, but every option exercised, any intervention suggested, has several consequences for the whole, and it is not possible to have only positive consequences.

However, the practical conclusion of this situatedness of hermeneutics is not to pretend that situatedness can be undone, but to engage in the project of hermeneutics with a better, more realistic understanding of what that project entails. Hermeneutics requires self-critical awareness of the limits of one's own ability as interpreter: one has to take a stand, but also has to know this to be a limited, perspectival, and correctable stand. For this reason, hermeneutics is open to other opinions (as discussed in § 2.3 above), even if afterwards these views are found to need correction, critique, or rejection. Realising that their thought emerges from being surrounded by things that are at stake, hermeneuts understand that in thinking too, things are at stake: it can borrow, but also become subservient; it can attempt to pinpoint the core of a matter and essentialise; it can make itself strong in defiance of what it opposes at the expense of its own subtlety; in attempting to convince the cultural other, it may succumb to extraversion, but in avoiding extraversion it may become narrowminded and dogmatic. African hermeneutics is traversed by a latent acknowledgement of the awkwardness associated with the situatedness of its own philosophical practice: it is caught between oral tradition and written practice, between traditional culture and contemporary universities, between African history and people's contemporary lifeworld and the potential and pitfalls of Western scholarship, between thorough reflection in pursuit of deep understanding and the need for strategic action. This has an impact on the way African hermeneuts conceive of their own practice, and can be found in many ideas that capture the conflicting demands of these oppositions: "philosophemes" in Okere, a "fusion of horizons" as reinterpreted by Serequeberhan, or "translating" in Diagne.

A lot is at stake and there are no guarantees of a good outcome. Given the risks associated with the practical implications of hermeneutics, some authors prefer to extend the detour out of action (and some may never succeed in making a real, explicit return to practice); others are constantly driven by the desire to have their thought feed back into practice in rapid succession.

To explore this return to practice, one has to consider practice in its full complexity, ranging from the resumption of initiative to the transformation of institutions. And this is what I now turn to.

4.3. The spectrum of practical engagement

Provided that one understands philosophising as one action among others, there is no reason to accuse it of navel-gazing or misconstruing its own nature, when it is presented as a response to the context of action. Below, I come back to the correct demarcation of hermeneutics' potential in relation to action, but let us first consider that range of conjunctions of philosophy with practice.

Hardly any author is such a sharp observer as Eboussi Boulaga of the most minute forms of action that reside in philosophy. He understands how mimicking the "master's" philosophical discourse (but doing so with an internal *irony*), is already the start of a micro counter-initiative. This unspoken insubordination is an exercise in adopting an alternative stance, one from which the broader strategy of transfunctionalisation of that discourse may be built up.

This insight is valuable for another reason. It points to the role of philosophy in cultivating an alternative *self-awareness*, and to the possibility of *self-affirmation*. In some contexts, saying that philosophising is a form of practice may be a platitude. For African philosophers generally, taking to the pen is an act of self-affirmation. In this regard, Fanon's emphasis is particularly apposite: the point of restoring self-confidence is not merely to gain recognition of one's humanity from others, but to affirm *oneself* to oneself and one's peers first, and only then, as far as is necessary, to carry this momentum through, to self-affirmation in the face of others.[38]

Gaining an unhumiliated self-awareness after (or amidst) destruction and finding a foothold for self-affirmation are the initial components of quests for initiative, for acting once again on one's own terms, and for gaining at least some space for autonomy. For this reason, the hermeneutic turn to culture and tradition is first to be understood as an act of *defiance* against the value system of imperial powers, and not necessarily as an act of conservatism. (I affirmed this in the conclusion to the chapter on Okere; despite Eboussi Boulaga's harsh criticism of ethnophilosophy, he grants this as its moment of truth.) Clearly, the return to tradition may fall into the trap of succumbing to conservatism or culturalism. But for hermeneuts, generally, tradition is properly grasped only when it is understood as an occasion for de-ossification, re-taking, creation, invention, and so on. All these terms may, initially, evoke a milieu of working with books, but there is no reason to limit it to this milieu (as Okolo and Serequeberhan argue explicitly). Part of the expectation behind hermeneutics is that re-interpreting humiliated traditions (including traditions of practice) serves the practical aim of self-affirmation and of generating perceptive interpretations of the current socio-political reality, which can then feed into the resumption of initiative on one's own terms.[39]

In line with this point, hermeneutics has the critical task of identifying the undue freezing of culture or of ideas, of reconstructing the histories by which it came about (see Mudimbe), and of working to dismantle such solidification. Rooted in an understanding of human agency's historicity, contingency, and complexity, hermeneutics deploys its tools against the "mummification" of traditions, against all forms of simplification, essentialism, context-independent thought, and simplistic explanations (as already pointed out in § 2.1). And as my critical engagement with authors throughout this book has demonstrated, their philosophical contribution is at its weakest where this principle has been abandoned. It is truer to the spirit of hermeneutics to consider the institutionalisation of essentialised views of local "cultures" or foreign "civilizations" as part of the destructive machinery that remains at work in the present context. Not that this insight is visible only from a philosophical perspective. Consider, for instance, the accurate articulation by Mahmood Mamdani of this principle: "From a reified language fortifying a despotic authority, custom needs to be rethought as a thread of life, not only one that makes us but also one that we make."[40]

The relevance of this exposing and dismantling of such essentialised ideas stretches as far as the effect of such ideas: from common language to political programmes, from legal principles to journalism, from the terminology of social sciences to the symbolic representation of social relations—in short, everywhere that language takes on institutional forms. This implies that hermeneutics strives to accompany all practical engagement with reality, *with the means proper to it*, which includes *interpretation, critique, genealogy* and *translation*. This work of accompaniment extends into all dimensions of life together in modern states, and applies to the values that subtend technological and economic development (as Diop and Okolo argue), to reflection on the best kinds of curriculum design and forms of education, to analysis of local or international conflict and strategies by which to respond to it, to the distribution of resources and the limitation of damage to the environment. Wherever there is discrimination, exploitation, marginalisation, or humiliation, there is a need to interpret social problems. And wherever such abuses are identified, the question arises of how it is possible to respond to them. There is an interpretative dimension to changing institutional culture, transforming legislation, sensitising children and adults, mobilising international solidarity, identifying the risks of technological inventions and of the unprecedented use thereof, exploring old and new media by which people's affective, aesthetic, practical, or intellectual attitudes towards the world are modified, and inventing strategic practices directed at oneself and others (cf. Serequeberhan). All of these actions require insight into the ambiguous potential of transfunctionalisation, creative translation, re-taking tradition, and simply autonomous use of reason—in other words, hermeneutic work. One may say that the intention of hermeneutics in all this is not being self-serving, but being *supportive* in the restoration of maximal autonomy. This core vocation to support a return to the source of initiative has been convincingly articulated by Serequeberhan and Okolo, and their point stands, even when people have different views on how that initiative is to be taken.

Overall, the supportive function of hermeneutics consists then in a more *deconstructive* and a more *constructive* moment (as several authors have argued). The deconstructive task applies to the whole domain of things from which people have to be liberated. This requires the interpretation of unfair geopolitical relations, economic exploitation, warped historiography, the circulation of biased news reporting, ethnic and religious conflict, racism, sexism, and other forms of discrimination in all their guises, and so forth. The constructive task draws from the common understandings that circulate in society, and from the array of traditions and forms of knowledge available to the contemporary reader in identifying diverse possibilities for interventions. This identification, in turn, requires assessments of each possibility's risks and potential, possible alliances in pursuit of goals, the evaluation of means and strategies, and so forth.

It is difficult to deny that the deconstructive and constructive tasks of hermeneutics are driven by the conviction that in everything meaningful, there is something at stake—as I have explained above. This raises the question of which kind of ethics then binds hermeneutics. I come back to this question in § 5, below, but before doing so, I would like to examine more directly what is meant by characterising the role of hermeneutics in liberation as "supportive".

4.4. *Understanding the ambiguous practical profile of hermeneutics: ambition and self-restraint*

In the previous section we have seen that hermeneutics takes up an ambitious task that stretches from a vast critical, deconstructive interpretation of the past and of current states of society to a constructive contribution on the whole scope of practical initiatives. These initiatives in turn range from the smallest acts of defiance and self-affirmation to massive projects of development or the reconfiguration of international political relations. Pursuing such an ambitious vocation can lead to catastrophe if it is not accompanied by a very clear awareness of the limitations of hermeneutic work, to which I have alluded above as its "supportive" role. This role is incompatible with overestimating what hermeneutics can do, and it requires self-insight and self-restraint. For this reason, it is appropriate to take another look at what it means to assume the *role of interpreter*, which is clearly part of the package of tasks of philosophical hermeneutics.

Many of the authors studied here explicitly guard against overestimating the role that their scholarly work can play. It is only a *miniature* protocol (for Eboussi Boulaga) or *part* of the solution (for Diagne) or a *preparation* for action (for Okolo).[41] I take these examples as pointers to the *delimitation* of how hermeneuts have to *position* themselves socially if they want to remain consistent with their own insight into hermeneutics' embeddedness in social reality (described above, §§ 4.1 and 4.2).

As for the social embeddedness of hermeneutics, the capacity to *understand* is part of human existence in all parts of society, the *arts of interpretation* are usually more often set within specific social roles, practices, and institutions, and the opportunity to practice *philosophical hermeneutics* is almost exclusively tied to the position of scientific staff at universities. This fact has not escaped hermeneuts' attention. In various ways, they reflect on the social location of their role as academics, which, as a situated perspective, has to have an impact on the kind of view they offer on society and liberation. Whatever the regional differences may be, this role is shaped by its epistemological and institutional filiation with Western universities (see § 3.2, above) and other institutions with a distinct colonial history.[42] The typical profile of this role is that of a *mid-position* between two cultural and political worlds (explicitly dealt with by Serequeberhan and Diagne[43]). One has to be mindful of the professional distortions (or even undue self-justification) that such mid-positions may entail, but one also has to recognise that the university is one space in which the tension—indeed, friction—between the familiar and the strange can be debated and dealt with. Given that these positions exist and that people de facto have to play these institutional roles,[44] the more pressing question is then how to make the best of that social function.

Furthermore, African philosophy clearly illustrates how the specific *spatial location* of institutions can affect the variety of ways in which people can take up the social function of a university academic. Geographical associations or dissociations necessarily require corresponding adaptations of the repertoire of practices available to academics. The sheer distance between institutions and the cost of transport may make it difficult to cultivate collegial exchanges—the distance between the east and the west of the DRC is a speaking example. Administrative obstacles, sometimes bordering on harassment, may often add another obstacle to international exchange. But the physical space and the means of traversing it are also structured by divisions of the symbolic space. A strong illustration of this fact is the difficulty that philosophers in the anglophone and francophone spaces in Africa experience in establishing ties with one another. Finally, the geopolitical organisation of international relations that are established by foreign funding creates divergent effects of linking (between African scholars and academia in different countries) and of disjuncture (between African scholars whose academic orientation may diverge widely because of their different foreign exposure). The divergent trajectories of philosophers who are partially oriented to the United States, France, South Africa, or China,[45] because of their doctoral funding, illustrates this point.[46]

These references show not only how location has an impact on the practices of academic hermeneuts, but also how that impact can display regional similarities. Such similarities are one reason not to dissociate the *region*, Africa, from our understanding of African philosophy.

Nevertheless, as I have argued in spelling out some of the consequences of Serequeberhan's stance, the situatedness of a philosopher should never be reduced to location, since views and concerns from all over the world can be transmitted by media and thus be integrated into people's most intimate concerns, wherever they are. From this perspective then, the term African philosophy has much more to do with a set of *concerns*.

But hermeneutic practices also have a *temporal location* that characterises the social role of hermeneuts. Whereas *understanding* cannot be detached from practice, the *arts of interpretation* assume some distance from everyday practice, and *philosophical hermeneutics* as a meta-reflection is constituted by further distance. In other words, interpretation and hermeneutics do not engage immediately, but require some postponement before tying back into practice. Above, I have referred to this fact by typifying hermeneutics as an exercise in patience. This raises questions about the disjuncture, or even tension, between the temporal demands of practice and the time needed for rigorous interpretation. Here the philosopher has to respond soberly.

Even under the most trying circumstances, people have an *understanding* of what surrounds them, and retain some capacity for reflective *interpretation*, and they engage in action on the basis of these understandings and interpretations. However, I would grant that the more urgent the practical demands are, the less place there is for patient practicing of the arts of interpretation, and especially for philosophy of any kind. Of course, hermeneuts can reflect on what happens when people have to work out how to address the challenges of a situation and make decisions under pressure, but this is different from acting in those circumstances. Philosophy, and philosophical hermeneutics in particular, has its place typically where people can afford to stand back to do research and reflect. If one grants this argument, the question is then rather to consider how interpretation and philosophical hermeneutics tie back into practice. In this sense, hermeneutics is a long-term investment. Insistence on the practical aims of hermeneutics should not seduce one into construing it as a form of direct mobilisation.[47] Any person with an acquired ability to practise the arts of interpretation or philosophical hermeneutics has to decide how much of these intellectual practices are needed in a context of varyingly urgent social matters.

To conclude, the spatial and temporal locations of hermeneutics thus affect the setting of hermeneuts in social practices, in specific social roles, and in webs of power with which these roles may be linked in any particular society. What the practices of hermeneutics can hope to achieve is facilitated or constrained by the web of their interactions with other social practices (as discussed above).

Full awareness of the social role of interpreter and hermeneut thus obliges one to assume an attitude of self-restraint and realism in pursuit of the very ambitious vocation of hermeneutics.[48]

In the previous two sections I have examined possible hermeneutic engagement for continued liberation (§ 4.3), and how responding to this vocation has to impact on hermeneuts' sensitivity to their own embeddedness in society (§ 4.4). These two points in turn prompt us to clarify the nature of the ethical commitments involved in both these points.

5. Hermeneutics and ethics

It is difficult to imagine how hermeneutics could aim at liberation, and do so in a socially aware way, without some normative commitment. And yet, nothing so far has indicated that hermeneutics has the means by which to lay the foundation for an ethics. True, hermeneutics can and should interpret conflicting moral judgements, examine the socio-historical formation of ethical values, institutions, and traditions, and analyse the workings of normative authority. But *hermeneutics is not a meta-ethics*. It is also true that some of the arts of interpretation are practised in explicit fidelity to certain traditions (for example, Islamic hermeneutics, Biblical hermeneutics), which may invest those practices with specific ethical views. However, one cannot avoid reflecting on what the plurality of such ethical traditions means for hermeneutics: juxtaposing them has to lead either to the dilemma of mutual limitation, or to the question of their compatibility. In both cases, the only way to proceed would require restriction or temporal suspension of that fidelity to assume a meta-perspective that would have affinities with philosophical hermeneutics. And here again, philosophical hermeneutics may interpret the differences, but does not dispose of the ultimate standards against which to measure contradictory claims. In this sense, philosophical hermeneutics is *ethically agnostic*.

But there is another perspective on the relation between ethics and hermeneutics—one that we have already touched upon above (see § 2.3).

Scrutiny of the constitution of hermeneutics reveals that it cannot remain perfectly ethically neutral. The most rigorous pursuit of the task of interpretation and hermeneutics is *premised on a number of commitments*. This is what I want to clarify here.

First, I argue above (§ 4.2) that hermeneutics as a philosophy is born from the awareness that *something is at stake* in a specific context. One can, of course, respond complacently to those stakes, but that amounts to a performative contradiction: what is *understood* to be important is *responded to* as if it is not. Any response that takes seriously that which is at stake in a situation would want that response to have some practical relevance, even if this response is only to set aside time for studious labour on the problem. The realisation that something is at stake is, therefore, the primary ethical impulse behind hermeneutics. This is abundantly illustrated throughout this book, as we see how hermeneuts take the traumatic dimensions of contemporary social life as a call to work for modes of living together in which people can be increasingly free from humiliation, oppression, exploitation, and domination. These are the more explicit and ambitious pursuits of the general impulse to respond to what is at stake.

What links *awareness* of what is at stake with *care* for that which is at stake is acceptance of the notion that *some things in human life are better than others*. Clearly, there are a myriad of smaller and bigger matters that may thus elicit people's concern. This fact pushes one into the domain of uncertainty, which hermeneutic strives to clarify. However, amid this uncertainty some experiences are so atrocious that people would generally concur that these experiences are absolutely *incompatible* with the value of individual human life.[49] The hermeneuts discussed in this book have all made an implicit or explicit appeal to their readers' recognition that there is something in human existence that may never be violated. This is why the orientation of African hermeneutics towards a history of trauma on the African continent does more than clarify this trauma and the conditions of life that result from them: it furthers our understanding of injustice everywhere in the world. Achille Mbembe has articulated this point in a thought-provoking manner: instead of seeing Africa as a kind of waiting room adjacent to the world of real events (as the developmentalist view on the continent would have it), much of what is happening in Africa can be seen as the vanguard of the severest forms of the injustices that are gradually spreading across the world (this refers to his thesis of the world "becoming black"[50]).

Thus, as hermeneutics strives to respond to the fact that there are things at stake in social life, and accepting that some things in human life are better than others, references to grotesque trauma serve as important pointers. They are negative pointers, in the sense that they say what we reject. But the density of human life is such that it is much too complex to address using only these guides.

One could, of course, try to translate these negative claims into positive ones. This would require making explicit precisely which aspects of human existence that we value are destroyed in such events: what is not to be destroyed has to be protected, cared for, and promoted. In this way, the flipside of any reference to historical trauma is an implicit understanding of human flourishing. But generally, cultural traditions contain pictures of what should count as a "better life". I assume that while these pictures do not always overlap, hermeneuts of all kinds would subscribe to the basic idea that it is worth promoting some kinds of existence rather than others, and that interpretation could help to distinguish the myriad differences between the two. In this sense, hermeneutics is committed to an *ethics of a flourishing life*. However, at this point, hermeneutics is immediately faced with its limitations regarding ethics, since commitment to an ethics of a flourishing life is always pursued in terms of richer and wider traditional understandings of human flourishing.[51] Thus, while they are guided by this *minimum* ethical commitment, hermeneutics rather seeks to engage with the complexities that arise from different socio-historical experiences of life and different traditions of interpreting the good life.[52] Intellectual honesty obliges the hermeneut to recognise that any engagement in this field of ethical complexity can only be undertaken from a limited, and moving, perspective.

However, granting the hermeneut's situatedness does not mean restricting the work of interpretation to the confines of the insurmountable walls of one's own perspective. Instead, it is typical of philosophical hermeneutics to compare positions and traditions, to try to offer insight into their contradicting claims, and, where needed, to critique them. The destructive and constructive tasks of hermeneutics respond to this commitment: they aim at removing what prevents human flourishing and facilitate what enhances the quality of human life. This work has to be driven by an aspiration to find ethical views that are valid beyond the limits of present perspectives and traditions. I guess that such work can be undertaken only by anticipating future improvement. And this anticipation would always reflect some minimum assumptions about human nature. Earlier I introduced the notion of adherence to some general ideas about human nature as a constitutive fact of hermeneutics (§ 2.2); here it appears again, but now also as a normative commitment.

But this pursuit of ethical validity beyond the limits of present perspectives and traditions may find some of its resources in the views of others. And in as far as reflection in this direction relativises one's own values and that of others, it seems to reflect a tacit commitment to an anthropological generality about which one tries to find views in common. In other words, this work of translation between different value systems is made possible by the anticipation of a commonality of value that can be established, without sacrificing one's commitment to the stake of human flourishing. This commonality entails that some communication is possible about what is at stake in life, in other words: the minimum human similarities make translation and the construction of commonality possible. In this way, commitment to the translatability of views is not only required for hermeneutics as such, but forms part of its minimum normative commitment.

But I have abstracted these proto-ethical dimensions of hermeneutics from tremendously complex processes of understanding, interpretation, and hermeneutics. There are, and should be, different views on how one is to respond to this call in hermeneutic work and how to flesh it out in practice.

Since hermeneuts know themselves to be situated and since they pursue the re-establishment of practical initiatives by the broader society, they cannot want to elevate themselves to a position of sovereign teacher and judge. Earlier in the discussion, I have pointed out that the hermeneutic relation to others is constituted by an "ethic of humility" (§ 2.3). Considering their orientation to practice, hermeneuts have to be aware of fulfilling only one social role among diverse others, and leave action to social role players in their respective domains. More generally, the possibilities of hermeneutic support for liberation are created by, and limited to, the position of interpreters in each particular society. One may call this hermeneutics' *ethic of self-constraint* provided that this realism about the hermeneut's social situation is not misconstrued as abolishing the ambitious task of involvement, or the courage to offer critique as much as is necessary. The ethic of humility and the ethic of self-constraint make sense only under the assumption that promoting translation, debate, and commonality is possible and would serve the ethic of human flourishing.

To conclude, philosophical hermeneutics is *constitutively ambiguous regarding ethics*. On the one hand, hermeneutics is not a meta-ethics, and does not dispose over the means by which to found one. Practising hermeneutics requires some suspension of one's fidelity to specific normative traditions. On the other hand, the very constitution of philosophical hermeneutics has proto-ethical implications: (a) knowing that things are at stake in human life, (b) the ethical rejection of atrocious conduct, (c) the pursuit of human flourishing[53] of life, (d) a practical commitment to some human generalities and the possibility of finding some commonality through practical acts of translation—such are the constitutive moments of hermeneutics that already comprise an ethics. In as much as hermeneutics is not committed to such an ethics, it is itself an obstacle to the destructive and constructive tasks of hermeneutics.[54] On the other hand, such commitments are entirely compatible with the hermeneutic task of interpreting people's particularity, situated as they are in conflicting traditions, with all the effort to explore the difficulties of communication and ideological distortions of ideas, with full awareness of the possibility or reality of the manipulation of others, and of the difficulty to establish strategic alliances, and with all the uncertainty about the creative pursuit of liberation in specific socio-political contexts.

This tension between commitment and uncertainty accounts for the hermeneut's ethic of self-questioning and non-humiliation of the other to which I referred in Chapter 1, and the ethics of humility and of self-constraint invoked just now. But it also accounts for the fact that hermeneutic practice does not amount to fatalism, but rather to a renewed effort to find the appropriate means for critique and engagement.

6. Hermeneutics among the strategies for liberating the world

In conclusion, I want to come back to the question of the existence and significance of a specific strand of African philosophy named hermeneutics. In Chapter 1, I unpacked the complexity of this question by considering the place accorded to hermeneutics in different typologies. Each typology offers an understanding of hermeneutics, even if sometimes only implicitly by neglecting it. I do not wish to arbitrate on who has the most accurate description and whose view best serves African philosophy in general. That is a question I leave to the readers, hoping that this book equips them better to develop an informed view. However, even with this proviso, a few remarks on where this book has taken us are in order.

Samuel Oluoch Imbo[55] points out that defining African philosophy is a matter not only of scholarly work, but also of academic politics. I concur. And the same holds for drawing up typologies. Above, I argued that everything hermeneutic is inscribed in social life and is thus intertwined with the possibility of exercising and undergoing power. Why would this be different for hermeneutics as a branch (or not) of African philosophy? Each typology is a blend of honest striving towards accurately rendering the available material, and interpretation of the relative importance of the material documented.

Suspending judgement on African hermeneutics' place in any typology still allows one to appreciate the philosophical contribution of the body of work collected and discussed here. When Okere wrote his pioneering study, the question of the possibility of African philosophical hermeneutics was still considered to be relevant. Today, that question is outdated: the possibility has been realised, among others, by the authors reviewed in this book. Indeed, as I have made plain from the beginning, this whole book amounts to an affirmation of the value of hermeneutics in African philosophy. From a general philosophical perspective, the authors studied in this book demonstrate the breadth and depth of problems identified, and their concerted effort to respond to these problems in the most radical way, resulting in an impressive wealth of ideas. Moreover, nothing indicates that the questions with which hermeneuts grapple are of relevance to their subdiscipline or to philosophy only. One rather gets the impression that whatever problem one may deal with, it is open to hermeneutic questioning. The rooting of hermeneutics in the expanse of human existence may account for this far-reaching implication of hermeneutics. Hermeneutics thus holds a mirror to African philosophy of its directions, potential, and vocation. This is a treasure to be transmitted and worked on, and not only by students in Africa or its diaspora. While the specificity of this body of work warrants the continued use of the term "African" for it (but then in the complex ways I have commented upon above), one cannot fail to notice the similarity of this body of work to what many people may claim for their forms of thinking anywhere in the world. Many philosophers hope to support the common human aspiration for freedom from the place in the world in which they happen to live. And for this, African philosophical hermeneutics offers them a wealth of supporting ideas.

With this point in mind, and having now considered major representatives and tried my hand at an independent contribution, I want to come back to the words by Hountondji with which I chose to open this book: "Without any doubt, the problem of African 'philosophy' refers us back to the problem of hermeneutics."[56] This comment, made in 1969, almost in passing, is one of the earliest uses of the term hermeneutics in African philosophy. Setting aside the context in which Hountondji wrote those words, we may today appropriate his claim as a challenge. Who is the "us" referred back to hermeneutics now? To which kind of hermeneutics are "we" referred? And what is *the* problem of hermeneutics?

Globalisation, an increasing awareness of connectedness, the destabilising of a simplistic world order, a realisation of the devastating effects of economic "development" on parts of humanity—the lived experience and foundational questions from which African philosophy emerged—pose a question not only to Africans (on the continent or spread over the world), but to everybody who takes this set of concerns seriously. I would thus argue that the "we" referred back to hermeneutics is in principle the whole of humanity. However, a serious response to the question of who this "we" is, requires one to avoid a simplistic, moralising "we", spontaneously bound in some kind of universal brother- and sisterhood. This "we" can be grasped only as a complex plurality of expressions, of power differentials, of histories of trauma and pride, humiliation and self-confirmation, oppression and exploitation—in short, the very question of who "we" is meant to be has to be the outcome of interpretative effort, which opens up to a politics of establishing commonalities.

This is already part of the response to the second question, regarding the nature of hermeneutics "we" are referred to. "We" need a hermeneutics as a complex tool by which to increase or challenge our existing understanding of this world in which we live. Since "we" refers not merely to minds and bodies, but also to people bound in a myriad of ways, mediated by practices and institutions—from the most laudable, to the most abject—we need any mode of thinking that could increase our understanding of ourselves, in such a way that we can make most of what we have inherited, but also open us up to life-advancing possibilities in the future. Hermeneutics holds the potential to assume part of this task.

On the basis of everything I have argued above, I would posit that the ultimate problem of hermeneutics—the third question derived from Hountondji's words—is how to pursue the possibility of a better life together, without violence to diversity, in a world that we have inherited and that in so many ways steers in the direction of worsening inhumanity. In this pursuit, our existing modes of understanding, our arts of interpretation and philosophical hermeneutics, are part of the problem, in as far as they may promote prejudice and essentialism, or fail to oppose them. But they are also the wellspring for all strategies to liberate us. What full liberation is remains a question of interpretation, and interpretation is indispensable for mustering all our means to pursue liberation as if we were one humanity.

This measure (of promoting a better life together) applies not only to the contribution of hermeneutics—a limited contribution, as even its best proponents understand it to be—but to the whole of humanity. Dedication to specific contexts, to specific people, and specific problems, opens up towards concern for humanity. This seems to be a lesson from the shifting perspectives of hermeneuts, who are devoted to translatability and human generality. This idea finds an echo in authors as divergent as Fanon and Diagne, Gilroy and Eboussi Boulaga. My contention is that the significant contributions to this aspiration that have been studied in this book deserve to be received everywhere in the world.

Notes

Preface. Approaching African hermeneutics

1. Cf. Ernst Wolff, "Four Questions on Curriculum Development in Contemporary South Africa", *South African Journal of Philosophy* 35, no. 4 (2016): 444–459; Ernst Wolff, "Adam Small's Shade of Black Consciousness", in *Philosophy on the Border: Decoloniality and the Shudder of the Origin*, ed. Leonard Praeg (Pietermaritzburg: UKZN Press, 2019), 112–147; Ernst Wolff, *Mongameli Mabona. His Life and Work* (Leuven: Leuven University Press, 2020); and relevant parts of Ernst Wolff, *Lire Ricœur depuis la périphérie. Décolonisation, modernité, herméneutique* (Brussels: Brussels University Press, 2021) and Ernst Wolff, *Between Daily Routine and Violent Protest. Interpreting the Technicity of Action* (Berlin: De Gruyter, 2021).
2. Paulin Hountondji, *African Philosophy: Myth and Reality* (London: Hutchinson, 1996).
3. Martin Heidegger, *Being and Time: A Translation of Sein und Zeit*, trans. Joan Stambauch (Albany: State University of New York Press, 2010).
4. Anthony Giddens, *The Constitution of Society: Outline of the Theory of Structuration.* (Cambridge: Polity, 1984), 374.
5. It should be clear from the typologies that I use that my focus is on philosophy from the African continent—I do not include the wider (mostly North American) Africana philosophy. However, I acknowledge that Serequeberhan, Diagne, and Mudimbe, who figure in this book, did sojourn in America for extensive periods.
6. The reader will notice that I have not included African philosophy in languages other than English and French. Work in other language areas lies outside my field of competence. Texts in Arabic raise a completely different set of historical, contextual, and interpretative issues relating to the prevalence of Islamic thought; lusophone philosophy represents only a very small fraction of African philosophy. Nor do I consider the philosophical traditions of ancient Egypt, Ethiopia, or modern South Africa. A comprehensive perspective on the wealth of African modes of thinking is offered by F. Abiola Irele and Biodun Jeyifo (eds.), *The Oxford Encyclopedia of African Thought* (Oxford: Oxford University Press, 2010).

Chapter 1. Introduction: Hermeneutics as a trend in African philosophy

1. "Le problème de la 'philosophie' africaine nous renvoie, de toute évidence, au problème plus général de l'herméneutique." Paulin Hountondji, "Une littérature aliénée" [1969], in *Sur la "philosophie africaine". Critique de l'ethnophilosophie* (Paris: Maspero, 1977), 28; *African Philosophy: Myth and Reality* (London: Hutchinson, 1996), 189n16. I have not yet identified any earlier reference to hermeneutics in African philosophy.
2. See discussion below.
3. For the purposes of this outline, it is unnecessary (and not really feasible) to identify from where I initially picked up the key idea(s) for each point, or, conversely, for which points I rely on my own arguments.

4   Henry Odera Oruka, "Four Trends in Current African Philosophy" [1978], in *Trends in Contemporary African Philosophy* (Nairobi: Shirikon, 1990), 13–22.
5   Henry Odera Oruka, *Sage Philosophy: Indigenous Thinkers and Modern Debate on African Philosophy* (Leiden: Brill, 1990).
6   Oruka, *Sage Philosophy*, xx–xxi.
7   Kwasi Wiredu, "African Philosophy, Anglophone" (1998), in *Routledge Encyclopedia of Philosophy*, Taylor & Francis, https://www.rep.routledge.com/articles/thematic/african-philosophy-anglophone/v-1.
8   Curiously, although Wiredu thus discusses implicit hermeneutics, authors who explicitly present their work as contributions to hermeneutics (see below) are not even mentioned in the *Routledge Encyclopedia of Philosophy* entry on African philosophy, by any of the three authors: Kwame Appiah in his overarching introduction, Wiredu in his entry on anglophone African philosophy, and Abiola Irele in his entry on francophone African philosophy—see. Kwame Appiah, "African Philosophy" (1998), in *Routledge Encyclopedia of Philosophy*, Taylor & Francis, https://www.rep.routledge.com/articles/overview/african-philosophy/v-1 and Abiola Irele, "African Philosophy, Francophone", in *Routledge Encyclopedia of Philosophy*, Taylor & Francis, https://www.rep.routledge.com/articles/thematic/african-philosophy-francophone/v-1.
9   Kwasi Wiredu, "Introduction: African Philosophy in Our Time", in *A Companion to African Philosophy*, ed. Kwasi Wiredu (Malden and Oxford: Blackwell, 2004), 1–28.
10 Barry Hallen, *A Short History of African Philosophy* (Bloomington and Indianapolis: Indiana University Press, 2002). The content is the same as Hallen's treatment of hermeneutics in his chapter "Contemporary Anglophone African Philosophy: A Survey", in Wiredu's *A Companion to African Philosophy*, 99–148. In his paper, Bekele Gutema, "Hermeneutics and African Philosophy" (published 25 June 2014, available only in podcast: https://international.ucla.edu/lai/article/141276, last accessed 2 February 2024) links hermeneutics in African philosophy to contemporary debates about post-colonialism. He uses Oruka's typology, but singles out Okere, Okolo, and Serequeberhan as significant hermeneuts, and adds Cabral and Fanon to the list. In this, he probably follows Serequeberhan, whom he then discusses critically. His presentation ends with an understanding of hermeneutics as an intercultural debate about common global problems, in a way similar to that of Bruce Janz, discussed below.
11 Hallen, *A Short History of African Philosophy*, 53.
12 Hallen, *A Short History of African Philosophy*, 38.
13 Oruka, *Sage Philosophy*, xx.
14 Cf. Hallen, *A Short History of African Philosophy*, 56.
15 His main contemporary European hermeneut in this context is Gadamer (cf. Hallen, *A Short History*, 58, 59–61). The historical account of central Africa by Nkombe Oleko and Alfons Smet, "Panorama de la philosophie africaine contemporaine", in *Mélanges de philosophie africaine, bibliographie, histoire, essais* (Recherches Philosophiques Africaines, 3) (Kinshasa: Faculté de Théologie Catholique, 1978), 264, 279, points to the significance of Ricœur, whom Hallen mentions only in passing in connection to the work of Okolo Okonda (Hallen, *A Short History of African Philosophy*, 63).
16 There is no chapter on hermeneutics in Tommy L. Lott and John P. Pittman (eds.), *A Companion to African-American Philosophy* (Malden: Blackwell, 2006). However, the contribution in that volume by Albert G. Mosley, "African Philosophy at the Turn of the Century" (192–196), briefly discusses African philosophical hermeneutics and adds to his list of prime contributors to the field Serequeberhan, Okolo, Fanon, and Mudimbe, but also the American authors Leonard Harris and Lucius Outlaw. The little that Lucius Outlaw and Chike Jeffers, "Africana Philosophy", in *The Stanford Encyclopedia of Philosophy* (revised version published 23 May 2017, Fall 2022 Edition), eds.

Edward N. Zalta and Uri Nodelman, https://plato.stanford.edu/archives/fall2022/entries/africana say about hermeneutics follows the same pattern: hermeneutics is considered something specific to authors from the African continent (rather than Afro-American scholars), despite some of Outlaw's own publications, which could have been cited here.

17 Segun Gbadegesin, "On the Idea of African Philosophy", in *African Philosophy: Traditional Yoruba Philosophy and Contemporary African Realities* (New York: Peter Lang, 1991), 1–16.
18 Segun Gbadegesin, "Current Trends and Perspectives in African Philosophy", in *A Companion to World Philosophies*, eds. Eliot Deutsch and Ron Bontekoe (Malden: Blackwell, 1997), 548–563.
19 Adeshina Afolayan and Toyin Falola (eds.), *The Palgrave Handbook of African Philosophy* (New York: Palgrave-Macmillan, 2017), 688.
20 Afolayan and Falola, *The Palgrave Handbook of African Philosophy*, 767.
21 Afolayan and Falola, *The Palgrave Handbook of African Philosophy*, 785.
22 Peter Amato, "On Vernacular Rationality: Gadamer and Eze in Conversation", in *The Palgrave Handbook of African Philosophy*, 303–313.
23 Thaddeus Metz, "Contemporary African Philosophy", in *Oxford Bibliographies Online*, https://www.oxfordbibliographies.com/display/document/obo-9780195396577/obo-9780195396577-0164.xml?rskey=xLMq1I&result=1&q=african+philosophy#firstMatch (published 29 June 2011, last accessed 7 August 2021).
24 Issac Ukpokolo, *Themes, Issues and Problems in African Philosophy* (Cham: Springer, 2017), 2 (my emphasis).
25 Ukpokolo, *Themes, Issues and Problems in African Philosophy*, 283.
26 Jonathan Chimakonam, "History of African Philosophy", in *Internet Encyclopedia of Philosophy*, https://iep.utm.edu/history-of-african-philosophy/ (last accessed 25 September 2024). The details of his additions and broader perspective are not relevant for my current purpose.
27 Ademola Kazeem Fayemi, "Hermeneutics in African Philosophy", *Filosofia Theoretica* 5, no. 2 (2016): 2–18.
28 Bruce Janz, "Hermeneutics and Intercultural Understanding", in *The Routledge Companion to Hermeneutics*, eds. Jeff Malpas and Hans-Helmuth Gander (London: Routledge, 2015), 474–485.
29 Janz, "Hermeneutics and Intercultural Understanding", 475–476 (numbering added).
30 Cf. Janz, "Hermeneutics and Intercultural Understanding", 477.
31 Nkombe Okelo and Alfons Smet, "Panorama de la philosophie africaine contemporaine", 263–282. This text is based on earlier studies by both authors. Lucius Outlaw and Chike Jeffers, "Africana Philosophy", in *The Stanford Encyclopedia of Philosophy* are unusual among recent anglophone authors in picking up on this text.
32 Nkombe and Smet, "Panorama de la philosophie africaine contemporaine", 267–271.
33 Nkombe and Smet, "Panorama de la philosophie africaine contemporaine", 279. Elsewhere, they state that hermeneutics does not only come from Western philosophy, but that it was also present in African wisdom (cf. 266). Unfortunately, they do not develop this point.
34 In this context, it is worth mentioning the synopsis by Tshiamalenga Ntumba, who associates himself explicitly with the current of hermeneutics. Although his overview, "Die Philosophie in der aktuellen Situation Afrikas", *Zeitschrift für philosophische Forschung* 33, no. 3 (July—September 1979): 428–443, is much less informed than that of Nkombe and Smet, it is nevertheless interesting for comparison. Tshiamalenga's article, which was published a year after Nkombe and Smet's "Panorama de la philosophie africaine contemporaine", adopts a very wide view of African philosophy, by including also African Islamic philosophy. This inclusion anticipates the plea years later by Kasereka Kavwahirehi, "Francophone Philosophy", in *The Oxford Encyclopedia of African Thought*, eds. F. Abiola Irele and Biodun Jeyifo (Oxford: Oxford University Press, 2010),

231–235 (discussed below). Tshiamalenga's survey covers four trends: (a) movements of thought on African identity (Afro-American "African Personality" and Negritude), (b) socialism, in which he distinguishes forms from Sub-Saharan Africa and from Egypt, (c) "traditional African philosophy", where he simply juxtaposes ethnophilosophy and hermeneutics (or the "Existentiell-hermeneutische Richtung", as he also calls it) as two major forms of philosophising at the time, but considers hermeneutics as to some extent a corrective of ethnophilosophy—nevertheless, he stops short of attributing to hermeneutics the role of a synthesis, as Nkombe and Smet do (it is also noteworthy that Tshiamalenga considers hermeneutics very prominent in the context of the then Zairian philosophy, a point to which I will return later), (d) the debate about "African philosophy".

35   V. Y. Mudimbe, "African Philosophy as an Ideological Practice: The Case of French-Speaking Africa", *African Studies Review* 26, no. 3/4 (September–December 1983): 133–154.

36   Mudimbe takes Nkombe and Smet to task for the logical terminology in which they express the relation between African wisdom, Western philosophy, and African philosophy. While one may grant that this almost metaphorical use of technical terms is perhaps not the best way to make their point, to my mind Mudimbe is mistaken in applying that terminology on the level of *truth claims*. Nkombe and Smet used it as a figure for the relation between *whole traditions*—the overlap of which is not given, but that is created in African philosophy. For this reason, I will not engage Mudimbe further on this point.

37   Mudimbe, "African Philosophy as an Ideological Practice", 140.

38   Mudimbe, "African Philosophy as an Ideological Practice", 148–149n4.

39   Mudimbe, "African Philosophy as an Ideological Practice", 145.

40   Mudimbe, "African Philosophy as an Ideological Practice", 146.

41   Mudimbe, "African Philosophy as an Ideological Practice", 137, 142.

42   Mudimbe's essay dates to 1983. Three decades later, he came back to the same questions in a text co-authored with Barry Hallen, "Acerca de la filosofía Africana" ["On African Philosophy"], *Ruth* 10 (2012): 19–62. A large part of this essay (cf. 45–62)—and here the discussion of trends of African philosophy is relevant—overlaps with Mudimbe's 1983 essay. More precisely, it is simply a translation of the earlier essay, up to the question in the quotation above: "How is African philosophy in the strict sense presented?" This is followed by the section in which hermeneutics is embedded. In fact, there are only two new insertions of additional literature that is said to present (a) reflection by philosophy on its own practice, (b) themes of cultural philosophy, and (c) philosophy practices from a cosmopolitan point of view (cf. 58). The whole discussion is rounded off with a few more books containing recent English overviews (cf. 62). For the rest, Mudimbe's text has been taken over as is. This leads to at least one important conclusion and one question. The way in which Mudimbe reuses his schema of African philosophy can only be understood as a confirmation of the correctness of the views he held in 1983, and that they have remained relevant in 2012. The question does arise, however, of where this leaves his coauthor, Hallen, in respect of the different forms of African philosophising and the place of hermeneutics in it.

43   Kavwahirehi, "Francophone Philosophy", 231–235.

44   Kavwahirehi, "Francophone Philosophy", 233–234.

45   Mwembo Mutunda, *La Quête du sens dans la philosophie africaine contemporaine. L'Herméneutique Zaïroise et le problème de grille de lecture* (Lubumbashi: Presses Universitaires de Lubumbashi, 1991). I have not been able to obtain a copy of this book, and have had to rely on the critical assessment of it by Jules Emonga Lomomba, "De l'herméneutique zaïroise. Jalons d'une philosophie de l'histoire de la philosophie africaine contemporaine", *Revue Philosophique de Kinshasa* 6, no. 10 (1992): 129–136. However, given its systematic composition and critical comments, this article is itself a valuable document for African philosophical hermeneutics. For this reference, I acknowledge

Herman Lodewyckx, "Hermeneutics in Intercultural Horizons Using H.G. Gadamer. Applied to the Problem of African Philosophy", https://www.academia.edu/12439400/Hermeneutics_and_African_Philosophy (last accessed 27 March 2021).

One finds further confirmation of this point in Jean Onaotsho Kawende, *Appartenance et distanciation: De H.G. Gadamer et P. Ricœur à l'herméneutique africaine* (Louvain-la-Neuve: Presses universitaires de Louvain, 2016), see especially 165–176.

46   Elvis Elengabeka, "L'Herméneutique au carrefour des rationalités et son impact sur le 'savoir' africain", in *Philosophies et cultures africaines à l'heure de l'interculturalité. Anthologie, Tome 2*, eds. Michel Kouam and Chrisitan Mofor (Paris: L'Harmattan, 2011), 155–170. The thesis that I summarise here is not completely worked out in the chapter. For my present purpose, I set aside the central place Elengabeka accords the relation between philosophical hermeneutics and Christian theological hermeneutics, as well as the space devoted to European development.

47   *Nokoko* 6 (2017) (issued by the Institute of African Studies at Carleton University).

48   Dia Mbwangi Diafwila, "Introduction: African Philosophy is a Methodical Discourse", *Nkoko* 6 (2017): 9–14, here 11–13.

49   The English translation, Benoît Okolo Okonda, "From the Hermeneutics of Traditions to the History of Ideas in the Context of Orality", trans. Dia Mbwangi Diafwila, *Nkoko* 6 (2017): 49–80.

50   Louis-Dominique Biakolo Komo, "The Hermeneutical Paradigm in African Philosophy. Genesis, Evolution and Issues", *Nkoko* 6 (2017): 81–106.

51   Biakolo Komo, "The Hermeneutical Paradigm in African Philosophy", 81.

52   Grégoire Biyogo, *Histoire de la philosophie africaine*. 4 volumes (Paris: L'Harmattan, 2006).

53   V. Y. Mudimbe and Kasereka Kavwahirehi (eds.), *Encyclopedia of African Religions and Philosophy* (Cham: Springer, 2021).

54   Heinz Kimmerle, *Philosophie in Afrika, afrikanische Philosophie. Annäherungen an einen interkulturellen Philosophiebegriff* (Frankfurt: Campus, 1991).

55   See also Zacharie Habimana Makamba (ed.), *Courants actuels de la philosophie africaine* (Louvain-la-Neuve: Academia-Bruylant, 2002).

56   Frederick Ochieng-Odhiambo, *Trends and Issues in African Philosophy* (New York: Peter Lang, 2011).

57   Ochieng-Odhiambo, *Trends and Issues in African Philosophy*, 189–212.

58   A somewhat similar outcome results from Kai Kresse, "Zur afrikanischen Philosophiedebatte. Ein Einstieg", *Polylog* (2000), https://lit.polylog.org/2/ekk-de.htm (last accessed 18 October 2013). He identifies developing an African hermeneutics as one of three core "projects" or domains of research in African philosophy—the two others being documenting traditional wisdom and establishing a philosophical competence that engages with the political and techno-scientific actuality of Africa. As representative initiators of each project, Kresse cites Okere, Oruka, and Wiredu respectively. These three projects are seen as distinct from the larger spectrum of African philosophy because they are attempts to overcome the strong opposition between "African" traditionalists and "philosophical" modernists. However, he then devotes a section to each of the major proponents of three projects: Oruka, Wiredu..., but not Okere, nor even Tshiamalenga and Nkombe (whom Kresse considers the most important hermeneuts), while he does mention the critique of discourse in Mudimbe and Appiah. He gives no explicit rationale for proceeding in this way. It is thus unclear whether the readers are invited to read Mudimbe and Appiah as the most important contemporary representatives or as extenders of the project of African philosophical hermeneutics.

59   To be fair, Kai Marchal, the author of that chapter, is aware of the magnitude of hermeneutics outside of the West and invokes African studies, cf. Kai Marchal, "Hermeneutics. Non-Western Approaches", in *The Cambridge Companion to Hermeneutics*, eds. Michael N. Forster and Kristin Gjesdal (Cambridge: Cambridge University Press, 2019), 286–303, here 288–289.

60 Malpas and Gander, *The Routledge Companion to Hermeneutics*, 474–485.
61 According to the patronymic practice in the Democratic Republic of Congo, the surname is Okolo.
62 Elizabeth Mburu, *African Hermeneutics* (Bukuru: HippoBooks, 2019).
63 Stanley Uche Anozie, *Hans-Georg Gadamer and African Hermeneutic Philosophy* (Chisinau: Generis Publishing, 2020).
64 Raphael Okechukwu Madu, *African Symbols, Proverbs and Myths. The Hermeneutics of Destiny* (New York: Peter Lang, 1992).
65 My approach is fairly similar to that of Grégoire Biyogo, *Histoire de la philosophie africaine*, Tome 2, 126.
66 Jean Onaotsho Kawende devotes a substantial proportion of his book to this question, cf. Kawende, *Appartenance et distanciation: De H.G. Gadamer et P. Ricœur à l'herméneutique africaine*.
67 When Basile-Juléat Fouda's 1967 doctoral thesis was republished much later, its new subtitle profiled the book as a contribution to hermeneutics: *La Philosophie négro-africaine de l'existence: herméneutique des traditions orales africaines*. Paris: L'Harmattan, [1967] 2013. However, the original subtitle was Dynamique rationnelle et pancalisme ontologique. Moreover, given the strong ethno-philosophical leaning of this work I am reluctant to give it a central place in my study on African philosophical hermeneutics and therefore postpone studying this book to a later occasion.

Chapter 2. On the threshold: from cultural philosophemes to African hermeneutics—Theophilus Okere

1 Theophilus Okere, *African Philosophy: A Historico-hermeneutical Investigation of the Conditions of its Possibility* (Lanham: University Press of America, 1983). Sole page numbers refer to this book.
2 Theophilus Okere, *Can There Be an African Philosophy? A Hermeneutical Investigation with Special Reference to Igbo Culture* (PhD thesis, Catholic University of Leuven, 1971), 1.
3 *African Philosophy* does not explain Okere's motivation for publishing "Culture and Philosophy" (Part 2 of the original thesis) alone under the new title mentioned above. Does the omission of Part 1, "An Outline of Igbo Culture", represent a decision by Okere, and a tacit affirmation that it contained no original research and only a synopsis of existing scholarly work? Or was it motivated by practical concerns related to the conditions of publishing? For my current purposes, the response to this question is immaterial, since it will have no bearing on our understanding of the argument he offers in his book. I therefore limit my reading to the book that Okere offered on its own terms.
4 Cf. "How in practice could a black African philosophy develop form a black African culture? It is, of course, going to be the challenge to *future* philosophers." Okere, *African Philosophy*, 119 (my emphasis).
5 Rome from 26 March to 1 April 1959.
6 Okere is fully aware that it is not simple to accept both these claims at the same time: "It is, however, a difficult matter to know how a philosophical tradition can itself arise from a non-philosophical background. This would be the aim to pursue in African philosophy unless it is to become a mere branch of the European tradition" (*African Philosophy*, 125).
7 Unfortunately, Okere does not spell out the political implications of his hermeneutics. However, he is clearly aware of its significance: "The possibility of an African philosophy raises the question of the *validity and universality of truth* and of the *communicability* of cultures and their respective philosophies. Is truth relative? It seems this conclusion is inevitable. The historicity and relativity of truth—and this always means truth as we can and do attain it—is one of the main insights of the hermeneutical revolution in philosophy and it is on it that this thesis hangs. But is this relativity such that mutual understanding is impossible? This need not be" (*African Philosophy*, 124, my emphasis).

8   Okere does not give us a systematic introduction to the nature of culture, either in *African Philosophy*, or in his thesis *Can There Be an African Philosophy?* For a more systematic treatment of culture, see Okere's essays, "Culture and Religion" of 1973 and "Culture" of 1975 Both were republished in Okere's *Philosophy, Culture, and Society in Africa* (Nsukka, Nigeria: Afro-Orbis, 2005). I refer to these essays in the endnotes below.
9   See the discussion of Mudimbe in Chapter 5, § 3 below.
10 "Primitive mentality" refers to the degrading anthropology of Lucien Lévy-Bruhl. The word "Bantu", commonly used in early African philosophy, has become pejorative in South Africa.
11 In *African Philosophy*, Okere looks at "Igbo culture" to consider the conditions for an Igbo philosophy (see 115). However, one can recognize the difficulty of speaking about Igbo culture as a single entity in the anthropological first part of his original doctoral thesis. Okere calls his exposition "An outline of Igbo culture", but he confirms that "Igbo culture is not homogenous" and that he follows anthropologists who have "classified the various Igbo-speaking peoples into Northern, Southern, Western, Eastern and North-East regional groups, on the principle of general cultural affinity" (Okere, *Can There Be an African Philosophy?*, 3).Thereby, he approaches cultural homogeneity on a more local, regional scale and weakens Igbo "identity" to "affinity". However, Okere does not always apply this carefully qualified form of cultural description in the second part of his thesis, published in 1983 as *African Philosophy*.
12 In hermeneutics, the word "pre-judice" is often written with a hyphen to refer to a spontaneous initial judgement.
13 Elsewhere, Okere clarifies his traditionalist position as follows: "Though cultures are continuously changing, they are essentially conservative. There is no change except in continuity. No African culture has remained totally unaffected by European contact but there is none which has entirely given way before it. [...] [A]ll change is in continuity, but [...] most changes are selective." Okere, *Philosophy, Culture, and Society in Africa*, 29, similarly, 38.
14 Okere's doctoral thesis consists of a synopsis of literature on Igbo culture and philosophical hermeneutics. One would thus have expected that he would deal more extensively with how non-philosophy transforms into philosophy. However, as he indicates in the preface (Okere, *Can There Be an African philosophy?*, III), he leaves the task of relating culture and hermeneutics to part 2 of the thesis (which became *African Philosophy*) where it comprises only pp. 460–474.
15 One element of such an exploration could consist of scrutinising indigenous knowledge. Although Okere's thesis offers examples of indigenous knowledge, it never becomes a distinct object of study in the thesis or in *African Philosophy*. On the topic of indigenous knowledge, see the undated chapter, "Indigenous Knowledge" in Okere, *Philosophy, Culture, and Society in Africa*, 74–83.
16 Okere's critique of ethnophilosophy is quite different from Hountondji's. Hountondji's (early) position can be summarised with the formula: African philosophy is myth and reality; myth, in so far as there is no collective African philosophy; reality, in so far as a literature is produced in which philosophical claims are made (about elements of tradition and culture). By contrast, Okere's position is that African philosophy should be a hermeneutics of culture and a hermeneutic philosophy. Culture is non-philosophical, spontaneous, traditional, and less self-reflexive, but contains philosophemes; philosophy is situated in particular cultures, but reflects critically on that embeddedness.
17 Privileging European philosophy is exactly what Okere rejected. In his interview with Obi Oguejiofor, he juxtaposes the fascination that Western philosophy had on him and his refusal of the idea that the authors of this tradition simply spoke for humanity as a whole. See Theophilus Okere, "My Philosophical Odyssey", in *African Philosophy and the Hermeneutics of Culture: Essays in Honour of Theophilus Okere*, edited by Josephat Obi Oguejiofor and Godfrey Igwebuike Onah (Münster: LIT Verlag, 2005), 353–360, here 355.

18 Cf. "Just as language limits what a poet can do with it as well as offers him conditions of more possibilities of inventiveness, so does culture both channel the philosopher's interpretation as well as offer him infinite possibilities for creation of meaning." Okere, *African Philosophy*, 66. I take note of the male bias in this and other quoted passages, but will render all citations as they were originally published.
19 Apart from the gendered wording prevalent in Okere's writing—as it is in practically all of his contemporaries' texts—one needs to note his anthropologising appropriation of Heidegger's ontological thought.
20 For Okere's understanding of the concept "world" and its implications for hermeneutics, see especially *African Philosophy*, 48.
21 For Okere's understanding of "pre-judice" and its implications for hermeneutics, see *African Philosophy*, 58–59.
22 I follow the conclusion of *African Philosophy*. In speaking about the possibility of African philosophy, the reader has to bear in mind that this point was initially stated in 1971.
23 It is not entirely clear why Okere resorts to the expression "black Africa", particularly in the conclusion of *African Philosophy*. It is likely that this term does not have much to do with pigmentation or the social construction of racial categories. More likely is that he wants to delimit his thesis: falling outside of his focus are the philosophies of people of Western origin who live on the African continent and the philosophies of people thinking from a Muslim cultural background. Such a delimitation is not entirely convincing, because of the existence of Islam in "black Africa". Nevertheless, given that for Okere the principles of hermeneutics are anthropological in nature, everything he writes about philosophy is valid for all people.
24 As we have seen from Okere's critique of ethnophilosophy, there is no way by which to "automatically deduce a philosophical system from a culture" (*African Philosophy*, 8). Likewise, it is as absurd to try to derive the diverse Greek philosophies from Indo-European language(s) and custom(s) as it is to do so from "Bantu" languages and customs.
25 Most of them already do so to varying degrees and for those who don't, this question remains simply open. This is part of Okere's point when he exclaims: "it would be [...] absurd to [...] recommend to the whole [African—EW] continent as a precondition to having a philosophy, first of all, to demythologize, in order to enter decisively into the age of complete reflection, in order to be at last able to distinguish between subject and object, between the self and the other, between the natural and the supernatural, between time and space, and in order to evolve a complete idea of liberty" (119).
26 This word is quite unexpected, because Okere never outlines his methodology, and it would remain an arduous task for as long as he remains committed to the understanding of hermeneutics he derives from Heidegger and Gadamer.
27 Strictly speaking, Okere has not argued for the absence of reflection in non-philosophical tradition. I read his point as applying to the most challenging case, or to rephrase his words: philosophy becomes the gradual appropriation by reflective reason of this mass of tradition, *even up to and including the unreflected elements*.
28 Okere asks how an African philosophy may look and how it would be different from a Western philosophy. However, on closer inspection, he compares not different philosophies, but different cultural philosophemes.
29 The closest to an exception I could find is after Okere discusses how Igbo and Indo-European languages each deal with the notion of being: "This need not imply that an Igbo cannot understand the notion of Being or a philosophy based on this notion. It means, however, that a philosophy original to this culture would not take its orientation from a concept so strange to it" (*African

Philosophy, 124). Much later, in 2004, Okere articulated his view on a related subject, namely that of the ambiguous role of philosophy in intercultural dialogue. See Okere, "Philosophy and Intercultural Dialogue", in *Philosophy, Culture, and Society in Africa*, 60–73.

30 Okere uses the emergence of Indian philosophy as analogy for the emergence of African philosophy (cf. *African Philosophy*, 126–127).
31 Later in this book, in Chapter 4, § 2, I point out that Sophie Oluwole adopts a similar position.
32 Elsewhere, Okere recognises the social reality of religious pluralism in his own society; see *Philosophy, Culture, and Society in Africa*, 43. Although conceding the fact of cultural pluralisation, Okere's own assessment of it remains clear: "Pluralism has as it were stolen the soul out of our culture" (*Philosophy, Culture, and Society in Africa*, 44). This echoes his disapproval of cultural métissage evoked earlier in this chapter (*African Philosophy*, 127). In all fairness, the brunt of his critique is aimed at Westernisation rather than other forms of cultural mixing.
33 The central role of culture in philosophical questioning is also reflected in Okere's reading of Heidegger: Okere is clearly more interested in Heidegger's view of understanding as rooted in life circumstances, than Heidegger's view of understanding as grasping not yet realised potential of existence.
34 Okere's double view on one's relation to a culture is also reflected in his other writing. On the one hand, the fact that human beings are cultural beings affiliates them with specific social groups: "each one in his own social group, has got his own culture. There is no such thing as a cultureless person. For us human beings to be is to be in a social group and to be in a social group is to have a culture." On the other hand, cultural heritage is not a fate: "we cannot be expected to appropriate our past without any discrimination". *Philosophy, Culture, and Society in Africa*, 32.
35 Elsewhere, Okere gives a more qualified view of cultural homogeneity, emphasising the socio-cultural facts of selection and mixing. He sheds no tears for the cultural constraints of what he called the pre-colonial "ethnic ghetto" (*Philosophy, Culture, and Society in Africa*, 35).
36 Elsewhere, Okere articulates the circumstances in which African philosophers must work with equal force: "Our culture has been changing at a near revolutionary pace since our first contact with the white man, almost 500 years ago. The slave trade, commerce in oil, colonization and Christian evangelization, urbanization and industrialization have followed one another in uninterrupted succession. Moreover, colonial history has tied the political fortunes of our people to those of our neighbours in a way that now seems irreversible. [...] There is no calling back yesterday, what has not survived will not survive." *Philosophy, Culture, and Society in Africa*, 43–4.
37 See *Philosophy, Culture, and Society in Africa*, 29.
38 See the title of chapter 2 of *African Philosophy*: "Culture and Philosophy: A Question of Hermeneutics".
39 Unnumbered first page of the Preface in Okere, *Philosophy, Culture, and Society in Africa*.
40 "This self-interpretation which is also a self-assertion, is no doubt the best way to restore self-confidence to a humiliated culture" (*African Philosophy*, 128).
41 The nature of this political stance is the same as what Okere assumes in justifying a conference on indigenous knowledge, when he writes: "Therefore our purpose in convoking this symposium is not for the mere reason of establishing a difference, not for continuing the divide between western knowledge and [African] indigenous knowledge. Rather it is first, *to recognize and valorize for ourselves our own indigenous knowledge* and take off from there as from our starting point. It is also to help us mark the limits of western narrowly scientific knowledge and be mentally prepared to *combat its reductionism, its hegemony, its strangling and impoverishing monopoly of orthodoxy*. Hopefully it will enable us to integrate our two sources of knowledge since the two meet in us and our future lies in their harmonious merger. It is likely that a healthy merger will help us forge

a more inclusive, holistic and sustainable knowledge of our environment and better-sustained development.

If we succeed in laying such a foundation we shall be helping in achieving the most significant form of people *empowerment*; nay of *independence* beyond any dreams of our people since strangers enslaved us in our land." *Philosophy, Culture, and Society in Africa*, 82 (my emphasis).

Chapter 3. Interpretation as a resource for political resistance: Serequeberhan between generality and particularity

1. Tsenay Serequeberhan, *The Hermeneutics of African Philosophy: Horizon and Discourse* (London and New York: Routledge, 1994). Sole page numbers refer to this book.
2. Similarly, "philosophy in general and African philosophy in particular is, above all else and necessarily, a hermeneutical thinking through of its own lived historicalness" (118). And again, "we will see that philosophy, African or otherwise, is a situated critical and systematic interpretative exploration of our lived historico-cultural actuality. In this regard it is a radically presuppositional and reflexive discourse" (3). On "existence", see Tsenay Serequeberhan, *Our Heritage: The Past in the Present of African-American and African Existence* (Lanham: Rowman & Littlefield, 2000), ix.
3. Two valuable summaries of the book's content are given, see 10 and 117.
4. This formulation captures how Serequeberhan receives Fanon in this book, instead of reprising Fanon's conception of himself.
5. The ability to articulate our understanding of the world around us is "the inherently interpretative character of human existence as such". Serequeberhan, *Hermeneutics of African Philosophy*, 1.
6. In elaborating this claim, Serequeberhan draws from Heidegger in an anthropologising reading of the latter's early ontology, in a way reminiscent of Okere. I do not develop this point.
7. This reference to the German philosopher is called for by the place Serequeberhan accorded to him in this part of his argument.
8. Serequeberhan made two of Towa's essays available in English under the title, *Marcien Towa's African Philosophy: Two Texts* (Asmara: Hdri, 2012).
9. Serequeberhan, *Our Heritage*, 41.
10. Serequeberhan's nuanced view on the relation between European philosophy and human nature is confirmed elsewhere in his writings. For instance, he claims that "we can categorically affirm that the question of African philosophy is 'less a borrowing from [or imitation of] European culture than a retrieval, a rejuvenation and re-valorizing of an *ancient heritage*, and, more profoundly, a re-conquest and re-affirmation of our *generic human identity*'". Serequeberhan, *Our Heritage*, 52, citing Marcien Towa, *L'Idée d'une philosophie négro-africaine* (Yaoundé: Editions Clé, 1979), 79. Serequeberhan also develops this position by critically self-relativising of African particularity: "the humanity of those negated by the metaphysically sanctioned violence of European conquest is itself a *specific actualization of human existence* that does not arrogate to itself the hubris of cultural-historical solipsism". *Our Heritage*, 69 (my emphasis).
11. See Serequeberhan, *Hermeneutics of African Philosophy*, chapter 2 and § 6, below.
12. See also Serequeberhan, *Our Heritage*, 57–58, on "generic humanity".
13. See Serequeberhan's entirely valid remark that Heidegger's philosophy is a "product of a systematic hermeneutic of modern European existence" (20). However, Serequeberhan also insists on the fact that the historical contingency of this mode of philosophical expression is to be distinguished from the human reality to which it refers (see 132n30).
14. The details of his argument are telling: "The reader should thus not be surprised to find, throughout this study, positive references and appropriations, as well as critical rejections of the

European philosophic tradition. For ultimately, as Cornel West correctly points out, this obsessive (Afrocentric?) effort to bracket Europe at all costs is itself the product of our encounter with and interiority to Europe. To be a Westernized African in today's post-colonial Africa means ultimately to be marked/branded—in one way or another—by the historical experience of European colonialism. We should not try to 'bide' from this all-pervasive element of our modern African historicity. Rather, our efforts to surmount it must begin by facing up to and confronting this enigmatic actuality. This then is the hermeneutic task of this study, for ultimately the antidote is always located in the poison!" (11)

15 As proof of the positive side of the philosophical practice common to all humanity, consider the climax of chapter 4 of *The Hermeneutics of African Philosophy*, which consists of a declaration of what African philosophy should be as a radical emancipatory hermeneutics. When this is realised, Serequeberhan affirms, African philosophy "will become a radical and emancipatory hermeneutic inventory of our post-colonial African inheritance". And he adds a reason: "For as Foucault tells us: 'philosophy is precisely the challenging of all phenomena of domination at whatever level or under whatever form they present themselves—political, economic, sexual, institutional, and so on'" (115).

16 An idea that is echoed with reference to Cabral (see 113).

17 In this context, "professional philosophers" is a technical designation, referring to African scholars who had a formal university education, most likely in Western universities and in Western philosophy, which is the epistemic competence from which they practise the discipline. Therefore, the critique of "professional philosophy" does not aim at the fact that some authors pursue a profession in philosophy, but rather scrutinises the implications of a more universalistic understanding of philosophy advanced by these people (see 124).

18 This point can be supported by the fact that Serequeberhan edited an anthology of African philosophy: Tsenay Serequeberhan, *African Philosophy: The Essential Readings* (St. Paul: Paragon, 1991).

19 Elsewhere, Serequeberhan defines Eurocentrism as "a pervasive bias in modernity's self-consciousness of itself. It is grounded at its core in the metaphysical belief or idea (*Idee*) that European existence is qualitatively superior to other forms of human life." Tsenay Serequeberhan, "The Critique of Eurocentrism and the Practice of African Philosophy", in *Postcolonial African Philosophy*, ed. Emmanuel Eze (Oxford: Blackwell, 1997), 141–161, here 142.

20 Serequeberhan's critique of Okere is problematic (125–126). He attributes to Okere the idea that precolonial Africa is devoid of philosophy. This is an unfortunate simplification that seems to overlook the key notion of "philosophemes" by which Okere assumes a much more complex view on the presence/absence of philosophy in African societies. On may well wonder if Serequeberhan's way of attributing philosophy retrospectively to African societies succumbs to the "honorific" sense of philosophy that he himself rejects.

21 Explicitly formulated: "In their [Fanon's and Cabral's] work, African philosophical hermeneutics finds a living example of its vocation" (114).

22 In *Muntu in Crisis* Fabien Eboussi Boulaga advances similar critique of ethnophilosophy and "school philosophy", measured according to their failure to respond to people's need for practical self-affirmation. This is discussed in Chapter 5, § 4 below.

23 See again Serequeberhan, *Our Heritage*, 41: "Indeed, beyond our ethnic identities, the heritage of the differing African liberation movements makes possible for us a historical and political world in which we all share as Africans. This 'sharing' does not presuppose any kind of racial, mystical, or metaphysical African oneness. It only calls for the recognition that, beyond color and race, our being African is grounded in a shared history of subjugation, struggle, and political liberation: a history we affirm, choose to perpetuate, and aim to further expand on and consolidate!"

From this, Serequeberhan derives a narrative understanding of (African) identity in *Our Heritage*, 42, 44.

24 Serequeberhand takes this citation from Frantz Fanon, *Toward the African Revolution* (New York: Grove Press, 1988), 44. Serequeberhan advances a similar argument in *Hermeneutics of African Philosophy*, 48. The challenge for Serequeberhan is to overcome these polarising distinctions, without succumbing to a philosophy of universalism. It is a combination of Heidegger and Fanon that allows him to do so.
25 For a more in-depth exploration of Serequeberhan's perspective on the European Enlightenment, see the studies in Tsenay Serequeberhan, *Contested Memory: The Icons of the Occidental Tradition* (Trenton: Africa World Press, 2007).
26 The last chapter of Serequeberhan's *Contested Memory* develops his thinking on international relations, where the core of the argument is expressed as follows: "in a contracting world of politicoeconomic interdependence, weak countries can survive only to the extent that the norms of international legality—i.e., the contractual relations that guarantee mutual justice and recognition—nullify the permanent threat incarnated in the military-political might of 'powerful' states". *Contested Memory*, 170.
27 Serequeberhan expands his critique of Nkrumah with a critique of the similar defects he sees in Hountondji. I focus only on the former case.
28 This critique of Nkrumah already appears in Tsenay Serequeberhan, *The Eritrean People's Liberation Front: A Case Study in the Rhetoric and Practice of African Liberation* (Boston: William Monroe Trotter Institute, University of Massachusetts, 1989), 8–13.
29 For Serequeberhan's reading of Marx, see *Contested Memory*, chapter 4.
30 Still, I don't think this is how Senghor saw it. In his world of plural essential races or civilisations, the complementarity between them does not allow for a "normal" version, all versions being equal. But even then the question remains whether anybody (or any African person) should feel recognised or flattered by reading Senghor's description of Africans. I wouldn't. Serequeberhan wasn't. But others were.
31 See, for instance, Olúfẹ́mi Táíwò, *How Colonialism Pre-empted Modernity in Africa* (Bloomington: Indiana University Press, 2010).
32 Serequeberhan takes this term from Gramsci.
33 See the recapitulation of these problems in 14–15 and 18.
34 As Serequeberhan claims "lived situatedness of philosophy is not a blemish but the source of philosophical reflection as such" (135n67). This takes nothing away from the generality of philosophy, which is the obverse of particularity. The diverse, particular situatedness of each philosopher may always serve as a source of reflection.
35 But it is clear in places that Serequeberhan is not thinking about the mediation of a philosopher's situatedness. When defending himself against the critique that hermeneutics may be a foreign importation, he retorts by analysing how "philosophic discourse itself originates from and is organically linked to the concrete conditions-of-existence and the life-practices of the horizon within and out of which it is formulated" (17). How concerns from over the world can really and legitimately be introduced into our "living actuality" forms a significant blind spot in *Hermeneutics of African Philosophy*.
36 About his location in the United States, Serequeberhan notes: "African philosophy, as practiced on this side of the Atlantic, then, is not, in my view, rendered impotent by the distance from which it speaks. In fact, given the academic and political difficulties on the continent, distance allows one a favorable horizon within which critical questions can be properly explored. It establishes a material detachment that is fruitful in exploring that which is closest to our spiritual concerns." *Our Heritage*, 36.

Likewise in *Contested Memory*, Serequeberhan approvingly cites Foucault, who spoke about working outside of France during the time of the Algerian war: "While that event had very important repercussions in the intellectual world and in all of French culture, I experienced it somewhat like a foreigner. Moreover, by *observing the facts like a foreigner*, I managed more easily to understand the absurdity and to discern *with great clarity* what the necessary conclusion of that war would be." Michel Foucault, *Remarks on Marx* (New York: Semiotext[e], 1991), 74, cited in Serequeberhan, *Contested Memory*, xxi (Serequeberhan's emphasis). Serequeberhan then comments on this passage: "Those of us who are stepchildren, permanent *inside-outsiders* to Europe as *indigenous-foreigners*, see 'with great clarity' Europe's metaphysical entanglement. For we are the living, breathing, corporeal incarnations of this mélange, of this tangle."

37 See also *Our Heritage*, 77n5, where one finds, perhaps, an explanation for Serequeberhan's reticence to elaborate on this point: he attributes Ethiopia's dominance over Eritrea to the influence of the United States. Some support for his attitude is provided in *Contested Memory*, 177–178, and evoked again in Serequeberhan's interview with Richard Marshall, "The Contesting Memory of African Philosophy", *3:16*, https://www.3-16am.co.uk/articles/the-contesting-memory-of-african-philosophy?c=end-times-archive, 12 August 2018 (last accessed 3 January 2023).

38 Serequeberhan insists, against Castoriadis, that South Africa was made possible by the West (see *Hermeneutics of African Philosophy*, 142n3).

39 On this point there is complete agreement between Serequeberhan and Eboussi Boulaga, as we will see later.

40 In *Our Heritage*, Serequeberhan cites Okolo: "Praxis unlatches the hermeneutic process and gives it an orientation. Hermeneutics, in its turn, offers praxis a cultural self-identity, necessary for ideological combat" (*Our Heritage*, xiv).

41 Serequeberhan's aim is not to undo, negate, or hide Western philosophy, but to hasten the demise of its exaggerated universalistic claims (see 128n30). However, Serequeberhan simplifies the matter by adding: "After all, when all is said and done, this is the lived heritage which buttressed and gave ethical and metaphysical endorsement to the expansionist adventures of a colonialist Europe" (11). This condemnation of Western philosophy is in line with Serequeberhan's understanding of Eurocentrism, in which European/Western philosophy is nothing but a continuity of past blindness and violence.

42 See also: "Hence, in addition to *expanding*—through our contributions—and *appropriating* the European heritage of the Left, the struggle for African freedom at a more fundamental level is aimed at *overcoming* European dominance and reclaiming the politico-historic space of African existence which has been obliterated by European colonialism" (38, my emphases).

As an example of this line of thinking, Serequeberhan claims (in the context of anti-colonial counter-violence) that "all Fanon does is to articulate a prevalent theme of European philosophy in the context of Africa's experience of the modern Europeanized world". (75). However, taking this claim literally would seriously disrupt Serequeberhan's view of European philosophy explained thus far.

43 See also Serequeberhan, *Our Heritage*, 55.

44 Elsewhere, Serequeberhan works with a related, but still different, distinction: instead of actuality-ideality, that of actuality-possibility: "the work of theory is aimed […] at hermeneutically seeking out and elucidating the *possible* in the *actual* eventuation of lived existence". *Our Heritage*, 76.

45 How the anti-slavery movement formed part of European Enlightenment does not come into Serequeberhan's view.

46 Serequeberhan never mentions, for instance, violence in or between pre-colonial polities. Consequently, the reader is led to understand that, in Serequeberhan's view, any such violence may by implication be considered trivial or insignificant for the hermeneutics of contemporary Africa.
47 For an alternative rendering of Africa's history of modernisation, see again Olúfẹ́mi Táíwò, *How Colonialism Pre-empted Modernity in Africa*.
48 It is certainly no trivial point that Serequeberhan sets aside a discussion in chapter 3 of "Fanon's originative discussion of violence in the first section of *The Wretched of the Earth*" (56). However, judging from the citations and references to the book in the end notes, Serequeberhan actually indiscriminately inserts references to other parts of the book, more than once doing violence to Fanon's chronology.
49 See again Serequeberhan's *Contested Memory*.
50 The "stagnant actuality of neo-colonialism [...] is nothing more than the *de facto* renegotiation of the colonial status. That is why, as we noted earlier, all that is said of colonialism also holds true, in every essential, of neocolonial Africa" (82, see also 67). The exact same claim is made elsewhere with some support cited from Basil Davidson (cf. 89).
51 Here I am not thinking of all kinds of writing—Diagne's insistence on a centuries' old tradition of written Islamic philosophy serves as caution. I rather have in mind the publishing of novels, a fact that Diagne himself associates with the colonial and post-colonial milieu (cf. his discussion on literature of translation below, Chapter 5, § 5).
52 But note that in *Our Heritage*, Serequeberhan gives a cryptic assessment of the role of Islam in North Africa: despite colonisation and exploitation, it preserved the cultural heritage and even helps to oppose Western hegemony (see *Our Heritage*, 1). However, according to Serequeberhan, this happens through "fundamentalist movements aimed at a frozen, archaic, and arcane past", which seems to contradict his understanding of a return to a "purer" cultural source.
53 However, we know that even as early as chapter 2 of Fanon's book this Manichaeism no longer holds so purely. See also Serequeberhan, *Hermeneutics of African Philosophy*, 82.
54 Under the circumstances of extreme oppression sketched by Serequeberhan, where the colonised is defeated and the colonist wins everything (cf. 71), it is not clear what space remains for this claim: "The colonized, on the other hand, knows that he is human and the incarnation of a distinctive civilization" (70–71).
55 The role of this social category in post-independence politics and continued liberation is discussed below.
56 Serequeberhan quotes this phrase from Fanon (in 71), but one recognises here the dangers of breaking the chronology of Fanon's exposition. A longer reading of Serequeberhan would have to deal with the divergences from Fanon, a question to which Serequeberhan hardly pays any attention. That he diverges from Fanon is obviously no problem. However, he has to justify his bold claims. To name but one example: for Serequeberhan (probably following Cabral) where the urban elite contributes to liberation, they will not divest themselves from their elite cultural capital and hence there will be much more of question of *two* horizons to fuse, whereas Fanon envisaged an integration of the urbanites into the rural masses.
57 Mariangela Barker, a former student of mine, drew my attention to this fact.
58 Executing this task is a long-standing project of Serequeberhan. See, in this respect especially, *Contested Memory*. One finds a good description of this "de-structive" procedure in *Contested Memory*, 28n87.
59 Serequeberhan's reference is to Hannah Arendt, *Between Past and Future* (New York: Penguin Books, 1980), 4.

60 My critique here is not of Serequeberhan's insistence on violence, but of his unhermeneutic, unqualified recourse to it. If my reading is correct, then the problem is not (as Serequeberhan claims) Arendt's misunderstanding of Fanon on violence, or that she had no sympathy for colonised Africans' aspirations to the same kind of liberty claimed by Europeans of the resistance. The problem is that Serequeberhan fails to appreciate the fundamental difference between Fanon and Arendt. But even if one were to side with Arendt, this does not yet close Serequeberhan's case against the importance of counter-violence, since, at most, she helps us consider public debate. To schematise: for Serequeberhan liberation resides in the moment of "organized *violence*"; for Arendt it resides in "*organized* violence". This is not a trivial issue: if Arendt is right, it raises an entire set of questions about legitimate and strategically efficient means of resistance, questions on which Serequeberhan barely touches. The fault of under-interpretation—the application of a "pre-established framework" as if it held "automatically and of necessity" to all contexts of which Serequeberhan accused Nkrumah (in 34 and 35)—can now be laid at Serequeberhan's feet, when he affirms that "the colonized does not choose violence. Violence is not a choice" (78). In short, according to Serequeberhan, across the African continent, and under all political conditions of colonisation and neo-colonisation, the rule of the recourse to violence holds *automatically* and *of necessity*. One could also say that, in attributing "rehumanisation" to the effect of violence alone, Serequeberhan negates the possibility that Africans can—like the passage from Arendt suggests—humanise by acting in peaceful concert. In this way Serequeberhan perpetuates the myth of the violent barbarians, who act out of immediacy and mechanical spontaneity, a way of thinking reminiscent of the essentialism he identified in Senghor. As an alternative, Serequeberhan could well have adopted the idea of acting in concert from Arendt, in order to better articulate his ideas on violence with those of African traditions of democratic exchange, to which he furtively refers (150–151n35).

61 See also Serequeberhan, *Our Heritage*, 70.

62 The "fusion of horizons" is a technical term from Gadamer's hermeneutics, to which Serequeberhan gives his own articulation.

63 Serequeberhan cites this phrase from Fanon, *Toward the African Revolution*.

64 Phrases cited from Fanon, *Toward the African Revolution*. See also 106. Similarly argued with reference to Césaire in Serequeberhan, *The Eritrean People's Liberation Front*, 22.

65 This passage is a citation from Fanon, *The Wretched of the Earth* (New York: Grove Press, [1961]1968), 246.

66 Compare Serequeberhan's view that "the necessity of violence in the colonial situation arises out of the violent nature of this situation itself" (in *The Eritrean People's Liberation Front*, 14) with his own critique of *necessity* in his debate with Nkrumah. Here, Serequeberhan regards Nkrumah's framework of (Eurocentric) Scientific Socialism as insufficiently hermeneutic because it presumes to be "automatically and of necessity" valid (as discussed above).

67 There is some confusion of anti-colonial and post-independence struggles in this discussion (see *Hermeneutics of African Philosophy*, 99), because Lumumba, Fanon, and Cabral are cited, even though they had little experience with neo-colonial struggle.

68 When considering the colonial *context* of violence of which colonised people are the victims, it is correct to say that "it is not our invention—it is not our cool decision". As an expression of the dire situation of the colonised, it is understandable. But this is not Serequeberhan's point on counter-violence.

69 Serequeberhan cites Fanon in *Hermeneutics of African Philosophy*: "The men coming from the towns learn their lessons in the hard school of the people, and at the same time these men open classes for the people in military and political education" (99).

70   However, in *The Eritrean People's Liberation Front*, the idea of practices of self-reliance is derived from liberation practice.
71   One sees here again, implicitly, Serequeberhan's refusal of Enlightenment-derived anthropological norms. However, the more general anthropology that subtends his own work seems to escape this problem, without Serequeberhan commenting on this.
72   Similarly argued in *The Eritrean People's Liberation Front*.
73   Serequeberhan agrees with Heidegger's idea of the polysemy of human existence. Serequeberhan even states: "Instead of being organic wholes, these 'new nations' are Euro-African hybrid constructions which do not arise out of the internal constancy of an indigenous historical formation" (105).
74   But then one may wonder how Serequeberhan can cite Cabral approvingly when the latter wrote about the "birth of new nations from human groups or from peoples who were at *different stages of historical development*" (104, my emphasis) or when Cabral depicts the armed struggle for liberation as a "forced march along the road to *cultural progress*" (cited in 109, my emphasis).
75   Both Okere and Okolo insist on this point.
76   Note that the role attributed in chapter 3 of *Hermeneutics of African Philosophy* to a faction of Westernised urbanites is now ascribed to *all* Westernised urbanites.
77   Serequeberhan's portrayal of Westernisation as inherently estranging poses a problem. On which basis could this lived historicity (as he would say) be said to be a self-negation? As long as this idea is not developed, it is as if Serequeberhan still works with the *original* African culture, which he explicitly denies.
78   Up to this point, the impetus of liberation comes from a conversion of some urbanites, while the masses contribute little more than energy.
79   I spell out the implications between brackets. This stance is worked out more explicitly in Serequeberhan, *Our Heritage*, chapter 1.

Chapter 4. Critique of African hermeneutic reason: interpretation triggered and oriented by praxis—Okolo Okonda

1   Benoît Okolo Okonda, *Pour une philosophie de la culture et du développement. Recherches d'herméneutique et de praxis africaines* (Kinshasa: Presses universitaires du Zaïre, 1986). This title translates as, *For a Philosophy of Culture and Development: Exploration of African Hermeneutics and Praxis*. Sole page numbers refer to this book. Following the patronymic practice in Zaire/DRC, the author's surname is Okolo.
2   In some places in *Pour une philosophie*, Okolo takes his ideas from his doctoral thesis, *Tradition et destin. Essai sur la philosophie herméneutique de Paul Ricœur, Martin Heidegger et Hans-Georg Gadamer* (PhD dissertation, University of Lubumbashi, 1979) ("Tradition and Destiny: Essay on the Hermeneutic Philosophy of Paul Ricœur, Martin Heidegger, and Hans-Georg Gadamer".) Some of the chapters that compose *Pour une philosophie* are based on pieces Okolo published before completing *Tradition et destin*. Finally, Okolo worked out some of the ideas that he had first defended before writing *Tradition et destin*. The intricate history of the genesis of ideas in *Pour une philosophie* will not occupy us in this chapter.
3   On praxis and action as synonyms, see 87.
4   Similarly Okolo, *Tradition et destin*, 6.
5   Okolo argues this point in agreement with Elie Phambu Ngoma-Binda. Okolo's criticism of what he sees as unproductive philosophy echoes the views of Okere and Serequeberhan.
6   Benoît Okolo Okonda, "From the Hermeneutics of Traditions to the History of Ideas in the Context of Orality", trans. Dia Mbwangi Diafwila, *Nokoko* 6 (2017): 68.

7   In distinguishing the centre from the periphery of global capitalism, Okolo draws on the work of Samir Amin.
8   For Okolo, the terms of "development" are often dictated by dominating countries (see 81).
9   Later, Okolo clarifies that revolutionary praxis entails neither class struggle nor civil war, but in essence radical opposition to under-development. See Okolo, "From the Hermeneutics", 50.
10 Okolo's scepticism of established developmental theory is rooted in his critique of neo-colonialism.
11 This claim is supported by Okolo's critique of "muzzling" [*muselage*] in "From the Hermeneutics", 66 (cited above) and to his critique of the bourgeoisie of the global periphery.
12 This feedback is required for development to become global, revolutionary, and driven by science (see 86).
13 And see Okolo, *Tradition et destin*, 3, 276.
14 Okolo explicitly derives his understanding of "text" from Paul Ricœur. Other traits of texts are also discussed in detail, following Jacobson and Todorov. See Okolo, *Pour une philosophie*, 35–36.
15 The separation of text and author has major implications for reading as part of tradition, in other words, by people who are not necessarily the original addressees of the text.
16 See Okolo, *Pour une philosophie*, 28, 43; *Tradition et destin*, 278.
17 Later, Okolo defines tradition as a "space of transmission [that] is not only the place where interpretation is deployed, but [...] also and above all the subject and object of interpretation". "From the Hermeneutics", 49.
18 See Okolo, *Pour une philosophie*, 38, 44; *Tradition et destin*, 280.
19 See Okolo, *Pour une philosophie*, 44, 52; *Tradition et destin*, 280.
20 Okolo stresses re-taking cultural tradition, and this reprise is not limited to culture. His entire reasoning is constructed in such a way that reprise applies to whatever presents itself to be read. *Reprise* does not mean accepting everything: discarding something can also be a re-taking.
21 Elsewhere, "hermeneutics" is used as an umbrella term for both reading and re-taking. See Okolo, *Pour une philosophie*, 100.
22 Cf. *Pour une philosophie*, 46: "From this point of view, the validity of an interpretation will be linked to the validity of a struggle: of its justice [*justice*] and its rightness [*justesse*]."
23 This proposition is formulated on page 39 of *Pour une philosophie*, where the subject is not only a reader but a "philosopher". Matching the two formulations invites us to understand re-taking as the eminently philosophical component in the complex social-scientific interpretative framework presented in Okolo's book.
24 See Okolo, *Pour une philosophie*, 45; *Tradition et destin*, 282–283 and § 4.3.a below.
25 Neither Okolo's reason for choosing this term, nor the appropriate way to translate it, is evident to me.
26 See Okolo, *Pour une philosophie*, 46; identical to *Tradition et destin*, 284–285.
27 Thus, we come back to the questions of validity (raised under § 3.2.b, above) and the verification function of worldviews (in § 3.3.a, above).
28 Okolo refers to Laurent Ankunde, "Philosophie et développement", in *Présence Africaine* 81 (1972): 3–17.
29 See Okolo, *Pour une philosophie*, 56; *Tradition et destin*, 3.
30 Elsewhere, Okolo identifies three dimensions of tradition: material support, interpretation, and transmission. See "From the Hermeneutics", 58, but this does not change the essence of his discussion.
31 See Okolo, *Tradition et destin*, 278; "From the Hermeneutics", 60.
32 See Okolo, *Pour une philosophie*, 26, 53, 105; *Tradition et destin*, 6.
33 See § 3.1.a, above; Okolo, *Tradition et destin*, 278.

34 See also Okolo, *Tradition et destin*, 3.
35 Therefore, all tradition or culture depends on the deposit; the deposit is one of the conditions for reading. In chapter XI of *Pour une philosophie*, Okolo resorts to Marxist phraseology to explain the factors involved in producing culture. The "superstructure of culture" depends on the "infrastructure of production", which makes culture possible, he claims. Therefore, "in the current context of Africa, we are faced with three kinds of culture that correspond to the modes of production at stake. Traditional cultures correspond to traditional modes of production. The culture of contemporary Africa, mirrors the difficult articulation between the dominated and declining traditional modes of production, and the dominant capitalist mode of production. Finally, the culture to be promoted on the basis of new modes of production" (96).

One cannot deny that productive forces play a central role in generating culture. But the way in which this is argued here does not fit with the rest of Okolo's philosophical framework. In Okolo's understanding of tradition/culture, anything categorised as superstructure and infrastructure belongs to tradition/culture; there is no extra-cultural or non-traditional infrastructure, which his deployment of the Marxist terminology leads one to believe. Instead, superstructure *and* infrastructure are combinations of tradition-as-deposit and tradition-as-reading. The terminological distinction between superstructure and infrastructure is not in agreement with his earlier declaration, which states that the text-like solidification of tradition allows one to reconstruct the rules for its production (34, referred to above), because this principle applies equally to whatever one may categorise as superstructure and infrastructure.

Nevertheless, my critique does not invalidate the distinction between different kinds of culture on the basis of economic conditions with which they are associated. Nor does it invalidate the idea that relations of production—or other conditions in which tradition is practised—have to be changed if culture is to be liberated. Finally, it remains valid that a discrepancy (*décalage*) can emerge between some of the conditions of cultural production and other forms of culture (see 96). However, all three of these claims would have to be rearticulated to fit with the more plausible *hermeneutic* view of culture and tradition in the rest of Okolo's book.
36 Identical to Okolo, *Tradition et destin*, 279.
37 The citation, which is made also in (33), is from V. Y. Mudimbe, "Réponse à J.L. Vincke sur quelques questions de méthode", in Jacques L. Vincke, *Le prix du péché. Essai de psychanalyse existentielle des traditions européenne et africainne* (Kinshasa-Lubumbashi: Mont-Noir, 1973), 35–53, here 51–52.This point is also made in Okolo, *Pour une philosophie*, 40; *Tradition et destin*, 278.
38 See Okolo, *Pour une philosophie*, 44; *Tradition et destin*, 281.
39 One way to deepen the discussion that follows is to consult Okolo's study of African receptions of Heidegger: "Afrikanische Heidegger-Rezeption und -Kritik", in *Zur Philosophischen Aktualität Heideggers 3: Im Spiegel Der Welt: Sprache, Übersetzung, Auseinandersetzung*, edited by Dietrich Papenfuss and Otto Pöggeler (Frankfurt: Klostermann, 1992), 264–272.
40 In other words, that "cultural thing called in the West 'philosophy'". Okolo, "From the Hermeneutics", 76.
41 Looking back on this part of his thought, Okolo later schematises: "It is necessary to free oneself from the ethnological gaze if one wants an authentic circularity. [...] History and hermeneutics will take the place of ethnology and ethnophilosophy." "From the Hermeneutics", 59. Taking Okolo's *Pour une philosophie* as a philosophical anchor, a new methodology for studying the history of ideas of particular ethnic groups is Okolo Okonda and Jacques Ngangala Balade Tongamba, *Introduction à l'histoire des idées dans le contexte de l'oralité. Théorie et méthode avec application sur l'Afrique traditionnelle* (Louvain-la-Neuve: Academia-L'Harmattan, 2018). This text offers a case study to prove the methodology.

42   The science lambasted in the following citation is ethnography: "Good will and revolutionary feelings [...] cannot, in a turn of hand, erase the fundamental trick [*ruse*] of a science that transforms fantasies into 'reality' so that an enslavement can live and survive" (66).
43   These categories are to be taken as examples. Our discussion earlier shows that Okolo has a more complex understanding of unjust social relations.
44   Cf. "Hermeneutics is theoretical by its process, it is ideological by the decision that triggers it, directs it and applies it" (100).
45   Similarly Okolo, *Pour une philosophie*, 46; *Tradition et destin*, 285.
46   Elsewhere, Okolo separates the task and function of hermeneutics from those of a critique of ideology (see 98–99).
47   Similarly, "From the Hermeneutics", 61–62.
48   Although destiny is an extension of identity, it is equally that which resists identity closing in on itself; it opens narrative identification with unexpected futures and with others. See Okolo Okonda, *Hegel et l'Afrique. Thèses critiques et dépassements* (Argenteuil: Cercle herméneutique, 2010), 108.
49   Destiny should not be taken to mean inevitable improvement. Okolo's whole exposition on identity and destiny militates against this. More accurate would be to say that destiny is at stake exactly *because one cannot say in advance* if people or a culture are on their way to improvement or degeneration within a specific period of time.
50   "[I]n a given situation, praxis assigns hermeneutics its place and its development. Praxis triggers the hermeneutic process and gives it an orientation. Hermeneutics, in its turn, offers to praxis a cultural self-identification, necessary to the ideological fight." Okolo, *Pour une philosophie*, 46; identical to *Tradition et destin*, 285.
51   Okolo, *Hegel et l'Afrique*, 105–115.
52   Sophie Oluwole adopted a similar approach to pre-colonial philosophy in Africa, as I indicate in discussing her work later.
53   One should be careful to note that this claim applies only to Okolo's examples of Tempels and Kagame.
54   I do not have the competence to determine if, or how, this declaration could have chimed with Zairean authenticity or Mobutism at the time. I can only observe that in Okolo's assertion that "[a]n unclosed or extraverted circle is inauthentic" (105), both "inauthentic" and "extraverted" allow for understandings other than those of the official doctrine.
55   In Okolo's *Tradition et destin*, 277n13, ethnophilosophy is included in the family of African hermeneutics without further commentary. However, in *Tradition et destin*, 279n16, Okolo anticipates the coming of a "hermeneutic critique of ethnophilosophy".
56   The same double-sided appraisal of ethnophilosophy is found later in Okolo and Ngangala, *Introduction à l'histoire*, 14–16.
57   I follow the two discussions in *Pour une philosophie*, 21 and 26f.
58   Elsewhere, I devote a shorter discussion to Okolo's philosophy of proverbs, with which part of the present argument overlaps. Cf. Ernst Wolff, *Between Daily Routine and Violent Protest. Interpreting the Technicity of Action* (Berlin: De Gruyter, 2021), 181–185.
59   I take this paragraph verbatim from: Wolff, *Between Daily Routine and Violent Protest*, 183.
60   See also Okolo, "From the Hermeneutics", 63; Okolo and Ngangala, *Introduction à l'histoire*, 12–13.
61   These three parts are captured by the names of the subsections of chapter I of *Pour une philosophie*. Okolo and Ngangala offer a revised approach in the form of four hypotheses on the textuality, usage, and interpretation of proverbs in *Introduction à l'histoire*, 73–74.
62   Following the patronymic practice in Zaire/DRC, the family name is Nkombe.

63   Nkombe's study covers a wider range of figures of speech. Following Okolo, I delimit the discussion to proverbs.
64   See also, "[Nkombe] thus manages to organize the main experiences of muntu [humans—EW] around six oppositions: vacuity and fullness; tensions towards and closing in on oneself; belonging and appropriation; necessary intersubjectivity and free intersubjectivity; valorising distance and negative distance; mission and accomplishment. This translates the tension of the ontological structure of the muntu and the moments of their fundamental processes" (19).
65   This effect is the perlocutionary dimension of the utterance of proverbs.
66   Okolo speaks here not about the flux of events in the past, but rather about the scientific study and critical recording of those events, namely historiography, which translates events into text.
67   Okolo, *Tradition et destin*, 282.
68   Or "sociocryonics", to use Olúfẹ́mi Táíwò's term.
69   Whence Okolo's (and Ngangala's) insistence on combining *two* disciplines in the history of ideas: history and the sociology of knowledge. See *Introduction à l'histoire*, 72. The sociology of knowledge is overshadowed, in *Pour une philosophie*, by the recurrent emphasis on history, but studying the social power dynamics of knowledge is always part of what Okolo understands to be the task of history.
70   Some of Okolo's arguments in *Pour une philosophie* are informed by self-critical publications in ethnology or cultural anthropology. However, he does not focus on this kind of intra-disciplinary change. Later, Okolo (with Jacques Ngangala) comes back to some of the significant self-critical publications of the 1970s. See *Introduction à l'histoire*, 9–10. One may read this volume as the authors' own contribution to cultural anthropology.
71   See, for instance, where Okolo situates "the work in the intersection between hermeneutics and praxis" (59).
72   Similarly, "hermeneutics and critique invite each other and [their relation] is founded in the work itself" (59).
73   Ouologuem's novel was translated by Ralph Manheim as *The Wages of Violence* (London: Secker & Warburg, 1968) and *Bound to Violence* (London: Heinemann, 1971). Okolo uses the terms "re-taking", "breaking", and "transcending" [*reprise, rupture, dépassement*] also in his reading of this novel.
74   Here and below, I cite Okolo's word as is without translating it.
75   As Okolo argues, "Y. Ouologuem seems to tell the Nègre that his enemy is first of all himself; he is the first other of himself, his first aggressor; he is his own negation before any other negation" (61).
76   Okolo implies that Fanon did not deal with the problem of an ambiguous identity. Fanon may well have resisted the image of Africans presented by négritude, but by obliterating pre-colonial violence, his focus on the Manichaean colonial order and his advocacy of humanising violence as the only response to it, depends implicitly on a portrayal of Africans as devoid of any history of compromises (61–62). Okolo's point is not Fanon's, namely how to respond to colonial violence, but to question a certain vision of African identity.
77   Okolo does not think that there is something like a particularly African literary criticism, but reintroduces the adjective "African" here, too, to refer to a domain of relevance (see 58).
78   Cf. "The African tradition assures the 'Africanness' of African philosophical hermeneutics by providing the material to be treated, the issues [*problématiques*] and philosophical approaches. As a result, the problem arises out of the restoration of the past that the hermeneutical concern of appropriation has made us forget. [...] The history of philosophical ideas is one of the conditions of an African philosophical hermeneutics. African hermeneutics, left to itself, can only die as hermeneutics if it is not supported by a science of history applied to ideas, which science will give it a subject, a question [*problématique*] and an approach of its own." Okolo, *Pour une philosophie*, 45, identical to *Tradition et destin*, 281–282.

79 Cf. "The interest in going to the past is aroused by the present situation: a hermeneutical situation which is at the same time a *situation of praxis*. It is for us a *question of spiritual and material survival. We feel invaded by a culture that has powerful means to expand and dominate. We are also among those who are starving and suffering from material deprivation.* This situation is long-standing and still exists." Okolo, *Pour une philosophie*, 28 (my emphasis).

80 The question of the meaning and possibility of a "general hermeneutics" is dealt with in *Tradition et destin*, 274–276.

81 See also *Tradition et destin*, 2.

82 "Extrovert", but not therefore "extraverted".

83 Earlier, Okolo articulated his view of the relationship between European hermeneutics and other forms of hermeneutics. Even when it does not mention hermeneutics from other regions of the world, European hermeneutics is "not closed; it opens to other hermeneutics than those considered; it constitutes for the theorist a way of access to other theories and a framework for a recasting of the theory in view of a greater generality". *Tradition et destin*, 277.

Chapter 5. Implicit hermeneutics: origins, constitutions, projects

1 I refer to Cheikh Anta Diop, *Alerte sous les tropiques: articles 1946–1960: culture et développement en Afrique noire* (Paris: Présence Africaine, 1990). In the current chapter, where page numbers are given without other author identification, the page numbers refer to Diop's text. Where two page numbers are separated by a stroke, the number marked with an asterisk refers to the English translation *Towards the African Renaissance: Essays in African Culture & Development, 1946–1960*, trans. Egbuna P. Modum (London: Karnak House, 1996).

2 I do not develop a complete assessment of Diop's ideas here. The discussion later does include some critical observations on his work, and an indication of how my critique relates to Diop's general framework.

3 The reader needs to retain only the principle, namely that description is open to critique. For the rest, Diop's earliest essays are arguably questionable on this point. He frequently equates cultural "mixing" with "contamination", without any clear justification. However, he advocates the contemporary strategic advantages of using printing, radio, and the cinema (cf. 37), without discussing why or how the appropriation of these media does not amount to submission to the hegemonic power of European cultures and languages.

4 In a regrettable slip of self-reflexive vigilance, Diop admonishes African novelists who write in French: "It is easy to see when a writer is mainly trying to express himself correctly in French, to demonstrate an unexpected literary talent or to exhibit his mastery of grammatical subtleties rather than expressing ideas that are useful to his community" (34/*34)—seemingly forgetting that he himself is writing this critique in French. Should we apply his own criterion to him and suspect that he never wrote for (francophone) Africans? Moreover, these words of Diop unfairly critique those fellow Africans who, knowing very well the tragic reasons for which French became prevalent in Africa, nevertheless use it to communicate among one another. The problem is compounded when Diop claims, a page later, that there was, for the time being, no other means to communicate widely. If there are no other means, why should people first think about why and for whom they think? Why strategise in the absence of options? Below, we see that, while Diagne is not ignorant of the pitfalls of speaking the "master's" language, he highlights the possibility of non-subservient appropriation and "insemination" of the colonial language.

5 Diop did not recognise immediately that he was duplicating some of these cultural politics of domination *within* Africa by maintaining that "there are in Africa, not six hundred but only four

5   languages capable of being developed to become instruments for the expression of the entire African thought" (37/*37). However, we can trace the complexification of his own view elsewhere (cf. 110–112).
6   Cf. 110, 118.
7   On the one hand, it is regrettable that Diop did not elaborate on these implications. On the other hand, where he did so, contemporary readers may well have differed from him: "And we remain convinced that the undeniable benefit [*bienfait incontestable*] of colonisation is this secular [*laïque*] rationalism which enables us to see things outside their religious connotations and thus to free ourselves intellectually" (44/*44, translation corrected).
8   Regrettably, Diop does not consider whether this implies a kind of cultural imperialism. At that stage of his life, his view seems to waver between a kind of African *terra nullius* filled from Egypt, and the "colonization" of Africa by the Egyptian ancestors of all Africans (51), which should count as a source of "legitimate pride" (51/*53) for Africans.
9   A longer study would follow Diop's development in chronological order.
10 Given a number of awkward arguments, one cannot characterise Diop's thought as a whole as hermeneutic. Here I am thinking of (a) the recurring deployment of essentialism (cf. "mentality of a people" 35/*35, translation modified), (b) the identification of the most remote historical origins of contemporary cultural phenomena without a proper genealogy to trace the subsequent developments (e.g. 25–26), (c) the idea that civilisation emerged in one place from whence it spread to the rest of humanity (48), until then lost in "barbarism [*barbarie*]" (48/*50), similar argument 106/*110, where people are called "savages", and this while he critiques "the" Western manuals' view of African history, which identifies the third-century Ghanaian empire as the central important starting point, and "[t]he textbooks [that] teach us that beyond Ghana there was nothing [*c'est la nuit noire*]" (116/*121), which is precisely Diop's own argument.
11 In my discussion of Oluwole, I use several texts, for which the full bibliographical information is given in the select annotated bibliography at the end of the chapter.
12 My own impetus to study Oluwole's work from this perspective came from the article of Fayemi Ademola Kazeem, "Sophie Oluwole's Hermeneutic Trend in African Political Philosophy: Some Comments", *Criticism* 13 (2013): 158–177.
13 We will see Diagne's partial objection to such a position, which consists in emphasising written traditions of thought in Africa (thinking especially of Islamic scholarship in north-west Africa and contemporary written publications).
14 We also find this difficult procedure in Okolo.
15 This is not dissimilar to how I work with hermeneutics in African philosophy throughout this book. My provisional characterisation is given in Chapter 1, § 1.
16 This point is similar to one advanced by Okolo in working on proverbs.
17 Oluwole's point is not that this tradition speaks, once and for all, for all African tradition, but that it can be used as a token example or a "specimen" (Oluwole, "Culture, Gender", 100).
18 In assuming this position, Oluwole adopts a traditionalist view on culture quite similar to that of Okere.
19 However, she is not always consistent on this point.
20 The only way this declaration could be compatible with her other pronouncements about the nature of African philosophy would be to propose a distinction between the question about the nature of philosophy (in "Philosophy and Oral Tradition", 101, Oluwole explicitly states that African philosophy is not about determining African identity, as I have pointed out above) and the question of whether African philosophy has a beneficial effect on society (which would consist of the impact of African philosophy on Africans' self-recognition, as is argued here).

21 However, if I read correctly, the significance of this argument does not depend on traditional modes of reasoning playing an important role in contemporary societies any longer.
22 "Authentic African views about the male–female relationship in their societies became blurred by Western ideology and the unquestioned assumption that sexism occurred under similar parochial conditions of male chauvinists in all human societies" ("Africa", 104, similarly, "Culture, Gender", 119).
23 Oluwole is actually referring to *government* as she initially defined the terms when she writes about "the concept of governance as that of exercising political power or control. The latter was experienced under some tyrants and later under colonialisation" ("Democracy and Indigenous Governance", 421).
24 See Chapter 4, § 7.1, above.
25 It is shocking to see that Oluwole, in a discussion of contemporary society, could speak about the rights of slaves without questioning the legitimacy of slavery in the least.
26 This is what she does in a much more prudent formulation of her conviction: "It is my fervent belief that African youths may still learn to draw some inspiration from different aspects of their intellectual heritage" ("The Cultural Enslavement", 103).
27 She makes this point even though, in education, students have to learn to combine the best of different worlds, as we have seen above (cf. "The Cultural Enslavement", 104). This tendency to pure essences cannot be upheld in terms of an accurate description, and carries unexamined judgements into the argument.
28 She writes: "The need to look back into traditional African philosophical ideals and the ways these affected their principles of organising society will be misplaced and consequently misleading if it is meant to be a call for a wholesale acceptance of all or even particular philosophies and cultural paradigms in ancient African societies. The need to look back is, to me, necessary so that contemporary African scholars do not, without adequate scrutiny of their own intellectual heritage, continue to accept without question the superior wisdom of Western scholars who are basically ignorant of our existing social orders which they intend to change" ("Culture, Gender", 118).
29 The references here are to Valentin Yves Mudimbe, *The Invention of Africa: Gnosis, Philosophy, and the Order of Knowledge* (Bloomington: Indiana University Press, 1988). Sole page numbers refer to this book.
30 It is difficult to determine what precisely "gnosis" refers to in *The Invention of Africa*. While the introduction seems to define gnosis as traditional modes of knowing (cf. ix), the conclusion defines "gnosis" as "both the scientific and ideological discourse on Africa" (187). Here I follow the introduction. My exposition of the three terms of the subtitle that follows is supported by Mudimbe's own claim in *The Idea of Africa* (London: Currey, 1994, xiii–xiv), where he claims that there are three levels of discourse in all societies: everyday exchanges, the sciences, and meta-science and critique.
31 How Mudimbe situates himself in relation to philosophy and his own African background can be deduced from a response to critics of his earlier books: "I only hope that some people would agree that the task of bringing philosophy to some of its own limits and metaphors in social science, and that of questioning philosophy's ambiguous contacts with unphilosophical discourses, justify my commitment not to philosophy, nor to an *invented Africa*, but to what it essentially means to be an African and a philosopher today" (xi).
32 In *The Idea of Africa* Mudimbe gives a clear exposition of this first task of critique: "I have been trying to understand the powerful yet invisible epistemological order that seems to make possible, at a given period, a given type of discourse about Africa—or, for that matter, about any social group in Africa, Asia, or Europe. [...] [I]t describes the processes and products of scientific consciousness. But, on the other hand, it tries to restore what eluded that consciousness: the influences that affected it, the implicit philosophies that were subjacent to it, the unformulated thematics, the

unseen obstacles; it describes the unconscious of science. This unconscious is always the negative side of science—that which resists it, deflects it, or disturbs it" (Mudimbe, *The Idea of Africa*, xiv).

33 Mudimbe came back to this point again in *The Idea of Africa* to clarify that, "[f]rom this perspective, it is obvious that to approach the question 'What is Africa?' or 'How do we define African cultures?' one cannot neglect a body of knowledge in which Africa has been subsumed by Western disciplines such as anthropology, history, theology, or whatever other scientific discourse, as I have tried to demonstrate very concretely in *The Invention of Africa* and in *Fables and Parables* [...]" (Mudimbe, *The Idea of Africa*, xiv).

34 A curious exception is the discussion of Blyden in chapter 4, where Mudimbe explains: "Blyden's work is *not* analyzed as sign or symbol of something else, but only in terms of its own density and spiritual limits, as it reveals its own irreducibility and specificity" (99, my emphasis).

35 We see a similar way of proceeding in Eboussi Boulaga, although the latter's study is more narrowly focused on forms of philosophy (see § 4, below).

36 In Mudimbe's own formulation: "This orientation has two consequences: on the one hand, an apparent attenuation of the originality of African contributions and, on the other, an overemphasis upon external procedures, such as anthropological or religious influences" (x).

37 A curious fact about chapter 2 of *The Invention of Africa* is that Mudimbe seems to consider borrowing from Foucault as a matter of course, whereas he repeatedly criticises Lévi-Strauss. One gets the impression that Mudimbe takes from Lévi-Strauss primarily a kind of intellectual *stance*.

38 In explaining the notion of "amplification", Mudimbe explains that it "implies direct or indirect causal relations" (36). However, it would be incorrect to think that he is claiming that European discourses simply are the causes of an African discourse or that an African discourse is merely the local consequence of European discourse. If there is an echo of the detached scholarly stance of Foucault or Lévi-Strauss in Mveng or Hountondji, this echo is found first in the assumption of a critical and independent verbalisation of own's own views ("prise de parole", 36).

39 Hence the following detail on *amplification*: "Mveng seems to be carrying Foucault's project further than the French philosopher himself would have. Hountondji emphasizes the necessity of considering Africanity as a *fait*, in the sense of an event. Its demythification should sustain a critical reinterpretation of an African history invented from its exteriority. Hountondji's invitation to *appauvrir* (impoverish or weaken) the very notion of Africa implies a radical break in African anthropology, history and ideology. The convergence with Levi-Strauss's and Foucault's predicaments is clear" (37).

And on *filiations*, he adds: "In these enterprises one notes a remarkable mediation between the rigor of a philosophical exercise and the fantasies of a political insurrection: the text commented upon is a mirror which reveals the self to the reader or commentator" (43).

40 This dichotomous kind of thinking did not emerge upon Europe's contact with Africa. It existed in Europe before colonisation in chauvinistic relations between urbanites and rural people, between Western Europeans and Eastern Europeans, between the social elite and factory workers, and in many other forms. It is a pity that Mudimbe did not examine this reduplication and augmentation.

41 This is also reflected where all African originality is attributed to importations from elsewhere, even when this is not from Europe (cf. 13).

42* They are called two "kinds" (19), but I think it would be more correct and descriptively more plausible to call them two dimensions or "aspects of ethnocentrism" (20).

43 Here we think about African authors and the case for this filiation to European (philosophical) practices is most strongly made by Eboussi Boulaga.

However, all epistemic traditions have epistemological filiation. It refers to the simple fact that nobody creates out of nothing that which their knowledge claims are made of. Instead, people engage in practices within relations of transmission and acquisition from what they receive from their predecessors. In other words, claims-making comes from practices that are shaped in form and content by epistemic traditions. Such traditions reflect continuity, but not determinacy; similarity, but not identity. Filiation thus refers to the remnants of a broad scientific paradigm in a scholar's work, in as far as he/she still draws on that paradigm, consciously or not.

44 In as far as that is the case, it seems appropriate to exonerate epistemological filiation from the specific moral judgement entailed in the term "ethnocentrism"; it is "ethnocentric" in a descriptive way.

45 When Mudimbe defines ethnocentrism as "the belief that scientifically there is nothing to be learned from 'them' unless it is already 'ours' or comes from "us'" (15), this definition actually applies only to this second dimension of ethnocentrism.

46 However, his discussion does not develop beyond the statement of a hypothesis.

47 Consider, for instance, the fact that "the Western tradition of science, as well as the trauma of slave trade and colonization, are part of Africa's present-day heritage" (78). This view is typical of all African hermeneutics, where "African" denotes a particular way of receiving this heritage in the light of shared experience (although it cannot be reduced to this heritage).

48 The non-European roots of négritude and authenticity are explored in chapter 4 of *The Invention of Africa*, where Mudimbe is "concerned with a practical question in the precise field of the history of African ideologies: in what sense can we accept Senghor's and Lynch's statements about Blyden as the precursor of *négritude* and 'African Personality'?" (99, and see the conclusions on 133). I do not deal with Mudimbe's chapter 4 here.

49 As a first orientation, Mudimbe fairly simplistically considers missions part of the colonial machinery (cf. 45). I do not go into the historical material that contradicts this, but a thorough study has to include the different roles played by missions, and the different missions as they related to specific colonial enterprises. Besides, elsewhere, he is quite sympathetic to missions.

50 What he calls "echo or negation" in this quotation is similar to his notion of "amplification", which we encountered above, but whereas "amplification" has a markedly positive meaning, "echo or negation" spans the breadth of all tendencies.

51 "Ironically, it was during this period [since the 1950s] that positive and sympathetic contributions on African religions were produced in anthropology" (56). Mudimbe cites a substantial list of references to European anthropological studies in support of this claim. However, since European anthropology was, up to that point in his argument, presented exclusively as an agent of violent othering, these references account for a turn in anthropology that comes as a complete surprise in Mudimbe's presentation. It is similarly unexpected when Mudimbe points out valuable contributions by missionaries as amateur anthropologists (cf. 64–67), which does not align comfortably with his characterisation of missions as part of the "colonizing structure". References to the "anthropological and missionary commitments to African values" (88) make it difficult to relate this significant rehabilitation to his initial damning assessment of European anthropology and missionary work.

52 Below (§ 5.2) we see how Diagne takes up the same point with his idea of an "insemination" of the "master's" discourse or creative translation, and how Eboussi Boulaga develops it through his idea of a "transfunctionalization" of inherited philosophical discourse.

53 Hence, Mudimbe's portrayal of the similarity between Tempels and Kagame: "Their argument, in its demonstration, runs parallel to primitivist theories on African backwardness and savagery. If there is a dividing line between the two, it is a blurred one established primarily as a signifier of sympathy or antipathy" (151). One notes that the same figures of thought can be advanced from a sympathetic *and* a hostile stance.

54 Mudimbe lifts the veil regarding his own position when he writes: "[A]s the School of Kinshasa has demonstrated, it is not at all certain that Hountondji and his fellow anti-ethnophilosophers are neocolonialist devils preventing people from affirming their otherness. Strangely enough, his responses to criticisms [...], reflect a well-balanced philosophical and nationalist imagination: 'as Gramsci rightly used to say, only truth is revolutionary' [...]" (162).

55 However, as a general characterisation of the three hermeneutic authors studied in this volume, Mudimbe is mistaken in claiming that a "hermeneutical school appeared in this context as the site of a more culturally oriented research in African *theology*" (173, my emphasis). It holds perhaps, in the background, for Okere, but it does not hold for either Okolo or Serequeberhan.

56 This is how I understand Mudimbe's claim that "anthropology, [is] both a challenge and a promise" (186, an idea that is rearticulated in *The Idea of Africa*, xiv–xv).

57 Making Europeans the object of African gaze, in Sartrean terms, as mentioned above.

58 "Theories of cultural hybridism, schizophrenia, and other metaphoric diseases [...] seem, therefore, to be by-products of a normative conception of history" (195). Stripped of this normative imposition, one recognises that "acculturation is not an African disease but the very character of all histories" (196).

59 I follow the Cameroonian practice of referring to him also simply as Eboussi Boulaga. I wrote this study of Eboussi Boulaga at the same time as the chapter, Ernst Wolff, "Working under Cover. Eboussi Boulaga and the Practice of Social Critique", in *Philosophy in the Shadow of Racism* (forthcoming). While these are two independent arguments, they share the same interpretation of Eboussi Boulaga's thought, and it was not possible to avoid some overlap.

60 The references in this chapter are to Fabien Eboussi Boulaga, *La crise du Muntu. Authenticité africaine et philosophie* (Paris: Présence Africaine, 1977). Where two page numbers are separated by a stroke, the number marked with an asterisk refers to the English translation *Muntu in Crisis: African Authenticity and Philosophy*, preface by Kasereka Kavwahirehi (Trenton: Africa World Press, [1977] 2014).

61 See also his approach to this point in Eboussi Boulaga, *L'affaire de la philosophie africaine. Au-delà des querelles* (Paris: Editions Terroirs/Karthala, 2011), 219.

62 This is a point we have also seen clearly in Diop and Serequeberhan.

63 In Oluwole's mind, this would be a reductive view on the sources of African wisdom; Diop would also object that precolonial wisdom—notably that of ancient Egypt—is thereby bypassed. However, there is nothing in Eboussi Boulaga's position that prevents him from adopting insights from the sources highlighted by Oluwole or Diop.

64 In both the initially impartial collection of discourses and the subsequent interpretation of these discourses as signs of broad socio-political phenomena, Eboussi Boulaga's approach is quite similar to that of Mudimbe. It is his explicit orientation to the fate of Muntu that distinguishes Eboussi Boulaga from Mudimbe.

65 On this point, Eboussi Boulaga is close to Serequeberhan. In Chapter 3 of the current book, we saw how Serequeberhan measured philosophies in terms of their capacity to orient people anew to the source of initiative.

66 This hermeneutic critique of ethnophilosophy could be explored further by examining Eboussi Boulaga's reading of their rhetoric and philosophies of history (33–41/*28–37 and 67–81/*65–79).

67 Translating this expression will always be difficult. The English translator opted for the free rendering "the mind acts" (*179).

68 Those disciplines corresponding to the outward movement Eboussi Boulaga calls "mediating", because they help to relate the spirit to the material that is studied; those corresponding to the inward movement he calls "mediated", because they depend on the previously established relation or mediation.

69 Cf. "The working out of a common denominator is the outcome of the recollection of violence undergone together. And it is first of all perceived as writing negatively, as the togetherness effectuated by common passion" (145/*143). In this point, Eboussi Boulaga agrees with Serequeberhan.
70 Again his proximity to Okolo is evident.
71 One may reformulate the task of the transfunctionalisation of Western philosophy in Mudimbe's terms as working through the first sense of orientation to Europe ("epistemological filiation"), but ridding it of its ideological connection to an ideology of Eurocentrism.
72 By situating theorising within practice, Eboussi Boulaga affirms the practice orientation of Okolo and even more specifically the action-initiative orientation of Serequeberhan. This position also invites us to study further the links between *Muntu in Crisis* and Eboussi Boulaga's later socio-political writings.
73 Souleymane Bachir Diagne, *De langue à langue. L'hospitalité de la traduction* (Paris: Albin Michel, 2022). Sole page numbers refer to this book. A translation by Dylan Temel is forthcoming at Other Press under the title *From Language to Language. The Hospitality of Translation*.
74 All translations are my own.
75 When speaking about the "comparabilité" (122) of two languages, Diagne probably also has in mind the etymological sense of "appearing next to each other at the same time".
76 This expression is taken from Antoine Berman.
77 This is a reference to the title of Antoine Bermann's book, *L'Épreuve de l'étranger. Culture et traduction dans l'Allemagne romantique* [The Test of the Foreign(er). Culture and Translation in German Romanticism]*: Herder, Goethe, Schlegel, Novalis, Humboldt, Schleiermacher, Hölderlin* (Paris: Gallimard, 1984).
78 Diagne does not include the translations made by missionaries in this category, but I will not discuss his critical views here (cf. 73–74).
79 Diagne's point implicitly contradicts Cheikh Anta Diop's understanding that using the colonial language almost inevitably leads to a kind of extraversion, contamination, or subservience (as we saw above).
80 Diagne discusses this term in length in his chapter 3.
81 Speaking of object of art, Diagne writes: "Once deterritorialized, they don't 'speak', but they can insinuate themselves as 'forces' in artistic unconsciouses, which then have to give them true expression" (98).
82 Diagne presents this term with reference to Roger Bacon (115–116). The origin and implications of the term are complex, and I do not explore the term in detail here.
83 For more detail see Diagne in *Open to Reason* (especially chapter 2) and *Le Fagot de ma mémoire*, 63–64 where the line of transmission is traced as far back as Timbuktu in Mali (see full references in the select annotated bibliography).
84 If I read this correctly, this terminological distinction is not explicitly present in *De langue à langue*, but the idea is certainly reflected in the book's argument. The distinction, which Diagne derives from Merleau-Ponty, occurs in several places in his writing, for example, Souleymane Bachir Diagne, "L'universel latéral comme traduction", in Philippe Büttgen, Michèle Gendreau-Massaloux, and Xavier North (eds), *Les Pluriels de Barbara Cassin ou le partage des équivoques* (Lormont: Le Bord de l'Eau, 2014), 243–255.
85 In the context from which this quotation comes, this insight is attributed to Abu Bishr Matta.
86 How Diagne derives this from Quine is discussed at length (21–40).
87 To this I could add the discussion of translation in religion (as in chapter 5 of *De langue à langue*), which I do not discuss here.

Chapter 6. Conclusion: hermeneutics as commitment

1 Part of what I present here was developed in thinking along with the authors examined in this book (I indicate this where applicable throughout this chapter). However, the argument in the chapter goes beyond what I developed in this way, and reflects views that have evolved in my thinking in the course of my academic life. It is not possible to give credit for each point—for many of them, I can no longer recall where I picked up an idea for the first time, or whether the thought is one that I have come up with myself. Let this note serve as recognition for those to whom it is due.

2 The theme of human beings as historical and interpretative beings, which covers the entire discussion of Serequeberhan, corresponds to this point.

3 We saw, for instance, how Mudimbe distinguished three levels at which knowledge circulates: everyday interactions, the sciences, and meta-science or critique; cf. Mudimbe, *The Idea of Africa*, xiii–xiv.

4 There is widespread agreement about this among hermeneuts. We saw this very explicitly in Mudimbe.

5 This is also pointed out by Eboussi Boulaga and, to a lesser extent, by Diagne.

6 Arguably the best confirmation of my position can be found in Okolo, who repeatedly stressed the ambiguities of interpretation and the complexities of thinking from shifting perspectives.

7 This term, which is particularly appropriate for the use I want to make of it in hermeneutics, is inspired by Elísio Macamo (ed.), *Negotiating Modernity: Africa's Ambivalent Experience* (Dakar, London, and Pretoria: Codesria Books and others, 2005).

8 On this point see Ernst Wolff, "Hermeneutics and the Capabilities Approach: A Thick Heuristic Tool for a Thin Normative Standard of Well-Being", *South African Journal of Philosophy* 33, no. 4 (2014): 487–500. There I reworked an argument derived from Michael Walzer, "Moral Minimalism", in *Thick and Thin: Moral Argument at Home and Abroad* (Notre Dame and London: University of Notre Dame Press, 1994), 1–20, here 9.

9 Souleymane Bachir Diagne, "L'universel lateral comme traduction", in *Les pluriels de Barbara Cassin ou le partage des équivoques*, edited by P. Büttgen, M. Gendreau-Massaloux, and X. North (Lormont: Le Bord de l'Eau, 2014), 243–255. The term "universalism" can be accepted in this context only when it is considered as a practical stance of openness to the other, and not as an exaggerated generalisation of one's own views.

10 See, for instance, how Serequeberhan argues for the specificity of African philosophy against the background of universal philosophy.

11 This corresponds to the exercise of generosity attributed to hermeneutics in the preliminary sketch of hermeneutics (cf. Chapter 1, above).

12 Elsewhere I have examined the top-down and bottom-up models of legitimate critique in a reading of Eboussi Boulaga's *Muntu in Crisis*—cf. Ernst Wolff, "Working under Cover. Eboussi Boulaga and the Practice of Social Critique", in *Philosophy in the Shadow of Racism* (forthcoming).

13 Recognising the significance of distantiation in relation to belonging is one of Ricoeur's most important contributions to hermeneutics. The intellectual origins of his work on this concept include his own contribution to debates on decolonisation and intercultural philosophy—cf. Paul Ricœur, "Introduction", in *Les Cultures et le temps. Au carrefour des cultures* (Paris: Payot/Les presses de l'Unesco, 1975), 19–41, here 35. To understand the significance of this point, cf. Ernst Wolff, *Lire Ricœur depuis la périphérie. Décolonisation, modernité, herméneutique* (Brussels: Éditions de l'Université de Bruxelles, 2021), chapter VI, § 1.2.

14 Below I discuss the practical relevance of this functioning of hermeneutics, when I consider the spectrum of the engagement of hermeneutics in socio-political problems (see § 4.3).

15 Okolo claims explicitly that our relation to tradition is caught up in the tension between familiarity and strangeness; I adopt an even broader perspective on this tension.
16 Elsewhere I have indicated the relevance of this point for philosophising across traditions, cf. Ernst Wolff, "Intercontinental Philosophy: Thinking in and for a Plural World" (forthcoming), where I draw inspiration from Bernhard Waldenfels, *Phenomenology of the Alien*, trans. T. Staehler (Evanston: Northwestern University Press, 2011).
17 This point is forcefully made in Taiwo's critique of sociocryonics, in Olúfẹ́mi Taiwò, *How Colonialism Pre-empted Modernity in Africa* (Bloomington and Indianapolis: Indiana University Press, 2010) and in Mamdani's critique of indirect rule, summarised in Mahmood Mamdani, "Race et ethnicité dans le contexte africain", *Actuel Marx* 2, no. 38 (2005): 65–73.
18 None of the authors studied highlights the ambiguity of philosophy itself as clearly as Okolo and Eboussi Boulaga do. They arrive at this conclusion in different ways from one another and from me.
19 Although he did not develop this point of uncertainty, as a basic insight about (African) hermeneutics, the point can be found as far back as Okere's initial study.
20 This series of procedures is not exclusive to hermeneutics, but can be found in different forms in the broad movement of self-affirmation through writing in Africa and the African diaspora. See, for instance, Achille Mbembe, *Critique de la raison nègre* (Paris: La Découverte, 2015), 52–55.
21 One may claim that hermeneutics reveals the intercultural presuppositions of all philosophy. In the case of African hermeneutics, this point is reflected in the way in which Janz embedded his discussion of African hermeneutics in a broader discussion of intercultural philosophy (cf. Chapter 1, § 2.1, "Other contemporary views").
22 However, we have seen how some authors too hastily identify the "familiar" from which they start out, for example, when Okere or Oluwole overstate the homogeneity of their own culture, or when Serequeberhan narrows down his "stock-taking" of the present horizon of action to fit a simplified schema of perpetrators of violence and non-violence.
23 Serequeberhan, for instance, does this by associating the particularity of African culture with philosophy, the core of which has to be a universal ability.
24 Elsewhere I have already used this kind of argument on the performative character of philosophy. See Ernst Wolff, *Martin Versfeld. A South African Philosopher in Dark Times* (Leuven: Leuven University Press, 2021), 216. I drew this concept from Martin Saar, "Genealogische Kritik", in *Was ist Kritik?*, eds. Rahel Jaeggi and Tilo Wesche (Frankfurt-am-Main: Suhrkamp, 2009), 221–246.
25 As stated above, I take most of this idea from Diagne, but similar positions can be found in Fanon, Serequeberhan, and Mbembe—see references in Wolff, "Intercontinental Philosophy".
26 Fayemi writes, in an otherwise valuable article: "After extensive study of Heidegger, Ricœur and Gadamer, Okere, a prominent African philosopher, attempted a hermeneutical engagement with Igbo culture. He advocates a specifically African form of hermeneutics." Cf. Ademola Kazeem Fayemi, "Hermeneutics in African Philosophy", *Filosofia Theoretica* 5, no. 2 (2016): 2–18, here 7. My point is not the fairly trivial one that, in reality, part 1 of Okere's doctoral thesis is devoted to Igbo culture, and part 2 to the relation between culture and philosophy. The real point is that this order reflects Okere's logical prioritisation of everyday culture above scholarly work, which is decisive for our understanding of hermeneutics. It is only because Fayemi inverts the order that he can insist so strongly on hermeneutics as a method.
27 Of course, Mudimbe also identified a pathological form of filiation, but that is not my point here.
28 A. J. Smet, *African Philosophical Bibliography/Bibliographie de la philosophie africaine/Bibliografie van de afrikaanse wijsbegeerte*, https://sites.uclouvain.be/sisp/sites/philafr/default.htm. Last updated on 2 June 2004 (last accessed 9 April 2024).

29 I have argued a similar point in Ernst Wolff, "Four Questions on Curriculum Development in Contemporary South Africa", *South African Journal of Philosophy* 35, no. 4 (2016): 444–459, especially 448–454.

30 Here one thinks of Okolo's view of tradition as half-material, half-spiritual, and where "the spirit exists only supported by a steady [*fixé*] deposit, and this deposit has meaning only by the spirit which vivifies it" (*Pour une philosophie*, 56).

31 At the same time, Oluwole cannot resist the temptation to spend a great deal of energy on interpreting ancient traditional culture, at the expense of an equally serious engagement with the problems of the day. Whatever the virtues of traditional wisdom may be, I do not think that these can be demonstrated or that we can benefit from them without corresponding probing work on the contemporary reality.

32 As we have seen, for instance, in Serequeberhan, who, on the one hand, makes his critique of European thought explicit while drawing from it, but, on the other hand, hardly touches on positive changes in European thought. In this respect, Mudimbe's view on long-term developments in African and European thought is more consistent.

33 See further Ernst Wolff, *Between Daily Routine and Violent Protest: Interpreting the Technicity of Action* (Berlin: De Gruyter, 2021), especially chapter 1.

34 Oluwole explicitly places pre-colonial oral *traditions* at the centre of her understanding of African philosophy, rather than the big historical catastrophes. Nevertheless, her aim of rehabilitating these traditions can be understood only against the backdrop of colonisation.

35 Oluwole's insistence on starting with oral traditions predating trauma is an important caution not to cut short the full scope of hermeneutic material and practice in Africa. But even this affirmation of the most distant, accessible traditions still gains its meaning from the perspective of the present context of action.

36 This point is developed, for instance, by Okolo, when he theorises the tension between identity and destiny, or sees philosophising as balanced between its positive and negative ideological potential. I came to similar conclusions, arguing from a different angle, in Wolff, *Between Daily Routine and Violent Protest*, 159–160.

37 Evidently, the same holds mutatis mutandis for importations and borrowings from outside of the West.

38 This makes of self-affirmation something other than extraversion.

39 In Okolo's terms, the affirmed identity is stretched between history and destiny.

40 Mamdani, Mahmood, *When Victims Become Killers: Colonialism, Nativism and the Genocide in Rwanda* (Princeton: Princeton University Press, 2001), 277.

41 Admittedly, we have seen promises relating to the potential of hermeneutics several times in this book, promises that are exaggerated when applied to the sole resources of philosophical hermeneutics. However, such claims become more realistic if one considers how hermeneutics (philosophical or other kinds of hermeneutics) can stimulate human initiative (as Serequeberhan argues) or science (notably development sciences, in Okolo, but many forms of social science for which African hermeneuts of all kinds seem to have a predilection: Oluwole, Diop, Mudimbe). Thus, the point is again to understand how hermeneutics is to be situated *in relation to* other social practices of knowledge generation.

42 This claim is made from a historical point of view. Today, a more detailed account of university practices should consider a wider range of interactions with academic role-players from a much wider range of regions of the world.

43 See also the more general claim about travelling, engaged intellectuals as generators of a modern black imaginary—Mbembe, *Critique de la raison nègre*, 54–55, who makes his point with reference

to Paul Gilroy, *The Black Atlantic: Modernity and Double Consciousness* (Cambridge: Harvard University Press, 2000).

44 One hardly ever hears any advocate of the decolonisation of universities calling for the abolition of the university as an institution. Indeed, often the very practice of advocates for decolonisation stand in an easily demonstrable epistemological filiation with the practices they critique—this is obviously noted as a feature, and is not a delegitimation of the basic concerns of decolonisation (cf. Ernst Wolff, "Four Questions on Curriculum Development", pp. 453-454).

45 Here one may consider the fact that the explicit practice of hermeneutics as a philosophical subdiscipline is more prevalent in Francophone African philosophy than in Anglophone African philosophy. Generally, this may be ascribed to a stronger historical orientation of Francophone African philosophy to German and French philosophy. However, there are contributions in English to hermeneutics (see Okere, with his one foot in Belgium, and Serequeberhan, with his one foot in the United States), and the German-French orientation is not required to recognise hermeneutics as a valid trend in African philosophy, as is significantly demonstrated by Oruka's typology.

46 The context from which this African philosophical hermeneutics arose and its modes of reproduction and transformation are of great significance to the present point, but pursuing this question in depth would go beyond the scope and aims of the present study. Nevertheless, it is worth mentioning the kind of detail that one would have to attend to: the typical background of the founding authors, the kind of education they had, the role of the (Catholic) Church and other religions in providing funding and/or institutional homes, the kind of teaching the authors received and which they in turn gave, the formation of a tradition through the studying of texts by young researchers, the kinds of libraries and books available to the relevant African researchers and students, the requirements set by foreign donors for bursaries, the influence of European/American university set-ups for those who wrote their doctorates and/or taught in such countries, and so forth. These issues have received relatively little attention in the scholarly literature, but see Heinz Kimmerle, *Afrikanische Philosophie im Kontext der Weltphilosophie* (Nordhausen: Traugott Bautz, 2005), and Mudimbe, *The Invention of Africa*. Both works deal with African philosophy generally.

47 Okolo, whose understanding of ideology accords it a mobilising function, would not contradict this view.

48 Evidently this attitude is ambiguous: it could either be accepted as realistic, sober work on practical problems, or it could be construed as a pretext for a sterile, scholarly detachment from reality. I comment further on this attitude in § 5 below.

49 This does not mean that all people always act in accordance with this insight. In war, for instance, the lines people draw between what is acceptable and what is unacceptable are often blurred. This increases the uncertainty of the situation, resulting in traumatic disorientation. Indeed, many would see such a trauma of disorientation as itself an injury to human life, confirming my initial point. If people are indifferent to heinous violence under more normal circumstances, they may well implode the work of hermeneutics as a whole.

50 Mbembe, *Critique de la raison nègre*. Granting this principle does not amount to agreeing that there is only one history or one source of injustice in this world.

51 In other words: every hermeneut may have his/her own "thick" views on this, but the very practice of hermeneutics requires commitment to a "thin" understanding of human flourishing.

52 Extreme forms of dehumanisation are important to hermeneutics in the sense that they serve as points of orientation that could attract very wide consensus. In this sense, these events are hermeneutically simple. But human history is filled with many more forms of injustice, the meaning of which is not quite as evident as in these extreme cases. In all, interpreters have to distinguish the simpler from the more complex cases. Ascribing too much complexity to cases where a straightforward normative judgement is appropriate may serve as justification for violence; ascribing

simplicity to complex cases may amount to one-sidedness. One has to be careful not to pretend that all forms of necessary and even urgent opposition to current unfreedoms are of equal importance. At the same time, adopting a complex view on "liberation" prohibits one from metaphorising the severest forms, which may not be our own present condition, as if it applies *pars pro toto* to all forms of unfreedom. The quest for the most encompassing liberation requires accurate descriptions of the problems, and such descriptions should reveal the divergent forms of "liberation" required by our present condition, and help us to make realistic assessments as academics.

53 Clearly, this does not exclude the flourishing of any other species, the ecosystem, the earth, or entities other than material beings. But that is not the point here.

54 In this regard, one would do well to review the pages where Okolo makes it clear that philosophy can itself be an obstacle, not only to philosophy, but to the furthering of human life.

55 Samuel Oluoch Imbo, *An Introduction to African Philosophy* (Lanham: Rowman & Littlefield, 1998), 43–46.

56 Paulin Hountondji, *African Philosophy: Myth and Reality* (London: Hutchinson, 1996), 189n16.

Index

Abraham, William 57
Achebe, Chinua 43, 105f, 109
Afolayan, Adeshina 30, 291
African, Africanness 25, 27, 51, 57, 79f, 102, 151, 153, 172, 175-178, 183, 185, 198-200, 210, 219, 235, 263, 286, 292f, 308, 310, 312f
agency 227f
Agzenay, Asma 240
ambiguity, ambiguous 53f, 59f, 64, 83, 99, 113, 126, 145, 158, 201, 206, 217, 219, 223, 234, 238, 251, 259-262, 264, 267-269, 272-273, 277f, 285, 297, 308, 311, 316f, 319
Amin, Samir 179, 305
amplification 162, 200, 203, 210, 258, 312f
Amselle, Jean-Loup 241
Ankunde, Laurent 136, 148, 305
Anozie, Stanley Uche 43, 294
Appiah, Kwame 290, 293
appropriation 22, 35, 37, 62, 64f, 67, 76, 82, 84, 86, 102, 114, 120, 124, 130-132, 134f, 139-141, 143, 150, 167, 178f, 196, 202-204, 210, 213, 215f, 221, 223, 225, 228-230, 235, 237, 254, 260f, 264f, 267-269, 287, 296-298, 301, 308f
arbitrariness, arbitrary 15, 78, 253, 272
archaeology 55, 141, 198, 207f
Arendt, Hannah 109, 302f
art(s) 60f, 133, 139, 142, 169, 183, 202, 216, 223, 226, 229f, 233, 245, 248f, 255f, 258, 269-271, 278, 280f, 288, 315
autonomy 13, 101f, 130f, 133, 165, 213, 216, 222, 237, 256, 272, 275, 277

Bacon, Roger 234, 315
Barker, Mariangela 57
belonging 57, 71, 105, 154, 157, 183, 185, 194, 247, 259f
Bermann, Antoine 315
Biyogo, Grégoire 38, 293f
Bongmba, Elias Kifon 31

Cabral, Amílcar 76, 82f, 85f, 89, 100, 103, 110, 114-119, 121, 290, 299, 302-304

capitalism 125f, 135, 169, 171, 176, 185, 302, 305f
centrifugal 40, 244, 250
centripetal 41, 244, 250
Césaire, Aimé 51, 57, 103-106, 117, 121, 205, 223, 303
Chimakonam, Jonathan 31, 291
colonies, colonization 33, 42, 51, 55, 69, 75f, 81f, 85, 88f, 91f, 94f, 97, 100-114, 116-120, 125-127, 151, 158f, 168, 171f, 177, 183, 185, 192, 200f, 204f, 209, 211-214, 217, 222f, 228f, 234f, 260f, 268, 272, 279, 297, 299, 301-303, 308f, 310-313, 315, 318
common, commonality 13, 20f, 29, 40, 48f, 52, 55f, 58, 60, 81f, 84, 88, 97, 117, 120, 137, 168, 182f, 185, 188, 213, 215, 219f, 223, 235f, 238, 244, 248, 253-255, 258f, 263-265, 272, 276f, 284-287, 290, 299, 315
confusion, disturbance 20, 78, 100, 196, 209, 245f, 253, 312
contradiction 23, 55f, 68, 106, 115, 130, 135, 141f, 146, 159, 161-168, 172-174, 186, 189, 203, 207, 213, 237, 253, 282
Coquery-Vidrovitch, Catherine 239f
creation, innovation 23, 36, 62, 64f, 67f, 81, 84, 91, 115, 132-135, 137, 141f, 155, 157, 159, 162, 165-167, 170, 178f, 183, 185, 189, 198, 210, 220, 223f, 228, 230, 231, 233, 238, 248, 251f, 256, 258, 262, 266f, 269, 276f, 285, 296, 313
critique, criticism 13f, 17, 22, 24, 26, 30, 32f, 35f, 40, 42f, 46, 49-52, 57, 64, 68, 76, 79, 81-85, 87-92, 94f, 98f, 102, 119f, 123, 125, 136, 142, 147, 151, 154-160, 168-174, 179, 182-184, 187-189, 191f, 195-200, 202, 205f, 208f, 212-215, 217f, 223f, 231, 234, 236f, 244, 247, 250, 252, 255-258, 261f, 266, 269, 274, 276, 278, 283-285, 292f, 297-300, 305, 307-312, 314-319
culture 13, 21, 31, 33, 45-72, 85, 88, 99f, 104f, 111, 118f, 123-125, 127, 129-131, 134, 137-143, 145, 147, 149-152, 155, 157, 160, 162, 169, 171, 175-177, 179, 181, 183, 188, 190-201, 203, 205, 209f, 213, 221, 225f, 228, 230, 233-238, 246f, 255, 257f, 260f, 264f, 267f, 271-277, 294, 298, 301, 304-307, 309, 312, 317, 318

Dadié, Bernard 228
De Waelhens, Alphonse 56
deposit 124, 131, 137-141, 153, 175, 179, 306, 318
Descartes, René 79
destiny 97, 101, 124, 135, 138, 145, 152f, 168, 219, 220, 307, 318
determined 47, 80, 115, 130, 134-136, 145, 151, 202, 206, 214, 229
development 35f, 40, 46, 53, 58, 101, 107, 116, 123, 136, 138, 142f, 145, 147-151, 153, 155, 159, 174, 178, 191, 201, 206, 209f, 236, 250, 261, 277f, 282, 287, 293, 298, 305, 307, 318
deviations (*écarts*) 83, 210, 217f, 221, 223f, 238, 251
Diafwila, Dia Mbwangi 293, 304
Diagne, Souleymane Bachir 42, 121, 180, 182, 224-235, 238, 241, 248, 251, 254-256, 258, 260f, 274, 278f, 288f, 302, 309f, 313, 315-317
Diop, Birago 228
Diop, Cheikh Anta 42, 57, 182-187, 208, 234-236, 239, 248, 260f, 277, 309f, 314f, 318
disciplines 14f, 31, 37, 78, 86, 127, 133, 147, 151, 166, 186, 197, 200, 209, 215f, 244f, 248-250, 299, 308, 312, 319
discourse 31, 36, 68, 76f, 79, 85f, 88, 91, 93, 95, 101-104, 116, 132, 138, 141, 146, 178, 197-201, 213f, 216, 218, 222f, 226, 237f, 248, 252, 258, 265, 275, 293, 298, 300, 311-314
distanciation, take distance 22, 257
distortion 17, 78, 107, 197, 232, 264, 279, 285
double hermeneutic 13, 245
Du Bois, W. E. B. 57
dynamic 112, 137, 142, 144f, 179, 152, 154, 227, 261, 308

Eboussi Boulaga, Fabien 42, 50, 57, 68, 182, 185, 205f, 210-224, 235, 237, 241, 247, 250, 255, 257f, 260-262, 264, 266, 268, 272, 275f, 278, 288, 299, 301, 312-317
Elengabeka, Elvis 37, 293
Elengu, Alphonse Pene 36
Empowerment 62, 150, 216, 298
epistemological filiation 183, 200-203, 205, 208, 210, 221, 237, 259, 263, 265-267, 279, 312f, 315, 317, 319
essential, essentialism 32, 48, 67, 69, 78f, 86f, 93, 95, 97f, 107, 115f, 148, 182f, 187, 189, 195f, 199, 234f, 252, 261, 267, 274, 276, 288, 300, 302f, 310, 311

estrangement 78, 99f, 105, 111, 113, 260, 262, 304
ethics 22, 31, 91, 127, 129, 139, 161, 164, 170, 173, 205, 215, 217, 226, 231, 233f, 238, 244, 251, 254f, 278, 281, 283-285, 301
ethnophilosophy 13, 26f, 33, 35f, 38, 50-52, 54, 57, 66, 68, 71, 75, 84-87, 89, 94, 97f, 119f, 123, 125, 132, 143f, 156-163, 168f, 175, 179, 188f, 195, 206, 212-215, 218-221, 223, 237, 247, 250, 266, 276, 292, 295f, 299, 306f, 314-84
Eurocentrism, ethnocentrism, Euro-normativity, chauvinism 46, 48f, 81f, 85, 87f, 90-93, 97f, 109, 120, 192, 197, 201f, 204, 209, 213, 231, 234, 299, 301, 303, 311-313, 315
Europe, European – 46, 48f, 85, 88, 90f, 93, 97f, 109, 192, 197, 201f, 209, 213, 231, 234, 299, 301, 303, 311-313, 315
existence 13, 17, 26, 28, 59, 61f, 75-79, 82-87, 89, 93, 95, 102, 105, 107-109, 114-116, 118-120, 130, 134, 145, 150, 154f, 157, 181, 185f, 189, 192, 194, 211, 216, 222, 232f, 249, 252f, 259f, 264f, 269, 278, 282f, 285f, 296-301
explication/explaining 22, 55, 66, 103, 106, 248, 252, 257, 276, 301
exploitation 104, 106f, 110, 125, 127, 148, 155, 171, 176, 185, 199, 222, 255, 264, 277, 282, 287
Eze, Emmanuel Chukwude 30

Fall, Papa Abdou 241
Falola, Toyin 30, 291
familiarity 62, 66, 68, 138, 142f, 172, 175, 226f, 229, 231, 233, 238, 244, 246f, 259-265, 267, 279, 317
Fanon, Frantz 57, 76, 83, 86, 88, 94, 103f, 106-110, 112f, 115, 118f, 121, 233f, 275, 288, 290, 298-303, 308, 317
Fayemi, Ademola Kazeem 31, 239, 291, 310, 317
Foucault, Michel 115, 199f, 210, 240, 299, 301, 312
Fouda, Basile-Juléat 294
Fraiture, Pierre-Philippe 240
freedom 26, 42, 75, 90, 94f, 101, 110-116, 120, 148, 152, 183, 193, 212, 216, 266, 286, 301
Freud, Sigmund 55
fusion of horizons 104, 110-118, 120, 274, 303

Gadamer, Hans-Georg 30, 40, 43, 61f, 81, 100, 112, 266, 290, 296, 303, 313
Gander, Hans-Helmuth 294
Gbadegesin, Segun 29f, 40, 291
genealogy 42, 133, 221, 255f, 264, 276, 310

general, generality 20f, 23, 48f, 51, 55, 61f, 65, 72, 75-83, 85-87, 89f, 92, 96, 115-120, 148, 151, 168, 173, 185, 190, 208, 211, 216, 223, 233, 236, 244f, 249, 251-255, 264, 269, 284-286, 288, 300, 304, 309
generosity 22, 65, 171, 233f, 238, 316
Giddens, Anthony 13, 245, 289
Gilroy, Paul 288, 31
global 59, 89, 101, 110, 119, 126, 176, 178, 264, 268, 287, 290, 305
Gutema, Bekele 290
Gyekye, Kwame 27f, 40, 42

Habermas, Jürgen 266
Hallen, Barry 27-29, 31f, 37, 40, 290, 292
Hebga, Meinrad 205
Hegel, Georg Wilhelm Friedrich 50, 55f, 104
Heidegger, Martin 13, 49f, 56, 61f, 78, 81f, 92, 143, 266, 289, 296-298, 300, 304, 306, 317
Hesiod 69
Heywat, Walda 79
historiography 38, 133, 137, 145, 147, 158f, 166-169, 200, 255, 277, 308
Homer 69
homogeneity 15, 52, 55, 67f, 144, 176, 203, 213, 247, 255, 295, 297, 317
horizon 21, 68, 76f, 79, 82, 88, 95f, 99f, 103f, 110-118, 120, 135, 141, 155, 199, 216, 233, 274, 300, 302f, 317
Hountondji, Paulin 13, 19, 44, 47, 51, 57, 68, 81, 92, 119, 143, 156f, 168, 200, 206, 223, 287, 289, 295, 300, 312, 314, 320
Hume, David 104

identity, identification 14, 50, 64-68, 82, 95, 108, 124-126, 128, 138, 144, 149-154, 172, 175-179, 183-186, 189, 203, 206, 210, 212, 220, 223, 225, 237, 255, 265, 273, 276f, 292, 295, 298f, 301, 307f, 310, 313, 317f
ideology 26, 33-36, 53, 89, 126, 136, 138, 144, 146-154, 156, 158f, 164-166, 178f, 185, 197, 202-204, 206, 213f, 237, 273, 285, 301, 307, 311-313, 315, 318f
Imbo, Samuel Oluoch 286, 320
in-between 46, 50, 56, 88, 138, 142f, 152f, 164
individual 16, 23, 31, 45, 51-53, 55, 60, 65, 67f, 70, 72, 96, 110, 115, 135, 137, 146, 151f, 154, 162f, 190, 192, 216, 224, 250, 282

intercultural 31f, 190, 290, 297, 316f
interpretation 13-15, 20-23, 41, 48, 60-62, 64, 75, 78, 82, 90-92, 106, 118, 120, 124, 130-132, 134, 136, 138-141, 145, 154-156, 158, 161, 164, 167, 170, 176, 178, 181f, 184f, 199, 203f, 212, 215f, 220, 222, 224f, 231f, 234-236, 238, 243-246, 248-251, 253-259, 262, 268-273, 276-278, 280-284, 286, 288, 296-298, 303, 305, 307, 313f, 316
intracultural 32, 48
Irele, Abiola 289-291

Jahn, Janheinz 209
Janz, Bruce 31f, 39, 290f, 317
Jeffers, Chike 290f
judgement 22, 24, 31, 42, 65, 164, 178, 188f, 196, 199, 207f, 258, 262, 281, 295, 311, 313, 319

Kagame, Alexis 50f, 145, 307, 313
Kane, Cheikh Hamidou 105f, 109
Kant, Immanuel 79, 104
Kavwahirehi, Kasereka 36f, 240f, 250, 291-293, 314
Kawende, Jean Onaotsho 293f
Kimmerle, Heinz 39, 293, 319
Kinyongo, Jeki 37
Kisukidi, Nadia Yala 241
Komo, Louis-Dominique Biakolo 38, 293

language 13, 17, 21, 27, 235, 29, 31, 40-42, 51f, 55, 66, 71, 81, 157, 159f, 181-185, 187, 189, 204, 224-233, 235f, 238, 245f, 251, 254, 258, 260, 262, 264, 271f, 276, 289, 296, 298, 309f, 315
Lévi-Strauss, Claude 199f, 210, 312
Lévy-Bruhl, Lucien 93, 205, 295
liberation, emancipation 33, 36, 67, 76, 80, 86, 88f, 91, 95, 99-103, 105, 108, 110-113, 115f, 118-120, 129, 136, 142, 149f, 150, 156, 174, 182, 185, 187, 193, 196, 203f, 206f, 214-217, 223f, 234f, 244, 256, 269, 277-279, 281, 284f, 288, 299f, 302-304, 306, 320
Lodewyckx, Herman 293
Lomomba, Jules Emonga 292
Lott, Tommy 290
Lukács, Georg 56

Macamo, Elísio 316
Madu, Raphael Okechukwu 31f, 43, 294
Malpas, Jeff 294

Mamdani, Mahmood 276, 317f
Marchal, Kai 293
Marx, Karl 55f, 90-92, 104, 108, 114, 147, 150, 153, 203, 206, 300, 305
Mbélé, Charles Romain 241
Mbembe, Achille 32, 282, 317-319
Mbiti, John 50f
Mburu, Elizabeth 43, 294
meaning 13, 20-23, 27, 29, 35, 46, 53, 60f, 64, 66f, 77f, 100, 102, 118, 123f, 127f, 130-132, 137, 139-142, 146, 149, 153-155, 157f, 164-167, 174, 178f, 183, 185, 189, 198f, 218f, 223, 225-227, 235, 245-248, 252-254, 257, 259-263, 269, 273, 278, 296, 309, 313, 318f
Memmi, Albert 108
Merleau-Ponty, Maurice 315
method, methodology 22, 29, 31f, 36-38, 40, 51, 64, 79, 84, 145, 165, 187f, 199f, 205, 221, 249, 256, 296, 306, 317
Metz, Thaddeus 30, 291
misunderstanding 32, 78, 83, 86, 99f, 104, 194, 245, 303
mixing, métissage 27, 35, 142, 183, 195, 203, 210, 229, 261, 297, 309
modern, modernisation 38, 55, 68, 70-72, 78, 85, 90, 94, 101, 103f, 106f, 116, 118, 125f, 134, 147, 150, 171, 176, 184, 206, 209, 220, 230, 248, 274, 277, 289, 293, 298f, 301, 302, 318
monoculture 56f
Mosley, Albert 290
Mudimbe, V. Y. 29f, 32, 34-36, 42, 51, 72, 141, 179f, 182, 197-210, 221, 230, 235, 237, 240, 248, 250, 257f, 261, 264f, 276, 289f, 292f, 295, 306, 311-319
Muntu 211f, 215, 221-223, 237f, 265, 308, 314
Mveng, Engelbert 200, 312
Mwembo, Mutunda 37, 292

neo-colonialism 80f, 95, 97, 100-102, 106-113, 116, 125, 127, 158 302f, 305, 314
neo-culture 209f, 230, 237
Njoh-Moellé, Ebénézer 146, 161-166, 180, 194
Nkombe Oleko 25, 33-40, 72, 146, 161, 163-166, 180, 194, 239, 250, 290-293, 308
Nkrumah, Kwame 57, 81, 83, 89-94, 104, 114, 119-121, 300, 303

non-philosophy 32, 45, 49-51, 54-58, 60, 62f, 65, 67f, 71, 133, 246, 294-296
normative 87, 89, 92, 100f, 116f, 164, 178, 199, 211, 256f, 262, 273, 281, 284f, 314, 319
Nyerere, Julius 59

Obenga, Théophile 239
Ochieng-Odhiambo, Frederick 39, 293
Oguejiofor, Josephat Obi 72, 295
Okere, Theophilus 15, 29f, 32, 38-73, 84f, 156, 181, 208, 233, 247, 250, 268, 272, 274, 276, 286, 290, 293-299, 304, 310, 314, 317, 319
Okolo Okonda 15, 17, 29, 36-42, 78, 100, 123-181, 183f, 194, 198, 200, 208, 218, 233, 257f, 261, 264, 267-269, 274, 276-278, 290, 293, 301, 304-310, 314-320
Oluwole, Sophie 24, 42, 187-197, 234-236, 239f, 250, 255, 260f, 268, 297, 307, 310f, 314, 317f
Onah, Godfrey Igwebuike 72
oral, orality 20, 24, 26, 123f, 130, 137, 139, 141, 157, 159-162, 167-169, 177, 179, 188-195, 233f, 236, 248, 260, 266, 272-274, 318
orientation 86, 88-91, 124, 136, 155, 158, 177, 188, 201, 212, 216, 219, 256, 258f, 261-265, 267, 272, 282, 284, 296, 301, 307, 312, 314f, 319
Oruka, Henry Odera 19, 25-31, 33, 43, 52, 73, 190, 240, 290, 293, 319
Orunmila 190
Outlaw, Lucius 88, 290f
Owolabi, Kolawole 32

Pan-africanism 33
particularity 27, 59, 75, 79-81, 87f, 90f, 96, 100, 123, 159, 175f, 178, 214, 217, 224, 226, 231, 254, 265, 285, 298, 300, 317
perspective 76, 93, 99, 101, 114, 116, 124, 136, 142, 144, 146, 149f, 154f, 169f, 179, 181f, 186, 190, 196f, 199, 201, 208, 215, 217, 225, 233, 238, 243, 246, 248, 250, 254, 256f, 260, 268, 274, 276, 281, 283f, 286, 288, 316, 318
philosophemes 63-68, 70f, 247, 274, 295f, 299
Pittman, John 290
Plato 56, 69
plurality, pluralism 47f, 52, 55f, 68-70, 72, 116f, 164, 203, 220, 226, 245, 250-254, 257-260, 281, 287, 297

politics 13, 21, 23, 31, 33, 36, 42, 46-48, 51, 53f, 59, 63-65, 67-72, 75-80, 84, 89, 92-96, 98, 100, 102f, 112, 114, 119f, 125, 129, 132, 135, 137, 139, 144, 146, 150f, 157, 161, 170, 176, 178, 181, 183-187, 191, 193-197, 200f, 203-205, 210, 212, 215f, 219, 225, 229f, 236f, 249, 252, 257, 264f, 269, 276-279, 285-287, 293f, 297-303, 309-312, 314-316

poor, poverty 71, 126, 128, 162, 184

post-colonial 36, 43, 75, 86, 88, 95-97, 105, 119f, 128, 258, 290, 299, 302

power(s) 23, 66, 67, 89, 107, 116, 128, 146, 157, 158, 162, 171, 176, 183-185, 191, 193, 199, 202, 204, 206, 209, 211-216, 218, 220, 222-225, 238, 251f, 264, 269, 271f, 275, 281, 286f, 300, 308f

practice(s), praxis 13, 20-23, 31, 33f, 40-42, 48, 52, 63f, 66, 77f, 85, 87-90, 101, 103, 114f, 118, 123-130, 135-137, 140, 142-144, 147-159, 165f, 169f, 174, 176-179, 184, 189f, 196, 201f, 205-208, 212, 214-220, 221-223, 225, 228, 228, 231, 235-238, 244-246, 248f, 251f, 255-258, 260, 262f, 264-281, 284f, 287, 292, 294, 299-301, 304, 307-309, 312-315, 318f

practices of freedom/liberation 75f, 110, 112, 114-116, 119f

pre-colonial 100, 105, 116, 157, 162, 167-169, 171f, 188f, 195, 267f, 272, 297, 299, 302, 307f, 314, 318

pre-judice, prejudgement 24, 33, 51, 54, 60, 62, 114, 157, 204, 288, 295f

Presbey, Gail 240

professional philosophy, school philosophy 26, 75f, 84, 94, 97f, 119f, 168, 212, 214f, 218f,, 237, 266, 299

project, projection 35, 37, 52, 64, 67, 89, 94, 107, 112, 118f, 124, 127, 129f, 133-136, 145, 149, 152f, 157, 169, 181, 188, 190, 216, 220, 228, 233, 243, 250, 274, 278, 293

protocol of action 221f, 238, 268, 278

proverbs 123, 132, 160-168, 172, 178f, 194, 247, 307f, 310

pure, purity 69, 111, 120, 126, 151f, 160173f, 177, 179, 183, 195, 200, 262, 167, 273, 302, 311

question 14, 21f, 24, 27, 34, 37f, 41, 45, 48, 50f, 53, 56-58, 60, 62-64, 66-68, 71, 78, 85, 90f, 94, 99, 103f, 112, 119, 172f, 191, 195, 204f, 221, 225f, 233, 248f, 285-288, 303, 309, 312

reading 124, 130-136, 139f, 141, 145, 149f, 152-154, 157f, 161, 166, 178f, 199, 208, 212, 270, 305f

reject, rejection 51f, 55, 59, 61, 64, 68, 71, 76, 81f, 88, 91f, 98, 117f, 128, 135, 137, 143, 153, 169, 173, 175, 186, 188, 191, 195f, 199, 209, 214f, 231, 247, 250, 254, 269, 274, 283, 285, 295, 298f

relativity, relativism 48f, 52, 61f, 88, 93, 119, 164, 170, 183, 190, 196f, 203, 227, 230-232, 236, 238, 243, 252, 258, 270f, 294, 298

re-taking (*reprise*) 116, 124, 131-138, 140-143, 145, 149f, 152f, 157f, 161, 166f, 170f, 174, 176-179, 200, 218, 251, 258, 267, 276f, 305, 308

revolution, revolutionary 61, 118, 124-129, 131, 142f, 149, 153, 159, 294, 297, 305, 307, 314

Ricœur, Paul 40, 49, 62, 266, 290, 305, 316f

risk 49, 83, 99, 110, 127f, 150f, 165, 216, 274, 277

rural, rural population 100, 110-113, 116-118, 120, 184, 302, 312

Saar, Martin 317

Sadji, Abdoulaye 228

science(s) 14, 21, 33, 35f, 48, 66, 68, 91, 100, 125f, 128f, 133, 145-150, 153, 158, 161, 166, 182f, 185-187, 199-203, 206-209, 226, 245, 248, 250, 255, 260, 263, 276, 305, 307f, 311-313, 316, 318

self-affirmation 42, 47, 59, 66, 125, 138, 174, 197, 203, 211-213, 217-219, 223f, 237f, 256, 258, 260, 262f, 268, 275f, 278, 299, 317f

Sen, Amartya 90

Senghor, Léopold Sédar 59, 81-83, 89-94, 97f, 119-121, 228, 300, 303, 313

Serequeberhan, Tsenay 15, 29f, 32, 38-40, 42, 73, 75-121, 181, 185, 208, 250, 257f, 260-262, 268f, 272, 274, 276f, 279, 289f, 298-304, 214-219

situated, situatedness, contextuality 21, 25, 30, 45, 61, 66-68, 70, 75, 77, 79, 80, 82, 87f, 90f, 95-97, 118, 120, 129, 132, 155, 164, 177f, 184f, 187f, 196, 201, 206, 208, 211-213, 215, 217, 219, 224, 235-237, 246, 254f, 271, 273f, 279f, 283-285, 289, 295, 298, 300, 303, 307, 309, 315, 318f

slavery, enslavement 33, 105, 171, 188, 191, 193f, 272, 297f, 307, 311, 313

Smet, Alfons 25, 33-37, 39f, 250, 266, 290-292, 317

socio-political 42, 68, 70, 75, 77f, 84, 95, 103, 119f, 125, 135, 178, 181, 183, 186f, 194, 196, 201, 210, 212, 225, 229, 236f, 249, 251f, 259, 269, 276, 285, 314, 316

Socrates 53, 189f
Sodipo, John Olubi 27-29, 31f, 40
solidarity 89, 119, 126, 150, 155, 163f, 268, 277
spirit 59, 69, 124, 127, 137, 140, 153, 179, 200, 215-217, 224, 238, 254f, 273, 300, 309, 314, 318
stakes 55, 61, 100f, 152f, 159, 167, 169, 184, 206f, 222f, 236, 261, 263, 273f, 278, 282-285, 306f
static 68, 78, 137, 142, 144f, 153, 179, 209, 220, 247, 258
stock-taking 95, 97, 100, 105f, 117, 126, 259, 272, 317
strangeness, foreign 23, 33, 53, 62, 66, 69, 71, 105, 111, 125f 138, 142f, 172, 175, 177, 184, 206, 226f, 229, 231-233, 244, 248, 254, 259-265, 267, 276, 279, 296, 300f, 317, 319
symbols, symbolic 22, 62, 69, 107, 109, 111, 132f, 146, 164, 167, 183-185, 191, 193, 236, 238, 245, 270f, 276, 279, 312 123f
synthetic, synthesis 15-17, 24, 33-37, 40, 93, 117f, 157, 191, 207, 216, 220, 243f, 250

Táíwò, Olúfẹ́mi 121, 292, 300, 302, 308, 317
Tempels, Placide 50f, 84, 159, 307, 313
text 24, 30, 32, 41, 124, 130f, 133f, 137-140, 157, 160, 170, 178f, 213, 225, 236, 238, 305f, 308,
Thiérard, Hélène 242
Tongamba, Jacques Ngangala Balade 180, 306
Towa, Marcien 79, 82, 143, 156, 206, 298
tradition 19, 29, 32, 34, 41, 45f, 49, 52f, 55, 58-61, 63-65, 69f, 85, 88, 94f, 97, 99, 101f, 120, 125-127, 130-144, 147, 149f, 152-161, 166-172, 174-179, 181, 183, 186, 188f, 190-197, 205f, 209, 218-221, 223, 225, 228, 233f, 236-238, 243, 247, 249, 257f, 262f, 267f, 273-277, 294-296, 299, 302, 305f, 308, 310, 313, 317-319
traditionalism 55, 66f, 70, 187, 195f, 214, 293, 295, 310
tragedy 104, 110, 116, 195, 210, 272
transfer 225f, 229-231, 235, 238, 250, 261
transfunctionalisation 217-219, 221, 223f, 238, 258, 261f, 275, 277, 313, 315
translation 22, 42, 93, 120, 144f, 157, 182, 224, 235, 238, 244, 251, 254, 258, 261, 268, 274, 276f, 283-285, 288, 313, 315
transmission, transmit 22f, 53, 70, 91, 124, 130f, 137, 139, 141, 154, 159-162, 167, 179, 188f, 191, 194f, 201-203, 215, 220, 225f, 228, 230, 236, 246f, 264, 267, 270f, 272, 280, 286, 305, 313, 315

Tshiamalenga, Ntumba 37, 291-293
typology 15, 19, 25-31, 33, 35f, 39, 41, 106, 169, 285f, 289f, 319

Ukpokolo, Issac 31, 291
unanimism, concordism 52, 125, 137, 144, 156f, 159, 161, 169, 175, 195f, 205, 213, 237, 247, 250
uncertainty 17, 40f, 72, 99, 114, 172, 174, 196, 198, 238, 243f, 248, 259, 262f, 269, 282, 285, 317, 319
understanding 13-15, 19-24, 29, 31-33, 39, 52, 62, 69f, 77f, 82, 97, 116, 118, 120, 130, 152, 155, 59-161, 163, 181, 185, 194, 196f, 201, 208, 210, 215, 219, 221, 223-226, 228, 231-236, 243-255, 257-259, 261-263, 265, 267, 269, 274, 276-280, 282-285, 287f, 290, 294, 297-299
universalism, universality 27, 39, 47-49, 56, 59, 61, 72, 82, 84, 88, 90-92, 119, 123, 143, 157, 174f, 177, 179, 214, 218, 226, 231f, 234, 238, 254, 264f, 287, 294, 299-301, 316f
universalism, lateral 23, 232, 238, 254, 264f
urban, urban population, 109-114, 116-118, 120, 184, 195, 271f, 297, 302, 304, 312

Vergopoulos, Kosta 179
violence, counter-violence 56, 67, 67, 75f, 78, 83, 94, 101, 103-116, 118, 120, 123, 169, 171, 174, 179, 191, 193, 207, 210, 219, 227-229, 232f, 236, 238, 252, 260, 262-264, 272f, 288, 298 301-303, 307f, 313, 315, 317, 319

Waldenfels, Bernhard 317
Walzer, Michael 316
West, Cornel 299
Winch, Peter 49
Wiredu, Kwasi 27-30, 40, 42, 290, 293
Wolff, Ernst 241, 289, 307, 314, 316, 319
work (œuvre) 169-174, 177f
worldview 60, 64, 130, 134-136, 138, 144-146, 150, 153f, 157, 159, 162, 178f, 192, 206, 305
written, writing 13f, 20, 26, 71, 79, 87, 96, 106, 109, 130f, 139f, 167-169, 189, 191, 198-200, 205, 213, 228, 230, 233f, 252, 274, 302, 310

Ya'aqob, Zera 79

www.ingramcontent.com/pod-product-compliance
Lightning Source LLC
Chambersburg PA
CBHW051600230426
43668CB00013B/1918